Penguin Education

The Theory of the Firm

Edited by G. C. Archibald

Penguin Modern Economics Readings

General Editor

B. J. McCormick

Advisory Board

K. J. W. Alexander
R. W. Clower
G. R. Fisher
P. Robson
J. Spraos
H. Townsend

The Theory
of the Firm

Selected Readings

Edited by G. C. Archibald

Penguin Education

Penguin Education
A Division of Penguin Books Ltd,
Harmondsworth, Middlesex, England
Penguin Books Inc, 7110 Ambassador Road
Baltimore, Md 21207, USA
Penguin Books Australia Ltd,
Ringwood, Victoria, Australia

First published 1971
Reprinted 1973
This selection copyright © G. C. Archibald, 1971
Introduction and notes copyright © G. C. Archibald, 1971

Made and printed in Great Britain by
Richard Clay (The Chaucer Press) Ltd
Bungay, Suffolk
Set in Monotype Times

Contents

Introduction

It should be possible to explain quite clearly what one's subject matter is. Failure to do so is normally occasion for criticism; and confessed inability to do so should be occasion for embarrassment. Yet the fact is that the subject matter and scope of the 'theory of the firm' are neither obvious nor simply explained. It is doubtless no accident that in many universities there is no course with this title, but only 'price theory' or 'microeconomics', and perhaps 'industrial organization'. There is, however, some tradition that the theory of the firm is a suitable label for some recognizable subdivision of economics. Since it is *not* business administration, or operations research – or industrial organization – let us try to work out what it may be.

Economics is the study of allocation, of how societies solve their allocational problems, and how they might do better. That there is an allocation problem is due to the scarcity of resources that can serve alternative ends, and the fact that wants are insatiable. The economic problem in this sense is universal: it transcends time and space, and political or social organization. If, therefore, there is a theory of the firm, it must be a part of our theory of allocation (and, of course, income distribution; but income distribution is determined by resource ownership and resource prices, and a theory of allocation must explain resource prices in conjunction with commodity prices). From the universality of the economic problem, it also follows that if the theory of the firm proves to be a useful and recognizable portion of the theory of allocation (and distribution) in a Western or capitalist context, so it must in a communist context: there must be a Soviet analogy. (There is: see the Reading by Ames reprinted in Part Five.)

We need to be a little more specific about the allocation problem. At any moment of time, a society has a given endowment of resources: it has capital, land, buildings and equipment, inherited from the past (and among its allocation problems is the intertemporal one: how much to set aside from current consumption to add to the productive stock); it has a labour force, with training and skills inherited from the past (two more allocational problems: income versus leisure, or how many of the population are to 'participate', for how many hours per day; and how much to invest in training); and it has a stock of technical knowledge, or know-how, in part embodied in the design of existing equipment, and also inherited from the past. The knowledge and the endowments between them determine the production possibility set, the list of all the possible combinations of commodities that society could have. We now add consumers, with their preferences, and the stage is set. As the limerick has it: 'Who does what, and with which, and to whom?'

This is the subject matter of general-equilibrium theory. It was a great achievement to see that completely unregulated (anarchic) competition, in which each agent considered nothing but self-interest, could generate solutions. Walras saw this, although it has required modern mathematical techniques to *prove* that equilibrium solutions to a competitive system exist, and to investigate their efficiency (the contributions of Arrow and Debreu are probably the most important).

It will be noticed that the allocation problem was set out above without any mention of 'firms'. This is because of its universality: it exists whether there are firms or not, and however they may be owned and organized. Yet firms exist, and must fit in somewhere. Formally, we may think of them as intermediate agents, between resource owners and consumers, that perform certain organizational tasks. Resources are sold or hired *to* firms; commodities are bought *from* firms (by resource owners); and firms are black boxes in between. The black boxes turn out to be production functions, converting inputs to outputs. In neo-classical general-equilibrium theory, firms are completely described by their production functions.

It is easy now to see why the theory of the firm was initially hard to explain and classify. The formal theory of general equilibrium is extremely difficult to handle without important simplifications, particularly perfect competition. But in perfect competition firms have so little to do, particularly in the absence of technical change and uncertainty, that there is nothing worthy of a separate title. Something worthy of a separate title has, however, emerged as economists have worked on problems of obvious interest, and importance to resource allocation and income distribution, problems particularly of market structure. The result is a substantial body of literature which is conveniently brought together. It deals with production and costs, market structures, and entrepreneurial behaviour. Its subject matter is, of course, allocation and income distribution, but it deals, usually in partial equilibrium, with complications that general equilibrium theory has not yet managed to incorporate.

Much of the literature in the theory of the firm is concerned, directly or indirectly, with a question of fundamental importance: to what extent are the allocational and distributional results of our society determined by the 'underlying forces', resources, technology, and tastes, as they are in the purely competitive model, and to what extent are they influenced, or 'distorted', by departures from perfect competition? The answer to this essentially quantitative question is obviously of critical importance to our understanding, as well as our assessment, of our economy. It should be noted that it is a question in positive economics: its answer is logically prior to, and independent of, judgements of the welfare consequences. It is also a question that continually recurs, perhaps unexpectedly. This point may be illustrated by considering the familiar problem of 'relative shares': what determines the functional distribution of the national product between labour and capital? Suppose that the economy is perfectly competitive, or, better, that departures from perfect competition are quantitatively unimportant. Then, given tastes, the answer is simply 'technology and relative supplies'. But we may go further. Suppose that relative shares are constant over time (often alleged, but debatable). There is one production function, the Cobb-Douglas, with the property that, if factors are paid their marginal products, their relative shares are independent of their supplies. Thus constancy of relative shares is at least consistent with a world of perfect competition and Cobb-Douglas production functions (and knowledge of the share of wages – or capital – in the national income is sufficient to tell us the value of the required parameter of the function). Now suppose that relative shares are observed to vary, whether over time or cross-section, but that we stick to the equality of factor prices with marginal products. If we now assume a more complicated production function[1] of the same type as the Cobb-Douglas we may use our observations of relative shares (or value added per man and wages, assumed equal to marginal value products) to estimate the parameters of the production functions. The nature of the argument here is as follows: we assume something about markets, and then use our observations of relative shares to tell us about the otherwise unobserved technology which, on our assumptions, determined the relative shares. Whether this procedure (which is followed by Solow in his pioneering paper on technical change) is justified depends, of course, on the quantitative importance of market structure in influencing relative shares.

A diametrically different approach is provided by Kalecki in his explanation of the supposed constancy of relative shares (reprinted in Part Four). He starts by assuming that marginal costs in manufacturing are constant over the normal range of output, and then turn up sharply. Constancy of marginal cost (for which there is a good deal of evidence in manufacturing) is, of course, inconsistent with perfect competition. The degree of monopoly (reciprocal of the elasticity of demand in profit-maximizing equilibrium: see the paper by Lerner in the Further Reading to Part Three) determines the discrepancy between price and marginal cost (equals average direct cost in this case). So, given raw-material costs, the share of wages in value added depends on the degree of monopoly (which must be constant to explain constancy in relative shares). The nature of the argument here is as follows: we assume something about technology, and then use our observations of relative shares to tell us something about the otherwise unobserved imperfection of the market which, on our assumptions, determined the relative shares.

I would not at this point ask anyone to choose between the two procedures! In any case, *the* question of relative shares may have

1. This is the Constant Elasticity of Substitution, or CES, production function. Cobb-Douglas is the special CES case in which the elasticity is unity. If the elasticity is not unity, although constant, shares do depend on relative factor supplies and the whole analysis is more complicated. This is immaterial to our point, which is to contrast two approaches: assuming competition, and something about the technology (functional form), use observation to quantify the technology; alternatively, assuming technology and something about the market (not perfect) use observation to quantify the imperfection.

been inappropriately formulated in the first place, in spite of its traditional importance (to Ricardo, it was *the* question of political economy, and it was certainly central to Marx; but see the paper by Solow reprinted in Part Four, and the Introduction to Part Four). The discussion is intended illustratively: at every turn, we find that what we want is quantitative information on the relative importance of technology and market structure. The importance of Bain's pioneering work is that he is endeavouring to supply this information (see Part One). Harberger, in the paper reprinted in Part Three, tries another approach to measuring the quantitative importance of market imperfection.

It would be possible to open any volume on economics with a discussion of methodology, and it would be intolerable if all volumes so opened. Some, however, might feel that there was particular reason for a volume on the theory of the firm to open with methodological discussion, since most of the methodological disputes of the profession have for many years revolved round, or at least used as examples, issues in the theory of the firm. Some, too, feel that bad and unsound argument in the theory of the firm has driven them to methodological criticism as more general and economical than *ad hoc* criticism. Yet others would argue that doubtful propositions have been persuasively defended by plausible but mistaken methodological argument. In fact, the literature on 'methodological controversy with special reference to the theory of the firm' is so vast that it would require a special volume, whence none of it will appear here: there is an annotated bibliography at the end of this Introduction. Here, I shall simply take the risk of making some bold methodological assertions, and inviting the sceptical or curious reader to sample the bibliography.

1. Economics is an empirical science: we prefer theories that explain observable phenomena to those that don't.

2. It is always necessary to check theory with observation, and this by any means we can.

3. Intuition and *a priori* argument are not sufficient to check the correspondence between theory and observation (and asking people about their motivations is notoriously and obviously likely to elicit some funny answers).

4. To check, we must know what a theory *says* about observables. Theories don't 'say'; but they yield predictions in the form of 'if . . . then' statements, *conditional predictions* that can in principle be tested (profit-maximizing firms will reduce output if excise taxes are imposed on their products). *Comparative Statics* is the familiar method of extracting the predictions from a theory.

5. 'Theories' that do not yield conditional predictions are non-theories: the prediction 'if . . . then anything might happen' can never be wrong and is therefore consistent with any state of the universe, whence it can tell us nothing about the particular state we inhabit. (Some theories say: it all depends. If the dependence is specified, the theory is at least testable in principle, however difficult it may be to obtain the conditional information.)

6. If we have rival theories, we proceed by working out their predictions, looking for disagreement and a chance to conduct a critical experiment. (If there were no contradictory predictions, in what sense, if any, would theories incorporating different assumptions *be* rivals?) We then see which theory corresponds better to observation. This procedure is the only alternative to an argument of the form 'My theory's better than yours', 'It's not', 'It is', 'Yah', 'Boo!' (If we have a theory with no rival, we should probably try to design one, partly for the hell of it, and partly to sharpen up our possible tests.)

7. Finally, and probably redundantly: the impersonality of science does not depend on the superhuman detachment, devotion, and integrity of the man in the white coat. It depends on the fact that all his work can be checked by others: his logic can be tested and his experiments repeated. The impersonality of science is a social phenomenon. The 'act of creation' that led to a scientific innovation is personal and imaginative. The product depends on logic and observation, and is in the public domain. Economic theory is a logical construct from stated axioms; and the correspondence of any theory with the world is to be checked: personal belief is immaterial to the status of a theory.

From point seven it can be deduced that the adherence of an economist to a 'school' is not of great moment, save as loyalty and conflict may stimulate him to acts of creation. It is, in any case, an editorial duty to be eclectic. The selection of papers in this volume is intended, *inter alia*, to give some sample of interesting contemporary developments and schools.

Something more must be said about the principles of selection. First, I must explain three major omissions (besides methodology). The first is general-equilibrium theory. The reasons for this omission are several. In the first place, there is not much in the way of 'firms' in contemporary general-equilibrium theory. In the second place, the subject is developing in a new, and very powerful way, with the aid of new mathematical techniques. Some of these techniques are now being effectively applied to more mundane problems in the theory of the firm. An investment in techniques other than standard calculus is, however, required. The second major omission is of historical 'classics', papers such as Viner's 'Cost curves and supply curves' or Sraffa's 'The laws of returns under competitive conditions'. There are other reasons besides the fact that many of the classics are now readily accessible. In some cases the major results are now thoroughly incorporated into standard modern textbooks (Viner's paper is an example). In other cases, the paper is important because it initiated later developments, and the developed theory may be assessed on its own (Sraffa's paper is an example). I have done my best to point to the most important and interesting of the omitted classics in the Further Reading. The third systematic omission is of papers dealing with investment. The reason is that, following the publication of Keynes's *General Theory*, investment became a part of macroeconomics, along with the consumption function. In the last few years, there has in fact been a change. Economists are increasingly trying to develop their 'macro' investment relations from properly developed theories of decision-making at the micro level. Some very important work has already appeared, but it is technically demanding. Having, under a space constraint, to make some choices, I have omitted the whole of this important and difficult literature.

A fourth topic which is only casually included is welfare economics, a subject which could well have a volume to itself. It is closely related to general-equilibrium theory on the one hand and to market structure on the other. I have chosen two important and stimulating articles particularly relevant to the problems of market structure which are dealt with here.

There have been many developments in the theory of the firm in the last quarter of a century. In 1950 Boulding complained 'The usual marginal analysis treats the firm as if it had nothing but an income account; it has no balance sheet, no capital problems and no dynamics; it maximizes an odd variable called "net revenue", of which no accountant ever heard, and presumably lives happily ever after' (1950, p. 8). If, of course, the existing theory provided satisfactory explanations of the phenomena it was designed to explain, its neglect of (irrelevant) attributes of firms was a virtue, not a vice. But the papers reprinted in this volume will illustrate that many economists have been dissatisfied, that there are yet many unsolved problems, and many controversies

One controversy that is only partly represented here is over the firm's objectives. Alternatives to the traditional assumption of profit maximization may be divided into two main groups, models in which the firm maximizes either something else, or some more complicated function of profit and something else, and models in which the firm does not maximize at all. Models in the first group are presented here in Part Six. The second group is scarcely represented at all. Versions of the non-maximizing approach vary from the crude 'cost plus' doctrine to the sophisticated 'behaviourist' models of Simon and the 'Carnegie School'. The cost-plus school is not represented because it is so crude, and, in any case, is discussed by Stigler in the paper reprinted in Part Two. Omission of the work of the Carnegie School is more debatable. It would be imperative to include some sample of the work of Simon were it not for the fact that his paper 'Theories of decision-making in economics and behavioral science' is already available in Clarkson (1968). Further references to the work of the behaviourist school, and a critique by Machlup, will be found in the Further Reading. Perhaps it is best to say that this editor is fascinated by Simon's work, but much inclined to agree with Machlup (broadly, that it is difficult to obtain systematic predictions from these models), and that it would require a great deal of space to do justice to the subject. It should also be remarked that firms can only indulge themselves in the pursuit of objectives other than profit (as they do in the models of Baumol, Marris, etc. in Part Six), or indulge themselves by simply not making the effort to maximize ('satisfice', in Simon's terminology) if the market will let them. We thus return to the essential quantitative issue: how competitive is the economy? If there is a great deal of monopolistic shelter for many firms, their non-profit objectives are important; but if there is little shelter, the pursuit of other objectives cannot quantitatively be very important. It is in recognition of this point that Marris, who presents an alternative maximizing model in Part Six, rightly discusses the economics of the take-over bid.

It is hoped that the papers collected here will illustrate something of the development of techniques of analysis, which has been very rapid in the last quarter-century. Mathematical advances have made the theory of the firm operational and practically useful as it never was before (see Part Seven). The matter of the reader's technical equipment may, however, require a comment. The standard requirement for entry to an honours course in economics in a British university is only O-level mathematics. To have restricted the papers in this volume to those comprehensible to readers with only that equipment would have been to omit most of the modern classics. I have chosen, where I could, the least technically demanding of papers which were reasonably close substitutes, but there is no escaping some calculus and some statistics. These should, in any case, be part of the honours economics course. As explained above, papers (chiefly in general-equilibrium theory) requiring a modern set-theoretic approach have been omitted entirely. So have those dealing rigorously with optimization over time, and employing the calculus of variations (which helps to account for the omission of modern work on investment).

References

BOULDING, K. E. (1950), *A Reconstruction of Economics*, Wiley.
CLARKSON, G. P. E. (ed.) (1968), *Managerial Economics*, Penguin.

Further Reading

Methodology
Philosophy

K. R. Popper, *The Open Society and Its Enemies*, 2 vols. particularly chs. 3 and 11, Routledge & Kegan Paul, 3rd edn, 1957.

K. R. Popper, *The Poverty of Historicism*, Routledge & Kegan Paul, 1957; Beacon Press, 1957.

K. R. Popper, *The Logic of Scientific Discovery*, translated from the German, Hutchinson, 1959; paperback 1968; Basic Books, 1959.

R. B. Braithwaite, *Scientific Explanation*, Cambridge University Press, 1953; paperback 1968.

History of science

A. Koestler, *The Sleepwalkers*, Hutchinson, 1959; Macmillan, 1959; Penguin, 1968.

T. S. Kuhn, *The Structure of Scientific Revolutions*, University of Chicago Press, 1962.

By economists

L. C. Robbins, *An Essay on the Nature and Significance of Economic Science*, Macmillan, 2nd edn, 1935.

M. Friedman, *Essays in Positive Economics*, Essay One, University of Chicago Press, 1953; paperback, 1966; Cambridge University Press, 1954.

T. C. Koopmans, *Three Essays on the State of Economic Science*, McGraw-Hill, 1957.

A. G. Papandreou, 'Theory construction and empirical meaning in economics', *American Economic Review Papers and Proceedings*, vol. 53, 1963, pp. 205–10.

G. C. Archibald, 'Refutation or comparison?', *British Journal for the Philosophy of Science*, vol. 17, 1966, pp. 279–96.

A. A. Alchian, 'Uncertainty, evolution and economic theory', *Journal of Political Economy*, vol. 63, 1950, pp. 211–21.

E. T. Penrose, 'Biological analogies in the theory of the firm', *American Economic Review*, vol. 42, 1952, pp. 804–19.

R. G. Lipsey, *An Introduction to Positive Economics*, ch. 1, Weidenfeld & Nicolson, 2nd edn, 1966.

Science fiction

F. Hoyle, *The Black Cloud*, Penguin, 1960.

Non-Maximizing Models

'Full-cost' doctrines were advanced by Hall and Hitch, and Andrews.

See:

R. L. Hall and C. J. Hitch, 'Price theory and business behaviour', *Oxford Economic Papers*, No. 2, reprinted in *Oxford Studies in the Price Mechanism*, T. Wilson and P. W. S. Andrews (eds.), The Clarendon Press, 1951.

P. W. S. Andrews, *Manufacturing Business*, Macmillan, 1949.

The Hall and Hitch paper is criticized in the paper by Stigler reprinted in Part Two. A full review of 'cost-plus' is in:

R. B. Heflebower, 'Full costs, cost changes and prices,' *Business Concentration and Price Policy*, Universities National Bureau Committee for Economic Research, Princeton University Press and Oxford University Press, 1955.

The most exciting (and difficult) work of the Carnegie School will be found in the collected essays of Simon (of which only some are on economics):

H. A. Simon, *Models of Man*, Wiley, 1957; Chapman & Hall, 1965

For the theory of the firm, see:

R. M. Cyert and J. G. March, *A Behavioral Theory of the Firm*, Prentice-Hall, 1963.

K. J. Cohen and R. M. Cyert, *The Theory of the Firm*, Prentice-Hall, 1965.

A methodological critique is in:

F. Machlup, 'Theories of the firm: marginalist, behavioral, managerial,' *Americal Economic Review*, March, 1967, reprinted in *Readings in the Economics of Industrial Organisation*, D. Needham (ed.), Holt, Rinehart & Winston, 1970.

Part One
Production Functions and Long-Run Costs

If marginal costs in manufacturing plants are usually constant over the normal range of output, perfect competition is impossible. So it is if returns to scale are either increasing or only start to diminish at a scale large relative to the size of the market. Monopoly may be the consequence of cost functions, or industries may be more monopolized than technology requires: the choice between 'regulation' and 'trust-busting' might depend on this. British industry may be characterized by unexploited economies of scale, in which case there might be a pay-off to increasing the size of the market, as advocates of joining the Common Market argue, or it may not.

These are just a few of the reasons why knowledge about the shape of production functions (or cost functions) is important. It is not, however, easily gained. Economists have been finding constant marginal costs at the individual plant level for a generation. Others have been fitting functions of the Cobb-Douglas type (constant returns to scale; marginal products everywhere diminishing) to aggregate data with good results. The matter is not yet settled.

Two methodological points require mention.

1. Choose the smallest efficient (least cost) plant-size. Then you may double it, treble it, etc. If you incur increased costs when you try, there must have been some indivisible factor that was not actually doubled. Vice-versa, if you cannot halve, quarter it, etc., without increased average cost there must be an indivisibility. This argument is good *until* 'invisible' or 'non-measured' indivisible factors are appealed to to account for non-constancy: the argument then becomes simply

non-empirical, metaphysical (see the paper by Peston in Further Reading).

2. After reading Caleb Smith's survey, and Friedman's Comment, one might wonder if there was any reliable method left for finding out about long-run cost curves. Bain's overwhelmingly simple answer is: go and ask! Many of his sources, however, are confidential, which raises the question 'is not the evidence too private and personal to Bain to be admissible as scientific evidence?' The answer is no, because anyone can repeat his experiment, with a different (though private) sample of respondents. Notice, incidentally, that Bain was not asking about motivation: he was asking for professional estimates on matters of fact.

Applications of the 'survivor technique' are not included here. This technique is described by Stigler in an important paper (see Further Reading):

The survivor technique proceeds to solve the problem of determining the optimum firm size as follows: Classify the firms in an industry by size, and calculate the share of industry output coming from each class over time. If the share of a given class falls, it is relatively inefficient, and in general is more inefficient the more rapidly its share falls.

An efficient size of firm, on this argument, is one that meets any and all problems the entrepreneur actually faces: strained labor relations, rapid innovation, government regulation, unstable foreign markets and what not.

The problem that this approach is addressed to is therefore more akin to that of accounting for the observed size distribution of firms in an industry (see Part Six, and particularly the paper by Hart) than that of determining the shape of the production function itself. (It must, however, be noted that information about the production functions does not seem to be much help in solving the distribution problem.)

Starting with Solow's classic 1957 paper on production functions and technical change (see Further Reading), economists have been much concerned with estimating the contributions to economic growth of investment and technical change, respectively. This interest has produced an enormous literature on estimating production functions, and substantial contributions to some of the 'classic' problems involved. Thus Griliches has successfully adjusted inputs to allow for quality change (the education of the agricultural labour force in particular). He has also relaxed the assumption of constant returns in a competitive industry, explicitly assuming that US agriculture was not in long-run equilibrium in the period studied (farms were increasing in average size). All in all, it seems that empirical studies of the sources of economic growth are going to make a contribution to our knowledge of 'the firm'.

Further Reading

On the relationship between long-run costs and production function, see J. Viner, 'Cost curves and supply curves', *Zeitschrif für Nationalökonomie*, vol. 3, 1931, pp. 23–46; reprinted in the American Economic Association *Readings in Price Theory*, Richard D. Irwin, 1952, George Allen & Unwin, 1953.

For the relationship between returns to scale and indivisibilities, see F. Knight, *Risk, Uncertainty and Profit*, Houghton Mifflin, 1921; paperback reprint by Harper & Row, 1965.

On 'indivisible factors', etc., see M. H. Peston, 'Returns to scale', *Oxford Economic Papers*, n.s. vol. 12, 1960, pp. 133–40.

For the 'survivor technique' see G. J. Stigler, 'The economics of scale', *Journal of Law and Economics*, vol. 1, 1958 pp. 54–71.

Two useful and critical papers on the Cobb-Douglas production function are E. H. P. Brown, 'The meaning of the fitted Cobb-Douglas function', *Quarterly Journal of Economics*, vol. 71, 1957, pp. 546–60, and H. Menderhausen, 'On the significance of Professor Douglas's production function', *Econometrica*, vol. 6, 1938, pp. 143–53; 'A correction', *Econometrica*, vol. 7, 1939, p. 362.

The CES production function was introduced in K. Arrow, H. Chenery, B. Minhas, R. Solow, 'Capital-labor substitution and economic efficiency', *Review of Economics and Statistics*, vol. 43, 1961, pp. 225–50.

For technical change and the production function, see
R. M. Solow, 'Technical change and the aggregate production function', *Review of Economics and Statistics*, vol. 34, 1957, pp. 312–20;
Z. Griliches, 'Estimates of the agricultural production function from cross-sectional data', *Journal of Farm Economics*, vol. 45, no. 2, 1963, pp. 419–28;
and
Z. Griliches, 'The sources of measured productivity growth: United States agriculture 1940–60', *Journal of Political Economy*, vol. 71, 1963, pp. 331–46.

A fine survey of econometric estimates of production functions is
A. A. Walters, 'Production and cost functions: an econometric survey', *Econometrica*, vol. 31, nos. 1–2, 1963, pp. 1–66.

The estimation of both short- and long-run cost functions, rather than of production functions, is surveyed and extended in
J. Johnston, *Statistical Cost Analysis*, McGraw-Hill, 1960.

1 C. A. Smith

Empirical Evidence on Economies of Scale

Abridged from C. A. Smith, 'Survey of the empirical evidence on economies of scale', from Universities National Bureau Committee for Economics Research, *Business Concentration and Price Policy*, Princeton University Press, 1955, pp. 213–30.

At the outset the reader should be warned that only after what may seem an over-long introduction have I attempted to carry out the commission assigned me: to survey the available empirical information on the variation of cost with size of plant and company, to appraise the validity of the literature on economies of large-scale production, and to indicate what generalizations it will support.

The time available proved inadequate to anything approaching a comprehensive review of the scattered and uneven material. Only a sample of the literature on economies of large-scale production has been consulted and summarized and a very limited appraisal of individual studies undertaken. The validity of the available empirical information on the variation of cost with size of plant has been weighed in general on the total information, rather than in detail.

Based on the survey, the conclusion is that the generalizations that available empirical information supports are indefinite and disappointing. In part, this is because much information in government and trade association files has never been studied[1] but in part I suspect a more fundamental difficulty.

1. So far as I have been able to discover, very little information obtained by the national war agencies which might throw substantial light on this subject has been compiled and published in a usable form. The only exception of any importance is the Office of Price Administration Economic Data Series published by the Office of Temporary Controls. The material here presented, while it seems worthy of more study than it has received, is certainly less significant than the data we had reason to hope might emerge from the OPA files. The most needed research job today in the field of the relation of cost to size of plant and firm would be one done by a government agency with full access to the data accumulated during the war. If

Whenever the best answer to any question adduced by empirical investigators tells them little, the question should be re-examined. Because I was disappointed in the answers to the question, 'What generalization will the empirical evidence on economies of scale support?' I undertook the introductory analysis comprising so much of this paper. This re-examination may be divided into two parts.

First, what sort of problems arise when we seek empirical evidence of a relationship developed in deductive theory?

Second, what related questions might have more significant answers?[2] These two questions will be examined in some detail in the following Introduction to this discussion.

Introduction

The effort to obtain empirical evidence of relationships which have been developed in deductive economic theory encounters two sets of problems. The first centers around the widespread but fundamental misconception as to the nature of empirical facts. Certain empirical facts – the length of a table (under specified conditions), for instance – can be defined operationally. (That is, the process of measurement against a specified standard of length may be described.) Such facts have validity for any use where the operational process of measurement and the standard used are acceptable.

But there is another sort of empirical fact which has meaning only in terms of a complicated conceptual framework. That a particular empirical study shows or does not show economies of scale is an example of this. Only in terms of a carefully delineated concept can we say that particular evidence shows or does not show economies of scale. The Introduction to this paper first considers the concept of economies of scale and distinguishes this from concepts with which it easily may be confused in empirical work.

---

one of the small business committees of Congress, for instance, would put a modest research staff to work on this task, a monograph of very great value probably could be produced.

2. The author claims no originality in questioning the question asked. Such questions have been posed by the authors of some of the studies surveyed in the preparation of this paper.

The second set of problems centers around the elimination of variations in cost which do not result from differences in size of plant or firm. Simplifying assumptions are essential to the development of theoretical concepts. Inevitably, however, each simplifying assumption blocks the path toward an empirical investigation of the relationship which the theory states. In empirical investigation the complexities cannot be removed by a simple declarative sentence; nor can the empirical economist – like his empirical brethren in the laboratory sciences – remove complicating factors by carefully regulated experiments in which the factors are held constant. The second subsection of the Introduction to this paper discusses some of the more serious problems posed by factors other than scale which influence costs in the empirical studies of economies of scale.

The final subsection of the Introduction considers some questions closely related to economies of scale, in the hope of finding a more promising line of inquiry.

To give some precision to this discussion, economies of scale may be defined as equivalent to a falling long-run average cost function.[3] These economies can be considered either with respect to size of plants or of firms. The long-run average cost function of economic theory shows the long-run relationship between average cost and the output of one homogeneous product.

Questions of definition arise with respect to the terms 'average cost' and 'size'. Average cost includes (in the economist's definition) the imputed cost of capital or any other services supplied by the owners. Empirical data generally follow accounting practice and exclude dividend payments and other payments of 'profits' to owners from costs. Unfortunately, there is no reason to assume that costs covered by dividends are the same for all plants or firms making the same product. In fact there are reasons to think that there may be systematic variations in these costs with size of firm. Salaries of owners who are officers of corporations which show little relation to value of services rendered pose a similar problem of a possible systematic variation between costs recorded by

3. The long-run average cost function is the envelope curve to the short-run average cost function. Thus the capacity or size of a plant or of a firm is that output for which the short-run cost function and the long-run cost function coincide.

accountants and the economist's cost for firms of different size. When using empirical material to test economic theory, we must not forget these different concepts of cost.

To measure size in empirical studies of economies of scale is even more difficult. The measurement of output is unequivocal only if the output is homogeneous. In practice we do not find either plants or firms which, during a period of growth from small-scale to large-scale, produced one homogeneous product, nor do we find a group of plants or firms of widely different size which produce a single homogeneous product.[4] Output of plants and firms is in fact heterogeneous to a very substantial extent. Since the definition of economic theory has little relation to reality, let us explore the implicit definition of common usage.

When we talk about the size of a plant or firm we ordinarily mean its capacity to turn out its entire product mix, not its capacity to turn out one specific product. When we talk about cost in relation to size we ordinarily mean the cost of a specific product. We thus pose two problems: (1) What do we mean by cost for one of a group of products? (2) What are we doing when we relate the cost of one product to capacity to produce a multiplicity of products?

The cost of a number of products produced by a firm can be determined only on the basis of arbitrary allocations. In practice, empirical studies of economies of scale have accepted the cost allocations made by the firms studied. Unfortunately, the cost accounting techniques used by business are not nearly so highly standardized in most industries as are income accounting techniques. These have been subjected to at least two powerful standardizing influences which have not affected cost accounting techniques: the rules of the Bureau of Internal Revenue, and the pronouncements of the American Institute of Accountants, which shape accounting practices through the institution of outside auditors. In spite of the standardizing influences to which income accounting techniques are subject, the lack of comparability of

4. The reader should not conclude that data from even such plants or firms would, without surmounting further problems, yield an empirical counterpart of the theoretical long-run cost function.

balance sheet and income statement data of different firms lead the author of a well-known text on financial statement analysis to issue this warning:

The figures of one enterprise may be compared with those compiled for another only with great care. The combination of the financial statement data of different enterprises for statistical studies is usually unsatisfactory (Meyer, 1952, p. 44).

It is extremely unlikely that the cost figures obtained from the accounting records of a group of firms are really comparable. The student of empirical data on economies of scale is seldom in a position to make the figures comparable; he can only hope that there will be no incomparability systematically related to size. The dangers in using cost accounting figures in empirical studies of economies of scale are, I believe, greater than most economists realize, because their lack of familiarity with accounting practice leads them to underestimate the uncertainties of cost data.

The second problem posed by the comparison of cost for one product with size measured in terms of a multiplicity of products is a conceptual one. What relation, if any, is there between the concept of economies of scale as defined in economic theory (a relation between cost and size in plants or firms producing homogeneous output) and either (1) the concept of a relation between the cost of producing one of many products and the size of plants or firms measured in terms of composite output, or (2) the concept of a residual relation between cost and size after allowing for the effect of variations in other dimensions of output?

If the product mix of the composite output for the different observations of cost and size is highly similar, then we are seeking a relationship which might be regarded as similar to the concept of economies of scale as defined in economic theory. The problem is to distinguish sufficiently similar product mixes from those which are diverse. Here we must rely upon our own judgement and that of the investigator.[5]

5. Unfortunately, once an economist discovers data which might be used for an empirical study he is strongly inclined to use them, if it is at all possible, and to present the study 'for whatever it is worth'. Others, less familiar with the problems posed by the basic data, are likely to overrate the significance of the study.

Even if we accept similar product mixes[6] as the output in a study of the long-run cost output relation, the problem of measuring output remains. If all the elements of the product mix occurred in the same proportion at all different sizes of plant or firm any element might be used as the measure of output, and we might as well regard the output as homogeneous. The real problem of measurement of output arises because the elements of the product mix occur in different proportions for the different observations of cost and size. The use of a number of different dimensions of size, which might appear to be a way around this problem, is explored later and found to be generally impractical. Perhaps the most practical method of measuring the amount of a somewhat heterogeneous product mix is to use the familiar though arbitrary common denominator of economics – money value. We may at times wish to question price as a measure of output but at least it has the merit of being a market evaluation.[7]

There are at least two ways to get around the two problems posed by cost allocation and the relation between the cost of one part of output and size in terms of a composite measure of output. The first is to study the relation between cost per composite unit of output and scale in terms of the composite unit, i.e. if money value is used as the composite unit, the cost of a dollar of output at various dollar scales of output. The second is to regard output, and hence size of plant, as having many dimensions. Each of these routes around the problems will be explored in some detail.

The difficulties with studies of cost per dollar of output in relation to capacity measured in dollars of output are obvious.

6. What should be meant by product mix similarity? To require similar percentages of identical products would be too restrictive. Product mixes might better be regarded as highly similar even though no product in one is homogeneous with any part of the other if all the products are highly similar and are produced in highly similar percentages. Thus the output of Fords and of Chevrolets might be regarded as similar product mixes.

7. The use of this common denominator has the added practical advantage that general price-level changes will tend to move an observation of cost and size more or less along the function rather than almost at right angles to it as would occur if a physical measure of output were used with a money measure of costs.

Different firms may charge different prices for the same product. More serious questions arise when the price differences between similar products do not fairly represent differences in the 'quantity' of output. In spite of these obvious difficulties, studies relating cost per dollar of sales to dollar capacity for plants or firms which have similar product mixes may be preferable to those seeking to relate cost for a particular product to either a physical or a dollar measure of capacity. Further, the data needed to determine costs per dollar of output in relation to scale measured in dollars of sales are more generally available than are data needed to determine the relation between costs per unit of a particular physical output and size, though empirical economists have been afraid to use them. This reluctance may rest on no more secure basis than a greater familiarity with variations in price for the same product than with variations in costs allocated to the same product by different cost accounting systems or with the variability of product mixes within an industry.

The second way around the problems posed by cost allocation and by relating cost of a part of output to capacity to produce many different products is to regard output as having many dimensions. In a study of costs for airlines, Ferguson explores this method (1949). Ferguson, in summarizing his study, says that it 'avoids the assumption of a homogeneous product and deals explicitly with the problems of varying the quality and the product mix of output' (p. 1). Explicitly, the product is not conceived of as simply ton-miles or passenger-miles; speed and length of flight are introduced as measures of output characteristics. The introduction of additional dimensions of output results in complications which are more than computational.

On the surface, the problem of measuring somewhat heterogeneous output appears to be more manageable conceptually when the idea of several dimensions of output is introduced, but here new problems arise. First, what is the significance of one of several dimensions of output? Second, can the data support statistical procedures for separating the effects of variations in several dimensions?

We must realize that not all dimensions of output measure the size of plant or firm. It is easy to conceive of a scale relationship between costs per ton-mile and 'capacity' in ton-miles in which all other dimensions of output are held constant; but to conceive of the relation between costs per mile per hour and capacity in miles per hour *as a scale relationship* is bizarre. (Incidentally, capacity in miles per hour is a dimension for which cost increases rapidly with large 'scale'.) The whole problem of what is meant by 'scale' is cast in a different light when viewed as the dimensions of a single output. The usual notion of a larger plant or firm involves the production of a greater number of identical units of output. It is better to regard the other dimensions of output as elements in the heterogeneity of output. Interesting relations between cost and any of these dimensions of output may be discovered empirically, but they should not be regarded as cost–size relations.

It may be suggested that empirical study should seek an overall relationship between cost and all the various dimensions of output and size. One phase of this complex would be the cost-size relation. Output has too many dimensions to make this approach seem promising as an empirical method of deriving a cost–size relation. Ordinarily, observations are too few to indicate the shape of a cost–size relation after allowing for the effect of many other variables.

The multiplicity of dimensions of product is fantastic. Simply in terms of its physical characteristics, a product always has more than one dimension, and the dimensions of a product cannot be so limited. Among its other dimensions are consumer and trade acceptance of the brand name and the characteristics of its distributive system. Thus, although it may be possible to describe the outputs of a steel rolling mill by many fewer dimensions than the number of products, even the minimum number of dimensions probably would leave the problem of deriving a cost-output function statistically unmanageable.

Competing products may have quite different dimensions in these respects. The possibility of having a larger firm or plant may depend upon the existence of different dimensions for the product of the large-scale firm. A good example of the different non-physical dimensions of competitive products is found in a study of costs incurred by fourteen manufacturers of rubber tires. The data are presented by the Office of Temporary Controls (1947).[8]

8. A portion of this data is presented in an article by Blair (1948).

In August 1943 for the 6–16 four-ply synthetic rubber passenger car tire the selling, general and administrative expense for the four largest manufacturers was 65 cents more per tire than for the ten other manufacturers studied. This 69 per cent higher cost indicates a different dimension of the product. Whether or not we enjoy listening to the 'Firestone Hour' we must recognize that it helps give the Firestone tire a different dimension; that is, it makes it a different product. The higher cost of selling and administration is not just the result of the larger size of the firm, but of expenses undertaken to differentiate the product. These expenses may be necessary in order to have the larger firm or they may be profitable only for the larger firms. If the former, then the data may be regarded as revealing the cost-size relation for firms producing this product. On the other hand, if they are not necessary to the maintenance of the larger firms but are profitable for the larger firms though they would not be profitable for smaller firms, the data pertain to two products too dissimilar to reveal a cost-size relation.

Methods used to handle cost variations from causes other than economies of scale

Ideally, empirical evidence on economies of scale should be obtained by observing the variations in cost associated with different scales of plant or firm with all other cost influences constant. Since it is obviously impossible to find any such situation, the relation between average cost and the scale of plant or firm must be sought by other means. Two methods of study have been used which may be characterized as the statistical approach and the engineering approach.

In the statistical approach, the costs of the plant or firm as a unit or the costs allocated to some type of output are related to size. Other influences on cost either are ignored or allowed for by such techniques as deflation or multiple correlation. Though the details will not be discussed here, some inherent weaknesses of this approach will be considered.

First, statistical data show costs in relation to scale for the many different technologies actually used by plants or firms for which sufficient empirical evidence is available to make it possible to include them in a statistical study. If the technologies used by the different plants varied only because different sizes of plant require different technology, the data would be appropriate. But technology varies from plant to plant for other reasons. For example, some plants are old, others newly built while technological horizons have changed from year to year. Further, technologies were selected at various times because of different relative factor prices, or because of different demand expectations, etc. Statistical studies have limited significance because they regarded all or most of the plants or firms currently classified as part of the 'industry' as sufficiently homogeneous in technology to warrant grouping them together to derive a long-run cost function.

Another difficulty with the statistical approach is that it assumes that each cost-size observation used represents a point on the long-run cost function; that is, that every output studied is the optimal output for that plant or firm. This is an heroic assumption, but most studies make no attempt to eliminate any observations because they represent obviously non-optimal outputs. There is, perhaps, a tacit assumption that at any one time all plants or firms are operating in the same relation to optimal output and that their non-optimal function is similar to the optimal cost function. Simply to state these assumptions reveals their inherent dangers.

In the engineering approach, each element of the production process is studied to discover the relation between inputs and outputs at different scales for that process. The input-output relations of the processes are then combined to give the over-all input-output relations. The introduction of prices for the inputs transforms these relations into cost-output relations. Since this method of study is less familiar, two studies of economies of scale made from the engineering point of view will be discussed as examples of the method. These studies are presented in unpublished doctoral theses written independently but at about the same time at Harvard.

The first of these studies, already mentioned, was submitted by Ferguson (1949). The second was submitted by Chenery (1949). Both studies apply parts of the great mass of engineering observations of the relations between inputs and outputs to an analysis of over-all cost functions of both the short- and long-run variety. The technique of using engineering laws in discussions of economics of scale is not new[9] except in the thoroughness and precision with which it is applied, but this exact use opens exciting new vistas for the further study of economies of scale which can be made on the basis of the empirical relations developed by engineers.

Chenery, in the summary of his thesis, says

The purpose of this study is to determine the usefulness of physical laws for the economic analysis of production. It seeks to develop a method by which the type of calculation made by engineers in designing plants and equipment may be used to derive the general relations among productive factors expressed in the production function of economic theory (1949, p. 1).

Ferguson's conception of the subject for investigation, though it is essentially the same, is broader. He is concerned not only with the 'technical' but also with the 'institutional determinants of the amount of each type of input required and [with] ascertaining the quantitative input-output relationship so determined' (1949, p. 2). The author recognizes that the institutionally determined input-output relations are subject both to arbitrary changes and to changes which may be induced by a large or sudden change in this input or in other inputs. However, the inclusion of what have sometimes been called human engineering relations in the purview of engineering studies considerably broadens the usefulness of the technique.

Studies made by economists on the basis of observations by engineers avoid the problem which arises from the fact that the existing plant was built when different technological horizons existed, but they have similar limitations. They have been over-oriented toward the study of input-output relations in the elements of the presently utilized productive processes because these relations are the only ones thoroughly investigated by the engineers. The authors have recognized explicitly the fact that this narrowed the economic significance of their studies. The importance of this limitation is greatest if a change in scale or factor prices makes it more economical to adopt techniques, the input-

9. Economic discussions frequently have pointed out engineering laws which may lead to either economies or diseconomies of scale, e.g. that heat loss is proportional to the square of any one dimension while volume is proportional to the cube.

output relations of which have not been studied. Furthermore, engineering studies show ideal rather than actual relations of size and cost. This is good or bad, depending on what we want the cost function to reveal. Finally, the relation of factor cost to scale, if not explicitly studied, further limits the usefulness of the engineering studies.

The problem of cost and size of plant is more susceptible to study through the engineering approach than is the problem of cost and size of firm because the relations between the plants which make up a firm do not lend themselves to engineering study. These relations probably are dominated by the more or less unique considerations for each aggregation of plants into a firm.

The question to which we seek an answer

When we ask the supposedly precise scientific question, what is the relation of cost to size of plant or firm, we are usually concerned in fact with finding answers to questions which appear less precise: Are giant firms more efficient or do they prosper because of 'unfair' advantages? How much saving does the public get from giant firms? How?

Examination of the data that are available and that conceivably might be available shows that we cannot hope to make very satisfactory empirical studies of the long-run cost function. I believe that if we asked the student of the data to tell us in detail just what cost differences exist between different types and sizes of plant and firm and what causes, if any, he could discover for those differences, the information would go farther to clarify the practical questions to which we seek answers than would studies of the relation of cost to size.

Comments on a sample of the empirical studies

Before venturing on a statement of the generalizations which the empirical evidence warrants, some comments on a sampling of the material which has become available since 1940 will be presented. Earlier material on the subject was published ten years ago by the National Bureau of Economic Research (1943). This discussion provides, in my opinion, an adequate treatment of the material prior to 1940. The material published since 1940 enables us to fill in some portions of the picture drawn there. We still lack sufficient data for confident and precise generalization.

In 1941 a study prepared by the Federal Trade Commission was published. This presents substantial material each part of which, however, is rather briefly and superficially analysed. The results show that, in general, medium-sized business[10] is most efficient in the industries and instances studied. The material on costs of individual plants and companies in a number of industries shows that very seldom (one out of fifty-nine cases for companies, and two out of fifty-three cases for plants) did the largest plant or company show the lowest costs. These results, unfortunately, prove little since the much greater number of medium-sized, small and very small plants and companies included biases the results. This may be, in part, the result of more frequent accounting abnormalities among small and medium-sized businesses. Furthermore, we should expect to find that some small or medium-sized plants or companies had especially favorable cost conditions. These facts – coupled with a lack of detailed discussion and analysis of the material presented – (much of it rather sketchy) prejudice the scholarly mind against accepting the conclusions which seem to follow from the data in the monograph.[11]

On the other hand, a second look at the data reveals somewhat better evidence in support of the idea that small or medium-sized business is more efficient.

1. 'On the average, over one-third of the companies in every array' and 'over one-third of the plants in each cost array had . . . costs lower than that of the largest company' or 'plant'. Federal Trade Commission (1941, p. 12).

2. When data for companies or plants grouped according to size were used, in ten out of eleven cases when companies were studied, and in all five cases when plants were studied, the medium-sized group showed lowest costs (p. 12).

10. The classification 'medium-sized' is sometimes strained, e.g. Chrysler is called medium-sized when clearly the significant difference between Chrysler and Ford is in degree of vertical integration.

11. For a reasoned and highly critical review of this monograph see Blair (1942).

3. A few quick calculations on some of the cost data presented in arrays but not included in the grouped data mentioned above, show instances – although not an overwhelming predominance of cases – in which grouping the plants or companies would result in the medium-sized plants showing the lowest costs. The mass of data is so great and the conclusion of lower costs for medium-sized plants or companies so general that in spite of the fact that almost every individual study is subject to serious criticism it is necessary to give considerable weight to the findings.

There may be a bias in the data on cost and size of firm which prejudices our conclusions. It is entirely possible that, although almost always we find costs for the largest firms higher than for a group of medium-sized firms, it is not general. In those industries where cost continues to decrease with increasing size it is probable that all the medium-sized firms either have become giants and swallowed the other medium-sized firms or they have failed or shrunk into small firms. If this is the case, the sound generalization is not that medium-sized firms have, in general, lower costs than do large firms, but that in industries where both medium-sized and large-sized firms are found, the costs of the medium-sized firms are probably lower than those of the large firms. (But, let us not forget that 'medium-sized' here includes the Chrysler Corporation.)

A study by Steindl presents some interesting ideas and evidence on the general subject of size of plants and firms although it offers little bearing directly on our question. He shows, by the use of data from the *Statistics of Income*, that capital intensification accompanies increasing size of firm for all manufacturing industry as a group, for mining, for trade, and for most of the major subgroups of manufacturing. He rejects as unlikely the possibility that this showing of greater capital intensity for larger firms is caused only by differences in the products produced by small and large firms or by greater vertical integration of larger firms (1945, pp. 23–5). Steindl devotes a considerable part of his study to demonstrating that with capital intensification, the profit rate will fall beyond a certain point even if cost per unit of output continues to fall. He thus offers a possible explanation of the declining profit rates frequently found by Crum (1939) for the largest corporations in any industry which is consistent with the idea that unit costs are lower for larger companies. He also explores suggestively certain difficulties the large firm may face because of imperfect competition or oligopoly. The high selling and administrative costs of the four largest tire manufacturers, discussed earlier, is an example of this problem. He re-analyses the material on the growth of concentration in manufacturing and shows that although the percentage of wage earners in manufacturing establishments with over one thousand wage earners hardly changed from 1919 to 1937, establishments with two hundred and fifty to one thousand wage earners gained substantially relative to establishments with fewer than fifty wage earners (Steindl, 1945, p. 49). This loss by small manufacturing business he regards as a significant continuance of the concentration pattern which was so marked before and during the First World War.

Steindl, in his discussion of capital intensity, highlights the association of size with capital intensity. He asserts that 'large-scale economies are in reality *technically* inseparable from capital intensification, so that the greater plant, if it is to make use of large-scale economies, has also to use a greater proportion of capital to labor' (1945, p. 22). While we may admit readily that many large-scale economies require much capital there seems no *a priori* reason why a small-scale plant using the best available technology and facing the same relative factor prices should use relatively less capital.

Greater capital intensity in large-scale plants could result if small-scale plants have inadequate capital resources, or if their managers believe they can find more profitable uses for capital in horizontal expansion rather than in capital intensification. If few small-scale enterprises want to put capital into intensive investment, the capital-intensive technology for small-scale plants will not be as adequately developed and the appropriate capital-intensive machines will not be readily available to them. There are, also, other reasons why small-scale technology may be less well developed in general than large-scale technology. On the basis of all these factors, we may conclude that, if capital intensification, as a rule, leads to lower unit costs, a systematic difference in the capital intensity of the technology between plants of different sizes may prejudice seriously the unit-cost size relations which we discover empirically.

C. A. Smith 39

Many numbers of the Office of Price Administration Economic Data Series published in 1947 by the Office of Temporary Controls contain certain material on cost and size of firm.[12]

In a paper presented at the December 1947 meetings of the American Economic Association, Blair (1948) analysed data for several industries which show the lowest cost for groups of plants or companies smaller than the largest group. On the basis of this evidence he seems ready to make the generalization that both plants and firms which are larger than the lowest cost size are found in practice in a substantial number of industries. His conclusion is especially interesting in view of his attack, referred to above (Blair, 1942), on the similar conclusions drawn in the TNEC Monograph 13. It should be noted that he attaches great significance to the growth of new 'decentralizing' techniques which have improved the position of plants and firms of less than maximum size.

A study by Florence (1948) presents a great deal of information on subjects related to that here under survey. He shows that in many industries the predominant size of plant is not large. More specifically, he shows that highly localized industry generally has medium-sized plants. If predominance of a plant size less than that of the largest firms may be taken as an indication of a certain sort of efficiency (even if not of lowest average cost) for medium-sized firms, his data clearly establish substantial areas in which medium-sized firms are 'efficient'.

There also is scattered evidence, some of it of very high quality, on the relation of cost and size. Unpublished Harvard doctoral

12. Study 10, on rubber tire and tube manufacturers, cited earlier, shows costs divided into several categories for nine products for two size groups of firms. Study 7 on retail furniture stores shows operating expenses as a percentage of sales for three size groups in metropolitan and non-metropolitan areas. Study 12, on fresh fruit and vegetable wholesalers, gives cost figures for four cost categories for five size groups of wholesalers for each of three types of wholesaler. Study 13, on women's underwear and nightwear, gives cost figures for two different years by five cost categories for six size groups of manufacturers. Study 26 on grocers retail chains and wholesale, gives expense as a percentage of sales by size groups for a considerable number of time periods. Other studies in this series contain similar data. Detailed appraisal of this mass of material would be a major task which, so far as I know, has not been undertaken.

theses by Ferguson (1949) and by Chenery (1949) have already been mentioned.

Conclusion

It is both difficult and dangerous to generalize on the basis of the scattered and heterogeneous empirical material on economies of scale. The following generalizations, however, appear to be warranted by the evidence I have examined in the preparation of this paper and in my connection with the preparation of chapter 10 of the earlier National Bureau of Economic Research Study (1943).

1. With increasing size of plant, at least from small to medium size, average cost of production declines as size increases if factor costs are held constant.

2. There is no substantial evidence that the decline in unit costs stops before the maximum size of plant available for study if factor costs are held constant and the product is the same. On the other hand, the little evidence available does not refute the idea that the long-run cost curve even with factor prices constant turns up at some attainable size. We can hardly hope to find an answer to this question as to whether there is in practice a plant so large that the costs of producing a specific product increase even if factor prices are held constant because:

(a) Factor costs, especially labor costs, seem to vary with size of plant. Generalization is hazardous and must be based primarily upon studies not concerned with determining the long-run cost function because most of the studies of the long-run cost function have not given this problem careful consideration. Generally, wage rates are found to be higher in the larger plants while probably raw materials (exclusive of assembly costs) and almost certainly capital, are cheaper.

(b) Assembly costs and distribution costs per unit decline for a time with increasing size of plant but usually start to increase within the range of size of plant available for study.[13]

These increases in factor prices and in assembly and distribution costs result in cost increases which make it impractical to

13. This conclusion is based primarily on studies of plants engaged in first stage agricultural processing, but there is no evidence to indicate that it is not generally applicable.

build plants which might be large enough to have higher average cost. Therefore, we have no opportunity to study the costs of such giant plants.

The hypothesis that the long-run cost function for the production of a product typically turns up at some very large size cannot be subjected to empirical verification. Even if one or two products should be found for which the cost elements which are supposed to be impounded in *ceteris paribus* do not in practice increase so as to prevent practical businessmen from expanding and the giant plants which they then built showed higher unit costs (*ceteris paribus*), it would be foolhardy to generalize on these instances. Furthermore, if the range in size of plants in practice stops (because factor prices and assembly and distribution costs increase) within the range in which the cost of producing a specific product is still decreasing when factor prices are held constant, the hypothesis that the long-run cost function eventually turns up is not very meaningful even if it could be proved. The fact that there is no substantial evidence that the long-run cost function for plants does not continue to decline up to the largest sizes found in practice if factor prices are held constant (a generalization apparently justified by the evidence) seems to have much greater significance for economists.

3. With increasing size of firm, the best documented generalization about average cost is that when factor costs are not held constant and outputs which are not the same but are sold competitively are considered as similar, costs decline with increasing size of firm up to a rather high point but that frequently and perhaps generally beyond a certain size of firm, costs again increase. But there is no satisfactory basis for distinguishing types of product for which the long-run cost function of the firm rises within the range of firm size actually found in practice.

References

BLAIR, J. M. (1942), 'The relation between size and efficiency of business', *Rev. econ. Stats.*, vol. 24, pp. 125–35.

BLAIR, J. M. (1948), 'Technology and size', *Amer. econ. Rev.*, vol. 38, pp. 121–52.

CHENERY, H. B. (1949), 'Engineering bases of economic analyses', Harvard University Library.

CRUM, W. L. (1939), *Corporate Size and Earning Power*, Harvard University Press.

FEDERAL TRADE COMMISSION (1941), *Relative Efficiency of Large, Medium-Sized and Small Business*, Temporary National Economic Committee, monograph no. 13.

FERGUSON, A. R. (1949), 'A technical synthesis of airline costs', Harvard University Library.

FLORENCE, P. S. (1948), *Investment, Location and Size of Plant*, Cambridge University Press.

MEYER, J. N. (1952), *Financial Statement Analysis*, Prentice-Hall.

NATIONAL BUREAU OF ECONOMIC RESEARCH (1943), *Cost Behaviour and Price Policy*.

OFFICE OF TEMPORARY CONTROLS (1947), *Survey of Rubber Tire Manufacturers*, OPA Data Series 10.

STEINDL, J. (1945), *Small and Big Business*, Oxford University Institute of Statistics, monograph no. 1.

2 Milton Friedman

Theory and Measurement of Long-Run Costs

M. Friedman, 'Comment', from Universities National Bureau
Committee for Economics Research, *Business Concentration and Price
Policy*, Princeton University Press, 1955, pp. 230–37.

I have great sympathy with Caleb Smith's conclusion that the
right questions have not been asked of the data on the costs of
firms of different sizes. My quarrel with him is that he does not go
far enough. I believe that cross-section contemporaneous accounting data for different firms or plants give little if any information
on so-called economies of scale. Smith implies that difficulty
arises because the observed phenomena do not correspond
directly with the theoretical constructs; because there is no single,
homogeneous product, and so on. I believe that the basic difficulty is both simpler and more fundamental; that the pure theory
itself gives no reason to expect that cross-section data will yield
the relevant cost curves. Some of the bases for this view are suggested by Smith in his discussion, but he stops short of carrying
them to their logical conclusion.

No specialized factors of production

Let us consider first the simplest theoretical case, when all factors
of production are unspecialized so there are numerous possible
firms all potentially alike. This is the model that implicitly or
explicitly underlies most textbook discussions of cost curves. For
present purposes, we may beg the really troublesome point about
this case – why there is any limit to the size of the firm – and
simply assume that there is some resource ('entrepreneurial
ability') of which each firm can have only one unit, that these
units are all identical, and that the number in existence (though
not the number in use) is indefinitely large, so all receive a return
of zero.

In this case, the (minimum) average cost at which a particular
firm can produce each alternative hypothetical output is clearly

defined, independently of the price of the product, since it depends entirely on the prices that the resources can command in alternative uses. The average cost curve is the same for all firms and independent of the output of the industry, so the long-run supply curve is horizontal, and hence determines the price of the product.[1] In the absence of mistakes or changes in conditions, all firms would be identical in size, and would operate at the same output and the same average cost. The number of firms would be determined by conditions of demand. In this model, the 'optimum' size firm has an unambiguous meaning.

Suppose this model is regarded as applying to a particular industry. Differences among firms in size (however measured) are then to be interpreted as the result of either mistakes or changes in circumstances that have altered the appropriate size of firm. If 'mistakes' are about as likely to be on one side as the other of the 'optimum' size, the mean or modal size firm in the industry căn be regarded as the 'optimum'; but there is no necessity for mistakes to be symmetrically distributed, and in any event this approach assumes the answer that cross-section studies seek.

What more, if anything, can contemporaneous accounting data add? Can we use them to compute the average cost curve that was initially supposed to exist? Or even to determine the size of firm with minimum average cost? I think not. Consider a firm that made a 'mistake' and is in consequence, let us say, too large. This means that the average cost per unit of output that would currently have to be incurred to produce the firm's present output by reproducing the firm would be higher than the price of the product. It does not mean that the current accounting cost is – even if there have been no changes in conditions since the firm was established, so that original cost corresponds to reproduction cost. If the firm has changed hands since it was established, the price paid for the 'good will' of the firm will have taken full

1. This neglects some minor qualifications, of which two may deserve explicit mention: first, the irrelevance of the output of the industry depends somewhat on the precise assumptions about the source of any increased demand; second, strictly speaking, the supply curve may have tiny waves in it attributable to the finite number of firms. On the first point, see Brumberg (1953).

account of the mistake; the original investors will have taken a capital loss, and the new owners will have a level of cost equal to price. If the firm has not changed hands, accounting costs may well have been similarly affected by write-downs and the like. In any event, cost as computed by the statistician will clearly be affected if capital cost is computed by imputing a market return to the equity in the firm as valued by the capital market. In short, differences among contemporaneous recorded costs tell nothing about the *ex ante* costs of outputs of different size but only about the efficiency of the capital market in revaluing assets.

In the case just cited, data on historical costs would be relevant. However, their relevance depends critically on the possibility of neglecting both technological and monetary changes in conditions affecting costs since the firms were established. A more tempting possibility is to estimate reproduction costs. This involves essentially departing from contemporaneous accounting data and using engineering data instead, in which case there seems little reason to stick to the particular plants or firms that happen to exist as a result of historical accidents.

Under the assumed conditions, the unduly large firms would be converting themselves into smaller ones, the unduly small firms into larger ones, so that all would be converging on 'the' single optimum size. Changes over time in the distribution of firms by size might in this way give some indication of the 'optimum' size of firm.

Specialized factors of production

The existence of specialized factors of production introduces an additional reason why firms should differ in size. Even if output is homogeneous, there is no longer, even in theory, a single 'optimum' or 'equilibrium' size. The appropriate size of firm to produce, say, copper, may be different for two different mines, and both can exist simultaneously because it is impossible to duplicate either one precisely – this is the economic meaning of 'specialized' factors. Or, to take another example, Jones's special forte may be organization of production efficiently on a large scale; Robinson's, the maintenance of good personal relations with customers; the firm that gives appropriate scope to Jones's special ability may be larger than the firm that gives appropriate scope to Robinson's.

It follows that in any 'industry', however defined, in which the resources used cannot be regarded as unspecialized, there will tend to be firms of different size. One could speak of an 'optimum distribution of firms by size', perhaps, but not of an 'optimum' size of firm. The existing distribution reflects both 'mistakes' and intended differences designed to take advantage of the particular specialized resources under the control of different firms.

The existence of specialized resources not only complicates the definition of 'optimum' size; even more important, it makes it impossible to define the average cost of a particular firm for different hypothetical outputs independently of conditions of demand. The returns to the specialized factors are now 'rents', at least in part, and, in consequence, do not determine the price, but are determined by it. To take the copper mine of the preceding paragraph, its cost curve cannot be computed without knowledge of the royalty or rent that must be paid to the owners of the mine, if the firm does not itself own it, or imputed as royalty or rent, if the firm does. But the royalty is clearly dependent on the price at which copper sells on the market and is determined in such a way as to make average cost tend to equal price.

The point at issue may perhaps be put in a different way. The long-run conditions of equilibrium for a competitive firm are stated in the textbooks as 'price equals marginal cost equals average cost'. But with specialized resources, 'price equals marginal cost' has a fundamentally different meaning and significance from 'price equals average cost'. The first is a goal of the firm itself; the firm seeks to equate marginal cost to price, since this is equivalent to maximizing its return. The second is not, in any meaningful sense, a goal of the firm; indeed, its avoidance could with more justification be said to be its goal, at least in the meaning it would be likely to attach to average cost. The equality of price to average cost is a result of equilibrium, not a determinant of it; it is forced on the firm by the operation of the capital market or the market determining rents for specialized resources.

Consider a situation in which a group of competitive firms are all appropriately adjusted to existing conditions, in which there is no tendency for firms to change their output, for new firms to enter, or for old firms to leave – in short, a situation of long-run equilibrium. For each firm separately, marginal cost (long-run and short-run) is equal to price – otherwise, the firms would be seeking to change their outputs. Suppose that, for one or more firms, total payments to hired factors of production fall short of total revenue – that average cost in this sense is less than price. If these firms could be reproduced by assembling similar collections of hired factors, there would be an incentive to do so. The fact that there is no tendency for new firms to enter means that they cannot be reproduced, implying that the firms own some specialized factors. For any one firm, the difference between total receipts and total payments to hired factors is the rent attributable to these specialized factors; the capitalized value of this rent is the amount that, in a perfect capital market, would be paid for the firm; if the firm were sold for this sum, the rent would show up on the books as 'interest' or 'dividends'; if it is not sold, a corresponding amount should be imputed as a return to the 'goodwill' or capital value of the firm. The equality between price and average cost, in any sense in which it is more than a truism, thus reflects competition on the capital market and has no relation to the state of competition in product or factor markets.

For simplicity, the preceding discussion is in terms of a competitive industry. Clearly, the same analysis applies to a monopolistic firm with only minor changes in wording. The firm seeks to equate marginal cost and marginal revenue. The capital market values the firm so as to make average cost tend to equal price. Indeed, one of the specialized factors that receives rent may be whatever gives the firm its monopolistic power, be it a patent or the personality of its owner.

It follows from this analysis that cross-section accounting data on costs tell nothing about 'economies of scale' in any meaningful sense. If firms differ in size because they use different specialized resources, their average costs will all tend to be equal, provided they are properly computed so as to include rents. Whether actually computed costs are or are not equal can only tell us something about the state of the capital market or of the accounting profession. If firms differ in size partly because of mistakes, the comments on the preceding simpler model apply; historical cost data might be relevant, but it is dubious that current accounting cost data are. And how do we know whether the differences in size are mistakes or not?

The definition of cost

The preceding discussion shares with most such discussions the defect of evading a precise definition of the relation between total costs and total receipts. Looking forward, one can conceive of defining the total cost of producing various outputs as equal to the highest aggregate that the resources required could receive in alternative pursuits. Total cost so estimated need not be identical with anticipated total revenue; hence *ex ante* total cost, so defined, need not equal total revenue. But after the event, how is one to classify payments not regarded as cost? Does some part of receipts go to someone in a capacity other than as owner of a factor of production?

All in all, the best procedure seems to me to be to define total cost as identical with total receipts – to make these the totals of two sides of a double entry account. One can then distinguish between different kinds of costs, the chief distinction in pure theory being between costs that depend on what the firm does but not on how its actions turn out (contractual costs), and the rest of its costs or receipts (non-contractual costs). The former represent the cost of factors of production viewed solely as 'hired' resources capable of being rented out to other firms; the latter represent payment for whatever it is that makes identical collections of resources different when employed by different firms – a factor of production that we may formally designate 'entrepreneurial capacity', recognizing that this term gives a name to our ignorance rather than dispelling it.

Actual non-contractual costs can obviously never be known in advance, since they will be affected by all sorts of accidents, mistakes, and the like. It is therefore important to distinguish further between expected and actual non-contractual costs. Expected non-contractual costs are a 'rent' or 'quasi-rent' for entrepreneurial capacity. They are to be regarded as the motivating force behind the firm's decisions, for it is this and this alone that the firm can seek to maximize. The difference between expected and actual non-contractual costs is 'profits' or 'pure profits' – an unanticipated residual arising from uncertainty.

Definitions of total costs that do not require them to equal total receipts generally define them as equal either to contractual costs alone or to expected costs, contractual and non-contractual, and so regard all or some payments to the 'entrepreneurial capacity' of the firm as non-cost payments. The difficulty is, as I hope the preceding discussion makes clear, that there are no simple institutional lines or accounting categories that correspond to these distinctions.

Smith mentions the possibility of relating cost per dollar of output to size. Presumably one reason why this procedure has not been followed is that it brings the problems we have been discussing sharply to the surface and in consequence makes it clear that nothing is to be learned in this way. If costs *ex post* are defined to equal receipts *ex post*, cost per dollar of output is necessarily one dollar, regardless of size. Any other result must imply that some costs are disregarded, or some receipts regarded as non-cost receipts. Generally, the costs disregarded are capital costs – frequently called 'profits'. The study then simply shows how capital costs vary with size, which may, as Smith points out, merely reflect systematic differences in factor combinations according to size. One could with equal validity study wage costs or electricity costs per unit of output as a function of size.

The use of physical units of output avoids so obvious an objection; clearly it does not avoid the basic difficulty and, as Smith points out, it introduces problems of its own. The heterogeneity of output means that any changes in average cost with scale may merely measure changes in the 'quality' of what is taken to be a unit of output. In so far as size itself is measured by actual output, or an index related to it, a much more serious bias is introduced tending toward an apparent decline of costs as size increases. This can most easily be brought out by an extreme example. Suppose a firm produces a product the demand for which has a known two-year cycle, so that it plans to produce one hundred units in year one, two hundred in year two, one hundred in year three, etc. Suppose, also, that the best way to do this is by an arrangement that involves identical outlays for hired factors in each year (no 'variable' costs). If outlays are regarded as total costs, as they would be in studies of the kind under discussion, average cost per unit will obviously be twice as large when output is one hundred as when it is two hundred. If, instead of years one and two, we substitute firms one and two, a cross-section study would show sharply declining average costs. When firms are classified by actual output, essentially this kind of bias arises. The firms with the largest output are unlikely to be producing at an unusually low level; on the average, they are clearly likely to be producing at an unusually high level, and conversely for those which have the lowest output.[2]

Size distribution of firms

It may well be that a more promising source of information than cross-section accounting data would be the temporal behavior of the distribution of firms by size. If, over time, the distribution tends to be relatively stable, one might conclude that this is the 'equilibrium' distribution and defines not the optimum scale of firm but the optimum distribution. If the distribution tends to become increasingly concentrated, one might conclude that the extremes represented mistakes, the point of concentration the 'optimum' scale; and similarly with other changes. Whether, in fact, such deductions would be justified depends on how reasonable it is to suppose that the optimum scale or distribution has itself remained unchanged and that the emergence of new mistakes has been less important than the correction of old ones. None of this can be taken for granted; it would have to be established by study of the empirical circumstances of the particular industry, which is why the preceding statements are so liberally strewn with 'mights'.

The relevant question

I share very strongly Smith's judgement that one of the main reasons why the evidence accumulated in numerous studies by able people is so disappointing is that insufficient attention has been paid to why we want information on so-called economies of scale; foolish questions deserve foolish answers. If we ask what size firm has minimum costs, and define 'minimum costs' in a sense in which it is in a firm's own interest to achieve it, surely the obvious answer is: firms of existing size. We can hardly expect to get better answers to this question than a host of firms, each of

2. This is the general 'regression fallacy' that is so widespread in the interpretation of economic data.

which has much more intimate knowledge about its activities than we as outside observers can have and each of which has a much stronger and immediate incentive to find the right answer: much of the preceding discussion is really only a roundabout way of making this simple point.

Reference

BRUMBERG, R. (1953), '*Ceteris paribus* for supply curves', *Econ. J.*, vol. 63, pp. 462–7.

3 Joe S. Bain

Economies of Scale, Concentration and the Condition of Entry

J. S. Bain, 'Economies of scale, concentration and the condition of entry in twenty manufacturing industries', *American Economic Review*, vol. 64, 1954, pp. 15–39.

Ever since the merger movement of the late nineteenth century, American economists have been recurrently interested in the extent to which large size is necessary for business efficiency. Was the merger movement necessary; was the rule of reason economically justifiable; can this or that concentrated industry be atomized without loss of efficiency? These continue to be important questions to students of recent industrial history and contemporary antitrust policy. In the last three decades, with the notion that plant or firm size is related to efficiency formalized in long-run average-cost or scale curves, there has been much speculation and some inquiry concerning the shapes and positions of those scale curves in various industries and the placement of existing plants and firms on them.

To the economist *qua* economist, a knowledge for its own sake of the scale curves in particular industries is obviously unimportant. Only idle curiosity could justify his learning without further purpose how many barrels of cement a plant should produce to attain the lowest unit production cost, or how many passenger cars an automobile firm should make to minimize its production costs. But inferences which can be drawn from such knowledge may be important in several ways.

First, the proportion of the total output of its industry which a plant or a firm must supply in order to be reasonably efficient will determine the extent to which concentration in that industry is favored by the pursuit of minimized production costs. In any industry, the minimal scales of plant and of firm which are required for lowest production costs – *when these scales are expressed as percentages of the total scale or capacity of the industry* and are taken together with the shapes of the scale curves at smaller capacities – determine the degree of concentration by plants and firms needed for reasonable efficiency in the industry.

Second, the same relation of productive efficiency to the proportion of the market supplied by a plant or firm in any industry will have a profound effect on *potential competition*, or on the disposition of new firms to enter the industry. If a plant or firm needs to supply only a negligible fraction of industry output to be reasonably efficient, economies of scale provide no deterrent to entry other than those of absolute capital requirements. If, however, a plant or firm must add significantly to industry output in order to be efficient, and will be relatively inefficient if it adds little, entry at efficient scale would lower industry selling prices or induce unfavorable reactions by established firms, whereas entry at much smaller scales would give the entrant a significant cost disadvantage. In this situation established firms can probably raise prices some amount above the competitive level without attracting entry. In general, the 'condition of entry' – measured by the extent to which established firms can raise price above a competitive level without inducing further entry – becomes 'more difficult' as the ratio of the output of the optimal firm to industry output increases.[1]

Third, the amount of money required for investment in an efficient plant or firm – as determined by size – will affect the availability of the capital necessary for new entry. When the supplies of both equity and loan capital in the range needed for a unit investment are either absolutely limited or positively related to the interest rate, the number of dollars required to establish an efficient plant or firm will clearly affect the condition of entry to an industry.[2]

Finally, a comparison of the scales of existing plants and firms in any industry with the most efficient scales will indicate whether plants and firms are of efficient size, or whether or not the existing pattern of concentration is consistent with reasonable efficiency.

1. See Bain (1954) for a development of this theory.
2. But the absolute capital requirement for efficiency need not, as we move from one industry to another, be systematically related to the proportion of industry output needed for efficiency.

Have plant and firm concentration proceeded too far, farther than necessary, just far enough, or not far enough – from the standpoint of productive efficiency? A knowledge of scale curves is prerequisite to an answer.

Although information on the relation of efficiency to scale thus has some importance, relatively little has been done to develop this knowledge through empirical research; economists have relied mainly upon *a priori* speculations and qualitative generalizations of the broadest sort. A popular American view is that economies of large-scale plant do exist – and that the efficiency of plants as large as are built may be conceded – but that further economies of large multiplant firms do not exist, or if they do, are strictly pecuniary in character and hence not to be sought or justified as a matter of social policy.[3] At the extreme it is argued that increasing the size of the firm beyond that of an efficient plant does not normally lower costs at all, so that the scale curve is approximately horizontal for some distance beyond this point. The dominant British view, expressed by such writers as Steindl, Florence and E. A. G. Robinson, gives more credence to the alleged economies of large-scale firms. Both schools rely upon qualitative and substantially untested generalizations about productive and commercial techniques which supposedly determine the response of production costs to variations in the scale of plant or firm. Yet in spite of the extremely sketchy nature of this sort of knowledge, it is common to presume, for instance, that there are numerous examples of each of two sorts of oligopolistic industries – those where scale economies encourage a high concentration, and those where such economies do not but something else does (Fellner, 1949, p. 44).

Direct empirical investigation has not added much to our knowledge of scale curves. The principal studies employing accounting cost data are found in TNEC Monograph 13, and in later work by Blair (1942, 1948) of the Federal Trade Commission. Unfortunately the industries studied have been so few, the periods of time reviewed so remote and brief, and the use and interpretation of the statistical data in most instances so open to question that

3. See, e.g. Federal Trade Commission (1941, pp. 95–139). It may be noted that the income-distribution effects of strictly pecuniary economies may not be inconsequential in many settings.

no reliable generalization regarding scale curves can be drawn from this body of material. There is more available in the way of profit-rate data for firms of various sizes, but here the unsupported assumptions which are normally necessary to argue from higher profits to lower costs are so numerous as to vitiate any attempt to infer scale curves from profit rates. Somewhat more satisfactory information has been developed, for a very few industries only, through 'engineering' estimates of the scale curve for plant or firm. But in general our information is such that we are ill-prepared to say much about actual scale curves and their implications.

Scope of the present study

In the course of a recent general study of condition of entry to American manufacturing industries,[4] it has been possible to develop some further data on economies of scale therein. The portion of this information presented here concerns, for each of twenty selected manufacturing industries:

1. The relationship of the output capacity of a plant of lowest-cost size to the output capacity of the industry, together with the shape of the plant-scale curve at smaller sizes.

2. The relationship of the capacity of a firm of lowest-cost size to industry capacity, and the firm-scale curve at smaller capacities.

3. The absolute amount of money capital required to establish an optimal plant and an optimal firm as of the current decade.

These data have been developed almost entirely from managerial or 'engineering' estimates supplied by certain firms in the industries involved; precisely, they reflect estimates of scale economies and capital requirements which were prepared, in response to detailed prearranged questioning, either by or at the

4. I wish to acknowledge the generous assistance provided for this study since 1951 by the Merrill Foundation for the Advancement of Financial Knowledge, through a grant made to the Research Group on the Monopoly Problem at Harvard University, directed by Dean E. S. Mason. Acknowledgement is also due for the assistance in preceding years of the Bureau of Business and Economic Research, University of California, Berkeley, where essential initial background studies were undertaken.

56 Production Functions and Long-Run Costs

direction of high-level executives in these firms. The general procedure for securing such data included:

1. A lengthy preliminary survey of each of the twenty industries, based on available monographs, documents, and other published and unpublished secondary materials.

2. The subsequent preparation for each industry of a separate, special and rather lengthy series of questions designed to elicit certain information having bearing on the condition of entry.

3. Securing, after explaining the project involved and assuring confidentiality of replies, an advance offer of cooperation in answering these questions from executives in a large number of firms.

4. Actual submission of the questions, followed (except in those cases where cooperation was subsequently withdrawn) by obtaining answers, in writing or orally or both. The method used thus involved neither shot-gun dissemination of an all-purpose questionnaire nor post-prandial armchair quizzes, but rather a more or less hand-tooled questionnaire procedure in the case of each of twenty industries.

The questions submitted relative to scale economies in each industry were designed in general to elicit information concerning the minimal plant-size requisite for lowest unit costs and the shape of the plant scale curve at smaller sizes, the same information for the firm, and the capital required to establish a plant and a firm of most efficient size. Direct and (with exceptions to be noted below) explicit answers to these questions were normally secured. In many cases, there was abundant evidence in the length and documentation of replies of a careful estimating procedure; in some, figures submitted were frankly characterized as unsubstantiated armchair guesses, though in most of these the respondents were very well qualified to guess. By and large, the writer is inclined to feel, on the basis of checks against other sources and of comparisons of different and independent replies to the same questions, that this is generally a fairly reliable body of data, in which the bulk of individual industry estimates are likely to be fairly accurate. The data have the advantage, so far as they are reliable, of reflecting 'engineering' estimates in the sense that they represent expert *ex ante* predictions of the net relations of cost to scale, rather than an *ex post* comparison of gross cost results at different achieved outputs. Thus they refer in general directly to scale curves as understood in economic theory.[5]

The twenty manufacturing industries studied may be designated as those producing cigarettes, soap, distilled liquor, shoes, canned fruits and vegetables, meat products, passenger automobiles, fountain pens, typewriters, flour, rubber tires and tubes, refined petroleum products, farm machinery, tractors,[6] steel, copper, cement, gypsum products, rayon and metal containers. The sample was obviously not drawn at random. It was selected to obtain a maximum possible diversity of industry types consistent with the availability of data, but the fact that data have been more frequently developed for large and for highly concentrated industries than for others has resulted in some systematic differences between the sample and the whole population of manufacturing industries.

The following characteristics of the sample deserve brief note. First, it features large industries, with fifteen of the twenty having value products above a half billion in 1947. Whereas it includes only a little over 4 per cent of the total number (452) of manufacturing industries in 1947, it accounts for about 20 per cent of

5. The general time reference of all estimates is the period 1950 to 1952. From two to five such estimates were received in each of the twenty industries in question. Other sources of data which were available for some industries – such as comparisons of accounting costs or the personal estimates of authors of industry studies – have been deliberately neglected here in order to give a more uniform consistency to the data presented. The only other data presented here, and these largely for expository purposes, are plant and firm concentration data prepared from the 1947 Census of Manufactures. Since the engineering estimates which supply the bulk of our data were generally secured under guarantees of secrecy as to source, no acknowledgements or references to source can be supplied.

6. For present purposes only we follow the Census in the dubious experiment of segregating tractors from other farm machinery.

7. The total population of industries described, as well as all data on value products and on concentration by firms, is derived (except as otherwise noted) from the 1947 Census of Manufactures, and in particular from a special analysis of concentration prepared from this Census and published as an appendix in *Hearings, Subcommittee on Study of Monopoly Power, Committee on Judiciary*, H. R., 81st Cong., Serial 14, Part 2–B.

the value product of all manufacture in 1947.[7] Second, it contains a substantially larger proportion of moderately and highly concentrated manufacturing industries than the total population. Nine industries of the sample had 75 per cent or more of value product controlled by four firms, three had 50 to 75 per cent so controlled, eight had from 25 to 50 per cent, and none less than 25 per cent controlled by four firms.[8] In the total population of manufacturing industries, the corresponding numbers in the four concentration classes were 47, 103, 164 and 138. This bias must be recognized in interpreting findings.

Otherwise, the sample is fairly representative. Eight industries are classed as making consumer goods, eight producer goods and four goods bought by both producer and consumers. The outputs of eight are non-durable in use, whereas twelve are durable or semidurable. As to type of technique or process, five industries may be classified as engaged in processing farm products, and four minerals, three as chemical industries, five as manufacturing or assembling mechanical devices, and three as in miscellaneous fabrication.[9]

Optimal plant size and plant concentration

Our first question concerns the shape and position of the plant-scale curve (relating unit costs of production to the size of the individual factory or plant) in each of the twenty industries, and the apparent consequences of economies of large plants for entry and for seller concentration. We are interested initially in the scale curve reflecting the relation of production cost to the output or capacity of the plant *when the latter are expressed as percentages of the total output or rated capacity supplying the market to be*

8. In three of the twenty cases, value added rather than value product figures were used by the Census in calculating concentration. For automobiles, registration rather than Census figures are followed in describing concentration, in both the sample and the total population, because of deficiencies in Census data.

9. One further characteristic of the sample may be noted – Census industries have been selected which correspond fairly well to 'theoretical' industries, or for which industry concentration as computed tends to reflect closely the relevant theoretical concentration of corresponding or component theoretical industries. This matter is discussed at length in Bain (1951).

supplied by the plant. When output or capacity is expressed in these percentage terms, what is the lowest-cost or 'optimal' size of plant and what is the shape of the plant-scale curve at smaller sizes?

An initial clue to the potential importance of economies of large plants is supplied by certain data on plant size assembled in the 1947 Census of Manufactures. This Census shows for each of many industries the number of plants in each of several size-classes (size being measured by number of employees), and also the proportion of Census industry employment and of total industry 'value added' accounted for by each size-class of plants. From these data[10] certain inferences can be drawn about the sizes of existing plants. For exploratory purposes here I have tried to develop from them some upper-limit estimates of the plant sizes requisite for greatest efficiency in the sample industries, by computing first the average size of plants in the largest size-class in each industry (expressed here as the percentage supplied per plant of the total value added of the Census industry), and second the maximum possible average size (similarly expressed) of the largest four plants in the industry.[11] If we neglect such obvious limitations as those of using value-added data, these estimates may be considered maximum percentages of the national industry outputs requisite for efficiency, on the grounds that in nearly every case we refer to the average size of a few of the largest plants actually built, and that the firms operating them were not restricted from building them to optimal scale. That is, they are generally multiplant firms which could bring a single plant to optimal scale before adding another, if indeed they did not in some cases duplicate optimal technical units on a single location.

The results of these estimating procedures are as follows. Eighteen industries were examined (automobiles and copper

10. The data were previously used by the Federal Trade Commission (1947) for its study. The staff of the Commission has kindly made available its tabulated calculations on plant concentration as based on the Census data.

11. The latter figure is derived in general by attributing to all but the first four plants in the largest size-class the minimum possible market share (i.e. for each the mean share of plants in the second size-class) and by dividing the remainder of the total market share in the largest-size class among the first four plants.

being eliminated because of gross deficiencies in Census data); for the eighteen the number of plants in the largest size-class lay between 3 and 15 in all but three cases; in those three it was large enough to make our estimates quite hazardous. The average share of Census industry value added supplied by plants in the largest size-class ranged from 20·1 per cent (typewriters) to 0·7 per cent (shoes), with a median at 3·8 per cent. The maximum possible average share of the largest four plants ranged from 19·1 per cent (cigarettes) to 1·7 per cent (shoes), with a median at 7·9 per cent.

The character of the data is more fully revealed in the frequency distributions in Table 1. The first frequency column therein (f_1) classifies industries according to the market-share interval within which the average size of plants in the largest size-class of plants falls, market share being measured by the percentage of the Census industry value-added supplied by a plant. The

Table 1 Classification of Eighteen Census Industries according to Percentages of Industry Values-Added Supplied by the Largest Plants, 1947[a]

	Number of industries with the largest plant-size in the specified percentage interval	
Percentage of Census industry value added supplied by the average of the largest plants	When 'largest plant-size' refers to average size of plants in largest size class of plants (f_1)	When 'largest plant-size' refers to the maximum possible average size of the largest four plants in industry (f_2)
0 – 2·4	6	2
2·5– 4·9	5	4
5·0– 7·4	2	3
7·5– 9·9	3	2
10·0–14·9	1	3
15·0–24·9[b]	1	4
Total	18	18

a. From 1947 Census of Manufactures. The composition of sample is described in the text above.

b. The highest value in this class was 20·1 per cent.

Joe S. Bain 61

second frequency column (f_2) shows the same information when the plant size referred to in each industry is the maximum possible average market share of the largest four plants.

These findings, showing that in from seven to twelve of the eighteen Census industries (depending on the method of estimate) the value added of the largest plants amounted to over 5 per cent apiece of total industry value added and that in from two to seven cases the figure was over 10 per cent apiece, suggest an importance for economies of large-scale plant which is substantial in some of these industries and small in others. But a detailed interpretation of the findings is not justified for several reasons. First, value added in a single year is a rather unsatisfactory measure of 'scale' as that term is ordinarily understood. Second, the largest plants as identified by the Census may have resulted from building multiples of optimal technical units on single locations, and if so, the figures presented may overestimate optimal scales. Third, the data in question express the output of the plant as a percentage of the total national value added within the Census industry, whereas in fact the theoretical industry or separate market which a plant supplies may be somewhat smaller.[12] In these cases – where a Census industry is in fact made up of several theoretical industries corresponding to distinct regional markets or product lines – the 'percentage-of-industry-output' derived from Census data for large plants is very likely to be below the theoretically relevant figure,[13] and revisions are in order. We thus turn at once to direct engineering estimates of optimal plant sizes.

Table 2 reviews the engineering estimates of the optimal scales of plants for twenty industry groups. In each case, the plant size referred to is the minimal physical production capacity of plant required for lowest production costs, this capacity being expressed as a percentage of total national capacity within the Census industry. In each case also the costs referred to are total production costs, including costs of outshipment where the latter are strategic to the determination of optimal plant scale.

12. It may also conceivably be larger, as in the case where imports are omitted from Census data or where the Census industry is too narrowly defined, but these contingencies are not realized in any important degree in this sample.
13. It will be if the plant specializes as to area or product line.

Table 2 Proportions of National Industry Capacity contained in Single Plants of Most Efficient Scale, for Twenty Industries, per Engineering Estimates circa 1951

Industry	Percentage of national industry capacity contained in one plant of minimal efficient scale	Industry	Percentage of national industry capacity contained in one plant of minimal efficient scale
Flour milling	$\frac{1}{10}-\frac{1}{2}$	Rubber tires and tubes[g]	3
Shoes[a]	$\frac{1}{7}-\frac{1}{2}$	Rayon[h]	4–6
Canned fruits and vegetables	$\frac{1}{4}-\frac{1}{2}$	Soap[i]	4–6
Cement	$\frac{4}{5}-1$	Farm machines, ex tractors[j]	4–6
Distilled liquors[b]	$1\frac{1}{4}-1\frac{3}{4}$	Cigarettes	5–6
Petroleum refining[c]	$1\frac{3}{4}$	Automobiles[k]	5–10
Steel[d]	$1-2\frac{1}{2}$	Fountain pens[l]	5–10
Metal containers	$\frac{1}{2}-3$	Copper[m]	10
Meat packing:[e]		Tractors	10–15
fresh	$\frac{1}{50}-\frac{1}{8}$		
diversified	$2-2\frac{1}{2}$		
Gypsum products[f]	$2\frac{1}{2}-3$	Typewriters	10–30

a. Refers to shoes other than rubber.

b. Capacity refers to total excluding brandy. Costs refer explicitly to four-year whiskey, packaged but ex tax.

c. Optimal balanced integration of successive processes assumed. Outshipment largely by water assumed; optimal scale may be smaller with scattered market and land shipment.

d. Refers to fully integrated operation producing flat rolled products.

e. Percentages are of total nonfarm slaughter; diversified operation includes curing, processing, etc.

f. Combined plasterboard and plaster production assumed.

g. Purchase of materials at a constant price assumed; production of a wide variety of sizes assumed.

h. Refers to plant producing both yarn and fibre.

i. Includes household detergents.

j. Refers primarily to complex farm machines.

k. Plant includes integrated facilities for production of components as economical. Final assembly alone – 1 to 3 per cent.

l. Includes conventional pens and ballpoints.

m. Assumes electrolytic refining.

Table 3 summarizes the data of Table 2 by classifying industries according to the market-share interval in which the mean estimated size of an optimal plant falls, when size is measured as a percentage of the national industry capacity. These 'engineering' data seem generally more satisfactory than those previously developed from Census figures. They reflect rational calculations

Table 3 Classification of Twenty Industries according to
Percentages of National Industry Capacities contained in
Single Plants of most Efficient Scale (from Table 2)

Percentage of national industry capacity contained in a plant of optimal scale	Number of industries with optimal scale plant (per mean estimate) in the specified percentage interval (f_3)
0– 2·4	9
2·5– 4·9	2
5·0– 7·4	4
7·5– 9·9	2
10·0–14·9	2
15·0–24·9	1
Total	20

rather than historical happenstance, and designed plant capacities rather than transient additions to value of output, although they still reflect percentages of the national capacities of Census industries.

It appears from them that in nine of the twenty industries an optimal plant would account for a quite small fraction of national capacity (under $2\frac{1}{2}$ per cent), whereas in five others the fraction would run above $7\frac{1}{2}$ per cent. In general, the industries with slight economies of scale of plant are engaged in processing of agricultural or mineral materials, whereas greater plant economies are frequently encountered in industries making mechanical devices. The engineering estimates of the importance of economies of large plant present an over-all picture for these industries not greatly different from that derived by calculating average plant sizes in the largest plant-size intervals (column f_1 of Table 1), but they clearly ascribe less importance to such economies than the estimates of the maximum possible average sizes of the largest four plants in each of these industries (column f_2 of Table 1).

Before we interpret these findings, however, two further matters must be discussed: the shapes of the plant-scale curves at capacities short of the estimated optima, and the revisions in the estimates of optima which are needed if the division of Census industries into separate regions or product lines is recognized.

As to the shapes of plant-cost curves at capacities short of the estimated optima, relatively fragmentary information has been received. In four industries the plant-scale curve appears to be horizontal back to the smallest size considered, or ¼ per cent of national industry output; these are flour, shoes, canned fruits and vegetables, and 'fresh' meat packing. In ten cases – steel, metal containers, diversified meat packing, gypsum products, farm machinery, automobiles, fountain pens, copper, tractors and typewriters – quantitative estimates of the shapes of the plant cost curves are not available, although in some cases (e.g. diversified meat packing and metal containers) it is suggested that substantially smaller than optimal plants would entail only slightly higher costs, whereas in some others (e.g. typewriters, automobiles and tractors) a distinct rise in costs is suggested at half the optimal plant scale. For the seven remaining industries, the estimated relation of production cost to plant scale is shown in Table 4, where costs of 100 represent the lowest attainable costs.

Table 4 Relation of Production Cost to Plant Scale in Seven Industries

	Percentages of national industry capacity in one plant					
	5%	2½%	1%	½%	¼%	
Cement	100	100	100	115	130	⎫
Distilled liquor	100	100	100·5	101	102	⎪
Petroleum refining	100	100	102	104	107	Relative costs
Tires and tubes	100	100·3	103	104	105·5	of
Rayon	100	107	125	Very high		production
Soap	100	103	105	Above 105		⎪
Cigarettes	100	101	102	Above 102		⎭

A mixed picture again emerges. In some cases (liquor and cigarettes, for example) the rise of production costs at suboptimal scales is evidently quite small; in others (soap, petroleum refining, tires and tubes) it is moderate but by no means negligible; in some – e.g. rayon and cement – the rise is great.[14] One might

14. It will be noted that the industries with the highest degrees of plant concentration are generally those on which it has been most difficult to secure quantitative estimates of the shape of the scale curve. In general, our information on plant scale seems sketchier and perhaps less reliable at this end of the sample.

hazard the guess that in from a half to two-thirds of all the industries sampled the upturn of the plant-scale curve at suboptimal scales is such as to discourage very much smaller operations unless there are forces counterbalancing production cost disadvantages. In the other one-third to a half of cases, a wide variety of plant sizes might prosper indefinitely in only slightly imperfect markets.

The findings of Tables 2 and 3, however – reflecting as they do the percentages of national Census industry capacities supplied by single plants – can hardly be taken at face value so long as the suspicion remains that many Census industries may be broken into several separate and largely non-competing regional or product submarkets and that a plant may specialize in only one such submarket. In these cases the relevant measure of plant size must be the proportion of the capacity supplying a submarket which is provided by an optimal plant, and this proportion will be larger than the proportion of national capacity provided by the same plant.

In eleven of the twenty cases listed in Table 2, a revision of plant-size figures is in order because of the apparent division of the national market into distinct submarkets, coupled with plant specialization among them. In seven of these cases – flour, cement, petroleum refining, steel, metal containers, meat packing and gypsum products – the important segmentation of markets is geographical in character; national markets are broken into regions, and a single plant will mainly supply only one region. In the other four cases – shoes, canned fruits and vegetables, automobiles and fountain pens – markets are divided to a significant extent among distinct product lines. In all cases, the relevant measure of plant size is the percentage it may account for of the total capacity supplying any submarket it may supply.

The industries in which market segmentation is important are predominantly those for which the percentages of national industry capacities represented by single plants are quite small. The data for nine of the first ten industries in Table 2 require revision because of market segmentation, and only two for which revision is required lie in the range of high plant concentration nationally. Where technology does not give some importance to plant economies in industries of our sample, geography and product specialization (by plants) apparently do. Correspondingly, revised plant-size data showing percentages of individual submarket capacities will differ markedly from those in Tables 2 and 3.

To make the revision mentioned, the optimal plant capacity for each of the eleven industries involved has been restated first as a percentage of the capacity supplying the largest submarket identified, and second as a percentage of capacity supplying the smallest of the major submarkets identified. For example, four major regional markets were identified in the petroleum refining industry. The proportion of national capacity supplied by a single optimal refinery had been estimated at $1\frac{3}{4}$ per cent (Table 2); the corresponding percentages for the largest and smallest of the four major regional markets were $3\frac{1}{3}$ per cent and $11\frac{1}{2}$ per cent. In the fountain pen industry the proportion of aggregate national capacity supplied by an optimal plant was estimated at from 5 to 10 per cent. Dividing the market into high-price or gift pens and low-price pens including ballpoints (and recognizing differences in techniques for producing the two lines) the corresponding percentages become 25 to $33\frac{1}{3}$ per cent and 10 to $12\frac{1}{2}$ per cent.

When these revisions have been made for the eleven industries, and the results combined with the unrevised data for the remaining nine, we are prepared to present two frequency distributions parallel to that in Table 3 above. They classify industries according to the percentage of market capacity provided by an optimal plant, in the first case (column f_4 of Table 5) when the capacities of optimal plants in the eleven revised industries are expressed as percentages of the total capacities supplying the largest submarkets in their industries, and in the second (column f_5) when optimal capacities in the eleven industries are expressed as percentages of the total capacities supplying the smallest major submarkets identified. The last column in Table 5 repeats column f_3 from Table 3 for purposes of comparison.

Subjective judgements have inescapably influenced the content of columns f_4 and f_5, particularly in the identification of regions, the decision as to what is a 'major' region or product line, and the decision as to whether market segmentation is significant, but we have tried to follow available information and industry practice systematically. If there is a bias, it is in the direction of defining

Joe S. Bain 67

areas and product lines quite broadly, of considering only a few dominant areas for analysis, and of recognizing segmentation only if there is strong evidence supporting the recognition.

Interpreting Table 5 with appropriate reference to the earlier discussion of the shapes of plant-scale curves, we may emphasize the following conclusions about the importance of economies of

Table 5 Classification of Twenty Industries[a] by Percentages of Individual Market Capacities contained in a Single-Plant of most Efficient Scale

Percentage of individual market capacity contained in a plant of optimal scale	Number of industries with optimal plant scale in the specified percentage interval		
	Where percentage is that of the total capacity supplying the largest recognized submarket (f_4)	Where percentage is that of the total capacity supplying the smallest recognized submarket (f_5)	Where percentage is that of the total capacity supplying the national market (f_3 from Table 3)
0– 2·4	4	2	9
2·5– 4·9	5	2	2
5·0– 7·4	5	4	4
7·5– 9·9	0	1	2
10·0–14·9	5	3	2
15·0–19·9	0	2	0
20·0–24·9	1	2	1
25·0–29·9	0	2	0
30·0–34·9	0	1	0
35·0–40·0	0	1	0
Total	20	20	20

[a] The meat packing industry is considered for purposes of this table as only involving so-called *fresh*-meat packing.

large-scale plants within the industries of our sample. First, if the reference is to the largest submarkets of industries with segmented markets (plus the national markets of those with unsegmented markets), then in nine of the twenty cases an optimal plant would supply less than 5 per cent of its market, and in five additional cases less than $7\frac{1}{2}$ per cent. If this is true and if, further, the plant-scale curve is usually fairly flat for a moderate range of suboptimal scales, then in many of these fourteen cases the scale requirements for an optimal plant should not provide a serious deterrent to entry. A firm constructing one reasonably efficient plant should not ordinarily induce serious repercussions from established firms in its market.

On the other hand in six cases – gypsum products, automobiles, typewriters, fountain pens, tractors and copper – the proportion of the total capacity supplying either the national market or the largest submarket which is provided by a single optimal plant runs from 10 to 25 per cent. Precise data are largely lacking on the shapes of scale curves in these industries, but if they are much inclined upward at suboptimal scales (as is suggested qualitatively in several cases) then the economies of large plant should provide a very significant deterrent to entry to the markets in question. Further, a substantial degree of oligopolistic concentration by firms might easily be justified by the pursuit of plant economies alone. The substantial diversity of situations among industries of moderate to high concentration deserves considerable emphasis.

The picture changes markedly if our attention shifts in the case of the eleven segmented industries from the largest to the smallest major submarkets. Now we find that in eleven of the twenty cases (rather than six) the proportion of the relevant market capacity supplied by an optimal plant exceeds 10 per cent, and in six cases it exceeds 20 per cent. Plant economies sufficient to impede entry very seriously are potentially present in half or more of the cases, and high plant and firm concentration is encouraged by technology. The importance of plant economies thus potentially bulks large indeed in the smaller regional submarkets and the smaller product lines, whereas it is evidently less in the major submarkets and frequently so in the industries with relatively unsegmented national markets.

Optimal firm size and firm concentration

The extent to which further economies of large scale are realized if firms grow beyond the size of a single optimal plant has been a subject of controversy among economists. If a distinction is drawn between 'production cost' and other advantages of scale – so that sales promotion, price-raising, and similar advantages of big firms are properly distinguished from cost-savings in production and distribution – there is no general agreement among economists as to whether or to what extent the multiplant firm is more economical.[15] It thus may come as no surprise that business executives questioned on the same matter with regard to our sample of industries evidenced a similar diversity of mind. Very distinct differences of opinion relative to the existence or importance of economies of multiplant firms were frequently encountered in the same industry, and in a pattern not satisfactorily explicable in general by the hypothesis that the individual would claim maximum economies for his own size of firm. Any findings presented here on estimates of economies of large-scale firm should thus be viewed as extremely tentative.

Whatever the ostensible importance of economies of the multiplant firm, exploitation of them will not *necessarily* require the multiplant firm to control a larger proportion of any submarket than is needed for one optimal plant. In those instances where national markets are segmented regionally or by product lines, the multiplant firm *may* realize its economies while operating only one plant in each submarket. Then concentration by firms in individual submarkets is not further encouraged and entry is not further impeded[16] by economies of the multiplant firm. An optimal cement plant may supply about 1 per cent of national capacity, or percentages of regional capacity ranging very roughly from 5 to 30 per cent in eleven regional submarkets. The fact that a multiplant cement firm could secure lower costs than a single-plant firm by operating one optimal plant in each of the eleven regions – thus accounting for 11 per cent of national capacity – would not imply that it need have a higher proportion of capacity in any one region than a single-plant firm of optimal size. Except for an increase in absolute capital requirements, the assumed economies of the multiplant firm would not encourage regional market concentration or impede entry.

Suppose on the other hand that there are economies of multiplant firms which are to be realized through operating two or more optimal-size plants either in a single submarket or in a single

15. This disagreement is, as noted above, complicated further by difference of opinion as to whether the disputed economies are real or strictly pecuniary in character.
16. Except for the increase of absolute capital requirements.

Table 6 The Extent of Estimated Economies of Multiplant Firms in Twenty Manufacturing Industries

Industry	*Percentage of national industry capacity contained in one optimal plant*	*Estimated extent of multiplant economies (as a percentage of total cost)*	*Percentage of national industry capacity contained in one optimal firm*	*Average percentage share of the national market of first four firms in 1947*[a]
Group 1:				
Canned fruits and vegetables	1/4–1/2	None		6·6
Petroleum refining	1 3/4	None		9·3
Meat packing:[b]				
Fresh	1/50–1/5	None		
Diversified	2–2 1/2	None		10·3[c]
Fountain pens	4–10	None		14·4
Copper	10	None		23·1[d]
Typewriters	10–30	None		19·9
Group 2:				
Flour	1/10–1/2	No estimate		7·3
Distilled liquor	1 1/4–1 3/4	No estimate		18·7
Metal containers	1/2–3	No estimate		19·5
Tires and tubes	3	No estimate		19·2
Rayon	4–6	No estimate		19·6
Farm machines, ex tractors	4–6	No estimate		9·0
Automobiles	5–10	No estimate		22·5[e]
Tractors	10–15	No estimate		16·8
Group 3:				
Shoes	1/7–1/2	Small, or 2–4	1/2–2 1/2	7·0
Cement	4/5–1	Small, or 2–3	2–10	7·4
Steel	1–2 1/2	2–5	2–20	11·2[c]
Gypsum products	2 1/2–3	Small	27–33	21·2
Soap	4–6	1/2–1	8–15	19·8
Cigarettes	5–6	Slight	15–20	22·6

a. Market shares are average percentages of 1947 national values of shipments unless otherwise indicated.

b. Plant percentages refer to total of non-farm slaughter, firm percentages to wholesale fresh meat packing only.

c. Expresses average percentage of total value added rather than value of shipments.

d. Expresses average percentage of electrolytic plus other national copper refining capacity, 1947.

e. Expresses approximate average percentage of total 1951 passenger car registration.

unsegmented national market. This will evidently encourage a concentration by firms in the relevant submarket or national market greater than that encouraged by plant economies alone, and will further impede entry. If a single plant of most efficient size would supply 5 per cent of the relatively unsegmented national cigarette market, whereas a single firm operating three such plants could lower costs of production and distribution perceptibly, economies of the multiplant firm would favor greater effective concentration and provide further deterrents to entry to the cigarette industry.

Findings relative to the economies of multiplant firms, together with certain related data, are presented in Table 6. The second column therein repeats the estimates of percentages of national Census industry capacities required for optimal plants, from Table 2. The third column indicates the estimated extent of economies of multiplant firms (i.e. firms of sizes beyond those of single optimal plants), costs of distribution but not of sales promotion being included. The fourth column indicates the percentages of national industry capacities required for firms with lowest production plus distribution costs, while the final column shows the average percentage per firm of the national market supplied by the first four firms in 1947. The last provides a measure of actual concentration by firms. The estimates in question are entirely those of executives queried in connection with the investigation underlying this study.

The data presented in Table 6 shed light on two questions: to what extent do the economies of the multiplant firm tend to enhance concentration and impede entry, and to what extent is the existing concentration by firms greater than required for exploitation of economies of large plants and of large firms?

Concerning the first question a varied picture appears. In eight industries (Group 2 in Table 6) no definite estimate could be obtained of the extent, if any, of economies of the multiplant firm. This is in spite of the fact that in most of these industries the degree of concentration by firms substantially exceeds that requisite for exploitation of estimated economies of the large plant. In six industries (Group 1 in Table 6) it was the consensus that economies of the scale of firm beyond the size of a single optimal plant were either negligible or totally absent. In these cases estimated cost savings of the multiplant firm cannot justify concentration beyond that required by plant economies alone (either in submarkets or in unsegmented national markets) nor can they make entry any more difficult than it is already made by plant economies. With respect to the first four industries in the group, a multiplant firm with plants in several regions or product lines would, according to the estimates received, realize no net cost savings by virtue of this aspect of its organization. In the second three industries in this group, however, economies of the large plant alone are sufficient to support a high degree of concentration by firms and to impede entry.

In the remaining six industries (Group 3 in Table 6) perceptible economies were attributed to the multiplant firm. The extent of these economies is in no case huge, being characterized as slight or small in three cases and as in the two to five per cent range in the remaining three. Nevertheless, two or three percentage points on total cost can be significant in any industry if the ratio of operating profits to sales is not beyond five or ten per cent and if product differentiation and other market imperfections are not dominant. What further tendency toward concentration and what further impediment to entry would the existence of these economies imply?

The optimal multiplant firm as estimated in Group 3 of Table 6 includes two or three optimal plants in the soap industry, three or four in the cigarette industry, four or five in the shoe industry, and about ten in the gypsum products industry. Estimates for the steel and cement industries run all the way from one or two to ten plants per optimal firm, and the range of disagreement among authorities is wide. Applying these estimates, the proportion of national industry capacity needed for best efficiency in a multiplant firm is raised; but is the proportion of the capacity supplying any particular regional or product submarket also raised? It will not be if the efficient multiplant firm includes only one optimal plant per submarket, and it will be if it includes two or more per submarket or if the national market is unsegmented.

In Group 3 in Table 6 no more than one optimal plant per region is attributed to the optimal firm in cement or in steel, and the proportion of any regional market which need be supplied for efficiency is thus not increased by the incidence of economies of the multiplant firms. In the remaining four cases the conclusion is different. Soap and cigarettes have relatively unsegmented national markets, and the proportion of the market required for best efficiency is doubled, trebled or quadrupled by the emergence of economies of the multiplant firm. In shoes the assumed specialization to a single product line of the four or five plants needed for efficiency raises the requisite firm concentration by product lines by corresponding multiples. In the gypsum industry it was evidently assumed that an optimal firm would operate several plants in each of one or more major regions. In all of the last four cases, therefore, economies of the multiplant firm encourage greater effective concentration by firms and impede entry. But in these cases (possibly excepting shoes) the economies of the large firm were characterized as slight, so that the effects just listed may be weak.

With respect to the effect of the economies of multiplant firms on concentration and on entry, these conclusions appear. In eight of twenty industries in our sample, no estimate was obtained of the extent of these economies. In two-thirds of the remaining cases, economies of the multiplant firm were held either to be absent, or to take such a form that exploitation of them would not require higher proportions of market control by the firm in any submarket. In one-third of the remaining cases, some encouragement to higher concentration by firms in submarkets was provided, but it was a small encouragement in view of the generally slight economies attributed to the large firm. Economies of the large-scale firm apparently do not represent a major force encouraging concentration or deterring entry in this sample of industries. The data on which this guess rests, however, are far from adequate.

Our second question concerns the extent to which the existing degree of concentration by firms within industries is justified by the estimated economies of large plants and firms. This is a rather complicated question, and may be broken down into three subquestions:

1. Is the existing concentration by firms for national Census industries justified by the economies of single large-scale plants?

2. If not, is the existing concentration by firms nevertheless con-

sistent with no higher concentration within individual submarkets than is required by a single efficient plant – i.e. need there be more than one optimal plant per large firm in any one submarket?

3. In any case, to what extent is the multiplant character of large firms apparently justified by the economies of such firms?

A first approximation to answers to these questions may be made by taking the concentration figure in column 5 of Table 6 as a simple and crude measure of national industry concentration by firms.[17] On the basis of this measure, the answer to the first subquestion is simple and unsurprising – concentration by firms is in every case but one greater than required by single-plant economies, and in more than half of the cases very substantially greater. Generally it is only within some of the industries with very important economies of large plant – e.g. fountain pens, copper, typewriters, autos, tractors, farms machines – that concentration by firms has not been much greater than required by single-plant economies. Even in these cases it may be two or three times as great as thus required. In the other cases concentration by firms tends to be a substantial or large multiple of that required by single-plant economies. Remembering that we are dealing in general in this sample with the more concentrated industries, it might be said in summary that nearly all of the industries tended to become moderately or highly concentrated (by firms) whether economies of the single plant were important or not.

The second subquestion is whether the existing degree of concentration by firms is consistent or inconsistent with the existence of a single optimal plant per firm in each recognized submarket. In seven of the nine cases where the national market has been considered substantially unsegmented – copper, typewriters, liquor, tires and tubes, rayon, farm machines, tractors, soap and cigarettes – the degree of concentration by firms within a single market is greater than required by such plant economies, although in all but two of the seven cases (liquor and tires and tubes) it is greater by at most a multiple of three or four. This last is found

17. The average share of national industry output per firm for the first four firms obviously is smaller than the market share for the first firm, larger than that for the fourth firm, etc.

probably in part because economies of the large plant seem very important in most of these industries.

In eight of the remaining eleven cases – canned goods, petroleum refining, meat packing, fountain pens, metal containers, cement, steel and gypsum products – the degree of national concentration by firms is not grossly inconsistent with the larger firms on the average having but a single optimal plant per submarket in each of several submarkets. (*This is certainly not to deny that the largest single firms may have more than this and probably do; we refer only to the average of the largest four firms.*)

In the last three cases – flour, automobiles and shoes – the degree of concentration by firms exceeds by a multiple of two or three that required for each of the four largest firms on the average to have an optimal plant in each submarket. In general, our showing is that in ten of twenty industries the existing degree of concentration by firms, as measured by the average size of the largest four firms, is significantly greater than required for these firms to have only one optimal plant per submarket; in the other ten cases concentration is at least roughly consistent with such a condition.

The third subquestion concerns the extent to which the existing degree of concentration by firms is justified by the exploitation of economies of multiplant firms. We will go no further with this question here than a comparison of the fourth and fifth columns of Table 6 will take us. In Group 1 in that table, the alleged absence of any economies of multiplant firm implies that there is no justification in terms of costs for the excess of concentration by firms over that required for single efficient plants, although in one case (typewriters) the existence of an excess is uncertain, and in four others (all but copper) it is not necessarily accompanied by accentuated concentration in individual submarkets. Here, therefore, the lack of an evident cost justification for multiplant firms raises not so much the issue of concentration in separate markets as the issue of the other advantages and disadvantages of a diversified firm operating in each of several related submarkets.

In Group 2 no estimates of multiplant economies are available; we need say no more than that in five of eight cases (excluding metal containers, farm machines and tractors) there is a concentration by firms much greater than that required for efficient plants in each submarket, and that this requires evaluation from a cost standpoint. In only one of the industries in Group 3 (shoes) does the degree of concentration by firms seem to have clearly exceeded that required for economies of production and distribution by the large firm.

In the sample as a whole the existing degree of concentration by multiplant firms lacks a clear cost justification in perhaps thirteen of twenty cases although in seven of these we have a simple lack of any definite estimates. In two more cases the multiplant phenomenon is not very important. Further information is needed on this matter, particularly with reference to cases in which multiplant firm organization has increased effective concentration in individual submarkets or in unsegmented national markets.

Absolute capital requirements and entry

The effect of scale economies on the condition of entry so far emphasized is transmitted through their influence on the share of market output which an efficient plant or firm will supply. This impact is important, but it is not proportional to the importance of scale economies measured in such terms as the absolute number of employees or the absolute size of investment required for an optimal plant or firm. This is because the proportion of a market supplied by an optimal plant or firm (which determines the degree of oligopolistic interdependence between the potential entrant and established firms) depends not only on the absolute size of the plant or firm but also on the size of the market. Thus an investment of over two hundred million dollars might add only 1 per cent to national steel capacity, whereas an investment of six million dollars might add five or ten per cent to the capacity for producing fountain pens. In addition to the effect of scale economies on entry via the proportion of the market an efficient entrant will supply, there is a distinct and not closely correlated effect via the absolute size of the efficient plant or firm, or, to choose a popular measure, via the total money investment needed to establish such a plant or firm.

To determine the importance of scale economies in establishing sufficient capital requirements to impede entry seriously, we have queried the same sources on the investment requisite for the most

Table 7 Estimated Absolute Capital Requirements for Plants of Estimated most Efficient Scale, circa 1951, for Twenty Industries

Industry	Percentage of national industry capacity provided by one efficient plant (from Table 2)	Total capital required for one efficient plant [a]
Category 1:		
Flour milling	$\frac{1}{10} - \frac{1}{2}$	$700,000 to $3,500,000
Shoes	$\frac{1}{7} - \frac{1}{2}$	$500,000 to $2,000,000
Canned fruits and vegetables	$\frac{1}{4} - \frac{1}{2}$	$2,500,000 to $3,000,000
Cement	$\frac{4}{5} - 1$	$20,000,000 to $25,000,000
Distilled liquor	$1\frac{1}{4} - 1\frac{3}{4}$	$30,000,000 to $42,000,000
Petroleum refining	$1\frac{3}{4}$	$193,000,000 ex transport facilities
Meat packing [b]	$\frac{1}{50} - \frac{1}{5}$	Very small
	$2 - 2\frac{1}{2}$	$10,000,000 to $20,000,000
Tires and tubes	3	$25,000,000 to $30,000,000
Category 2:		
Steel [c]	$1 - 2\frac{1}{2}$	$265,000,000 to $665,000,000 [d]
Metal containers [c]	$\frac{1}{2} - 3$	$5,000,000 to $20,000,000
Rayon	$4 - 6$	$50,000,000 to $75,000,000 [e]
		$90,000,000 to $135,000,000 [f]
Soap	$4 - 6$	$13,000,000 to $20,000,000 [g]
Farm machines ex tractors	$4 - 6$	No estimate
Cigarettes	$5 - 6$	$125,000,000 to $150,000,000
Category 3:		
Gypsum products [h]	$2\frac{1}{2} - 3$	$5,000,000 to $6,000,000
Automobiles	$5 - 10$	$250,000,000 to $500,000,000
Fountain pens	$5 - 10$	Around $6,000,000
Copper	10	No estimate
Tractors	$10 - 15$	Around $125,000,000
Typewriters	$10 - 30$	No estimate

a. These estimates generally exclude anticipated 'shakedown losses' of new entrants, which in some cases may be large and prolonged.

b. The two rows of estimates refer alternatively to fresh and diversified meat packing.

c. Percentage of an efficient plant in the largest regional market may exceed 5 per cent.

d. Excludes any investment in ore or coal.

e. Acetate rayon.

f. Viscose rayon.

g. Excludes working capital.

h. Percentage of an efficient plant in the largest regional market may exceed 10 per cent.

efficient plant or firm in the twenty industries sampled. The findings relative to capital requirements for the large plant are fairly comprehensive, and are summarized in Table 7. Column 2 of this table shows the estimated percentage of national industry capacity provided by one efficient plant, and column 3 the total investment required to establish such a plant (ordinarily including working capital) as of about 1951. The industries are grouped according to the importance of scale economies from the previously emphasized percentage standpoint. The first category of industries are those in which a single efficient plant will supply no more than 5 per cent of the largest submarket or unsegmented national market; the second includes those where the corresponding percentage is 5 to 10 per cent; the third includes those where the percentage is above 10 per cent. We may thus observe the extent to which the 'percentage effect' of scale economies is of the same order as their 'absolute capital requirement effect'.

The findings in Table 7 speak fairly clearly for themselves, but a few comments may be in order. First, there is no evident correlation of the absolute capital requirements for an efficient plant with the percentage of market output supplied by it. The size of the market is an erratic variable forestalling such a correlation. Second, absolute capital requirements for an efficient plant in all the manufacturing industries examined are large enough to restrict seriously the ranks of potential entrants; even 500,000 dollars, the smallest amount listed, will not be forthcoming from savings out of salary or from the winnings in a poker game.

Third, the absolute capital requirements in some cases reinforce but in other cases weaken the 'percentage effect' on entry of economies of scale of plant. For each of the eight industries in category 1 in Table 7, for example, the percentage of market output supplied by a single plant seems small enough to provide no serious deterrent to entry. In three of these cases – flour milling, shoes and canned goods[18] – the absolute capital requirements are also so small that entry may not be seriously restrained thereby. But in four others, capital requirements ranging from ten to forty-two million dollars per plant provide a greater deterrent, and in one (petroleum refining) they impose a truly formidable barrier.

18. As well as in fresh-meat packing.

In the six industries of category 2, where the 'percentage effect' on entry of economies of scale of plant is moderate, it is strongly reinforced in four cases (possibly excepting metal containers, and farm machines, for which there is no estimate) by absolute capital requirements. The effect is very much increased in both the steel and cigarette industries. In the six industries of category 3, where the 'percentage effect' appears quite important, it is strongly reinforced in the cases of automobiles and tractors by absolute capital requirements, but in the fountain pen and gypsum industries capital requirements are relatively small. Thus a generally mixed picture regarding the dual effects of economies of large plant emerges.

The extent to which economies of multiplant firms as already noted increase the capital requirements for efficiency may be readily ascertained by comparing the findings of Table 6 with those of Table 7. Since the existence of such economies was denied in six industries, not estimated in eight others, and held to be slight in at least half the remaining six, detailed comment on this matter does not seem justified.

Conclusions

When the answer provided by empirical investigation to an initial inquiry concerning the values of certain economic data is that the values are highly irregular and variegated, and when the answer is therefore found only in a great array of numbers, any brief summarization of the findings may be difficult to make and misleading if attempted. Since this situation is encountered with respect to each of the major questions posed at the beginning of this paper, no comprehensive summary of findings will be attempted here. Certain salient conclusions may be restated briefly, however, in each case with the proviso that they may have general validity only so far as the sample of industries selected is generally representative of moderately to highly concentrated manufacturing industries in the United States.

Regarding the importance of economies of large plants, the percentage of a market supplied by one efficient plant in some cases is and in some cases is not sufficient to account for high firm concentration or to impede entry. Where it is, these economies might easily propagate high concentration and serious impediments to entry; the number of cases where it is sufficient increases as we refer to the smaller regional or product submarkets in various industries. A significant corollary of these findings is that the following popular horseback observations are apparently *not true*: that economies of scale of plant are never or almost never important in encouraging oligopoly or impeding entry, and that such economies always or almost always are important in these ways. The picture is not extreme in either direction and not simple.

The economies of large plants frequently erect formidable barriers to entry in the shape of absolute capital requirements. Moderately to very high barriers of this sort were found in all but four or five of the industries studied. The height of such barriers is not clearly correlated with percentage of the market supplied by a single plant, so that a relatively independent influence on entry is discovered.

The economies of large multiplant firms are left in doubt by this investigation. In half the cases in which definite estimates were received, such economies were felt to be negligible or absent, whereas in most of the remainder of cases they seemed slight or small. Perhaps the frequently expressed suspicion that such economies generally are unimportant after all is supported, and perhaps we are justified in saying that we have had difficulty in accumulating convincing support for the proposition that in many industries production or distribution economies of large firms seriously encourage concentration or discourage entry.

Our reference here has of course been strictly to the effect of the size of the plant or firm on the cost of production and distribution, and thereby on entry and on concentration. Needless to say, parallel studies of other factors bearing on entry, including the effects of scale on price and on sales promotion, are required for a full evaluation of the entry problem.

References
BAIN, J. S. (1951), 'Relation of profit rate to industry concentration',
   Q.J. Econ., vol. 65, pp. 297–304.
BAIN, J. S. (1954), 'Conditions of entry and emergence of monopoly',
   in E. H. CHAMBERLIN (ed.), *Monopoly and Competition and Their Regulation*, Macmillan.
BLAIR, J. M. (1942), 'The relation between size and efficiency of business',
   Rev. econ. Stats., vol. 24, pp. 125–35.

BLAIR, J. M. (1948), 'Technology and size', *Amer. econ. Rev.*, vol. 38, pp. 121–52.

FEDERAL TRADE COMMISSION (1941), *Relative Efficiency of Large, Medium-Sized and Small Business*, Temporary National Economic Committee, monograph no. 13.

FEDERAL TRADE COMMISSION (1947), *The Divergence between Plant and Company Concentration*.

FELLNER, W. J. (1949), 'Case 1-a', 'Case 1-b', 'Case 2', in *Competition among the few*, Knopf.

Part Two
Pricing and Market Structure

In a simple taxonomy, we might distinguish perfect competition imperfect or monopolistic competition, oligopoly (limiting case: duopoly), and simple or Marshallian monopoly. The taxonomy can easily be made more complex by distinguishing also according to the presence or absence of product differentiation and or advertising, and the ease of entry, etc. Taxonomy on these lines rapidly becomes boring, and distracts attention from the interesting problems. No attempt has been made to select papers according to this sort of classification of 'cases'. Selection has rather been based on ideas of what is important or interesting that I attempted to justify in the Introduction. Selection of papers for this Part has also been determined by the desire to include only papers that assume profit-maximization – alternative behavioural hypotheses are discussed in another Part. Any work, however important, the contents of which has become thoroughly incorporated in modern textbooks has been excluded. On this account, much important and interesting work has been left out: Chamberlin and/or Joan Robinson on the tangency solution, on advertising and product differentiation, on discriminating monopoly, etc.

The brief extract from Cournot is included partly to show how early (1838) calculus was applied to economic problems. The whole chapter is not reprinted. He continues by undertaking a comparative static analysis of his model (again, nearly a century ahead of his time), but his notation and method are relatively clumsy: there are now easier ways of learning how to do the job.

I have included two sections of a paper of my own on monopolistic competition. The omitted sections were devoted largely to a methodological critique of earlier criticisms of monopolistic competition. They occasioned some controversy, and I should not care to reprint them here without the criticisms that have been made of them (Further Reading gives the references). I hope that the sections reprinted here stand reasonably on their own.

The problem of oligopolistic interdependence is still perplexing. 'Conjectural variation' is one tool for dealing with it. It is neatly explained in the brief extract from a paper by Hicks reprinted here (the remainder is omitted on the grounds that its substance is in modern texts). Its importance is partly in unifying theory. Once one is familiar with the idea, it is easily seen that the Cournot model of duopoly involves a limiting case of conjectural variation (zero), as does Chamberlin's large-numbers case. The famous 'kinky oligopoly demand-curve' can be seen to be another limiting case of conjectural variation: zero up, and unity down. Stigler's paper is, of course, a classic, but it is worth reprinting on another ground too: it contains a critical review of much on oligopoly and 'full-cost pricing' that makes it possible to dispense with other, lengthy, papers!

The obvious omission here is any game-theoretic treatment of oligopoly. The reasons for this are two. The first is that, whatever its intrinsic interest, it has not so far been very successful. The second is that the most interesting work in the field known to me is Shubik's: his idea of a 'game for survival' is very powerful. Unfortunately, I simply could not make any extract from his book that would both give the key ideas and be reasonably self-contained (and brief).

Further Reading

The standard analysis of imperfect competition and monopoly is now in any textbook. None the less, the student should at least sample Chamberlin's book for himself. Suggestions here are to works dealing with particular controversies, or unsolved problems.

The major criticisms of Chamberlin's *Theory of Monopolistic Competition* are to be found in

R. Triffin, *Monopolistic Competition and General Equilibrium Theory*, Harvard University Press, 1940; Oxford University Press, 1940,

N. Kaldor, 'Mrs Robinson's "Economics of imperfect competition"', *Economica*, n.s. vol. 1, 1934, pp. 335–41,

N. Kaldor, 'Market imperfection and excess capacity', *Economica*, n.s. vol. 2, 1935, pp. 33–50,

N. Kaldor, 'Professor Chamberlin on monopolistic and imperfect competition', *Quarterly Journal of Economics*, vol. 52, 1938, pp. 513–29,

G. J. Stigler, 'Monopolistic competition in retrospect' in *Five Lectures on Economic Problems*, Longmans, 1949; Macmillan Co., 1950,

M. Friedman, 'The methodology of positive economics' in *Essays In Positive Economics*, University of Chicago Press, 1953; Cambridge University Press, 1954.

The three Kaldor papers are to be found together in
N. Kaldor, *Essays on Value and Distribution*, Duckworth, 1960; Free Press, 1960.

Chamberlin replied to some of these criticisms in
E. H. Chamberlin, 'The Chicago school' in *Towards A More General Theory of Value*, Oxford University Press, 1957.

The paper printed here as 'The comparative statics of monopolistic competition' constitutes two sections from
G. C. Archibald, 'Chamberlin versus Chicago', *Review of Economic Studies*, vol. 24, 1961, pp. 2–28,
and was followed by

G. J. Stigler, 'Archibald versus Chicago',

M. Friedman, 'More on Archibald versus Chicago',

G. C. Archibald, 'Reply to Chicago',
all to be found in *Review of Economic Studies*, vol. 30, 1962, pp. 63–71.

A controversy over the 'excess capacity theorem' has continued. See
H. Demsetz, 'The nature of equilibrium in monopolistic competition', *Journal of Political Economy*, vol. 67, 1959, pp. 21–30,

H. Demsetz, 'The welfare and empirical effects of monopolistic competition', *Economic Journal*, vol. 74, 1964, pp. 623–41,

G. C. Archibald, 'Monopolistic competition and returns to scale', *Economic Journal*, vol. 77, 1967, pp. 405–12,

H. Demsetz, 'Monopolistic competition: a reply', *Economic Journal*, vol. 77, 1967, pp. 412–20,

H. Demsetz, 'Do competition and monopolistic competition differ?', *Journal of Political Economy*, vol. 76, 1968, pp. 146–58.

A beautiful review of neo-classical duopoly theory will be found in the first three chapters of
W. J. Fellner, *Competition Among the Few*, Knopf, 1949.

The 'kinky oligopoly demand curve' was introduced by
P. M. Sweezy, 'Demand under condition of oligopoly', *Journal of Political Economy*, vol. 47, 1939, pp. 568–73, and

R. L. Hall and C. J. Hitch, 'Price theory and business behaviour', *Oxford Economic Papers*, vol. 2, 1939, pp. 12–45.

4 A. Cournot

Pricing by the Proprietor of a Mineral Spring

Excerpt from A. Cournot, *Researches into the Mathematical Principals of the Theory of Wealth*, translated by T. Bacon, Kelley, 1960, chapter 5.

For convenience in discussion, suppose that a man finds himself proprietor of a mineral spring which has just been found to possess salutary properties possessed by no other. He could doubtless fix the price of a *litre* of this water at one hundred francs; but he would soon see by the scant demand, that this is not the way to make the most of his property. He will therefore successively reduce the price of the litre to the point which will give him the greatest possible profit; i.e. if $F(p)$ denotes the law of demand, he will end, after various trials, by adopting the value of p which renders the product $p F(p)$ a maximum, or which is determined by the equation

$$F(p) + p F'(p) = 0. \qquad\qquad\qquad\qquad \textbf{1}$$

The product $\quad p F(p) = \dfrac{[F(p)]^2}{-F'(p)}$

will be the annual revenue of the owner of the spring, and this revenue will only depend on the nature of function F.

To make equation **1** applicable, it must be supposed that for the value of p obtained from it, there will be a corresponding value of D which the owner of the spring can deliver, or which does not exceed the annual flow of this spring; otherwise the owner could not, without damage to himself, reduce the price per litre as low as would be for his interest were the spring more abundant. If the spring produces annually a number of litres expressed by Δ, by deducing p from the relation $F(p) = \Delta$, we necessarily obtain the price per litre which must finally be fixed by the competition of customers.

In this simplest case, chosen for a type, the producer has no cost of production to bear, or the cost can be considered insignificant. Let us go on to that of a man who possesses the secret of a medical preparation or an artificial mineral water, for which the materials and labour must be paid for. It will no longer be the function $pF(p)$, or the annual *gross receipts*, which the producer should strive to carry to its maximum value, but the *net receipts*, or the function $pF(p) - \phi(D)$, in which $\phi(D)$ denotes the cost of making a number of litres equal to D. Since D is connected with p by the relation $D = F(p)$, the complex function $pF(p) - \phi(D)$ can be regarded as depending implicitly on the single variable p, although generally the cost of production is an explicit function, not of the price of the article produced, but of the quantity produced. Consequently the price to which the producer should bring his article will be determined by the equation

$$D + \frac{dD}{dp}\left[p - \frac{d[\phi(D)]}{dD} \right] = 0. \qquad\qquad 2$$

This price will fix in turn the annual net receipts or the revenue of the inventor, and the capital value of his secret, or his *productive property*, the ownership of which is guaranteed by law and can have commercial circulation as well as that of a piece of land or any material property. If this value is nil or insignificant, the owner of the property will obtain no pecuniary profit from it; he will abandon it gratis, or for a very small payment, to the first comer who seeks to develop it. The value of a litre will only represent the value of the raw materials, the wages or profits of the agents who cooperate in making and marketing it, and the interest on the capital necessary for development.

The terms of our example prevent our admitting in this case a limitation of the productive forces, which would hinder the producer from lowering the price to the rate which would give the *maximum* net receipts, according to the law of demand. But in a great many other cases there may be such a limitation, and if Δ expresses the limit which the production or the demand cannot exceed, the price will be fixed by the relation $F(p) = \Delta$, as if there were no cost of production. The cost, in this case, is not borne by the consumers at all; it only diminishes the income of the producer. It falls not exactly on the proprietor (who, unless the inventor or first holder – a question of original conditions with which theory has nothing to do – acquired the property, himself or through his agents, for a value proportioned to its revenue), but on the property itself. A decrease of this cost will only be to the advantage of the producer, so far as it does not result in the possibility of increasing his producing power.

Let us return to the case where this possibility exists, and where the price p is determined according to equation 2. We shall observe that the coefficient $d[\phi(D)]/dD$, though it may increase or decrease as D increases, must be supposed to be positive, for it would be absurd that the *absolute* expense of production should decrease as production increases. We shall call attention also to the fact that necessarily $p > d[\phi(D)]/dD$, for dD being the increase of production, $d[\phi(D)]$ is the increase in the cost, $p\,dD$ is the increase of the gross receipts, and whatever may be the abundance of the source of production, the producer will always stop when the increase in expense exceeds the increase in receipts. This is also abundantly evident from the form of equation 2, since D is always a positive quantity, and dD/dp a negative quantity.

In the course of our investigations we shall seldom have occasion to consider $\phi(D)$ directly, but only its differential coefficient $d[\phi(D)]/dD$, which we will denote by $\phi'(D)$. This differential coefficient is a new function of D, the form of which exerts very great influence on the principal problems of economic science.

The function $\phi'(D)$ is capable of increasing or decreasing as D increases, according to the nature of the producing forces and of the articles produced.

For what are properly called *manufactured articles*, it is generally the case that the cost becomes proportionally less as production increases, or, in other words, when D increases $\phi'(D)$ is a decreasing function. This comes from better organization of the work, from discounts on the price of raw materials for large purchases, and finally from the reduction of what is known to producers as *general expense*. It may happen, however, even in exploiting products of this nature, that when the exploitation is carried beyond certain limits, it induces higher prices for raw materials and labour, to the point where $\phi'(D)$ again begins to increase with D.

Whenever it is a question of working agricultural lands, of mines, or of quarries, i.e. of what is essentially real estate, the function $\phi'(D)$ increases with D; and, as we shall soon see, it is in consequence of this fact alone that farms, mines, and quarries yield a net revenue to their owners, long before all has been extracted from the soil which it is physically able to produce, and notwithstanding the great subdivision of these properties, which causes between producers a competition which can be considered as unlimited. On the contrary, investments made under the condition that as D increases $\phi'(D)$ decreases, can only yield a net income or a *rent* in the case of a monopoly properly so-called, or of a competition sufficiently limited to allow the effects of a monopoly collectively maintained to be still perceptible.

Between the two cases where the function $\phi'(D)$ is increasing and decreasing, there falls naturally the one where this function reduces to a constant, the cost being constantly proportional to the production, and where equation 2 takes the form

$$D + \frac{dD}{dp}(p-g) = 0.$$

The case must also be pointed out where $\phi(D)$ is a constant, and $\phi'(D) = 0$, so that the price is the same as if there were no cost. This case occurs more frequently than would be suspected at first glance, especially where we have to do with production under a monopoly, and where the value of the number D receives the extension of which it admits. For instance, in a theatrical enterprise D denotes the number of tickets sold, and the cost of the enterprise remains practically the same, without reference to the number of spectators. For the tolls of a bridge, which is another monopolistic investment, D denotes the number of passengers; and the costs for repairs, watching and bookkeeping will be the same, whether the crossing is much or little used. In such cases the constant g disappears, equation 2 becomes the same as equation 1, and the price p is determined in the same manner as if there were no costs.

5 John R. Hicks

Duopoly

Excerpt from J. R. Hicks, 'Annual survey of economic theory: the theory of monopoly', *Econometrica*, vol. 3, 1935, pp. 12–16.

We have suggested that the demand curve for a particular product of a particular firm will usually be kept highly elastic by the incursion of other producers selling small quantities of highly competitive products, if the first firm raises its price. But if they do so, will not the first firm retaliate on them?

Two cases have thus to be distinguished. The first is when the other potential producers are fairly numerous. In this case, they are not likely to be much deterred by the fear of retaliation. For although the first firm may find it profitable to turn its attention to some other product if it meets with competition in the line it had first chosen, the chance of that other product being highly competitive with the products of any particular other producer is small.

In the other case, when the other potential producers are few, the fear of retaliation is likely to be more serious, and it may very well stop poaching.

The difficult problem which arises from the relations of a very small number of competing firms has been much studied in recent years, but there has not yet developed any very close agreement on the solution. Largely owing to the difficulty of the problem, it has been chiefly studied in its most simple case, that of two firms producing an identical product – duopoly.[1]

The theory of duopoly has a long history; and here we can do no more than allude to the classical theory of Cournot, and the displacement of Cournot's theory by the criticisms of Bertrand and Edgeworth, which form the ancient history of the subject.

1. Chamberlin, however, has made at any rate a preliminary investigation of the more complex cases where several firms are involved. See his sections on 'oligopoly' (1933, pp. 100, 170).

Edgeworth's solution, based on 'the characteristic freedom of the monopolist to vary price', involved such peculiar assumptions about costs that it could hardly have held the field forever. The post-war period therefore saw a renaissance of Cournotism, led by Amoroso (in *Lezioni d'economica matematica*) and Wicksell;[2] this movement is represented also by the chapter on 'Mehrfaches Monopol' in Schneider's book.[3] In the next stage, criticisms of both the Cournot and Edgeworth solutions were offered by Zeuthen and by Chamberlin,[4] it then became clear that each of the rivals had pointed the way towards a possible solution, but that even together they did not exhaust the list.

A very convenient line of approach, which sets these alternative solutions in their places, and so opens a path towards a general theory, can be developed from a hint given in Bowley (1924, p. 38). It is this approach which appears to be gaining ground at present. Its main principle can be expressed as follows.[5]

The marginal revenue, which a duopolist endeavors to equate to his marginal cost, is

$$\frac{d}{dx_1}(px_1),$$

where x_1 is his output, and $p = f(x_1+x_2)$, x_2 being the output of his rival. Thus

$$MR_1 = \frac{d}{dx_1}(px_1) = p + x_1 f'(x_1+x_2) + x_1 f'(x_1+x_2)\frac{\partial x_2}{\partial x_1}.$$

The marginal revenue curve which confronts the duopolist is thus in part dependent upon a quantity $\partial x_2/\partial x_1$, which we can only interpret as the degree to which the duopolist expects his rival to expand (or contract) output, if he himself expands his output by an increment dx_1. Since $f'(x_1+x_2)$ is negative, a negative value of $\partial x_2/\partial x_1$ will raise the adjusted marginal revenue curve of the

2. Wicksell (1927).

3. Schneider (1932), ch. 4.

4. Zeuthen (1930), ch. 2; Chamberlin (1933), ch. 3, which substantially reproduces his article (1929).

5. The following owes much to some yet unpublished work by W. M. Allen, of Oxford.

duopolist, and thus be favorable to an expansion of output; a positive value will favor a contraction.

The conception of these 'conjectural variations', $\partial x_2/\partial x_1$ etc., has been analysed in very general terms by Frisch (1933). There is, in the short period, no need for any particular degree of consistency between the conjecture of the first duopolist $\partial x_2/\partial x_1$, and that of the second $\partial x_1/\partial x_2$.

The equation of marginal revenue and marginal cost thus determines the output of the first duopolist, once the output of the second duopolist, and the first duopolist's conjecture as to the variation of this output are given. For any particular type of conjecture, we can thus construct a 'reaction curve', similar to that employed by Cournot, giving the preferred output of the first duopolist, corresponding to each possible output of the second. A similar reaction curve can be constructed for the second duopolist, and the intersection of the two will give the point of equilibrium.

In the majority of cases, these reaction curves will be negatively inclined;[6] and in the majority of these cases, the inclination will be such that an increased output by the other duopolist will react

6. The condition for negative inclination is that

$$1+\frac{hx_1}{x}\left(1+\frac{\partial x_2}{\partial x_1}\right)$$

should be positive; where h is the 'adjusted concavity' of the market-demand curve. (That is to say,

$$h = \frac{(x_1+x_2)f''(x_1+x_2)}{f'(x_1+x_2)}.$$

cf. Robinson 1933, p. 40). Since we may assume that in all sensible cases,

$$1+\frac{\partial x_2}{\partial x_1}$$

is positive, it follows that the reaction curve will be negatively inclined in all cases when h is positive (when the demand curve is convex upwards) and also for a considerable number of cases when h is negative. It has been further shown by Allen that in such cases of negative inclination, the slope of the reaction curve will also (for reasons of stability) be numerically less than 1, excepting when there is a high degree of asymmetry between the positions of the two duopolists. 'Normal cases' are defined as satisfying these two conditions, so that dx_1/dx_2, taken along the reaction curve of the first duopolist, lies between 0 and -1.

on the first in such a way as to increase the total output of both together. If we confine our attention to these *normal* cases, which are much the most likely to yield stable solutions, the more interesting assumptions about conjectures which have been made by recent writers fall into their places very simply.

1. If the conjectural variations are both zero, we have of course the Cournot case.

2. If one of the conjectural variations is zero, but the other duopolist takes as his conjectural variation the actual slope of the reaction curve of his rival, we have the case of an 'active' policy by one duopolist.[7] In *normal* conditions, this will make the conjectural variation of the active duopolist negative; thus, as compared with the Cournot case, it will raise his marginal revenue curve, increase his output, and (again in normal conditions) lead to an increased total output, and so a lower price.

3. If both duopolists act in this manner, each calculating conjectural variations from the other's Cournotian reaction curve, we have a curious case which has been investigated by Stackelberg (1933) and Harrod (1934). In normal conditions, once more, this will lead to a further expansion of total output, and a further fall in price.

4. There does not seem to be any reason why we should stop here. One duopolist may become doubly 'active', and calculate a conjectural variation from the reaction curve of his rival on the assumption that the rival is active. In most, though not (it appears) quite all, *normal* cases, this would lead to a further fall in price. The process becomes similar to one of price-cutting.

But once we are on the road of competitive price-cutting, it is reasonable to suppose that, sooner or later, one duopolist or the other would perceive that his conjecture that an increase in his output was leading to a contraction of his rival's was proving wrong. Once he acted on this, and constructed a conjectural variation based on this experience (and consequently a *positive* variation) the whole situation would be transformed. Price-cutting would give place to 'tacit combination'; positive conjectures,

7. Stackelberg (1933). This article also contains an important and ingenious extension of the theory to the case of several producers.

again in normal conditions, would give a higher price than that given by the Cournot equilibrium.[8]

The method just described is capable of extension to the case where the product of one duopolist is not a perfect substitute for that of the other. We have only to write $p_1 = f_1(x_1, x_2)$, $p_2 = f_2(x_1, x_2)$; the two sellers will now of course usually sell at different prices. We then have

Adjusted marginal revenue of first seller $= \dfrac{d}{dx_1}(p_1 x_1)$

$$= p_1 + x_1 \frac{\partial p_1}{\partial x_1} + x_1 \frac{\partial p_1}{\partial x_2}\left(\frac{\partial x_2}{\partial x_1}\right),$$

from which we proceed much as before. This highly general solution can be applied whatever is the relation between the demands for the products; it can thus be applied to cases where the products are complementary instead of competitive (see Edgeworth, 1925). Here $\partial p_1/\partial x_2$ will probably be positive, so that it is an anticipated consequential expansion of the other's output which will raise the marginal revenue curve of the first duopolist, and vice versa (see Professor Divisia's paper on duopoly summarized in *Econometrica*, June 1934 and *Revue d'Economie Politique*, May 1934).

8. Nicoll (1934). Nicoll's case of tacit combination emerges if we write
$$\frac{\partial x_2}{\partial x_1} = \frac{x_2}{x_1}, \qquad \frac{\partial x_1}{\partial x_2} = \frac{x_1}{x_2}.$$

References

BOWLEY, A. L. (1924), *Mathematical Groundwork*, Kelley.

CHAMBERLIN, E. H. (1929), 'Duopoly', *Q.J. Econ.*, vol. 43.

CHAMBERLIN, E. H. (1933), *The Theory of Monopolistic Competition*, Oxford University Press.

EDGEWORTH, F. Y. (1925), 'The pure theory of monopoly', *Papers II*, pp. 122–6.

FRISCH, R. (1933), 'Monopole, polypole, la notion de force dans l'économie', *Nationalökonomisk Tidoskrift*.

HARROD, R. F. (1934), 'The equilibrium of duopoly', *Econ. J.*, vol. 44, pp. 335–7.

NICOLL, H. J., (1934), 'Professor Chamberlin's theory of limited competition', *Q.J. Econ.*, vol. 48, pp. 317–37.

ROBINSON, J. (1933), *The Economics of Imperfect Competition*, Macmillan.

SCHNEIDER, E. (1932), *Reine Theorie Monopolitscher Wirtschaftsformen*, Tübingen.

STACKELBERG, H. VON. (1933), 'Sintra teoria del duopolie e del poliopolio', *Rivista italiana di statistica*.

WICKSELL, K. (1927), 'Mathematische Nationalökonomie', *Archiv fur Sozialwissenschaft und Sozialpolitik*, vol. 58, no. 2, pp. 252–81.

ZEUTHEN, F. (1930), *Problems of Monopoly and Economic Warfare*, Routledge & Kegan Paul.

6 G. C. Archibald

The Comparative Statics of Monopolistic Competition

Excerpt from G. C. Archibald, 'Chamberlin versus Chicago', *Review of Economic Studies*, vol. 24, 1961, pp. 9–28.

1

The object of this paper is to discover what testable predictions can be derived from the theory of monopolistic competition. If we want testable predictions, we must know how things change (it is not easy to see how we can hope to observe equilibrium conditions, although there are at least two well-known cases: the refutation of perfect competition by the observation that the rising-marginal-cost condition is not normally fulfilled, and the search for excess capacity in equilibrium). A static theory associates equilibrium values of the variables with given values of the parameters. We therefore attempt to derive predictions about associated changes: 'if this parameter increases (decreases), this variable increases (decreases)'. This is the familiar method of comparative statics.[1] Comparative statics may, however, be carried out at different levels of generality, with or without quantitative information about the functions of the system. The traditional programme of economics, what I call the Robbins-Samuelson[2] programme, is to endeavour to obtain qualitative predictions (direction of change) with only qualitative restrictions upon the functions. Thus we hope to obtain results by qualitative comparative statics, what Samuelson called the 'qualitative calculus'. He wrote:

1. The empirical testing of a comparative static prediction in general requires that we add a subsidiary dynamic assumption about the speed of response. Testing by trying to observe the fulfilment of equilibrium conditions, however, presents an even worse difficulty: we have to be prepared to say when the unit is in equilibrium.

2. Samuelson gave this programme formal expression (1947), but it is in the tradition of Marshall, and was given clear verbal expression by Robbins (see, for example, the discussion of statistical and quantitative work in ch. 5 of Robbins (1935).

The method of *comparative statics* consists of the study of the response of our equilibrium unknowns to designated changes in parameters ... *In the absence of complete quantitative information concerning our equilibrium equations, it is hoped to be able to formulate qualitative restrictions on slopes, curvatures, etc., of our equilibrium equations so as to be able to derive definite qualitative restrictions upon the responses of our system to changes in certain parameters* (p. 20).

The sentence I have italicized in fact describes something narrower than comparative statics: it describes specifically the programme of *qualitative comparative statics*, the hope that it will be possible to predict directions of change without quantitative information. Samuelson further described this programme:

In cases where the equilibrium values of our variables can be regarded as the solutions of an extremum (maximum or minimum) problem, it is often possible regardless of the number of variables involved to determine unambiguously the qualitative behaviour of our solution values in respect to changes in parameters (p. 21) (italicized in the original).

The purpose of this section is to apply the method of comparative statics to the model of a profit-maximizing firm 'in isolation', taking advertising and quality variation into consideration, in order to discover whether any *qualitative* predictions can be obtained. The conclusion is that, at this traditional level of generality, the model is almost empty: significant *qualitative* predictions cannot be obtained without *quantitative* information. As far as possible, the reasons for this failure will be explained in the text, but more detailed discussion and proofs must be left to the mathematical appendix to this section. In general, however, it appears that whether or not the qualitative method yields significant results depends upon the structure of the model in question.

Now to explore the qualitative content of Chamberlin's model, we must carry out the comparative static exercises so familiar from the study of perfect competition and Marshallian monopoly: we want to know the effects on price, quantity, quality, advertising expenditure, etc., of changes in demand, factor prices, tax rates, and so on. It is indeed surprising that this should be necessary now, about a quarter of a century after *The Theory of Monopolistic Competition* (1933) was first published: perhaps the fact that it is is the most serious criticism of both Chamberlin and his Chicago critics. But we cannot find predictions in Chamberlin's book for the simple reason that we cannot find the necessary comparative statics; and, when we try to do comparative statics, we find another handicap. If we want to do comparative static analysis on a system involving three (or more) variables, we must have the equilibrium conditions relating all three at once. But these Chamberlin does not present: instead, he illustrates the relationships between the variables a pair at a time. All we can really get from Chamberlin is that there will be a maximum, and that, at this maximum, all the necessary marginal equalities will hold, i.e. the conditions for a maximum will obtain.[3]

Many of the comparative static exercises presented below have, of course, been done by other writers: it would be ridiculous to pretend that the analysis here is all, or even mostly, original. Yet there has been a general tendency, in the literature on monopolistic competition, to ignore comparative statics, and to concentrate instead on alternative diagrammatic illustrations of familiar equilibrium conditions. There may, however, be a general reason for this: since the theory, broadly speaking, does not yield unambiguous predictions, many economists, concerned with a specific application or problem, and failing to obtain a prediction, may have given up the problem, instead of realizing that they had discovered something of general importance. Even Hahn (1959a, 1959b),[4] who has recently made a systematic and most welcome

3. This is about all we get from Brems, too (1951). To be told at length that there are equlibria (at which the marginal equalities hold) is not much help when we want testable predictions. Even a full statement of equilibrium conditions is valuable chiefly as a prerequisite to comparative statics.

4. I entirely subscribe to his opening remarks (1959a, p. 293): 'The literature on this subject [selling cost, price, and output decisions] is quite large. It appears to suffer from two deficiencies: it has not produced a simple diagrammatic technique to represent the decisions in question and it does not contain an adequate statement of the second-order conditions of a maximum. These two defects are related, since a major part of the writings in this field are "geometrical", and the non-availability of simple diagrams has led to a neglect of second-order conditions. Without these, however, the theory cannot be applied to an examination of such questions as the effects of excise taxes and/or of sales-cost taxes on the decisions of the firm, nor can the theory be said to be complete.' He therefore sets out to provide a simple diagrammatic technique, and to examine these questions. If only I found the diagrammatic technique simple! The second-order conditions here are left to the mathematical appendix.

attack on the comparative static properties of the model, has failed to point out to what extent his results depend on particular restrictive assumptions which are not altogether obvious, and he thus failed to point out that it is nearly impossible to obtain qualitative predictions from the model without quantitative information. It therefore seems worthwhile to present the analysis *de novo*; and this has the additional advantages of autonomy and consistency of treatment.

In this section I shall attempt the comparative static analysis for a single profit maximizing firm that advertises and varies the quality of its output, treating the firm in isolation; in the next section, I shall investigate the comparative static properties of Chamberlinian groups. Since there are at least three variables, price, quantity, and advertising expenditure or quality, the traditional methods of two-dimensional and verbal analysis are hardly adequate. I shall do what I can with them in the text, however, and relegate proofs to a mathematical appendix.

1. Consider first the effects of an increase in demand on a firm that advertises but does not vary quality. It is well known that, even in the case of a simple, or Marshallian monopolist, who does not advertise, the information that the revenue function has shifted to the right is insufficient to determine the direction of the price change. In the two-dimensional case, total revenue and output will increase,[5] and we may expect them to in the three-dimensional case as well. None of this is much help: we do not obtain a testable prediction about price, and the association of revenue and quantity when demand changes is likely to be produced by any plausible theory. Similarly, we cannot say in which direction advertising changes: if the demand surface shifts out, but we know nothing of the way in which it has been bent or tilted, we can no more say how advertising (a way of obtaining revenue) will change than we can say how price (another way of obtaining revenue) will change.

2. Still limiting ourselves to the case of advertising without quality variation, let us now consider the effect of variations in factor prices. To do this it is convenient to introduce a new con-

5. An increase in output involves an increase in total costs, and is therefore not worth undertaking unless, as a necessary but not sufficient condition, the increased output yields an increased total revenue.

cept, that of a 'factor of revenue'. Since revenue is a function of both the quantity of output and the quantity of advertising, I call both output and advertising 'factors of revenue'. If advertising is held constant, but output increased, revenue is also increased (so long as the demand curve appropriate to the given level of advertising is elastic, as it must be in the neighbourhood of a profit-maximizing equilibrium), and if output is held constant, but advertising is increased, revenue is also increased (because the price which will clear the market of a given output is increased). Thus output and advertising may be treated as substitutable factors of revenue, and for any given outlay, which may be devoted to advertising and output in different combinations, there will be a revenue-maximizing combination.[6] An increase in a factor price has the effect of making the factor of revenue, output, relatively more expensive; an increase in the price of the advertising medium makes the factor of revenue, advertising, relatively more expensive. There is obviously a close analogy here with the theory of production.[7] We know, however, that, while an increase in the price of one factor leads to substitution in favour of the other, there is an 'income effect' against both, so that we cannot say how

6. There is an obvious sense in which sales and advertising are complementary: if advertising is increased, sales are. But this involves increased total outlay; the point here is that they are alternative uses for any given total outlay.

7. I do not rely on the analogy with the theory of production: proofs of the propositions asserted here will be found in the Appendix. A diagrammatic technique may, however, be suggested. If advertising is measured on one axis and output on the other, iso-revenue curves and constant outlay curves may obviously be constructed, and the usual diagrammatic analysis carried out. In this case, however, there are difficulties over both the convexity of the revenue function and the concavity of the outlay function, the former due to what Hicks called the 'cross-effects' (1946, pp. 14–15), and the latter due to the possibility of 'bulk discounts' for advertising, increasing returns, etc. We may expect, and assume, diminishing marginal revenue to both advertising and output, but this is neither necessary nor sufficient for convexity: sufficient (but not necessary) conditions are that an increase in output does not diminish marginal revenue with respect to advertising, and vice-versa. We cannot assert *a priori* that the necessary conditions must be satisfied, and thus exclude the possibility of multiple equilibria, but it seems best at this stage to assume a unique and stable equilibrium and see what, if anything, follows. For convexity conditions see Allen (1938, pp. 340–45), and for the analogous propositions in the theory of production see pp. 369–74.

employment of the relatively cheaper factor changes without further knowledge. Employment of the relatively more expensive factor must fall, but, unless we know what happens to the relatively cheaper factor, we cannot even obtain a prediction about the direction of change in the ratio in which the two factors are combined. In fact, if we neglect 'cross-effects', we can predict that employment of the cheaper factor falls too, but this is still not enough to predict the change in the factor ratio (for which we require the initial proportions, and the relative effects on revenue of a change in each). The effects of an increase in the price of the advertising medium (investigated in the Appendix) are similarly unpredictable. The amount of advertising goes down; the direction of change in the quantity of output is predicted only if 'cross-effects' are neglected; the change in advertising expenditure per unit of output depends on the initial levels of, and changes in, both, and cannot therefore be generally predicted. Furthermore, *in neither case can the direction of change in price be predicted*, even if cross-effects are ignored. The reason is intuitively fairly obvious: a reduction in output, caused by an increase in a factor price, tends to push price up; the associated reduction in advertising tends to push it down; which force proves stronger depends on *relative magnitudes*, and cannot be predicted from purely qualitative considerations. Exactly the same argument applies, *mutatis mutandis*, in the case of an increase in the price of the advertising medium.

3. We now consider the effects of changes in tax rates. A specific indirect tax can be treated as an increase in the cost of the factor of revenue, output (since it varies with the quantity produced and nothing else). It is therefore completely analogous with the case of an increase in a factor price, just discussed, and yields no more results. An *ad valorem* tax is more complicated: it alters the relationship between both factors and revenue. In the two-dimensional, no-advertising case, we analyse it by moving the demand curve inwards and changing its slope. In this case a three-dimensional demand surface is moved inwards and changed in slope. Clearly, unless we know something about the effects on the rate of substitution between the factors advertising and output, and their relative costs (if physical returns are variable, the

relative expensiveness of output and advertising *must* change as the quantity of the former changes), it is going to be difficult to say much. In fact, if we cannot ignore 'cross-effects', we cannot obtain, in this case, any predictions whatever about the direction of change in the variables. Neglecting the cross-effect, then both advertising and output fall, but the change in price is still undetermined. The fall in quantity leads one to expect a higher price, the fall in advertising a lower, and, without knowledge of the relative strengths of their effects on demand and costs, it is impossible to predict the net result.[8]

4. Let us now consider the effects of changes in the data on the choice of product, assuming for simplicity that the firm does not advertise. Unfortunately most of the discussion of product differentiation has been only in terms of 'near' and 'far': it has been argued, for example, that firms will endeavour to create 'private markets', and use all the techniques of product differentiation, branding, and advertising, to separate these markets. An argument of this sort does not, however, constitute a model. If we ask: will a change in demand (or costs, or taxes) cause firms to produce closer or less close substitutes? we are simply not in a position to start to answer it.[9] If an object of monopolistic competition is to handle product differentiation in the sense of 'near' and 'far', it fails. Not only are there no testable implications, there is no theory from which we might try to derive them. Let us see, then, if we can do anything with less ambitious questions by confining ourselves to a model in which we have a continuous index of quality. The necessary assumptions are discussed by Dorfman and Steiner (1954), who consider '. . . a firm which produces a differentiated product whose quality can be measured (e.g. in terms of horsepower, tensile strength, denier, etc.) and whose rate

8. Hahn (1959a, p. 307) appears to obtain more definite results. They appear to be due to his assumption (p. 296, n. 3; but see also (1959b) which is unfortunately rather obscure) that the 'cross-effects' are negligible. He says that 'the contract effect ["income" effect of the tax] will normally tend to raise prices, but in one instance it will reinforce the substitution effect in lowering prices'. In the next paragraph he speaks of price (and output) as being 'in fact' reduced by the tax. I am in some doubt as to what his conclusion actually is.

9. Chamberlin suggests (1957, chs. 3 and 6) that the analysis of spatial competition may provide answers to analogous questions.

of sales per unit of time . . . is a continuous and differentiable function of price . . . and a quality index . . .'. They further assume that the cost of production is a continuous and differentiable function of the quality index (1954). This model cannot be used to investigate the effects of changes in factor prices that change the relative costs of different qualities, because they will alter the cost function, but it can be used to investigate the effects of changes, such as indirect taxes, that are independent of quality. (Dorfman and Steiner, following the usual tradition, confined themselves to an elegant investigation of some properties of the equilibrium conditions of the model: they did not inquire into its predictive ability.)

It is intuitively obvious that the comparative static analysis must be very similar to that of advertising: output and quality can be treated as substitutable factors of revenue; and the effect of an indirect tax is to raise the price of the factor output. Consider first a specific indirect tax. In the advertising case, neglecting cross-effects was a sufficient condition for predicting the direction of change in advertising but not in price; in this case, similarly, if we neglect cross-effects, we obtain the prediction that quality deteriorates, but still cannot predict the direction of change in price, which is pushed up by the reduction in output, and down by the deterioration in quality. Consider now an *ad valorem* tax. The intuitive expectation is that an *ad valorem* tax will cause a deterioration in quality (i.e. a concealed price increase), leaving the direction of the price change undetermined (lower quantity – price up; lower quality – price down). Once again, even this result can only be obtained if we ignore cross-effects.[10]

10. One other possible way of obtaining a prediction about product changes occurs to me. Suppose that a firm has two varieties of product which are substitutes in demand. Then they will also be substitutes in revenue, and the analysis is again similar to that of advertising. The firm produces all of one or some of both. If a change in the data causes one to become relatively more expensive, then, if both are produced, we expect that relatively less of the now more expensive one will be produced. If only one is produced then, if any change in produce occurs, it must be in favour of the now relatively cheaper variety. This is an obvious result; but if we cannot also point to changes in the data that will change the relative costs of the varieties, it is trivial too. The results of a change in a specific indirect tax is not certain: it changes the cost of units of both varieties equally.

5. Finally, consider the case in which we have both advertising and quality variation of the Dorfman–Steiner type. The results are fairly obvious: in the case of a specific tax, quantity falls, but the change in advertising and quality cannot be predicted without ignoring cross-effects; in the case of an *ad valorem* tax we cannot even predict a quantity fall without ignoring cross-effects; in neither case can we predict the direction of change in price without knowing which is stronger, the upward push from the fall in output or the downward push from the fall in advertising and quality.

I think it will be agreed that these results are very meagre. The difficulty with this part of monopolistic competition (or Chamberlin's extension of Marshallian monopoly theory, as we choose to call it) is not that the assumptions are 'wrong', but that, at the traditional level of generality, the implications are few and those few trivial. The implications we have obtained amount to little more than that if quantity, quality, or advertising be made more expensive, there will be less of it! The theory is not totally empty, but very nearly so. (Of course there may be some cases, some parameter shifts, that I have not tried and for which the results are unambiguous. I can offer no 'impossibility theorem': I can only show my own lack of success, and show that there are general reasons for it.) As it stands, however, this model of the firm will not provide an unambiguous answer to such a question as 'in what direction are the variables changed by an increase in a specific indirect tax?' Samuelson remarks that 'it is a poor theory indeed that will not answer so simple a question' (1947, p. 15).

Before we agree with Samuelson, let us consider the reasons for the failure. The programme of qualitative economics is, in fact, an extremely ambitious one – to deduce directions of change from

---

Similarly, the result of a change in an *ad valorem* tax is not certain: its results are unpredictable unless the demand surface is fully specified. All we can say is that, if one variety uses relatively more of a factor than the other, a change in the price of that factor will increase the cost of the first variety relative to the second, and we therefore expect it to diminish the ratio of the output of the first to the second. This result may not be trivial, but it is very obvious. It is the only comparative static result in the field of product differentiation that I have so far found, apart from the meagre results obtained from the Dorfman–Steiner model.

little more than the traditional assumptions that physical returns must diminish at *some* level of output, that returns to advertising must diminish at *some* level of advertising, and that demand curves slope down. It seems that we might blame the methodology that led us to expect 'something for nothing' (or very nearly nothing) rather than the theory that failed to provide it. All that has happened, after all, is that monopolistic competition has proved to be barren at a level of generality at which perhaps we should not expect much. Of course, the programme has been relatively successful in simple cases – Marshallian monopoly and perfect competition; but in both these cases the number of variables is smaller, and, in the second case, there are particularly convenient restrictions on the demand and cost functions for the individual firm. The qualitative calculus has failed in the Chamberlin case simply because the relations between the variables and the parameters are such that the traditional qualitative restrictions are not sufficient. Samuelson showed how this could happen;[11] and it is familiar from the theories of demand and production -- whenever substitution and income effects work in opposite directions, the results depend on relative magnitudes.

It is clear that purely qualitative assumptions may very often prove inadequate, and this has a methodological moral: we must give theory some facts[12] to help it to predict more facts. A failure

11. He wrote: 'In general, we should not expect to be able to determine the signs of the rates of change of our variables upon the basis of simple *a priori* qualitative restrictions on our equilibrium equations. . . . [This is because] the restrictions imposed by our hypothesis on our equilibrium conditions (stability and maximum conditions, etc.) are not always sufficient to indicate *definite* restrictions as to algebraic sign of the rates of change of our variables with respect to any parameter.

'Only imagine a change in a parameter which enters into all of a large number of equilibrium equations causing them simultaneously to shift. The resulting net effect upon our variables could only be calculated as a result of balancing the separate effects (regarded as limiting rates of change), and for this purpose detailed quantitative values for all the coefficients involved would have to be known' (1947, p. 19). None the less, he expected great things from the qualitative calculus!

12. In the absence of empirical evidence, restrictions on the functions are sometimes assumed because they are convenient, or 'seem reasonable' (cf. Hahn, 1959a). The trouble with this procedure is that, if the prediction that follows is then refuted by empirical test, we have no means of telling whether the fault lies with the theory or the particular restriction chosen.

of the Robbins–Samuelson programme is not necessarily a disaster: we learn from the analysis how much (or little) qualitative content a theory has, and what sort of empirical work is required to increase its testable content.

2

The problem of this section is to derive some comparative static predictions from the analysis of the group. This we can attempt without necessarily settling all the difficult questions about symmetry, uniformity, etc. We are simply asking the question: *given* a Chamberlin-group, what predictions follow?[13] This seems to be the easiest way of settling the controversy. If no predictions do emerge, we require a new or modified theory; if some are obtained, we have an opportunity of referring the whole matter to the test of fact. As it turns out, we do not obtain any comparative static predictions: we have a failure as complete as that of the last section. The reason is simply that the theory is incomplete: in the absence of a specified relationship between DD′ (the 'share-of-the-market' demand curve) and dd′ (the 'partial' demand curve), we have not even the minimum of qualitative information necessary for comparative statics. In an attempt to complete the theory I therefore introduce a relationship between DD′ and dd′ suggested by Kaldor; but even this proves to be insufficient to give the theory comparative static content.

Similarly, if a prediction obtained by arbitrarily neglecting 'cross-effects' is refuted, we have no means of telling where the fault lies. Restrictions are also sometimes chosen in order to make the theory predict something already known to be true. Unless there is some means of checking empirically on the restriction chosen, this procedure guarantees the theory against refutation!

13. It has been suggested that, since Chamberlin has apparently 'abandoned' the group, under the influence of Triffin's criticisms, this investigation is unnecessary. I have argued that many of the criticisms appear to be misdirected; but this is really beside the point: we have the theory of the group (from Robinson as well as Chamberlin) and we want to know what can be got out of it. It has also been suggested that Harrod's modifications to the theory render this inquiry otiose. But Harrod (1952) in fact constructed a different model by dropping the assumption of short-run profit-maximization. The comparative static properties of his model might well be investigated; but its existence is irrelevant to the comparative static properties of Chamberlin's model.

On the assumption that interdependence is ignored, the short-run predictions would be those of the last section – if the last section had yielded any. What we want now is to extend the analysis to the long-run in which the number of firms and the size of plant are allowed to change. It is obvious that the introduction of advertising and product differentiation (remember that we still have no *theory* of product differentiation as a form of inter-firm competition) will cause serious analytical difficulties even if they are not actually fatal to the predictive power of the theory. I shall therefore start by attempting to obtain some comparative static results for a group, ignoring advertising and the possibility of product change – that is, by trying to obtain some predictions from the model in the simplest possible case in which the difficulties are minimized.

1. What we now want is to answer questions of the following sort: when the number of firms is allowed to change, what are the effects on prices, size of plant, etc., of a change in demand? Of a change in costs? Of a change in tax? Remembering our defeat in the last section, where we considered the short-run adjustment of a single firm, let us try the effect of an increase in demand. It is well known that, at full equilibrium, the long-run average cost curve (LRAC) must be downward sloping (because this is tangential to the short-run average cost curve (SRAC) by construction, and the latter must be downward sloping) (see Kaldor, 1960, p. 63, n. 1 and Harrod, 1952, p. 127). From this we appear to have two results: first, that, so long as dd′ curves are downward sloping, we have unexploited economies of scale as well as excess capacity; and, second, that the long-run price must fall with increased demand. The first will be further discussed below; the second Kaldor has already shown to be wrong. The DD′ curves are moved to the right by the increased demand, and returned to the left by new entry. What happens to size of plant and price depends entirely on what happens to the elasticity of the dd′ curves as DD′ moves, i.e. on the effect of changing market size and share on the 'partial' demand curves for the individual firms.[14] Until some restrictions are imposed

14. See Kaldor, 'The effect of the entry of new competitors will not necessarily reduce the price of existing products; it may even raise them. The

on the behaviour of dd′ as DD′ moves, anything can happen.

Let us now try the effects of a change in costs, taking again the simplest possible case, a specific indirect tax which raises the SRAC curves everywhere by the same amount, as illustrated in

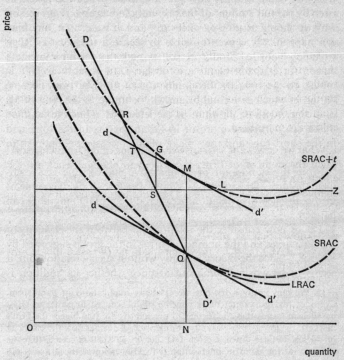

Figure 1

Figure 1, where the initial equilibrium is at Q and the tax is QM per unit. If we confine ourselves to parallel shifts in dd′, as Chamberlin does, tangency will occur at M, and the intersection of dd′ with DD′ (which is the locus of attainable positions) will

profits which the entrepreneur no longer earns will thus not be passed on to the consumer in the form of lower prices but are mainly absorbed in lower productive efficiency' (1960, p. 65).

occur at a point such as T, below the SRAC$+t$ curve. Hence no full equilibrium is possible until the number of firms is reduced, and DD′ shifted to the right. But how far must it shift? What happens to dd′ as DD′ shifts? If we retain the parallelism assumption, full equilibrium is only possible at M, when the price has risen by the full amount of the tax; but there is no *a priori* reason why we should assume parallelism,[15] and, if we drop it, anything can happen.[16] It is even possible to secure a tangency at R, in which case normal profits are still earned, there is no immediate reason for exit, but plants are too large. In general, as DD′ is moved to the right by the elimination of firms, dd′ may become flatter, in which case equilibrium will be found to the right of M, or steeper, with equilibrium to the left of M. Thus the tax may make price increase more or less than the tax in the long and in the short run, and may make plants increase or diminish in size.

From the standpoint of comparative statics, this is a complete failure. The model is empty because it is incomplete: in the absence of a relation between dd′ and DD′ anything can happen.

2. Let us now consider the relationship between the elasticity of the dd′ curves and the number of firms in the group suggested by Kaldor.[17] Since the theory is empty without such a relationship, it seems to be worth finding out at once whether its addition is

15. We may easily work out the elasticity implications of parallelism. Consider first horizontal displacements of dd′ caused by shifts in DD′: parallelism means that the further to the right is dd′ (the bigger the firm's market), the lower is its elasticity at any price. Consider now the elasticity of dd′ as it slides down a given DD′ curve: parallelism means that the elasticity at the point of intersection with DD′ is lower the lower is dd′ (slope unchanged, price lower, quantity greater), i.e. that the elasticity of the particular demand curve is lower the lower the market price. Either or both of these implications may correspond with the facts of a given case; but there is no *a priori* reason for supposing that they must.

16. See Mering (1942, pp. 71–7) for equally unsuccessful attempts to obtain any predictions from the model in this case, and substantially the same argument that is presented above.

17. Kaldor (1935 and 1938), both reprinted (1960). I attribute the idea to Kaldor, although it appears from Chamberlin's remarks that it may have been generally current in the 1930s, because it is explicitly set out and easily accessible in his work.

sufficient for the theory to yield some results.[18] Kaldor argues that an increase in the number of firms, by increasing the number of products in the group, increases the 'density' of the field of substitutes, and that this must increase the elasticity of demand for each individual product. This does not immediately establish a relationship between dd′ and DD′. If DD′ moves to the right because of an increase in total market demand, the changes in dd′ are still unspecified. Now, however, we expect the increased demand to attract new firms, making dd′, on Kaldor's argument, more elastic as DD′ shifts back to the left. We cannot, of course, tell whether it is more or less elastic than it originally was because the intermediate shift is unspecified. Hence, in order to give Kaldor's idea a trial, we must confine ourselves to cases in which the number of firms changes while total market demand does not. Then DD′ is shifted purely by the changed number of firms: and Kaldor's relation is that, as DD′ moves to the right (reduced number of firms), the dd′ curves become less elastic.

We now require a case in which the number of firms changes but total market demand does not, i.e. one in which the change results from a change in costs. The easiest cost change to handle is again a specific excise tax. Suppose that we again start from full equilibrium, at Q in Figure 1, and raise the SRAC curve by the imposition of a specific excise tax. Until and unless the number of firms changes, the locus of possible positions remains DD′. Where the new short-run equilibrium occurs depends on the shape of the family of dd′ curves: it is *possible* that the new equilibrium occurs at R, in which case normal profits are still earned. Assume, however, that, whatever does happen, it leads to subnormal profits, in which case the new short-run equilibrium must lie at a point such as S, intermediate between R and Q. At S the dd′ curve must be flatter than is the SRAC + t curve vertically above it at G (because, if it were steeper, the firm would expect a reduction in output to reduce the gap between average cost and average revenue, and S

18. Chamberlin rejects this relation, apparently on the grounds that the size or area of a market cannot be distinguished from the density with which it is populated (see Chamberlin, 1937; Kaldor's criticism, 1938 and Chamberlin's 'Reply' in 1938). My object here is not to try to settle the argument between Chamberlin and Kaldor (although, in fact, I find Kaldor's arguments most persuasive); it is merely to see if, when a serious deficiency in Chamberlin's theory is filled by Kaldor's relation, any results are then forthcoming.

could not be a position of equilibrium). Now firms leave the industry and DD′ shifts to the right. The reduction in the number of firms (and products: in this analysis the two must change together), according to Kaldor's relation, reduces the elasticity of the dd′ family. Can we now find a new position of equilibrium on SRAC+t, to the right of the present DD′ curve, where dd′ is less elastic than at S, but at the same time tangent to SRAC+t? This is not difficult. Imagine dd′ moving to the right along SZ. If it moves with a constant slope, its elasticity falls. But as we move to the right along SRAC, its slope is diminishing, i.e. changing in the direction of the slope of dd′. There does not, therefore, appear to be any reason why there should not be a tangency solution to the right of DD′ consistent with Kaldor's relation.

Now, have we any comparative static results? Can we say that the price increase after full adjustment will be greater or less than the short-run price increase, or if the average cost of production will be greater or less than before the tax was imposed? It appears immediately that the second question is unanswerable: the new equilibrium position may lie to the left or to the right of Q (bear in mind that S may lie anywhere on RQ). This can be interpreted as follows: the tax reduces total output but also the number of firms; whether the output of the individual firm rises or falls as a result cannot be predicted, and therefore the direction of change in the least-cost scale of plant, if any, cannot be predicted either. We can answer the first question only if we can exclude equilibria on RL (bear in mind that L may lie to the left or to the right of Q). We already know that we cannot exclude L. Consider now tangency at G. This would require a steeper curve than dd′ at S; but, with a higher price, its elasticity could be greater or smaller. But, in any case, we are now comparing elasticities at equal outputs instead of equal prices, and Kaldor's relation does not appear to justify this. The result is that we cannot exclude any point except R itself (trivially excluded by the fact that DD′ must shift). Hence, even with Kaldor's relation, we cannot predict how the full equilibrium values of price, output, and cost of production differ from those of short-run equilibrium. Hence we cannot compare the new full-equilibrium position with the old: the theory is still empty.

3. Since we have been unable to obtain comparative static results in the simplest possible case, without advertising or quality

variation, it is obvious that we shall obtain nothing in more complicated cases with additional variables. We may, however, reconsider the famous excess capacity theorem which has often been regarded as the most significant result obtained by Chamberlin, and the allocative implications of which have undoubtedly been responsible for much of the hostility to his work. In a recent article Demsetz has shown that, if advertising is introduced, full equilibrium does not necessarily involve excess capacity (1959).[19] Consider any given level of advertising expenditure, and the demand curve associated with it. The curve of average advertising expenditure is a rectangular hyperbola. Average total cost is obtained by adding this rectangular hyperbola to the curve of average production costs. Tangency between the demand curve and the average total cost curve may occur where the average production cost curve is falling *or rising*, so long as it is not rising fast enough to offset the effect of falling average advertising costs. If this is true for *any* level of advertising expenditure, it is true for the profit-maximizing level. Hence, when advertising is introduced, tangency is consistent with production at less than or more than minimum cost of production.[20]

19. I am indebted to J. R. Gould for the proof offered here, which I prefer to an earlier proof of my own. Demsetz's proof involves the construction of a '*mutatis mutandis* average revenue curve (MAR)' which relates price to quantity on the understanding that the optimum advertising expenditure is associated with it. Unfortunately this construction is useless for comparative static purposes: the demand conditions for the individual firm are altered by any change in market demand *or* costs (via their influence on the number of firms), so that the MAR curve, like the dd′ curve, will shift in an unspecified way whenever we try to analyse the results of a change in data.

20. Demsetz goes on to consider what happens if the minimum points on the curves of average production costs and average advertising costs do not occur at the same output. He suggests that, if selling costs start to rise before production costs, the firm will endeavour to move the selling cost curve by, e.g. acquiring trade names from other firms, while, if production costs rise first, the firm will build smaller plants, or sub-contract, while retaining its own market, brand, and curve of selling costs. What this amounts to is the well-known result that there may be economies of 'selling scale' as well as of 'producing scale', that the optimum producing scale may not coincide with the optimum selling scale, and that a system of subsidiaries and subcontracting can be devised to overcome the difficulty. Unfortunately, even if we assume that the *maximum maximorum* has been achieved, we still cannot do comparative statics because the necessary demand relationships are still unspecified.

If we introduce quality variation without advertising, we still have the excess capacity result. Consider the curve of average production costs for any given quality, and the demand curve associated with it. Normal profit requires tangency, and, so long as the demand curve is downward sloping, this involves excess capacity. Since this is true for any quality, it is true for the profit-maximizing quality. The difference between the two cases is due, of course, simply to the fact that in the advertising case we make the cost function additive, but not in the quality variation case. It is obvious that whenever there are two cost curves to be added together, equilibrium is consistent with production taking place to the left or to the right of the minimum point of either of them considered separately. So long, therefore, as advertising is handled in this way, the model yields no general excess capacity theorem. One result, however, we still have: if advertising is absent or unimportant, the excess capacity theorem stands, even if quality variation is possible.

It is obviously extremely difficult to prove that a model is empty, and, indeed, this model is not completely empty: all I can claim is that it yields, so far as I can discover, no *qualitative comparative static* predictions, and that this is the consequence of a general defect, the incomplete specification of the demand relationships within the group. I add to this that not even Kaldor's relation appears to fill the gap. Thus the appropriate criticism of monopolistic competition is not that the assumptions about the group are difficult: it is that, making the best of the theory, and assuming groups of the required sort, the theory predicts practically nothing about them, and thus affords inadequate opportunity for testing. This point appears to have escaped both Chamberlin and his methodological critics.[21]

Of course, if the number of variables is restricted, as it may be in some cases of special application, the model may yield some

21. I hope that nothing I have said will be understood to detract from Chamberlin's historical contribution. I have not enlarged upon the importance of *The Theory of Monopolistic Competition* to economic thinking simply because I have been concerned with current controversy and the present state of knowledge. And if I have said little about Mrs Robinson's contribution, it is not for want of appreciation, but because I do not wish to get side-tracked into the 'braces-suspenders' argument.

useful results. If, for example, prices are controlled above the equilibrium level, whether by the government, or by some collusive arrangement, we expect supernormal profits and new entry. In the absence of quality variation and advertising, price control and new entry obviously creates additional excess capacity in each firm. If competition is limited to quality variation, excess capacity still follows (Dorfman and Steiner, 1954, pp. 835–6). But these results, useful as they may be in particular cases, depend upon price being taken as a parameter rather than a variable, and are therefore not counter-examples to the general conclusion that the model is incomplete: if price is taken as a parameter, some additional knowledge about demand is obviously provided.[22] It seems probable, too, that there are other cases of the same type: some results must be forthcoming if, for example, entry is impossible, or advertising is banned and quality subject to regulation. But the model was designed to handle the more general problem, and this it will not do. The limited amount it will do may be seen from the following summary of the results of this section.

(a) Non-perfect competition is not a sufficient condition for monopoly profits, because of entry, and price-fixing will increase the number of firms instead of the profits of existing firms unless entry is controlled.

(b) In a normal-profit equilibrium without advertising, there will be short-run excess capacity and unexploited economies of scale.

(c) With advertising, normal profits are consistent with any position on the cost curves; if prices are fixed, this is still true, but fixed prices, quality variation, and no advertising give excess capacity in full equilibrium.

(d) So long as there are unexploited economies of scale, firms have a motive for trying to integrate, rationalize or do whatever else may be necessary to make their exploitation profitable.

(e) *We are unable to discover from this model the effects of changes in the data on the equilibrium price or size of plant.*

22. The literature is full of examples of specific applications in which some results are obtained because, e.g. price is fixed. Scitovsky, for example, analyses a case in which price is fixed and advertising not even mentioned (1952, pp. 349–51). He argues that new entry raises demand elasticities (this is Kaldor's relation), but not to infinity, hence there will be excess capacity.

Obviously if we could specify a demand relationship that completed the model, we should then, when we added advertising and quality variation, still be faced with the inadequacies of qualitative economics discussed in the last section.

It only remains to consider how we might proceed further with monopolistic competition. The outstanding implication of the last two sections is that we require more facts, not for their own sake, but in order to put into the theory sufficient content for it to yield significant predictions. Perhaps the most serious criticism of Chamberlin's critics is that they have concentrated upon *a priori* discussion of his assumptions, instead of on discovering what facts were needed to give the theory content, and endeavouring to obtain them so that they might test it. Discussion of the empirical material required is beyond the scope of this paper, but the results of the first section are a little discouraging: we need facts about the demand functions of individual firms (with respect to quality and advertising as well as price) which are likely to be very difficult to get. Hence it may be that, with the observational techniques at our disposal, the theory is not likely, at present, to be very fruitful. As for the theory of the group, it appears that, to proceed further, we require some knowledge of demand relationships within groups. This suggests both theoretical and empirical investigation.

Mathematical Appendix to 1 [23]

This appendix is a somewhat overdue application of the methods of the early chapters of the *Foundations* (1947) to some cases that Samuelson did not have occasion to consider. We have a maximizing model in several variables; our problem is to discover if our information is sufficient to determine the direction of change in the variables when a parameter is changed. It is in general obvious that we cannot expect much: the solutions will necessarily involve the second-order partial derivatives, both direct and cross, and, if we have little information about the former, we have less about the latter. We shall, however, at least discover what is the minimum information necessary to determine the direction of change. The main results are:

23. I am greatly indebted to Kelvin Lancaster, George Merton, and John Wise for generous help with this appendix.

1. In the case of a specific tax, the direction of change of quantity is unambiguously determined without the need for any additional information.

2. This is not true in any other instance. To determine the direction of change of quality and advertising when tax changes, it is necessary to assume that second-order cross-partial derivatives can be neglected; and this assumption is necessary in the case of an *ad valorem* tax to determine the sign of the quantity change.

3. In no case is the direction of change of price determined, even when cross-effects are ignored. This is because it is determined as a linear combination of the changes in quantity, advertising, and quality, which, in general, have opposite effects upon price.

In what follows, advertising and quality variation are first treated together and then separately. It will be noticed that the only difference between the two follows from the form of the cost functions assumed: in the case of advertising, the costs of production and of advertising are assumed to be independent. It would be possible to treat quality variation in this way, in which case there would be no analytical difference between it and advertising. The treatment offered here is intended to bring out any differences which may follow from the different forms of functions; but the association of one exclusively with advertising and the other exclusively with quality variation is largely a matter of terminological convenience.

The general case: advertising and quality variation
We assume a single-product profit-maximizing firm with demand and cost functions

$$p = \phi(x,q,v), \tag{1}$$

$$C = \Psi(x,q) + sv,$$

where
$p =$ product price,
$C =$ total cost,
$x =$ quantity of output,
$q =$ index of quality,
$v =$ quantity of advertising,
$s =$ price of a unit of advertising (for convenience this may be assumed constant without loss of generality).

Maximizing $R - C = x\phi(x,q,v) - \Psi(x,q) - sv$ **2**

yields $\phi + x\phi_x - \Psi_x = 0,$ **3a**

$\quad\quad\quad x\phi_q - \Psi_q = 0,$ **3b**

$\quad\quad\quad x\phi_v - s = 0.$ **3c**

It is now convenient to write

$a = 2\phi_x + x\phi_{xx} - \Psi_{xx},$

$b = x\phi_{qq} - \Psi_{qq},$

$c = x\phi_{vv},$

$f = x\phi_{qv},$

$g = \phi_v + x\phi_{xv},$

$h = \phi_q + x\phi_{xq} - \Psi_{xq}.$

In this notation

$$d^2(R - C) = a\,dx^2 + b\,dq^2 + c\,dv^2 + \quad\quad\quad \textbf{4}$$
$$+ 2f\,dq\,dv + 2g\,dx\,dv + 2h\,dx\,dq.$$

For a maximum, **4** must be negative definite, that is

$$a < 0, \quad \begin{vmatrix} a & h \\ h & b \end{vmatrix} > 0, \quad \begin{vmatrix} a & h & g \\ h & b & f \\ g & f & c \end{vmatrix} < 0 \quad\quad \textbf{5}$$

and, similarly, the principal minors of corresponding order have the same sign. We shall denote the third-order coefficient matrix of **5** by A.

We now wish to differentiate **3** with respect to the parameters. From inspection, it is obvious that nothing can be said about the effects of an increase in demand unless the changes in ϕ_x, ϕ_q, and ϕ_v are specified. If we wish to consider the effects of a change in costs of production, we must first introduce the production function, and the factor prices as parameters, and solve for the least cost combination of factors. We may avoid this labour, without loss, by considering the simplest form of an increase in costs, an increase in a specific indirect tax. We shall also be able to compare the results of an increase in s with those of an increase in a tax. We shall finally consider the effects of an increase in an *ad valorem* tax.

Introducing a specific tax at rate t, we merely add the term

$-tx$ to **2**, and $-t$ to **3a**. Differentiating **3**, thus modified, with respect to t and the variables x, q and v, we obtain

$$\left. \begin{array}{l} a\,dx + h\,dq + g\,dv = dt, \\ h\,dx + b\,dq + f\,dv = 0, \\ g\,dx + f\,dq + c\,dv = 0, \end{array} \right\} \qquad \qquad 6$$

the matrix of coefficients of the l.h.s. of which is A.

6 is solved by

$$\frac{dx}{dt} = \frac{bc - f^2}{|A|},$$

$$\frac{dq}{dt} = \frac{gf - hc}{|A|},$$

$$\frac{dv}{dt} = \frac{hf - gb}{|A|}, \qquad \qquad 7$$

and $\quad \dfrac{dp}{dt} = \dfrac{\phi_x(bc - f^2) + \phi_q(gf - hc) + \phi_v(hf - gb)}{|A|}$

(since $dp = \phi_x'\,dx + \phi_q\,dq + \phi_v\,dv$).

The solutions **7** constitute the set of consequences predicted by this model to follow from an increase in the tax. The question is whether qualitative knowledge of slopes and curvatures is sufficient to determine the signs of **7**, that is, to yield qualitative predictions.

We immediately obtain

$$\frac{dx}{dt} < 0 \quad \text{since } bc > f^2 \text{ (by 5)}.$$

This result is perfectly general.[24] *It is, however, the only unambiguous result at this level of generality: dq/dt and dv/dt are un*-signed unless the signs of second-order cross-partial derivatives are known; but not even this is sufficient to sign dp/dt, which is a linear combination of the other elements of the solution vector.

If we now arbitrarily assume that all second-order cross-partial derivatives are zero,[25] we may add to **5**

24. For a far more general proof that does not require the conventional assumptions of convexity and differentiability, see a forthcoming paper by Wise (1962).

25. Hahn, who does not consider quality variation, assumes ϕ_{xa} to be negligible (1959a, p. 296, n. 1; but compare 1959b). What he does not do is point out which of his subsequent results depend on this assumption. If the analysis offered here is correct, all save $dx/dt < 0$ must do.

$$f = 0, \qquad g = \phi_v > 0, \qquad h = \phi_q > 0,$$

which is sufficient to make dq/dt and dv/dt negative. It is not, however, sufficient to sign dp/dt, which is now reduced to

$$\frac{\phi_x bc - h^2 c - g^2 b}{|A|},$$

which cannot be signed without knowledge of relative magnitudes. The intuitive explanation is obvious: the reduction in quantity pushes price up, while the reduction in quality and advertising push it down; which is stronger cannot be determined at this level of generality. Qualitative economics fails to predict that a price will be increased by an increase in an indirect tax.

It might now appear unnecessary to continue with the separate investigations of advertising and quality variation. Consider, however, the reasons for the failure. In the first place, unless we are at least prepared to put the cross-partial derivatives equal to zero, we do not even know the signs of all the non-zero coefficients of the system of simultaneous linear equations obtained when the equilibrium system is differentiated with respect to a parameter; but even knowledge of all these signs is not a sufficient condition for determining the signs of the solution vector. The reason for this is intuitively obvious: expansion of the determinants involves subtraction, as well as multiplication and addition, so that signs are bound to depend on relative magnitudes. In the second place, however, we generally have some zero coefficients, and, if we have enough of them in the right places, some parts of the solution may be signed, as was dx/dt above. Thus, given the signs of non-zero coefficients, the extent to which the signs of the solution are unambiguously determined depends on the number and pattern of zero coefficients in the matrix.[26] But the pattern of zero coefficients will depend on the parameter chosen for variation, because the parameters do not, in general, appear symmetrically in all equations (thus compare 16 below with 6). Hence we cannot say that the qualitative calculus can never obtain results from maximizing models in, say, three or more variables: we apparently have to explore each case.

26. For a thorough investigation of these matters, see a forthcoming paper by Lancaster (1962).

Advertising only

In the absence of quality variation, the second equation of 3 disappears. **5** is replaced by[27]

$$a < 0, \qquad \begin{vmatrix} a & g \\ g & c \end{vmatrix} > 0$$

(we write B for $ac - g^2$), and, differentiating with respect to t, we have

$$\begin{aligned} a \, dx + g \, dv &= dt, \\ g \, dx + c \, dv &= 0, \end{aligned} \tag{8}$$

$$\left. \begin{aligned} \text{solved by} \quad \frac{dx}{dt} &= \frac{c}{B}, \\[2mm] \frac{dv}{dt} &= \frac{-g}{B}, \\[2mm] \text{which give} \quad \frac{dp}{dt} &= \frac{c\phi_x - g\phi_v}{B}. \end{aligned} \right\} \tag{9}$$

Once again, dx/dt is immediately negative, dv/dt is unsigned unless the cross-partial, ϕ_{xv}, is ignored, and dp/dt depends upon relative magnitudes.

We may now reconsider the problem of the effect of a tax change on the ratio of advertising expenditure to quantity produced. Differentiating,

$$\frac{d(v/x)}{dt} = \frac{x \, dv/dt - v \, dx/dt}{x^2}. \tag{10}$$

Plainly even if dv/dt and dx/dt are signed, **10** is not since dv/dt and dx/dt will have the same sign: **10** depends on the relative magnitudes of these expressions and of x and v. The analogy with the effect on the employment of two substitutable factors of production of a change in the price of one of them is obvious and complete. Thus suppose that we differentiate **3a** and **3c** with respect to s (the price of the advertising medium) instead of t.

27. The economic interpretation of these conditions is simple. $a < 0$ is the familiar condition that marginal revenue be falling faster than marginal cost. $c < 0$ is the obviously necessary condition that marginal revenue with respect to advertising is decreasing (cf. Hahn, 1959a p. 296, (i)).

We obtain

$$
\left.\begin{aligned}
\frac{dv}{ds} &= \frac{a}{B}, \\[2mm]
\frac{dx}{ds} &= \frac{-g}{B} \\[2mm]
\text{and} \quad \frac{dp}{dt} &= \frac{a\phi_v - g\phi_x}{B}.
\end{aligned}\right\}
\qquad \textbf{11}
$$

Exactly as before, the factor the price of which has risen falls in quantity ($dv/ds < 0$), the substitute falls if cross-effects are ignored, the change in price cannot be predicted, and neither, obviously, can the change in advertising per unit.

Quality variation only

The third equation of **3** disappears, **5** is reduced to

$$
a < 0, \qquad \begin{vmatrix} a & h \\ h & b \end{vmatrix} > 0
$$

(we write D for $ab - h^2$), and, differentiating with respect to t and solving, we obtain

$$
\left.\begin{aligned}
\frac{dx}{dt} &= \frac{b}{D}, \\[2mm]
\frac{dq}{dt} &= \frac{-h}{D}, \\[2mm]
\frac{dp}{dt} &= \frac{b\phi_x - h\phi_q}{D},
\end{aligned}\right\}
\qquad \textbf{12}
$$

with signs as before. The only difference between **9** or **11** and **12** arises from the fact that advertising is treated as a linear addition to cost, so that the only cross-partial in g is ϕ_{xv}, whereas the sign dq/dt depends upon h, which includes the cross-partial Ψ_{xq} as well as ϕ_{xq}.

The intuitive interpretation of **12** is clear. A quality reduction can be regarded as a concealed price increase, and therefore as an alternative method of absorbing the tax: quality falls, as does advertising (neglecting cross-effects), but whether it falls enough to offset the forces making for a price increase cannot be determined without quantitative information. In general, however, we might expect that, when the tax is increased, the firm lowers quality, raises price, or both, and that the less it does one the more it does the other. We might also expect that, the more sensitive is demand to quality changes, the less quality will change, because it does not have the effect of a concealed price change. These expectations may be checked by differentiating **12** with respect to ϕ_q (neglecting cross-effects, $\phi_q = h$). This yields

$$\left. \begin{aligned} \frac{\partial(dx/dt)}{\partial h} &= \frac{2hb}{D^2} < 0, \\[2mm] \frac{\partial(dq/dt)}{\partial h} &= \frac{-(ab+h^2)}{D^2} < 0, \\[2mm] \frac{\partial(dp/dt)}{\partial h} &= \frac{2hb(\phi_x-a)}{D^2}. \end{aligned} \right\} \qquad 13$$

13 does not fully confirm our expectations. The larger h, the larger the *absolute* change in x *and* q, but the effect on price is still undetermined.

The effect of changing an *ad valorem* tax

We cannot now even obtain the direction of change in x without knowledge of the cross-effects. To see this, replace **2** by

$$R-C = x\,\phi(x,q,v)(1-r) - \Psi(x,q) - sv, \qquad 14$$

where r is the rate of tax. Now instead of **3** we have

$$\left. \begin{aligned} \phi(1-r)+x\phi_x(1-r)-\Psi_x &= 0, \\ x\phi_q(1-r)-\Psi_q &= 0, \\ x\phi_v(1-r)-s &= 0, \end{aligned} \right\} \qquad 15$$

and, in place of **6**,

$$\left. \begin{aligned} a'\,dx + h'\,dq + g'\,dv &= (\phi+x\phi_x)\,dr, \\ h'\,dx + b'\,dq + f'\,dv &= x\phi_q\,dr, \\ g'\,dx + f'\,dq + c'\,dv &= x\phi_v\,dr, \end{aligned} \right\} \qquad 16$$

where the primes indicate that every demand term in each coefficient is multiplied by $1-r$. Now in **16** two non-zero terms replace the two zeros on the r.h.s. of **6** which were reponsible for the numerator-determinant of dx/dt collapsing to a principal minor. Hence every term appears in the expansion of the determinants, so that the signs of every element in the solution vector depend upon relative magnitudes. Putting all cross-effects equal to zero is necessary and sufficient to give $dx/dr < 0$ ($f' = 0$, g' and $h' > 0$), as well as dq/dr and $dv/dr < 0$. Of course, dp/dr is undetermined.

The reader may easily check for himself that, in the cases of advertising or quality variation alone, it is also necessary to neglect cross-effects to obtain the sign of dx/dr.

References

ALLEN, R. G. D. (1938), *Mathematical Analysis for Economists*, Macmillan.

BREMS, H. (1951), *Product Equilibrium under Monopolistic Competition*, Harvard University Press.

CHAMBERLIN, E. H. (1933), *The Theory of Monopolistic Competition*, Oxford University Press.

CHAMBERLIN, E. H. (1937), 'Monopolistic or imperfect competition?', *Q.J. Econ.*, vol. 51, pp. 557–80.

CHAMBERLIN, E. H. (1938), 'Reply', *Q. J. Econ.*, vol. 52.

CHAMBERLIN, E. H. (1957), *Towards a More General Theory of Value*, Oxford University Press.

DEMSETZ, H. (1959), 'The nature of equilibrium in monopolistic competition', *J. polit. Econ.*, vol. 67, no. 1, pp. 21–30.

DORFMAN, R., and STEINER, P. O. (1954), 'Optional advertising and optional quality', *Amer. econ. Rev.*, vol. 44, no. 5, pp. 826–36.

HAHN, F. H. (1959a), 'The theory of selling costs', *Econ. J.*, vol. 69, no. 274, pp. 293–312.

HAHN, F. H. (1959b), 'The theory of selling costs: a correction', *Econ. J.*, vol. 69, p. 826.

HARROD, R. F. (1952), *Economic Essays*, Macmillan.

HICKS, J. R. (1946), *Value and Capital*, Oxford University Press.

KALDOR, N. (1935), 'Market imperfection and excess capacity', *Economica*, vol. 2, pp. 35–50.

KALDOR, N. (1938), 'Professor Chamberlin on monopolistic and imperfect competition', *Q.J. Econ.*, vol. 52, pp. 513–29.

KALDOR, N. (1960), *Essays on Value and Distribution*, Duckworth.

LANCASTER, K. (1962), 'The scope of qualitative economics', *Rev. econ. Stud.*, vol. 29.

MERING, O. VON (1942), *The Shifting and Incidence of Taxation*, Blakiston.

ROBBINS, L. C. (1935), *The Nature and Significance of Economic Science*, Macmillan.

SAMUELSON, P. A. (1947), *Foundations of Economic Analysis*, Harvard University Press.

SCITOVSKY, T. (1952), *Welfare and Competition*, Allen & Unwin. pp. ix.

WISE, J. (1962), 'The effect of specific excise taxes on the output of the individual multi-product firm', *Rev. econ. Stud.*, vol. 29, no. 9.

7 George J. Stigler

The Kinky Oligopoly Demand-Curve and Rigid Prices

Excerpt from G. J. Stigler, 'The kinky oligopoly demand curve and rigid prices', *Journal of Political Economy*, vol. 55, 1947, pp. 432–47.

Just before the Second World War, the theory was advanced that there exists a kink in the demand curve for the product of an oligopolist and that this kink goes far to explain observed price rigidities in oligopolistic industries. The theory has rapidly gained wide acceptance: many economists give it some place in their theoretical system, and some economists make it *the* theory of oligopoly price.

The theory is an ingenious rationalization of the price rigidities that were reported in many statistical studies of prices during the thirties, and no doubt this explains its popularity. But no one, so far as I know, has examined in detail either the pure theory of the kinky demand curve or the degree of correspondence between the price patterns implied by the theory and the observed price patterns in oligopolistic industries. These two tasks will be undertaken in the two parts of this paper.

The formal theory
The received theory

The theory of the kinky demand curve was advanced independently and almost simultaneously by Hall and Hitch (1939) in England and Sweezy (1939) in America. The latter's version will be summarized first.

The Sweezy version. The market situation contemplated by Sweezy is one in which rivals will quickly match price reductions but only hesitantly and incompletely (if at all) follow price increases. This pattern of expected behavior produces a kink at the existing price ($= p_0$ in Figure 1) in the demand curve for the

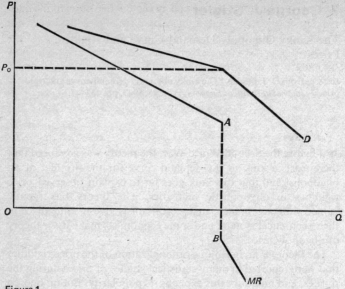

Figure 1

product of an oligopolist,[1] and the corresponding marginal revenue
curve will possess a discontinuity the length of which is proportional to the difference between the slopes of the upper and lower
segments of the demand curve at the kink.[2] Sweezy assumes that

1. The demand curve for the product of an oligopolist can be defined only
if the reactions of rivals to price changes are known. The upper branch of
the demand curve in Figure 1 represents the quantities that consumers will
buy from one oligopolist at various prices if rival producers set a price of
p_0; the lower branch represents the quantities that consumers will buy if
the rivals charge identical prices. This demand curve is objective in the sense
that it is consistent with the facts of the market if rivals behave in the specified
manner. Sweezy appears to view it as subjective because it is based upon
beliefs concerning rivals' price reactions which may have to be revised
(although no occasions for revision of beliefs are treated in his article).

2. With reference to Figure 1, if $f(x)$ is the demand curve, x_0 the output at
the kink, and subscripts 1 and 2 refer to the upper and lower segments of
the demand curve respectively,

$$A - B = x_0[f'(x_0 - O) - f'(x_0 + O)]$$
$$= p_0 \left(\frac{1}{\eta_1} - \frac{1}{\eta_2} \right).$$

126 Pricing and Market Structure

'the marginal cost-curve passes between the two parts of the marginal revenue curve,' so that fluctuations in marginal cost are not likely to affect output and price.

He considers also two other possibilities. An oligopolist may believe that secret price cuts will remain secret, in which case the demand curve becomes elastic throughout and the kink disappears. Or the oligopolist may be a price leader, so that price increases will be followed and the kink again disappears.[3]

Sweezy assumes that shifts in demand will not affect the price at which the kink occurs and argues that the results of increases and decreases of demand are asymmetrical:

1. An increase of demand will make the demand curve less elastic in its upper branch, since rivals are operating closer to capacity (Sweezy, p. 407),[4] and more elastic in the lower branch because rivals 'are less worried about losses in [of?] business'. If marginal costs are also shifting upward as demand increases, 'an increase in demand is more likely to lead to a price increase than to a price cut'.

2. A decrease in demand will have the converse effects – increased elasticity of the upper branch and decreased elasticity of the lower branch – so the discontinuity of marginal revenue will be increased and the oligopolists will be 'more anxious than ever' to hold to the existing price.

Except where price leaders exist or secret price concessions are possible, therefore, oligopoly price may rise in good times and will not be reduced in bad times.[5]

The Oxford version. Hall and Hitch conclude, after reporting interviews with some thirty-eight entrepreneurs on price policy

3. These possibilities, which are obviously mutually exclusive, are illustrated in the same diagram (Sweezy, 1939, p. 407, Figure 2). If the upper branch (for the price leader) and the lower branch (for the secret price cutter) were nevertheless joined, the resulting marginal revenue curve would again be discontinuous, but then maximum profits would never be secured at the price at which the kink arises.

4. Presumably the rivals' higher rates of production lead them to follow the price increase (although this reaction causes trouble; see below), or, if they maintain prices, the buyers are rationed.

5. The implications of Sweezy's theory for price rigidity were emphasized by Bronfenbrenner (1940).

that businessmen seek prices that cover average cost, regardless of marginal revenue and marginal cost (which they seldom know).[6] This 'full-cost' principle is apparently the result of tacit or open collusion, consideration of long-run demand and costs, moral conviction of fairness, and uncertainty of effects of price increases and decreases.[7] The particular results of the interviews need not be discussed here.[8]

The entrepreneur therefore sets a price that covers average cost (including 'profits') at the expected or some conventional output (see Figure 2). Increases or decreases of demand will usually shift the kink to the right or left and leave price unchanged, but there are two exceptions to this rule.

1. If the demand decreases greatly and remains small for some time, the price is likely to be cut in the hope of maintaining output. The chief explanation for this price cut is that one rival becomes panicky and his irrational behavior forces the others to cut prices.

2. If the average cost-curves of all firms shift by similar amounts, due perhaps to changes in factor prices or technology, this is 'likely to lead to a revaluation of the "full-cost" price' (p. 25). However, '. . . there will be no tendency for [prices] to fall or rise more than the wage and raw material costs' (p. 32).

The full-cost principle would suggest also that prices will vary

6. The treatment of entrepreneurial knowledge is contradictory. On the one hand, Hall and Hitch state that 'most of our informants werê vague about anything so precise as elasticity. . . . In addition, many, perhaps most, apparently made no effort, even implicitly, to estimate elasticities of demand . . . and of those who do, the majority considered the information of little or no relevance to the pricing process save perhaps in very exceptional conditions' (Hall and Hitch, 1939, p. 18). But, on the other hand, a majority of the entrepreneurs believed that price cuts would be matched and price increases would not be matched by rivals (p. 21, Tables 3 and 4) so they did act rationally on marginal principles (within a certain framework).

7. Several of these factors contradict the existence of a kink in the demand curve.

8. The questioning was not persistent and resourceful, nor were ambiguous answers clarified; for example, three entrepreneurs did not charge more than average cost because 'buyers technically informed about costs' (p. 21). Does this mean that buyers would otherwise enter into production of the article? Why was the same answer not given for unwillingness to sell below cost?

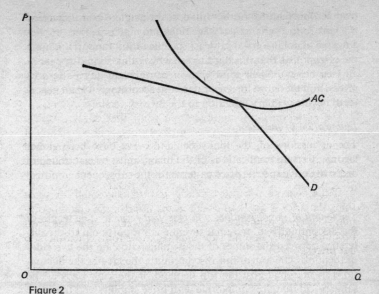

Figure 2

inversely with output, i.e. that high prices are necessary to cover the high average costs of small outputs. This price pattern is not followed, apparently, because the oligopolists (1) place a value on price stability, (2) are influenced by the kink and (3) wish to 'keep plant running as full as possible, giving rise to a general feeling in favor of price concessions' (p. 28).

Comparison of the versions. The Sweezy version is a consistent application of the kinky demand curve to price determination, without conflicting principles to modify its workings. The Oxford version embraces also the 'full-cost' principle (and apparently also the 'large-output' principle), although the possibilities of conflict between the two are manifold. Hall and Hitch resolve some of the conflicts by abandoning the kink (e.g. when prices follow production costs) and some by abandoning the 'full-cost' principle (e.g. when entrepreneurs do not raise prices in depression). They take no account of the difficulties raised by differences among the average costs of various oligopolists or of many other troublesome features of the 'full-cost' principle. Their thesis that the kink follows changes in wage rates and material prices implies a degree of collusion – or at least such beautiful rapport – among the oligopolists that it is hard to see why a kink should appear at all (see below). Their fluid version can explain any pattern of prices, and therefore forecast none, and accordingly I shall henceforth devote primary attention to the Sweezy version.

Elaboration of the theory

The discussions of the kinky demand curve have been rather laconic. Certain implications of the theory must be elaborated in order to derive specific price patterns for the subsequent empirical tests.

The length of the discontinuity in marginal revenue. The length of the discontinuity in marginal revenue is proportional to the difference between the slopes of the demand curve on the two sides of the kink. The longer this discontinuity, the greater the fluctuations in marginal cost (and in demand, if the kink stays at the same price) that are compatible with price stability and therefore the greater the probability of rigid prices in any interval of time. Some of the factors that affect the length of this discontinuity are:

1. The number of rivals (of a given degree of closeness, measured by the cross-elasticity of demand). We should expect that a price increase is more likely to be followed if there are few rivals than if there are many, because the rivals will realize that the temporary gains from holding down their prices will soon be erased. If this is so, the discontinuity will be short (in time) or non-existent when there are few rivals. The larger the number of rivals, the less likely are they to follow one oligopolist's price increases; on the other hand, the less likely are they also to match his price reductions, at least immediately. It seems probable, therefore, that the discontinuity is longest with an intermediate number of rivals, say, five to ten.

2. The relative size of rivals (of a given degree of closeness). When one firm (or an inner clique) is dominant in size, it will presumably be the price leader. When this firm increases its price, rivals are likely to follow (for individually they can sell as much as they

wish at the ruling price); when the firm cuts prices the rivals must follow. Hence the dominant firm will have no kink in its demand curve. The smaller firms cannot raise their prices above the leader's unless he is rationing buyers but can shade prices without being followed immediately or perhaps at all.[9] Again there will be no kink.

3. The differences among the rivals' products. The discontinuity will be longer, the more homogeneous the products, because customers will shift more rapidly to the low-price firm.

4. The extent of collusion. Should explicit collusion replace the stand-offish attitude visualized by the theory, the kink will vanish; there is no kink in a monopolist's demand curve.

Other factors affecting the length of the discontinuity in marginal revenue could be mentioned, for example, the number of buyers.[10] But these factors do not lend themselves to the type of

9. These conclusions can also be reached by a more mechanical application of kink theory. A rise of the dominant firm's price will so increase the demand of each small firm that marginal cost will intersect marginal revenue at an output less than that at which the kink occurs, so the small firm will also increase price. A reduction in price by a small firm will decrease the demand for the output of the dominant firm by so small an amount that probably no price changes will be induced.

10. Fewness of buyers is difficult to fit into the kink theory. If few buyers face a competitive supply, each will presumably believe that, if he raises his buying price, rivals will follow and the quantity supplied to him will not increase much; and, if he lowers his buying price, rivals will not follow and the quantity supplied to him will decrease greatly. Hence there will be a kink in the supply curve to the firm (which is illustrated by Bronfenbrenner, 1940). Combining this with oligopoly of sellers, presumably both supply and demand curves have a kink at the same price, which will be especially rigid.

But the whole argument is very elusive. If one buyer offered a higher price to a seller who assumed that his rivals would not follow a price increase, the seller would of course offer his entire output to the buyer, whose supply curve might therefore be extremely elastic for higher prices – the opposite of the above argument. And, conversely, if one seller offered a lower price to one buyer, who assumed that his rivals would be unwilling to reduce their buying prices, the buyer would snatch at the bargain so the seller's demand curve would be elastic for lower prices – again the opposite of the above argument. The difficulty is that the assumptions are inconsistent: if sellers believe that price reductions will be matched but price increases will not be matched and buyers believe the opposite, someone is likely to be wrong.

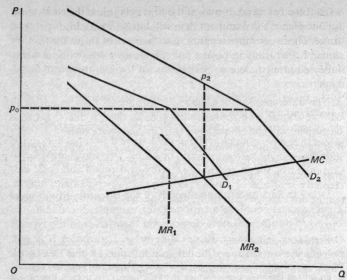

Figure 3

empirical tests that will be employed in the second part and will not be discussed.

The workings of the kink. In order to study the workings of the kinky demand curve, let us consider two producers (of equal size) of similar, but not identical, commodities. The initial demand and marginal revenue curves of duopolist A are given in Figure 3; they are denoted by the subscript 1. Assume now that the aggregate demand for the two commodities increases so that A's demand curve shifts to D_2, but marginal costs do not change. Then A will increase his price to p_2. What will duopolist B do?

If B's costs and demand are similar to A's, the former will simultaneously raise his price to p_2. But then D_2 must be redrawn above p_0 because this branch was drawn on the assumption that the rival's price was p_0. The situation becomes classical duopoly – with the usual wide range of possible patterns of behavior. It would be foolish to put a new kink in D_2 (as redrawn) at the level p_2. Experience has shown that the rival will follow a price increase, and businessmen will learn from this experience that there is no kink.

On the other hand, B may still find it profitable to stay at price p_0. But then his demand curve must shift to the right, for it was drawn on the assumption that A set a price of p_0 or less. If this demand shift leads B to set a new price, then A's demand curve must be redrawn. Again the existence of the kink is contradicted by experience.

The theory of the kinky demand curve explains why prices that have been stable should continue to be stable despite certain changes in demand or costs. But the theory does not explain why prices that have once changed should settle down, again acquire stability, and gradually produce a new kink. One possible explanation might be that a period of stability of demand and costs has created a tradition of stable prices, so that, when demand or cost conditions change materially, the kink has emerged to preserve price stability.

Other kinks and discontinuities. For present purposes it is not necessary to discuss additional implications of the theory of kinky demand-curves, but two are of sufficient interest to deserve brief mention.

The pattern of oligopolistic behavior underlying the kinky demand curve will also produce a discontinuous marginal cost curve. If one firm reduces its wage rate, for example, other firms will not follow, but these other firms will match wage increases. At the output corresponding to this input kink, there will be a discontinuity in marginal cost. A good part of the appeal of the kinky demand curve theory is that it is easy to draw demand and cost curves that lead to price stability. This appeal is definitely weakened if the marginal cost curve is also discontinuous, as the reader can readily verify.

The same general line of reasoning leads to kinks in the curves of other variables of policy – advertising, quality changes, etc. Indeed, the logic of the theory requires only that there be one variable – output – against which the discontinuities in the other variables may be displayed.

Alternative theories of price stability

Explanations of price stability are not common or prominent in the neoclassical price theory of Marshall's era. (The second part of this paper contains some evidence that bears on the question whether this is a cause for commendation or condemnation.) Of course it would be a grotesque caricature to describe this theory as requiring a change of price in response to every quiver of the demand or the cost curve. Three factors making for price stability were generally incorporated (without emphasis) into neoclassical theory.

Long-run considerations. In the long run the demand curve is usually more elastic because buyers can make changes in technology, commitments and habits that permit use of substitutes and because new rivals will be attracted at certain prices. Therefore an exorbitant current price may lose more (discounted) revenue in the future than it adds in the present. This type of consideration argues against raising prices greatly in short-run periods of inelastic demand but does not imply price rigidity.[11]

Administrative weaknesses in collusion. When a group of producers arrives at a mutually agreeable or tolerable price by collusion, this price will have a strong tendency to persist. When some of the firms will be injured by a price change (which must often occur when their costs, market areas and product structures differ), they will naturally oppose change. When all will gain from a price change, they will usually wish different amounts of change. Opening the question of prices may therefore lead to a pitched battle, and one can seldom be sure that things will stay in hand. Frequent resort to this area of political-economic determination must be avoided, so changes are postponed as long as possible. If they are postponed long enough, the need for them will pass.

Cost of price changes. The nature of the product and market may be such that small or frequent price changes cost more than they yield. There are costs of informing buyers of price changes: new lists, advertising, etc. If long-term contracts contain provisions that the buyer will receive any price reductions during the life of the contract, the short-run marginal revenue from a price reduc-

11. Marshall also had the doctrine that prices will not fall to prime costs in depression because of a fear of 'spoiling the market' (1920, pp. 374–6). He apparently assumed, in addition to oligopoly, that the long-run demand curve was inelastic for price reductions.

tion may be small or negative. Even when there are no contracts, price reductions may incur the ill will of early buyers of a 'style' good.

A comparison of the implications of the theories of price stability

There is no reason why the kinky demand curve cannot be joined with the other explanations of price stability. But there is also no purpose in adding it to the neoclassical theory unless it explains price behavior in areas where the other explanation is silent or contradicts the implications of the neoclassical theory in areas where both apply. For the empirical tests in the second part, the following differences between the implications of the kinky demand curve and the neoclassical theory will be used:

1. The kinky demand-curve theory is silent on monopolies, for the essential feature of retaliation by rivals is absent. Should monopoly prices be rigid, the forces that explain this rigidity (say cost of price changes) may suffice to explain an equal amount of price rigidity under oligopoly. Unless the factors making for monopoly price rigidity do not operate under oligopoly, we can dispense with the kink unless greater rigidity is found in the oligopolistic industries.

2. The discontinuity in marginal revenue will disappear, and with it the reason for price rigidity, if formerly independent firms enter into collusion. The neoclassical theory emphasizes the administrative weaknesses in collusion, on the other hand, and this argues for greater price rigidity.

3. Prices will be relatively flexible with very few and with many firms in the industry, and relatively rigid with a moderate number of firms (say, five to ten), according to the kink theory. The neoclassical theories of oligopoly are neither outspoken nor unanimous on this question, but there is a general suggestion that price flexibility increases continuously with the number of firms.

4. When there is a dominant firm or set of firms (acting together) in the role of price leader, prices should be more flexible than if there is no price leader, on the kink theory. The neoclassical theory is silent on this point.

5. Given the number and size configuration of firms, prices should

be more flexible the more heterogeneous the products, under the kinky demand-curve theory. The neoclassical theory has no such implication.

Empirical tests of the theory

One may submit to empirical tests either the assumption of entrepreneurial behavior underlying the theory of the kinky demand curve or the implications of the kink for price behavior. The former alternative requires an analysis of the sequence of price changes made by oligopolists in an industry; the latter alternative can be developed by a comparison of observed price rigidity with that prophesied by the theory.

The validity of the assumption

If price increases of one firm are not followed by rivals, but price reductions are followed, the oligopolists have a basis in experience for believing that there is a kink in their demand curves. If price reductions are not followed by rivals, or price increases are as closely followed, no such objective basis for a kink exists.

The cigarette industry (with three large firms) offers a good example of the type of experience that would create a belief in the existence of a kink. On 28 September 1918, the American Tobacco Company raised the list price of Lucky Strikes from $6 to $7·50 per thousand, but the rivals continued to charge the lower price. The sales of Lucky Strikes fell 31 per cent from September to November, when the price was reduced to $6, and continued to decline for several months.[12] The later price history in this industry, however, is not such as to create a belief in the existence of a kink:

20 April 1928: Reynolds (Camels) announced a reduction from $6·40 to $6 per thousand, effective 21 April. American Tobacco followed on 21 April and Liggett and Myers on 23 April.
4 October 1929: Reynolds announced an increase to $6·40, effective 5 October, and both rivals followed on that day.
23 June 1931: Reynolds announced an increase to $6·85, effective 24 June, and both rivals followed that day.

12. This episode is reported in detail in the forthcoming study of the American tobacco industry by William H. Nicholls.

1 January 1933: American Tobacco reduced its price to $6, effective 3 January, and both rivals followed that day.
11 February 1933: American Tobacco reduced its price to $5·50, and both rivals followed the same day.
9 January 1934: Reynolds increased its price to $6·10, and both rivals followed the same day.
(Federal Trade Commission, 1937, p. 448).[13]
These price changes, incidentally, were relatively larger than they appear: the manufacturer's net was smaller by a three-dollar tax and trade discounts.

The more complicated pattern of price changes for automobiles is illustrated for two leading firms in Figure 4. The prices of the two firms changed at different dates and by different amounts, and price increases were more nearly simultaneous than price reductions. Price experience in this field should not lead a firm to believe that price reductions will be matched immediately or

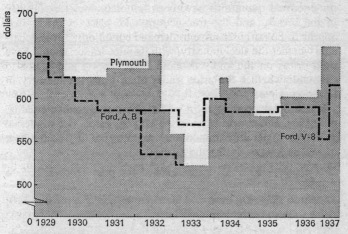

Figure 4   Factory prices of Plymouth and Ford four-door sedans June 1929 to May 1937

Source: Federal Trade Commission (1940, pp. 894–6).

13. The history of prices after 1934 follows essentially the same pattern, although Nicholls reports an unmatched and unsuccessful price increase by Liggett and Myers on 30 July 1946 – followed by a general increase on 14 October 1946, with American Tobacco the price leader.

wholly nor that in a period of business recovery rivals will fail to increase prices.

Six anthracite companies produced 62·5 per cent of the aggregate output in 1930, and eight companies usually produce 70 to 80 per cent of aggregate output (Fraser and Doriot, 1932, pp. 400, 401). The prices of seven companies, for each size of coal, are listed (in very large type) every week in the *Coal and Coal Trade Journal*. These prices are identical and they almost invariably change on the same day.[14] There is no evidence of a kink: prices change often in a marked, but by no means rigid, seasonal pattern.

Some direct evidence argues against the existence of a kink in the demand curve for steel produced by United States Steel: Bethlehem, for example, has faithfully followed the price increases (Temporary National Economic Committee, 1940, p. 10587). But the important evidence is indirect: there is no evidence of price rigidity within this industry. The official price lists and trade-journal quotations have been honored almost exclusively in the breach, and the transactions take place at prices that appear to be fairly sensitive to demand conditions.[15] It is debatable whether the steel industry, with its price leader, should have rigid prices on the kinky demand curve theory, and it is also debatable whether the price leader often leads the industry in lowering prices.

Three firms produce most of the dynamite used in mining, quarrying, and construction in the United States. The wholesale prices for 40 per cent ammonium dynamite, per fifty-pound bag, moved as follows during the thirties:

27 February 1933: All firms reduced the price from $12·25 to $10·50.

12 March 1934: Du Pont and Hercules reduced the price to $10; Atlas followed seventeen days later.

14. Occasionally there is a temporary discrepancy. For example, six companies announced prices of $4·70 per ton for pea-size coal in the 4 July 1929, issue; one company retained the previous price of $4·60. A week later the exception disappeared.

15. See especially the study made by the Bureau of Labor Statistics (1946). United States Steel officials testified before the TNEC that the Birmingham quotation had not been realized between 1932 and 1939 and that the general reduction in 1938 was merely a formal recognition of ruling prices (1940, pp. 10546, 10505; see also pp. 14141, 14172).

14 January 1935: All firms increased the price to $10·50.
7 May 1936: Du Pont and Hercules reduced the price to $9·50;
Atlas followed the next day.
8 May 1937: Du Pont and Atlas increased the price to $10·50;
Hercules followed three days later.[16]
Again there is no empirical basis for believing the kink exists.

Socony-Vacuum and Atlantic Refining are two important sellers of gasoline in the Boston area. Aside from three periods in 1934 and 1935 when Socony-Vacuum's price was less than Atlantic's, the prices of the two firms changed as shown in the accompanying list in the period 1929–37 (National Petroleum News, 1938).

Simultaneous price changes	40
Increases	22
Opposite	1
Decreases	17

Delay in following price increases	12
Days	
1	9
2	1
3	1
4	1

Delay in following price decreases	10
Days	
1	1
2	3
3	1
10	1
21	1
23	1
28	1
47	1

16. I am indebted to Edward W. Proctor of Brown University for the information in this paragraph, which was secured by correspondence with Du Pont, Atlas Powder and Hercules Powder. The three companies have headquarters in Wilmington; the latter two were created in 1912 by an anti-trust action.

It appears, then, that price increases are more nearly simultaneous than price decreases – the opposite of the kinky demand curve assumption.[17]

The most striking case of contradiction of the assumption of the theory, however, is provided by potash. On 1 June 1934, the American Potash and Chemical Corporation issued a price list that carried about 26 per cent reductions from the prices in the previous year. The other firms failed to follow. On 26 June the lower prices were withdrawn, and the company lamented:

It was expected that other potash producers would likewise announce their prices in accordance with long prevailing custom. No such announcements have been forthcoming. Under the circumstances this Company is compelled to withdraw the schedule of prices and terms referred to (1934, p. 49).

In these seven industries there is little historical basis for a firm to believe that price increases will not be matched by rivals and that price decreases will be matched. This indicates only that not every oligopoly has reason to believe that it has a kinky demand-curve, and most adherents of the theory would readily concede this.[18] On the other hand, here are seven industries in which the existence of the kinky demand-curve is questionable – a list that is longer by seven than the list of industries for which a prima facie case has been made for the existence of the kink.[19]

The validity of the implications

The kinky demand-curve would prove to be an incorrect or unimportant construction if oligopoly prices were as flexible as

17. I am indebted to Melvin D. Sargent of Brown University for the information on gasoline prices.

18. But apparently not all. Lange treats only of kinky demand-curves in his theory of oligopoly (1944, ch. 7); and Tarshis has recently done the same (1947, p. 139).

19. In the Conference on Price Research study (1943), it is stated: 'There is rather strong reason for believing that leading firms in the automobile, steel, agricultural implement and many other industries act upon approximately this view of the situation [i.e. that there is a kink in the demand curve]' (p. 278). The reason is not given. We have discussed automobiles and steel; agricultural implements will be taken up subsequently.

monopoly and/or competitive prices. It is not possible to make a direct test for price rigidity, in part, because the prices at which the products of oligopolists sell are not generally known. For the purpose of such a test we need transaction prices; instead, we have quoted prices on a temporal basis, and they are deficient in two respects.

The first deficiency is notorious: nominal price quotations may be stable although the prices at which sales are taking place fluctuate often and widely. The disparity may be due to a failure to take account of quality, 'extras', freight, guaranties, discounts, etc.; or the price collector may be deceived merely to strengthen morale within the industry. The various studies of steel prices, already referred to, contain striking examples of this disparity, and others can be cited.[20] We cannot infer that all nominally rigid prices are really flexible, but there is also very little evidence that they are really rigid.

The second deficiency is that published prices are on a temporal basis. If nine-tenths of annual sales occur at fluctuating prices within a month (as is true of some types of tobacco), and the remainder at a fixed price during the rest of the year, the nominal price rigidity for eleven months is trivial. With each price we ought to have the corresponding quantities sold: for a study of price rigidity, 'April' would better be the fourth one-twelfth of the year's sales than the fourth month of the year.

Despite these shortcomings, a comparison of the implications of the kinky demand-curve for price behavior with observable behavior (even if observable only in bulletins of the Bureau of Labor Statistics) has some value. If the theory cannot explain the pattern of rigidity of quoted prices among industries, there is no presumption that it would explain the pattern of transaction price rigidity among industries.

Our tests are made by comparing observed price rigidity in a group of industries with the relative rigidities forecast by the theory for industries with these market structures. We choose the period, June 1929, through May 1937, which embraces both a complete business cycle and the periods used in most empirical

20. See the industry studies of the Division of Research of N R A; the prices revealed in prosecutions under the Robinson-Patman Act; Nelson (1939, pp. 173–84).

studies of price rigidity. We require three types of information:

1. A list of oligopolistic industries. The two basic criteria are (a) a fairly precise knowledge of the industry structure, and (b) continuous price and output series. The industries are described briefly in the Appendix.[21] [Not included here. Ed.]

2. Some measure of expected price changes in the absence of restrictions on price changes. Shifts in demand are of primary (although far from exclusive) importance, and we measure them roughly by the coefficient of variation of production (or some related series) in 1929, 1931, 1933, 1935 and 1937.

3. A measure of price rigidity. The basic test used is frequency of change in the monthly price quotations; for the theory under examination implies that there will be *no* changes – not merely that the price changes will be small. This test is supplemented by the coefficient of variation of monthly prices for two reasons. First, the price series have technical features that lead to more numerous price changes than actually occur. They are often averages of weekly quotations, and hence show two changes in the monthly averages when a price change occurs within a month.[22] They are often averages of prices of several firms, and if each firm makes once price change the average can display as many changes as there are firms. Second, it can be argued that the kink is an exaggeration – that actually there is a sharp bend in the demand curve of the firm so that small price changes are what the theory prophesies.[23] But frequent small price changes would still be improbable because of the cost of making price changes.

The basic data that are used in the tests are summarized in Table 1. It will be observed that the two tests of price rigidity

21. More specifically, the oligopolies discussed by Wilcox (1940) formed the basic list. An industry was excluded if (a) necessary information was not available, (b) the industry was analysed in the preceding section, or (c) the firms were in known collusion throughout the period. In addition, many chemicals were excluded because of ignorance of substitution relationships.

22. Thus the BLS reports as eight changes the six changes made by Pittsburgh Plate Glass during the period.

23. To secure a sharp bend, we must assume that rivals will partly follow price increases and decreases that are small but fail to follow large increases and completely follow large decreases.

Table 1 Measures of Market Structure for Twenty-one Products and of their Price Flexibility and Output Variability June 1929–May 1937

Product	Number of firms in industry	Price leader	Price flexibility Number of price changes	Coefficient of variation	Coefficient of variation of output
Oligopolies					
Bananas	2	Yes	46	16	17
Boric acid	3	No	7	17	16
Cans	4	Yes	6	5	27
Cement	12	No	14	11	41
Copper	4	No	63	37	43
Gasoline*	11	No	84	22	16
Grain-binder	2	Yes	5	3	63
Linoleum	2	No?	12	9	30
Newsprint	9	No	6	16	16
Plaster	3	Yes	4	5	29
Plate glass	2	No	8	13	34
Plows	6	No	25	6	50
Rayon	8	No	26	30	34
Soap	3	No	9	12	7
Starch	4	Yes	20	12	13
Sulphur	2	Yes	0	0	24
Tires	8	No	36	9	16
Tractors	4	Yes	6	6	76
Window glass	3	No	20	21	24
Monopolies					
Aluminium	1		2	6	47
Nickel	1		0	0	35

* In Pennsylvania and Delaware.

differ substantially: the coefficient of rank correlation between number of price changes and coefficient of variation of prices is +0·69 for the nineteen oligopolies listed in Table 1.

Monopolies versus oligopolies. The monopolies listed in Table 1 are unsurpassed for price rigidity, despite the fact that their outputs varied more than those of most oligopolistic industries. This

George J. Stigler 143

finding, which could be supported by more cases,[24] suggests the possibility that the forces that make for price rigidity in monopolies are sufficiently strong to account for the lesser rigidity in oligopolies. One might argue that special factors are at work in monopoly, but the only two that come to mind are fear of governmental attention or action and the conservatism that comes with size. The former, however, is even more effective against oligopolies because of the importance of conspiracy in the antitrust laws, and the latter is presumably also a function of absolute size. It should be added that the neoclassical theory does not provide a satisfactory explanation for this extraordinary rigidity of monopoly prices.

According to the kink theory, there will be no kink when the oligopolists enter into explicit collusion; and hence prices would be expected to become more flexible. All empirical evidence contradicts this implication. Of our industries, at least two had periods of collusion. There was a combination of rayon producers to fix prices between 21 October 1931 and 23 May 1932 (Federal Trade Commission, 1939, p. 425): there were no price changes during this period, none in the preceding period of equal length, and four in the subsequent period of equal length. There are only two periods of protracted rigidity in the price series for copper: the first occurs under Copper Exporters (a Webb-Pomerene cartel), the second under NRA.

A number of examples are also provided by other industries. On 30 August 1932, the six important growers and canners of pineapple entered a ten-year agreement to restrict output and market through the Pineapple Producers Cooperative Association.[25] In the thirty-nine months preceding this date there were seventeen price changes in canned pineapples; in the subsequent fifty-seven months, eight changes. Prices of typewriters were very rigid during a period when the four important producers were

24. Thus, the price of magnesium was very rigid; the rentals of the International Business Machines Corporation have not varied (Wilcox, 1940, p. 106); the retail price of incandescent lamps of common sizes changed once or twice (United States Tariff Commission, 1939, p. 47); this was virtually a General Electric monopoly because of its licensing provisions.

25. 'The move brought all the island packers into complete accord and cooperation for the first time in history' (*New York Times*, 31 August 1932, p. 10); see also Shoemaker (1941).

charged with colluding (Wilcox, 1940, p. 140). During the period of operation of the midwestern oil pool (Madison Oil Case), prices 'displayed a rigidity without parallel in the history of the industry' (Wilcox, 1940, p. 136).

If the disappearance of the kink through collusion has a tendency to increase price flexbility, this tendency is completely submerged by the opposite effects of administrative limitations on cartel price policy.

The number of firms. The number of firms that enters into the formation of price policy is difficult to determine; a completely satisfactory determination would require knowledge of cross-elasticities of demand, the entrepreneur's knowledge and objectives, and similar data. As an unsatisfactory substitute for this information, we have been guided by two criteria: that sufficient firms be included to account for two-thirds to three-quarters of the output of the product and that the largest firm omitted from the count sell less than a tenth of the amount sold by the largest firm in the industry. Although these rules are arbitrary, they focus attention on relevant variables: if we do not include enough firms to account for a predominant share of output, the firms will not be able to control prices (attenuated oligopoly); and if we exclude firms large relative to those that are included, we may be omitting firms that are in the oligopolistic relationship. The precise number of firms, even by these arbitrary criteria, is in doubt in more than half the industries listed in Table 1, but it was thought better to give a single number than a range that invites mechanical averaging to secure a single number.

Our expectation, on the kink theory, is that a very few rivals will have relatively flexible prices because the impossibility of maintaining a price lower than a rival's will be evident. On the other hand, with many rivals the fear that price cuts will be matched is reduced, and again the kink disappears. We do not test this latter implication because it is identical with that of the neoclassical theory.

If the data in Table 1 are summarized by number of firms, we find a definite tendency for price flexibility to increase with the number of firms in the industry (Table 2). The coefficient of rank correlation between number of firms and number of price changes is $+0.41$, that between number of firms and coefficient of variation of prices is $+0.31$. There is virtually no relationship between fluctuations of output and number of firms, nor is the strength or direction of relationship between number of firms and price flexibility affected if industries with price leaders are segregated.[26]

Table 2

| Number of firms in industry | Number of industries in sample | Price flexibility | | Average of coefficients of variation of outputs |
		Number of price changes	Coefficient of variation	
2	5	14·2	8·2	33·6
3, 4	8	16·8	14·4	29·4
6, 8	3	29·0	15·0	33·3
9, 11, 12	3	34·7	16·3	24·3

Thus there is a weak tendency for a greater number of firms to be associated with a greater frequency and amplitude of price changes, the contrary of the implications of the kinky demand-curve.

Price leadership. The term, 'price leadership', is used in two very different senses in economic literature. In the one sense it refers to a dominant firm that sets the price, allows the minor firms to sell what they wish at this price (subject perhaps to non-price competition), and supplies the remainder of the quantity demanded. In the other sense, price leadership refers to the existence of a firm that conventionally first announces price changes that are usually followed by the remainder of the industry, even though this firm may not occupy a dominant position. For example, International Paper was for a long period the price leader in newsprint although it produced less than one-seventh of the output, and it was succeeded in this role by Great

26. The coefficient of rank correlation between number of firms and number of price changes is 0·37 for seven products with price leaders and 0·39 for twelve products without price leaders.

Northern, a smaller firm. This latter type of price leadership has been illuminatingly described by Swensrud of Standard Oil of Ohio:

In any territory all suppliers are watching the same things. They watch the statistical position of the industry as a whole, that is, production of crude oil and gasoline, sales of petroleum products, and stocks of crude oil and gasoline. . . . They watch the ambitions of competitors to increase their share of the business in the territory. They gage these ambitions by reports of salesmen on price concessions to commercial customers, by observations of the amount of business done by trackside operators and sellers of unbranded and locally branded gasoline, by the reports of salesmen as to competitive offers being made to dealers, and by reports of salesmen as to the extent of secret price cuts, discounts, and the like being offered by retailers. All these facts are constantly before local managers and central organizations.

Now suppose that secret price cutting by dealers in some particular area breaks out into the open in the form of a cut in the posted price because some dealer becomes disgusted with the uncertainty as to how much business he is losing to competitors granting secret discounts. As the openly admitted price reduction operates, the local officers of all suppliers are assailed with demands from dealers, relayed and in some instances emphasized by salesmen, for a reduction in the tank-wagon price. . . . The local manager of the leading marketer of course faces more demands than any other manager. He attempts to gage the permanence of the retail cut. Frequently local managers elect to make no change in the tank-wagon price. Ordinarily this decision springs from the conclusion that the local price war will soon run its course because it is not supported by weakness in basic markets. On other occasions the local manager concludes that the causes of the retail price cutting rest primarily on the availability of sufficient low-price gasoline so that the condition may be considered deep-seated, and he therefore authorizes or recommends a local reduction in the tank-wagon price. . . . Thus the particular local territory becomes a subnormal territory, that is, one in which prices are out of line with those generally prevailing in the marketing area.

The major sales executives of all companies watch carefully the number and size of subnormal markets. . . . If the number of local price cuts increases, if the number and amount of secret concessions to commercial consumers increase, if the secret unpublicized concessions to dealers increase, it becomes more and more difficult to maintain the higher prices. . . . Finally, some company, usually the largest marketer in the territory, recognizes that the subnormal price has become the normal price and announces a general price reduction throughout the territory. . . .

In summary, therefore, the so-called price leadership in the petroleum industry boils down to the fact that some company in each territory most of the time bears the onus of formally recognizing current conditions. . . . In short, unless the so-called price leader accurately interprets basic conditions and local conditions, it soon will not be the leading marketer. Price leadership does not mean that the price leader can set prices to get the maximum profit and force other marketers to conform (Farish and Pew, 1941, pp. 47–9).

The difference between these two types of price leadership from the viewpoint of the theory of kinky demand-curves is basic. The dominant firm has no kink in its demand curve because rivals have no reason for charging a lower price: they are permitted to sell as much as they wish at the leader's price (Stigler, 1940, p. 523). The second type of leader, the barometric firm, commands

Table 3

	Industries with leader	Industries without leader
Two-firm industries		
Number in sample	3	2
Average number of price changes	17	10
Average coefficient of variation of prices	6·3	11
Average coefficient of variation of outputs	34·7	32
Three- and four-firm industries		
Number in sample	4	4
Average number of price changes	9	24·8
Average coefficient of variation of prices	7	21·8
Average coefficient of variation of outputs	36·2	22·5

adherence of rivals to his price only because, and to the extent that, his price reflects market conditions with tolerable promptness. The widespread development of barometric firms is therefore explicitly a device to insure that there will be no kink, or that the kink will not prevent readjustment of price to important changes in cost or demand conditions.

Only the price leadership exercised by dominant firms, therefore, is relevant in testing the implication of the kinky demand-curve theory that there will be no kink when there is price leadership. Accordingly, we classify as industries with price leaders only those in which there is a relatively large firm, producing, say, 40 per cent of the output of the industry at a minimum, and more if the second largest firm is large (because otherwise the situation approaches classical duopoly). On this basis there are seven leaders among our nineteen industries (see Table 1), and they are compared with the remaining twelve industries in Table 3. Except for the number of price changes of two-firm industries (where bananas dominate the result), the prices of industries with price leaders are less flexible than those of industries without price leaders, despite the larger fluctuations of output of the former

Table 4

	Homogeneous products	Heterogeneous products
Number of products	13	6
Average number of price changes	23·4	15·5
Average coefficient of variation of prices	15·8	7·5
Average coefficient of variation of outputs	25·7	40·3

group. This is contrary to Sweezy's conjecture and is in keeping with the price rigidity found in monopolistic industries.

Goodness of substitutes. It is almost inherent in the methods of quotation of price statistics that most of the commodities examined in this article are nearly homogeneous. If products are rather heterogeneous, the significance of an average price becomes doubtful and the BLS does not report it. Of our nineteen industries, only six have products whose prices appear to differ significantly and persistently among firms: soap, tractors, grain-binders, plows, tires and linoleum. Their prices appear to change less often and less widely, on average, than those of homogeneous products as shown in Table 4. It should be noted that we might, with some justification, have designated our monopolies (aluminum and nickel) as oligopolies with differentiated products.

Conclusion

The empirical evidence reveals neither price experiences that would lead oligopolists to believe in the existence of a kink nor the pattern of changes of price quotations that the theory leads us to expect. The industries included in these tests are not very numerous, but they are sufficiently varied and important to suggest that similar adverse results would be secured from a larger sample.

But is this adverse conclusion really surprising? The kink is a barrier to changes in prices that will increase profits, and business is the collection of devices for circumventing barriers to profits. That this barrier should thwart businessmen – especially when it is wholly of their own fabrication – is unbelievable. There are many ways in which it can be circumvented. We have had occasion to notice the development of price leadership of the barometric variety as one device, and the old-fashioned solution of collusion is not always overlooked. In addition there is the whole range of tactical maneuvers that Neumann and Morgenstern's theory of games has uncovered. In the multi-dimensional real world there are many ways to teach a lesson, especially when the pupil is eager to learn.

References

AMERICAN POTASH AND CHEMICAL CORPORATION (1934), *Chemical Industries*.

BRONFENBRENNER, M. (1940), 'Applications of the discontinuous oligopoly demand curve', *J. polit. Econ.*, vol. 48, pp. 420–27.

BUREAU OF LABOR STATISTICS (1946), 'Labor Department examines consumers' prices of steel products', *Iron Age*, 25 April.

CONFERENCE ON PRICE RESEARCH (1943), *Cost Behavior and Price Policy*, National Bureau of Economic Research.

FARISH, W. S., and PEW, J. H. (1941), *Review and Criticism of Monograph No. 39*, Temporary National Economic Committee, monograph no. 39a.

FEDERAL TRADE COMMISSION (1937), *Agricultural Income Inquiry*, vol. 1.

FEDERAL TRADE COMMISSION (1939), 'Viscose Company *et al.*', *Federal Trade Commission Decisions*, vol. 25.

FEDERAL TRADE COMMISSION (1940), *Report on Motor Vehicle Industry*.

FRASER, C. E., and DORIOT, G. F. (1932), *Analysing our Industries*, McGraw-Hill.

HALL, R. L., and HITCH, C. J. (1939), 'Price theory and business behaviour', *Oxford econ. Papers*, vol. 2, pp. 12–45.

LANGE, O. (1944), *Price Flexibility and Employment*, Principia Press.

MARSHALL, A. (1920), *Principles of Economics*, Macmillan. 8th edn

NATIONAL PETROLEUM NEWS (1938), *Oil Price Handbook, 1929–37*, Cleveland.

NELSON, S. (1939), 'A consideration of the validity of the Bureau of Labor Statistics price indexes', in *The Structure of the American Economy*, National Resources Committee.

SHOEMAKER, J. A. (1941), 'Labor conditions in Hawaii', *Monthly Labor Rev.*

STIGLER, G. J. (1940), 'Notes on the theory of duopoly', *J. polit Econ.*, vol. 48, pp. 521–41.

SWEEZY, P. M. (1939), 'Demand under conditions of oligopy', *J. polit. Econ.*, vol. 47, pp. 568–73.

TARSHIS, L. (1947), *The Elements of Economics*, Houghton Mifflin.

TEMPORARY NATIONAL ECONOMIC COMMITTEE (1940), *Hearings, Pt 19: Iron and Steel Industry*.

UNITED STATES TARIFF COMMISSION (1939), *Incandescent Electric Lamps*.

WILCOX, C. (1940), *Competition and Monopoly in American Industry*, Temporary National Economic Committee, monograph no. 21.

Part Three
The Measurement and Effects of Monopoly

The diverse nature of the papers in this Part, and their intimate connection with papers in preceding and succeeding Parts, indicates the arbitrary nature of *any* attempted subdivision of the problems of 'production, pricing, and distribution': any proposition about production, pricing, or distribution involves assumptions about, and implications for, the other two. Nonetheless, some subdivision is helpful, and a few particular problems are emphasized in this Part.

It is possible that the most important lesson that has emerged from the whole story of monopolistic competition is a very simple one: the persistence of 'pure profit' (rent) has nothing to do with the slope of the demand curve, but depends exclusively on the existence of barriers to entry. Resource allocation, of course, depends on both. Thus we have attempts at definition and measurement of both the 'degree of monopoly' and 'barriers to entry', as well as attempts to evaluate the welfare consequences of monopoly.

The classical definition of the 'degree of monopoly' is due to Lerner (see Further Reading: his paper would have been reprinted here had a restrictive agreement not prevented it). Since price equals marginal cost under perfect competition, Lerner proposed as a measure of the degree of monopoly the proportional difference between market price and marginal cost. Thus the definition of the degree of monopoly, μ, is

$$\mu = \frac{p-c}{p},$$

where c is marginal cost. Equilibrium for a profit-maximizing monopolist requires that marginal cost equals marginal revenue.

The latter is, of course, equal to $p(1+1/\eta)$, where η is the (negative) elasticity of demand. Thus in equilibrium

$$c = p \left[1 + \frac{1}{\eta} \right]$$

and a little rearrangement gives

$$\mu = \frac{p-c}{p} = -\frac{1}{\eta}.$$

In other words, the degree of monopoly is measured as the reciprocal of the elasticity of demand (multiplied by -1). In the next Part, we see this result used by Kalecki in his explanation of the functional distribution of income. In this Part, we see Harberger measuring the cost of monopoly misallocation, assuming that the elasticities of the demand curves are unity. This poses a problem since, as we learn from Cournot, no monopolist with positive marginal costs can be in profit-maximizing equilibrium where the elasticity of his demand curve is unity.

The great empirical inquiry into the importance of barriers to entry, and their relation to profit rates, is Bain's. Here we have an extract from his book *Barriers to New Competition*, complementing his study of economies of scale in Part One. It will be noticed, incidentally, that Bain takes as his base point the perfectly competitive price, i.e. that equal to minimum average cost. This, as we know from Chamberlin's tangency solution, is not the price that would prevail in a monopolistically competitive industry into which entry were free. Bain also, of course, considers the importance of concentration. It is a property of Lerner's measure of the degree of monopoly that the corner grocery store may enjoy a higher μ-index than, say, British Oxygen or the Aluminum Corporation of America. As an alternative measure, many economists have studied 'concentration ratios' such as the proportion of industries' outputs contributed by the four largest firms. The concentration ratio too has its drawbacks as a measure of monopoly power (see Further Reading).

One omitted topic is the discussion of 'entry-preventing strategies' in the absence of barriers of the type measured by

Bain in his pioneering work. It has been suggested that firms that could earn profit would forego some of it to discourage entry (see Further Reading: Harrod, Sylos, Labini, Modigliani). It has also been pointed out that the threat of a price-war, backed up by ample reserves, might be cheaper and more effective! I find the omitted literature narrow and arbitrary compared with the rich variety of entry-preventing strategies discussed in Shubik's *Strategy and Market Structure*.

Many other relevant and important papers will be found in Hunter (1969).

References

HUNTER, A. (ed.) (1969), *Monopoly and Competition*, Penguin.

Further Reading

Lerner's classic paper is
A. P. Lerner, 'The concept of monopoly and the measurement of monopoly power', *Review of Economic Studies*, vol. 1, 1934.

On oligopoly and entry-preventing strategies, see
R. F. Harrod, 'Doctrines of imperfect competitition' in his *Economic Essays*, Macmillan, 1952; Harcourt Brace & World, 1953.
F. Modigliani, 'New developments on the oligopoly front', *Journal of Political Economy*, vol. 66, 1958, pp. 215–32.
P. Sylos-Labini, *Oligopoly and Technical Progress*, trans. E. Henderson, Harvard University Press, 1963; Oxford University Press, 1962, and, of course,
M. Shubik, *Strategy and Market Structure*, Wiley, 1959; Chapman & Hall, 1959.

Bain's research is fully reported in
J. S. Bain, *Barriers to New Competition*, Harvard University Press, 1963, and followed up in
H. M. Mann, 'Seller concentration, barriers to entry and rates of return in thirty industries, 1950–60', *Review of Economics and Statistics*, 1966, reprinted in *Readings in the Economics of Industrial Organization*, D. Needham (ed.), Holt, Rinehart & Winston, 1970.

Stigler reports a much weaker relationship between concentration ratios and profitability in chapter 3 of an important book:
G. J. Stigler, *Capital and Rates of Return in Manufacturing Industries*, Princeton University Press, 1963.

Concentration in British industry is discussed in
R. Evely and I. M. D. Little, *Concentration in British Industry*,
Cambridge University Press, 1960,
and in
A. Hunter, 'The Measurement of Monopoly Power', reprinted in
Monopoly and Competition, A. Hunter (ed.), Penguin, 1969.

A fine review of the measurement of concentration is
G. Rosenbluth, 'Measures of concentration' in Universities National
Bureau Committee for Economic Research *Business Concentration
and Price Policy*, Princeton University Press, 1955; Oxford University
Press, 1955. (This survey includes a comparison of concentration ratios
in British and American industries. One country engages in far more
trade than the other. Concentration ratios, at their best, measure
concentration among a group of producers, not necessarily the same
thing as concentration in any *market*.)

Harberger's work has been extended by
D. Schwartzman, 'The Burden of Monopoly' *Journal of Political
Economy*, vol. 68, 1960, pp. 627–30; 'The effect of monopoly:
a correction', *Journal of Political Economy*, vol. 69, 1961, p. 494.

Readers are likely to be surprised at the smallness of these estimates
of the loss due to monopoly distortion of resource allocation in US
industry. It is worth noting that it is of the same order of magnitude as
estimates of the allocative loss to Britain due to staying out of the
Common Market!
See
P. J. Verdoorn, 'A customs union for Western Europe: advantages and
feasibility', *World Politics*, vol. 6, 1954, pp. 482–500;
and
H. G. Johnson, 'The gains from freer trade with Europe: an estimate',
Manchester School, vol. 26, 1958, pp. 247–55. The latter explains why
these numbers generally are small. The gains to Canada from free
trade with the US have been estimated to be substantially larger. The
reason is that the authors of the Canadian study explicitly allowed for
scale effects, arguing that Canadian industry is in monopolistically
competitive equilibrium, with unexploited economies of scale (a model
discussed in Reading 6 above).
See
R. J. Wonnacott and P. Wonnacott, *Free Trade Between the United
States and Canada*, Harvard University Press, 1967.

8 Joe S. Bain

Barriers to Entry, Concentration and Profit Rates

Excerpts from J. S. Bain, *Barriers to New Competition*, Harvard University Press, 1956.

The importance of the condition of entry

This study analyses the character and significance of the 'condition of entry' to manufacturing industries; it is based on an investigation of the force of latent competition from potential new sellers in twenty such industries in the United States.

The investigation was made because of two beliefs:

1. That most analyses of how business competition works and what makes it work have given little emphasis to the force of the potential or threatened competition of possible new competitors, placing a disproportionate emphasis on competition among firms already established in any industry.

2. That so far as economists have recognized the *possible* importance of this 'condition of entry', they have no very good idea of how important it actually is.

If these are reasonable beliefs, it seems important to do two things – to develop systematic theory concerning the potential importance of the condition of entry as an influence on business conduct and performance, and to assess, in those ways that are open, the extent and nature of its actual importance. These are the main tasks of this study. In addition, we may read from our tentative findings some directions for the formulation of public policy toward business monopoly and competition. First, however, let us survey the facts and concepts which we are about to explore.

Actual competition versus the threat of entry

When competition is named as a regulator of enterprise outputs and prices, it is usually the competition among the firms already established in this or that industry which is emphasized. On the level of market conduct, detailed attention is given to whether the price-calculating policies of established firms are formulated independently or in the light of a 'recognized interdependence' with each other, whether or not there is collusion among these firms, and the extent to which collusion, if found, is imperfect. On the level of market structure, much emphasis is placed on those characteristics of the industry that presumably influence competitive conduct as among established rivals, and particularly on the number and size distribution of these rival sellers and on the manner in which their products are differentiated from one another. The immediate competition among established firms gets most of the attention.

This is true both of abstract economic theory and of the empirical investigations which implement, test or apply it. When conventional price theory treats the working of business competition, it devotes nearly all of its detailed analysis to the consequences of rivalry within various alternative conformations of established sellers, so much so that the effects of the actual or threatened entry of new sellers are generally mentioned, if at all, cryptically and almost as an afterthought. Similarly, empirical studies of market structure commonly center on seller concentration within established groups, product differentiation within these groups, and other determinants of the character of competition among established sellers. Most studies of individual industries refer, when discussing competition, almost entirely to rivalry among established firms.

Correspondingly, the condition of entry has generally received only nominal attention as a regulator of market conduct and performance. Typical versions of abstract price theory do recognize the long-run impact of an assumed 'free' or 'easy' entry of new firms to industries with many small sellers. But when they turn to the very important category of oligopolistic industries, they ordinarily fail to distinguish numerous possible alternative situations with respect to the condition of entry, and to identify and develop appropriate assumptions relative to the structural determinants of the condition of entry. They thus fail to offer any systematic predictions concerning the effect of variations in the condition of entry on the market conduct of established sellers and on industry performance in the long term. The theory of pricing in non-atomistic markets is generally too oversimplified to identify or distinguish potentially large and significant variations of behavior within the oligopolistic sector of industries.

Much empirical investigation of business structure and competition has followed the lead of abstract theory, and has been hindered by the fact that abstract theory provided few leads in the area of the condition of entry. Although investigations of the extent of existing seller concentration in various industries have become widespread in government agencies and elsewhere, measurement of the height and nature of barriers to entry has never been systematically undertaken. Studies of competitive conduct and performance have paid much attention to such matters as the role of the price leader in eliminating or canalizing competition among established sellers and in influencing the ultimate relation of price to cost in his industry, but ordinarily they have given much less attention to the extent to which established firms shape price policies in the light of their anticipation of new entry, by deciding whether or not to try to forestall it. In brief, neither the theoretically possible nor the actual significance of variations in the condition of entry has received much attention from economists.

A strong emphasis on actual competition among existing sellers is of course appropriate. Such competition, with its determinants, is most probably of first importance as a regulator of business activity. But the substantial neglect of the condition of entry is definitely unfortunate, since there is considerable evidence of the importance of the condition of entry as a co-regulator of business conduct and performance.

Let us understand the term 'condition of entry' to an industry to mean something equivalent to the 'state of potential competition' from possible new sellers. Let us view it moreover as evaluated roughly *by the advantages of established sellers in an industry over potential entrant sellers, these advantages being reflected in the extent to which established sellers can persistently raise their prices above a competitive level without attracting new firms to enter the industry.* As such, the 'condition of entry' is then primarily a structural condition, determining in any industry the intra-industry adjustments which will and will not induce entry.

Its reference to market conduct is primarily to potential rather than actual conduct, since basically it describes only the circumstances in which the potentiality of competition from new firms will or will not become actual. If we understand the condition of entry in this way, its possible importance as a determinant of competitive behavior is clear.

Conventional price theory has been quite explicit concerning the effects of one type of condition of entry – *free* or *easy* entry. It has deduced from reasonable premises the valid conclusion that in markets with many small sellers, easy entry in the long run will force price to equality with minimal average costs and will bring output to a level sufficient for supplying all demands at this price. When price theory has turned to markets with few sellers and to conditions of entry other than easy, it has ordinarily been inexplicit, cryptic or silent. But relatively elementary elaborations of received theory make it clear that variations in the condition of entry as it departs from the 'easy' pole may have a substantial influence on the performance of established firms in any industry.

Even in atomistically organized industries, barriers to entry may, under certain conditions, result in a long-term elevation of prices and profits and a restriction of output; if established firms are restricted in number and encounter diseconomies of scale, entry will operate to limit prices only after they exceed a certain super-competitive level. In oligopolistic industries, something additional is generally true. Each of the few large established sellers – whether they act collectively or singly – will appraise the condition of entry and, anticipating that entry may occur if price exceeds a given level, will regulate his price policies accordingly. There will thus be a sort of 'recognized interdependence' of actions not only among established sellers but between established sellers and potential entrants. In this event, variations in the condition of entry may be expected to have substantial effects on the behavior of established sellers, *even though over long intervals actual entry seldom or never takes place*. Elementary extensions of the deductive logic of conventional price theory thus suggest an important role of the condition of entry, and emphasize the desirability of finding how much in fact it does vary from industry to industry.

Empirical observation reinforces the impression that the condition of entry may be an important determinant of market behavior, especially in the case of oligopolistic industries. Examination of any considerable number of concentrated industries reveals great differences in market conduct and performance among them, in spite of the fact that in each a recognized interdependence among established sellers definitely appears to be present. Variations in the degree of seller concentration or of product differentiation among oligopolies may explain a part of these differences in behavior, but not all of them. The other most evident structural variation among oligopolies is that of the condition of entry, and from casual observation this variation seems to be at least loosely associated with variations in behavior. A more systematic empirical study of the importance of the condition of entry is thus indicated.

The meaning of the condition of entry

As suggested above, the condition of entry is a structural concept. Like some other aspects of market structure, it may be viewed as potentially subject to quantitative evaluation in terms of a continuous variable. This variable is the percentage by which established firms can raise price above a specified competitive level without attracting new entry – a percentage which may vary continuously from zero to a very high figure, with entry becoming 'more difficult' by small gradations as it does so. As the difficulty of entry (thus understood and evaluated) increases, some systematic variations in the behavior of established firms may be anticipated.

The preceding description is obviously unspecific in numerous details. On the ground that this is primarily an empirical study dealing with available data, and that we do not wish to fashion a precision instrument for use in ditch-digging, it does not seem profitable here to develop a very polished and detailed definition of the condition of entry. (The writer has taken some steps in that direction in an earlier article (Bain, 1954), and even the moderate degree of detail and precision attempted there seems out of place in the present setting.) Nevertheless, it seems useful to be somewhat more explicit by simply stating, without a detailed theoretical discussion, what is to be understood by various terms and notions expressed or implied in the definition so far presented.

Joe S. Bain 161

As stated, the condition of entry may be evaluated by the extent to which established sellers can persistently raise their prices above a competitive level without attracting new firms to enter the industry. The first term needing consideration is 'attracting new firms to enter the industry'. This implies some specific definition of the concept of *entry*, involving both the notion of the 'new firm' and of the meaning of the verb 'to enter'. As a first approximation, entry of a new firm may be taken to mean here the combination of two events: (a) the establishment of an independent legal entity, new to the industry, as a producer therein; and (b) the concurrent building or introduction by the new firm of physical production capacity that was not used for production in the industry prior to the establishment of the new firm. An addition to industry capacity already in use, plus emergence of a firm new to the industry, are thus required.

This definition excludes two related events from the concept of 'entry'. The first is the acquisition of existing producing capacity by a new legal entity, whether by purchase from a pre-existing firm, by reorganization involving a change of corporate name and structure, or through other means. Simple change of ownership or control of existing operating capacity is not considered as entry. The second exclusion is the expansion of capacity by an established firm. If, for example, a small established firm doubles its capacity, this is to be considered as a phase of competition among established firms rather than an act of entry. Growth of an already established rival firm in an industry is thus not considered as entry to that industry. Both of these exclusions are in some degree arbitrary, since the introduction of a new owner of old capacity may constitute a distinct change in a competitive situation, and since expansion of an established competitor may, from the standpoint of another established firm, have about the same significance as entry of a new firm with new capacity. Nevertheless, present purposes call for distinguishing competition among established competitors from the entry of new competitors, and we thus draw the lines indicated. As we proceed, we will have occasion to refer to the significance of events closely related to entry as defined.

Given these exclusions, a firm new to the industry may enter that industry by building new capacity to produce, by converting for use in this industry plants previously used in another industry, or by reactivating capacity that has been previously used in the instant industry but is currently idle. Any of these acts by a new firm, singly or in combination, will constitute entry, according to the definition, and will continue to do so, even though the new firm also acquires operating capacity from an already established firm. Acquisition of a going concern by a new firm, together with expansion of the facilities of the going concern, thus constitutes entry to the extent of the expansion. Detailed implementation of this definition would require further specifications, such as the duration of the idleness required to distinguish 'idle' plant from 'operating' plant, but from the preceding the general intent of our definition should be clear.

Thus we see that the condition of entry may be evaluated by the degree to which established firms can raise their prices above a competitive level without inducing new firms to bring added capacity into use in the industry. How many new firms or how big? For the moment we may say 'one or more' new firms and 'any size', although we will treat the subject directly when we consider the difference between the *immediate* and the *general* condition of entry.

The second crucial concept is the 'competitive level of prices', which, by definition, established firms may exceed more and more *without attracting entry* as the condition of entry becomes progressively more difficult. The 'competitive level of prices' is defined here as the minimum attainable average cost of production, distribution and selling for the good in question, such cost being measured to include a normal interest return on investment in the enterprise.

In effect, this is equivalent to the level of price hypothetically attributed to long-run equilibrium in pure competition. If equilibrium were of the stationary sort frequently described in theory textbooks, in which each firm produced regularly and uninterruptedly at its most efficient output, then this competitive price would equal the minimum attainable average cost (interest returns included) for the most efficient scale of firm when its capacity is always utilized at the optimal rate. In actual situations, where demand is unstable and uncertain and equilibrium is necessarily an adjustment to an average of varying situations over time, the competitive level of price and cost is elevated sufficiently to cover, for the most efficient scale of firm, the added costs of resulting periodic deviations from an optimal rate of utilization, and those coming from unavoidable errors in estimates of future demands, costs and the like.[1]

This competitive or minimum-cost level of price is a useful reference point for evaluating the condition of entry. Completely easy or unimpeded entry involves the inability of established firms to raise price above this level at all – persistently or on the average through time – without attracting new entry. If price may persistently exceed this level at all without inducing entry, then entry is somewhat impeded. The greater the persistent percentage excess attainable without inducing entry, the more difficult entry may be said to be.

It will be noted that this measure of the condition of entry refers to an independently defined standard of cost and not necessarily to the actual costs of firms established in the industry. It thus is a measure not simply of the profit margins they are able to establish without inducing entry, but rather of the margin between an entry-inducing price and minimal competitive costs as defined. There will tend to be a direct relationship between the two margins. But it is quite possible, for example, that in an industry where price could be substantially elevated above a competitive level without inducing entry, profits could nevertheless be absent because established firms were built to inefficient sizes.

A third term that must be considered is 'persistently'. We refer for our measure to the height of price which can be *persistently* attained by established sellers without inducing entry. This con-

1. Minimal costs as defined presuppose the use of optimal available production techniques. Where product differentiation and sales promotion are encountered, such costs also include sales-promotion costs as incurred according to profit-maximizing criteria. The distinction between the lowest attainable average cost for the firm (supposedly attained in purely competitive long-run equilibrium) and the close approximation to that lowest cost supposedly attained in equilibrium in monopolistic competition will be neglected in defining minimal cost throughout the following discussion. Hypothetically, the basic minimal cost level from which the condition of entry is measured should refer alternatively to the two levels, depending upon whether or not product differentiation is present.

dition is inserted deliberately to give a long-run and structural aspect to our definition of the condition of entry, rather than to make it merely reflect transitory and varying short-term conditions from year to year. By a persistent elevation of price relative to a competitive level, therefore, we mean one maintained on the average over a substantial period of time, long enough to encompass a typical range of varying conditions of demand, factor prices and the like. Such a period might normally be thought of as five or ten years. The definition thus refers, in brief, to the average relationship of the actual with a competitive price that can be maintained over a number of years without attracting entry. The relationship to entry of the short-run level of price – set only for a few months or year, for example – is deliberately neglected as erratic and without much significance in most industries.

We turn now to a very necessary elaboration of our definition of the condition of entry, designed to take into account (a) differences among established firms in an industry, and (b) differences among potential entrant firms. So far, we have referred to all established firms in an industry as an aggregate, and to entrant firms without reference to their number or identity. In so doing, we have spoken as if generally all established firms in an industry would charge a single price and have a single common competitive level of price or of minimum cost. Also, we have not recognized the existence or consequences of possible cost and other differences among potential entrant firms. Although both suppositions could be adopted for purposes of simplified theorizing, neither will be supported by fact, and thus it is necessary to elaborate the definition.

With respect to established firms, the complications are two. There may be a type of differentiation among their products which supports some system of differentials among their prices, so that actually they will at no time charge a single common price but rather maintain a certain regimen of different prices. And they may have somewhat different minimal costs to be used in defining the 'competitive' level of price, since there may be quality differences among their products or differential advantages in cost. In view of these cost and price differences, then, how do we define the maximum excess of price over competitive cost at which entry may be forestalled?

There is no simple answer, since existence of the sort of cost and price differences noted actually means that the condition of entry to an industry has become intrinsically a more complicated concept and cannot be fully measured by any single firm's difference between an actual and a competitive price. It could be measured fully only through an array of individual differences for all individual firms – i.e. margins of actual prices above minimal costs – which would be encountered when all firms had concurrently raised their prices just short of the point that would induce new entry. Since this theoretically satisfactory procedure of complex measurement is not practically useful, an arbitrary simplification is required.

We will tentatively suggest that, where interfirm differences exist within the industry, the condition of entry may be conveniently evaluated in the following terms. First, the relevant gap between price and minimal cost (just short of that sufficient to induce entry) will be the one encountered when all established firms elevate their prices concurrently by similar amounts or proportions, maintaining any customary competitive price differentials. (It will not refer to gaps associated with isolated hypothetical price increases by one or a few firms, since these would be relatively uninteresting.) Second, the condition of entry may then be measured specifically as the maximum gap between price and minimal cost at which entry may be forestalled, for the most favored established firm or firms in the industry, supposing concurrent price elevations by all established firms. (The 'most favored firm' may be identified as that with the largest price-minimal cost gap.) This single measure may be elaborated by any information revealing a significantly different gap for other established firms. Closer or more elaborate approximations seem unlikely to be implemented with data that are or can be made available.

Our next problem concerns differences among potential entrant firms. The condition of entry is measured by the long-run gap between minimal cost and price which the most favored firms can reach without attracting entry – but whose entry and how much? Do we assume that all entrants are alike and that there will be an unlimited and perfectly elastic supply of entrant firms if the entry-inducing gap is exceeded? If not, what do we assume about the number and size of entrants attracted as an entry-inducing gap is reached?

It is not realistic to assume that all potential entrants are alike either in their capacity to enter or with respect to the gap which will just induce them to enter. Nor can we assume that established firms are confronted by an indefinitely large supply of entrant firms if they exceed some critical price-to-minimal-cost gap. The more plausible assumptions are (a) that potential entrant firms may differ as to the gap which will induce them to enter, conceivably to the point where every potential entrant differs from every other in this respect; and (b) that any specific entry-inducing gap may induce only the entry of a finite number of firms. Then for any industry the condition of entry is fully measured only by a succession, within any range conceivably relevant to market behavior, of successively higher entry-inducing price-minimal cost gaps that will attract successive firms or groups of firms to enter industry.

We may therefore establish two complementary concepts: *the immediate condition of entry* and *the general condition of entry*. The *immediate condition of entry* refers to the impediments to entry by the firm or firms that can most easily or readily be induced to enter the industry in a given situation. This immediate condition is evaluated by the long-run price-minimal cost gap (for the most favored established firms) which is just short of sufficient (just sufficient at the margin) to induce the entry of what we may call the most favored potential entrant or entrants. At any stage in its development, each industry has some immediate condition of entry thus defined and evaluated, although the number of potential entrant firms referred to by the measure could vary greatly from industry to industry.

The *general condition of entry* then refers to the succession of values of the immediate condition of entry as entry to the industry occurs – to the distribution of price-minimal cost gaps just necessary to induce successively less favored firms or groups of firms to enter an industry consecutively, beginning with the most favored firm. At any stage in its development, each industry has a general condition of entry in prospect (as well as one past, or one faced by various established firms before entering the industry), reflecting the succession of entry-inducing long-run price-minimal cost gaps at which successive increments to entry are expected to occur. At one extreme, this condition might be represented in the sustained repetition of a single value of the immediate condition of entry, reflecting in effect a perfectly elastic supply of entry. At the other, it might be represented in a series of different values each of which referred to the entry of only a single firm. In most cases, the general condition of entry to an industry should be expected *a priori* to lie between these two extremes.

If the condition of entry refers to the conditions for the inducement to entry of successive finite numbers of firms, it should also logically refer to the *size* of each entry, viewed either as realized *ex post* or anticipated *ex ante*. That is, a full measure of each *immediate* condition of entry (successions of which define the *general* condition) must include not only a measure of the long-run price-minimal cost gap for principal established firms necessary to induce some increment to entry, but also a measure of the long-run scale (attained *ex post* or expected to be attained *ex ante*) of the firms included in that increment. Such a measure of scale might be expressed as a percentage of total industry output. If the scale to be attained by entrants is a range of alternative values depending on the choice alternative policies open to established sellers, then the condition of entry is measured in part by such a range of values.

The last elaboration on the measure of the condition of entry represents a refinement of an order not very useful for application to actual data. Nevertheless, it may be possible in evaluating various conditions of entry to make some general appraisal of the comparative scales likely to be attained by potential entrants if they enter, and of the circumstances, if any, that would limit their sizes.

The preceding elaborations and definitions of terms should make the general meaning of the condition of entry to an industry sufficiently explicit for our purposes here. It refers to advantages which established firms in an industry have over potential entrant firms; it is evaluated in general by measures of the heights of entry-inducing prices relative to defined competitive levels. One major matter that has not received attention in this definition, however, concerns the 'lags of entry', or time intervals consumed by entrants in making their entries effective.

Given any particular immediate condition of entry, as evaluated by some entry-inducing excess of price over a competitive level, there is still room for variation in the length of time an entrant firm requires to make its entry effective. For purposes of a first approximation we may say that entry is initiated when a new firm has taken more or less irrevocable steps to establish and use new capacity in an industry, and is completed when the firm has established and 'broken in' all production and other facilities necessary to permit it to produce in routine fashion at its planned rate of output. The 'lag period', then, is the time interval between these two dates, and may vary greatly from industry to industry. In the women's garment industry it might be only a few months; in the cement industry it might be a year or two; in the distilled liquor industry, more than four years would be required to develop aged stocks of whiskey.

The longer the lag period in question, the less influence any given threat of entry will be likely to have on established sellers. The fact that establishing a price at some given level may induce three new firms to enter the industry is more likely to deter established firms from setting so high a price if the entry will be made effective in six months than if it will be made effective in six years. The *effect* of any given condition of entry on market behavior will therefore be likely to vary with the length of the entry lags which accompany it.

Whether the 'value' of the condition of entry should be modified to reflect the length of entry lags seems principally a semantic issue. Because there is logically no unique method of combining measures of an entry-inducing price gap and an entry lag, we will follow the convention here of defining or evaluating the condition of entry to any industry without reference to entry lags – i.e. in terms of the excess of an entry-inducing price over a competitive level, whatever the lag. We will, however, consider data on entry lags as supplementary information useful in predicting the consequences of the condition of entry as defined. This procedure seems to place entry lags in their proper role in analysis.

The determinants of the condition of entry

Once the condition of entry has been so defined and measured, the next question is what *determines* the condition of entry to any industry. What is the nature of the advantages that established firms may possess, and what technological or institutional circumstances give rise to these advantages?

The identity of the immediate determinants of the condition of entry is suggested by considering the characteristics ordinarily attributed to a situation of theoretical 'easy entry'. In modern price theory, 'easy entry' is ordinarily conceived as a situation in which there is no impediment to the entry of new firms, in which established firms possess no advantages over potential entrant firms, or in which, more precisely, established firms cannot persistently elevate price by any amount above the competitive minimal-cost level without attracting sufficient new entry to bring price back to that level. The condition of entry, as we have seen, can be measured by the percentage by which the prices of established firms can exceed the competitive level without attracting entry. Then with easy entry, the immediate condition of entry has a value of *zero* at every point in any possible sequence of entry (each added entrant firm has no disadvantage relative to those already established), and the general condition of entry is correspondingly represented by a single zero value. Entry, of course, ceases to be easy and becomes more difficult as values of the condition of entry progressively in excess of zero are encountered, or as at one point or another in the progression of entry established firms can receive super-competitive prices without inducing entry.

The essential characteristics of the situation in which easy entry prevails should furnish a direct clue to the determinants of the condition of entry in general. For easy entry, three conditions must in general be simultaneously fulfilled. At any stage in the relevant progression of entry (a) *established firms have no absolute cost advantages* over potential entrant firms; (b) *established firms have no product differentiation advantages* over potential entrant firms; and (c) *economies of large-scale firm are negligible*, in the sense that the output of a firm of optimal (lowest-cost) scale is an insignificant fraction of total industry output. Let us see briefly what each of these conditions means and why it is important.

The condition that with easy entry established firms should have no absolute cost advantages means that, for a given product, potential entrant firms should be able to secure just as low a minimal average cost of production after their entry as established firms had prior to this entry. This in turn implies (a) that established firms should have no price or other advantages over entrants in purchasing or securing any productive factor (including investible funds); (b) that the entry of an added firm should have no perceptible effect on the going level of any factor price; and (c) that established firms have no preferred access to productive techniques. If these conditions are fulfilled, then established firms, if they should wish to elevate price above the competitive level without attracting entry, have no ability to do so by virtue of the fact that the *level* of their costs is any lower than potential entrant firms will be able to secure. Established firms (before entry) and the entrant (after entry) have costs on the same level for any given product. If product differentiation exists, the equivalent of this condition must be fulfilled.

The condition that with easy entry there should be no product differentiation advantage to established firms means either that there must be no product differentiation or that, if product differentiation is present, potential entrant firms should be able to secure a relationship of price to cost just as favorable as that enjoyed by established firms. Generally, if the possibility of differences in products, production costs and selling costs is recognized, the potential entrant firm should always be able to secure as favorable a relation of price to unit production plus selling cost as established firms, so that established firms can never make a profit when an entrant could not, or break even when an entrant would lose money. For this to be true, there must be no net price or selling-cost advantage accruing to established firms by reason of buyer preferences for their products, and also no price advantages in securing factors of production. The condition of lack of product differentiation advantages is obviously essential to easy entry, since otherwise established firms could raise their prices somewhat above the competitive level without creating a situation in which potential entrants could sell profitably.

The condition that there should be no significant economies to the large-scale firm means of course that an entrant firm, even if it enters at an optimal or lowest-cost scale, will add so little to industry output that its entry will have no perceptible effect on going prices in the industry. In order to avail itself of the lowest costs available to established firms, the entrant need not augment industry output enough to make the industry price less attractive; thus, the pursuit of economies of scale to the ultimate is possible and provides no deterrent to entry. The importance of this condition is evident when we consider the opposite possibility.

If, in order to enter at optimal scale, a firm must add a significant fraction to industry output, several possibilities are open. If established firms maintain their going outputs, entry at such a scale will tend in general to bring about a reduction of industry price. If they maintain or increase their prices, the obtainable market share for the entrant may very well be insufficient to permit optimal scale operations. Furthermore, retaliatory pricing by established firms may be engendered, and entry at a scale small enough not to disturb the market will require suboptimal scale and higher costs.

In one way or another, entry tends to be deterred sufficiently so that established firms are probably enabled to elevate price at least somewhat above the lowest-cost level without inducing entry. The potential entrant, if he enters at significantly large scales himself, will probably expect or fear either an industry price after entry which is somewhat below that which prevails before entry, or a market share involving costs above those of optimal scale.[2] Thus he will probably not be induced to enter by a somewhat super-competitive industry price. If he considers entry at insignificant scales, he will have costs above the competitive level and thus again will not be induced to enter by a somewhat super-competitive price. Significant economies of scale thus tend to impede entry, and their absence is generally essential to easy entry.

The three conditions just described are both necessary and sufficient for easy entry to exist. If this is true, it is clear that we have by implication identified the sources of departure from easy

2. Instances are logically conceivable in which a market share permitting lowest-cost scale could be secured by an entrant – e.g. where established firms were generally of super-optimal scale before entry, so that sellers in general would not be forced to suboptimal scales by sharing the market among more of them. But that this, plus the absence of some retaliation in price by established firms, should be found seems unlikely.

entry and the immediate determinants of the condition of entry as defined.

Departures of the condition of entry from the 'zero pole' of easy entry must be attributable to one or more of the following: (a) absolute cost advantages of established firms; (b) product differentiation advantages of established firms; and (c) significant economies of large-scale firms. Correspondingly, the heights of barriers to entry, or the 'values' of the condition of entry (expressed as the percentages by which established firms can set prices above a competitive level while forestalling entry), will clearly depend on the degree of these absolute cost and product differentiation advantages and on the extent of scale economies to large firms. The specific nature of these determinants of the condition of entry are presumably more or less obvious, but a brief summary of their character will serve to suggest the character of the institutional and other conditions from which they arise.

Absolute cost advantages to established firms will in general arise from one of three things: (a) the entry of a single firm may perceptibly elevate one or more factor prices paid by both established firms and the entrant firm, thus raising the level of costs; (b) established firms may be able to secure the use of factors of production, including investible funds, at lower prices than potential entrants can; (c) established firms may have access to more economical techniques of production than potential entrants, thus enabling them to secure lower costs. Such absolute cost advantages tend to give established firms a lower level of costs than the potential entrant, and thus enable them to set prices above a competitive level while still forestalling entry.

Product differentiation advantages of established firms result, of course, from the preferences of buyers for established as compared to new entrant products. What will constitute an effective product differentiation advantage will depend on the importance of economies of scale in production and selling in the industry. If there are no economies of scale, so that unit production plus selling costs are not increased by restricting output to very small amounts, a potential entrant firm may be said to be without disadvantage if he can receive as high a price relative to unit cost as established firms *at some output*, even though he is able to do so only at a much smaller output than established firms. (Existence of a large number of such potential entrants – even though each was restricted in sales volume – would provide easy entry.) Conversely, possession of an advantage by established firms in the case of no scale economies requires their ability to secure at some output a higher price or lower selling cost – or generally a higher ratio of price to production plus selling cost – than the most favored potential entrants can secure at any output.[3] Existence of such product differentiation advantages is possible and would confer on established firms the ability to elevate price above a competitive level while forestalling entry.

If there are some systematic economies of scale to the firm, so that unit costs of production plus selling decline relative to price over some range of outputs, absence of advantage to established sellers requires the ability of entrants in general to attain not only comparable prices but also to obtain them at comparable sales volumes and thus to secure comparable costs as well. Conversely, the possession of advantage by established firms would require only that they be able to sell at a higher price than potential entrants can at approximately optimal scales, even though potential entrants could gain a price parity at small and inefficient scales. In effect, entrants, in order to lack disadvantage, must not only get parity in price, but must get it at economically large sales volumes.

Not much more need be said of the nature of advantages to established firms that are inherent in substantial economies to the large-scale firm. The fact that an entrant must add significantly to industry output to attain lowest costs, and would have perceptibly higher costs at smaller outputs, bestows on established firms the ability to elevate price somewhat above the competitive level without attracting entry. The economies in question may be either those of large-scale production and distribution, or, as suggested in the preceding footnote, those of large-scale sales promotion. Clearly, the advantage of established firms is increased and the

3. A variant of this is that the potential entrants could, in the absence of scale economies *other than* price or selling-cost advantages of large-scale sales promotion, secure an equivalent price relative to unit costs, but only at an output constituting a significant fraction of the market. In this event the established firms would also enjoy some net advantage, although it would be attributable in some sense to the significance of scale economies *per se*.

condition of entry becomes more difficult both as the optimal scale of the firm becomes larger relative to the market, and as the rise of costs at smaller scales becomes steeper.

A question related to these immediate determinants of the condition of entry as we have defined it concerns the identity of the basic institutional and technological circumstances that give rise to the various immediate deterrents to entry. No exhaustive treatment is required here, but the following tabulation suggests the sorts of circumstances which typically give rise to impeded entry and which may logically be the subject of an investigation bearing generally upon the condition of entry:

Typical circumstances giving rise to an absolute cost advantage to established firms

1. Control of production techniques by established firms, via either patents or secrecy. (Such control may permit exclusion of entrants from access to optimal techniques, or alternatively the levying of a discriminatory royalty charge for their use.)

2. Imperfections in the markets for hired factors of production (e.g. labor, materials, etc.) which allow lower buying prices to established firms; alternatively ownership or control of strategic factor supplies (e.g. resources) by established firms, which permits either exclusion of entrants from such supplies, driving entrants to use inferior supplies, or discriminatory pricing of supplies to them.

3. Significant limitations of the supplies of productive factors in specific markets or submarkets for them, relative to the demands of an efficient entrant firm. Then an increment to entry will perceptibly increase factor prices.

4. Money-market conditions imposing higher interest rates upon potential entrants than upon established firms. (These conditions are apparently more likely to be effective as a source of advantage to established firms as the absolute capital requirement for an efficient entrant increases.)

Typical circumstances giving rise to a product-differentiation advantage to established firms

1. The accumulative preference of buyers for established brand names and company reputations, either generally or except for small minorities of buyers.

Joe S. Bain 175

2. Control of superior product designs by established firms through patents, permitting either exclusion of entrants from them or the levying of discriminatory royalty charges.

3. Ownership or contractual control by established firms of favored distributive outlets, in situations where the supply of further outlets is other than perfectly elastic.

Typical circumstances discouraging entry by sustaining significant economies of the large-scale firm

1. Real economies (i.e. in terms of quantities of factors used per unit of output) of large-scale production and distribution such that an optimal firm will supply a significant share of the market.

2. Strictly pecuniary economies (i.e. monetary economies only, such as those due to the greater bargaining power of large buyers) of large-scale production, having a similar effect.

3. Real or strictly pecuniary economies of large-scale advertising or other sales promotion, having a similar effect.

These circumstances are in a sense the ultimate determinants of the condition of entry to an industry. We have emphasized throughout that the condition of entry is a structural concept, and that it is evaluated by the extent to which established firms can, on the average over a long period, elevate price above a long-run competitive level while still forestalling entry. Consistently, the ultimate determinants of the condition of entry either reflect or refer directly to long-run structural characteristics of markets, and it is these which determine the condition of entry as we have defined it here.

If these are the determinants of the conditions of entry, we should be equally clear about the things that are *not* its determinants. The true determinants are the things that determine for established firms the possible price–cost relations which would and would not induce entry; they are not those things determining whether or not actual entry takes place at a particular time. Thus, although the persistent product-differentiation advantage of established firms is a true determinant of the condition of entry, the current and transitory relation of industry demand to capacity is not.

It is true, of course, that if an industry is currently plagued with heavy excess capacity (caused, for example, by a secular decline in demand against long-lived plants) prices may average below costs and no entry may take place for many years. But this does not necessarily mean that the condition of entry is therefore difficult, for it does not remove the fact that a persistent slight excess of price above minimal long-run average costs (perhaps unlikely to occur in this situation) could be sufficient to induce entry. We must thus in general reject current secular or cyclical movements of demand, capacity and cost as determinants of the condition of entry to an industry, just as we reject the current record of accomplished entry as direct or conclusive evidence of what the condition of entry is. Such things as the relationship of demand to capacity in an industry would affect the condition of entry as defined only so far as they persisted in a given state for some time, and so far as, in addition, they affected the manner in which potential entrants would react to given persistent differences between the actual price and a competitive price.[4]

We have by now frequently noted that the condition of entry to an industry is a structural and long-term condition. But that does not mean it is necessarily permanent and immutable. The basic structural characteristics of a market can change, and the condition of entry may then change in response. Thus the discovery of new deposits of a given natural resource might undercut the absolute cost advantage held by established processing firms which had controlled all previously known deposits; the development of a new product design by an outsider might reduce the product-differentiation advantages of established sellers of similar products; technological changes might either increase or decrease the economies of large-scale production in any line at any time. When such changes take place, the condition of entry to any industry will tend to be altered.

This raises the question whether the condition of entry and its determinants are sufficiently stable through time so that they may

4. The principal possible exception would occur if monotonic long-term secular movements in demand or cost, followed by lagging adjustments of industry capacity, caused potential entrants to react differently to given persistent differences between the prices of established firms and their minimal costs. That the reaction of potential entrants might be affected in this way seems entirely possible.

be viewed provisionally as quasi-independent long-run determinants of market behavior. If the condition of entry and its determinants change slowly through time and are not easily subject to deliberate alteration by the action of potential entrants, and if they thus represent primarily a structural framework for market behavior rather than a result of this behavior, this is a legitimate view. On the other hand, of course, is the possibility that the condition of entry is a sort of unstable will-o'-the-wisp rapidly changing through time, or that it is readily altered by the action of potential entrants. In this event, is should hardly be studied as a long-run structural determinant of market behavior.

It is definitely posited for purposes of the present study – on the basis of extensive empirical observation – that the condition of entry as defined and its ultimate determinants are usually stable and slowly changing through time, and are not generally susceptible to alteration by prospective entrants to various markets. Thus the condition of entry and the various specific advantages of established firms which fix its value may in general be viewed as long-run structural determinants of enterprise action.

This generalization, like many others about economic affairs, is, of course, true only subject to exceptions, or as a representation of a general tendency. Certainly the condition of entry has shifted fairly rapidly over time in a few industries, and certainly potential entrants periodically have succeeded in changing it to their advantage in some cases. Nevertheless, these exceptions seem infrequent and unusual enough to justify our proceeding on the basis of our assumption.

Only one specific exception may deserve special attention as we study various industries. In some industries (though definitely not in a majority of them), the ability of potential entrants to make effective product innovations has periodically broken down the product advantages of established firms and effectively eased entry to the markets in question. Here, the role of existing product preferences as structural determinants of action can be questioned. It will be interesting to see if we can identify some more fundamental determinants of the condition of entry in this area, in the shape of those things which determine whether or not potential entrants are likely to be in a position to make effective product innovations. [...]

The content and organization of the study

We have now defined the condition of entry, identified its determinants, and summarized theoretical predictions concerning its influence on business performance. The condition of entry to industries appears as a potentially significant dimension of market structure, with a substantial influence on the market behavior of business enterprises.

The predictions presented are 'theoretical' in that they are logical deductions concerning what the importance of the condition of entry should be; they are also highly general, in that they predict the consequences of various logically possible sorts of condition of entry rather than of specifically known sorts of condition of entry found in actual industries. Since a theoretical approach to the topic does have these limitations, in an empirical study of the condition of entry it would be desirable:

1. To ascertain in detail, for each of a large and representative sample of industries, the value of the condition of entry and the identity and relative importance of its various determinants.

2. To develop empirical generalizations concerning the extent and pattern of the differences in the condition of entry among industries, and concerning the relative and absolute importance as barriers to entry of economies of scale, product differentiation, and absolute cost differentials.

3. To test for associations of the condition of entry to market performance, and thus accept or reject various predictions concerning probable associations.

As is usual in economic investigations, our reach exceeds our grasp. Limitations of time and of data restrict the sample of industries studied; information on the character and determinants of the condition of entry in these industries is not entirely adequate; available performance data permit only a rather fragmentary testing for the association of the condition of entry to market performance. Thus restrained, we have been able in this study to analyse the condition of entry and its determinants for a sample of twenty American manufacturing industries, assembling relevant data already on hand and developing a considerable body of new data; to frame some inductive generalizations concerning the importance of various barriers to entry to the twenty industries; to assemble available data measuring certain aspects of market performance in these industries; and to make a few preliminary and partial tests for predicted associations of the condition of entry to market performance.

Although our findings are thus tentative, based on less than completely adequate data, and limited to a relatively small sample of industries, they seem to develop enough new information to justify presentation and discussion.

[In the next section, Professor Bain described the methods employed in assembling and analysing data. These are also described in his 'Economies of scale' paper (Reading 3), in which he reported on other results derived from the same study. The description of methods is therefore omitted here. Ed.]

Results

The results are set forth briefly in Tables 1 and 2 in which industries are ranked as having aggregate entry barriers either 'very high', 'substantial' or 'moderate or low'. It is hazardous to assign any absolute values to the entry barriers corresponding to these three rankings, but the very roughest sort of a guess would be as follows: (a) that in the 'very high' category, established firms might be able to elevate price 10 per cent or more above minimal costs while forestalling entry; (b) that with 'substantial' barriers, the corresponding percentage might range a bit above or below 7 per cent; (c) that in the 'moderate to low' category the same percentage will probably not exceed 4, and will range down to around 1 per cent in the extreme entries in this group. All the absolute magnitudes are quite speculative, because both of the 'guess-estimated' character of much of the basic data and of theoretical uncertainty concerning the effect on entry of certain estimated situations. [. . .]

The tabulation in Table 4 suggests that there is a distinct cleavage in average profit rates between industries with 'very high' entry barriers and all other industries; but that a similarly distinct difference within the 'all other' group is not apparent between industries with 'substantial' and 'moderate to low' barriers. The first difference would almost certainly prove to be statistically significant; the second probably would not. It thus appears that our prediction of the association of the condition of

Table 1 Summary of Relative Heights of Specific Entry
Barriers in Twenty Industries
(Higher Numbers Denote Higher Entry Barriers)[c]

Industry	Scale-economy barrier	Product-differentiation barrier[a]	Absolute-cost barrier	Capital-requirement barrier
Automobiles	III	III	I	III
Canned goods	I	I to II	I	I
Cement	II	I	I	II
Cigarettes	I	III	I	III
Copper	n.a.	I	III	n.a.
Farm machinery	II	I to III	I	n.a.
Flour	I	I to II	I	ϕ
Fountain pens	n.a.	I to III	I	I
Gypsum products[b]	n.a.	I	III	I
Liquor	I	III	I	II
Meat packing	I	I	I	ϕ or I
Metal containers[b]	n.a.	II	I	I
Petroleum refining	II	II	I	III
Rayon	II	I	I	II
Shoes	II	I to II	I	ϕ
Soap	II	II	I	II
Steel	II	I	III	III
Tires and tubes	I	II	I	II
Tractors	III	III	I	III
Typewriters	III	III	I	n.a.

a. Alternative ratings refer generally to different product lines within an industry.

b. Product-differentiation rating refers to the period subsequent to 1950. A rating of III is probably indicated for earlier periods.

c. Category III is, of course, open-ended.

entry to the profit rate is confirmed as far as it distinguishes 'very high' entry barriers from others, predicting higher profits with the first sort of barrier.

The tentative finding of no great difference in profit rates between industries of 'substantial' and 'moderate to low' entry barriers would potentially accord with our predictions *if* in most of the industries in the latter category the firms involved viewed entry as 'ineffectively impeded' – that is, viewed the barriers as low enough to encourage them to strive for relatively high, entry-attracting prices rather than to set prices sufficiently low to fore-stall entry. This could lead at least periodically to profit rates in

Table 2 Ranking of Twenty Manufacturing Industries According to the Estimated Height of the Aggregate Barrier to Entry

A. *Industries with very high entry barriers*	
Automobiles	Liquor
Cigarettes	Tractors
Fountain pens ('quality' grade)	Typewriters
B. *Industries with substantial entry barriers*	
Copper	Shoes (high-priced men's and specialities)
Farm machines (large, complex)	Soap
Petroleum refining	Steel
C. *Industries with moderate to low entry barriers*	
Canned fruits and vegetables[a]	Meat packing[a]
Cement	Metal containers[b]
Farm machinery (small, simple)	Rayon
Flour[a]	Shoes (women's and low-priced men's)
Fountain pens (low-priced)	Tires and tubes
Gypsum products[b]	

a. The barriers to entry for meat packing generally, and for major segments of the flour and canned goods industries, lie at the 'low' extreme.

b. Refers to period subsequent to 1950. Classification under group B is indicated for earlier periods.

this latter category roughly as high as those resulting from the entry-forestalling limit prices anticipated in industries with 'substantial' entry barriers, although such profits in the 'moderate to low' barrier category would then be expected to be associated with structural instability and recurrent excess capacity. This last condition is apparently met in at least three of the seven industries in the 'moderate to low' barrier category – cement, flour and shoes – and it is not ruled out in the case of meat packing and canned goods.

Table 3 Number of Industries of 'High' and of 'Moderate to Low' Concentration which have Industry Average Profit Rates[a] on Equity of Specified Sizes, 1936–40 and 1947–51

Size of industry average profit rate on equity (after income taxes) in percentage points	Number of industries with average profit rates in specified ranges of percentage points			
	1936–40		1947–51	
	Industries of 'high' seller concentration	Industries of 'moderate to low' seller concentration	Industries of 'high' seller concentration	Industries of 'moderate to low' seller concentration
25–25·9	1			
24–24·9				
23–23·9			1	
22–22·9				
21–21·9	1		1	
20–20·9				
19–19·9				
18–18·9	1		3	
17–17·9				
16–16·9				
15–15·9	2		2	
14–14·9			1	
13–13·9	2		1	1
12–12·9			2	1
11–11·9	1			2
10–10·9		1		1
9– 9·9	1			1
8– 8·9	2	1		
7– 7·9	1	1		
6– 6·9		1		
5– 5·9		1		1
4– 4·9				
3– 3·9		3		

a. Industry average profit rates are simple averages of the profit rates of dominant firms, as identified above.

The findings are thus potentially consistent with our hypothesis about the association of profit rates to the condition of entry in this crucial range. The available data, however, are not sufficient to permit us to say that the hypothesis (as far as it distinguishes 'effectively impeded' from 'ineffectively impeded' entry) has been either confirmed or disconfirmed. The only clear finding relates to the distinction between industries with 'very high' and lower absolute entry barriers. Industries with very high absolute barriers (and probably either 'blockaded' or 'effectively

Table 4 Number of Industries with 'Very High', 'Substantial' and 'Moderate to Low' Barriers to Entry which have Industry Average Profit Rates[a] on Equity of Specified Sizes, 1936–40 and 1947–51

Size of industry average profit rate on equity (after income taxes) in percentage points	Number of industries with average rates in specified ranges of percentage points					
	1936–40			1947–51		
	Industries with 'very high' entry barriers	Industries with 'substantial' entry barriers	Industries with 'moderate to low' entry barriers	Industries with 'very high' entry barriers	Industries with 'substantial' entry barriers	Industries with 'moderate to low' entry barriers
25–25·9	1					
24–24·9						
23–23·9				1		
22–22·9						
21–21·9	1			1		
20–20·9						
19–19·9						
18–18·9	1			2		1
17–17·9						
16–16·9						
15–15·9	2				2	
14–14·9					1	1
13–13·9		1	1		2	
12–12·9				1	1	1
11–11·9		1			1	1
10–10·9		1			1	1
9– 9·9		1				1
8– 8·9		2	1			
7– 7·9			2			
6– 6·9		1				
5– 5·9			1			1
4– 4·9						
3– 3·9		1	2			

a Industry average rates are simple averages of the profit rates of dominant firms, as identified above.

impeded' entry) seem to earn systematically greater rates of profit.

With respect to this finding, however, there remains a question. Is there an ascertainable *independent* influence of the condition of entry on profits, or on the contrary is there such an intercorrelation of the condition of entry and seller concentration that the separate importance of either alone cannot be ascertained?

Apparently, some independent or net influence may be ascribed to the condition of entry as apart from concentration. If the seller concentration of industries in the different entry-barrier categories in Table 4 is examined, the following appears. Although *all* five industries with 'very high' entry barriers have high seller concentration, it is also true that seven industries with only 'substantial' or 'moderate to low' entry barriers also have high seller concentration – not significantly different numerically from that of the first five – and that these seven have systematically lower profit rates than the first five. Among industries of high seller concentration, that is, the height of the barrier to entry seems to make a perceptible difference in profits.

Conversely, some independent influence may be ascribable to seller concentration *per se*. Within the 'substantial' entry barrier category the industries of high seller concentration seem on the average to have significantly higher profits than those of medium seller concentration, and within the 'moderate to low' category, a rough relationship of seller concentration to profits is again apparent. In effect, condition of entry and seller concentration are by no means perfectly intercorrelated, and both variables appear to have some independent influence on profit rates. All these conclusions, of course, rest on visual appraisal of tables and charts and not on statistical averaging and significance-test procedures.

The apparent independent influence of the condition of entry is illustrated in Table 5, which classifies the profit rates of the twelve industries *of high seller concentration* according to the heights of the barriers to entry to these industries. (It may be noted that no systematic or significant difference in seller concentration appears among the different entry-barrier categories.) There is a general appearance (stronger in 1936–40 than in 1947–51) that among industries of high seller concentration, those with very high entry barriers tended on the average to earn significantly higher profit rates than those with lesser entry barriers. This tends to confirm a part of our hypothesis concerning the relation of profits to the condition of entry. *It also suggests that seller concentration alone is not an adequate indicator of the probable incidence of extremes of excess profits and monopolistic output restriction.* The concurrent influence of the condition of entry should clearly be taken into account. When the possible associa-

Table 5

Table 5 Number of Industries, all of High Seller Concentration, with 'Very High', 'Substantial' and 'Moderate to Low' Barriers to Entry, which have Industry Average Profit Rates[a] on Equity of Specified Sizes, 1936–40 and 1947–51

Size of industry average profit rates on equity (after income taxes) in percentage points	Number of industries with average profit rates in specified ranges of percentage points					
	1936–40			1947–51		
	Industries with 'very high' entry barriers	Industries with 'substantial' entry barriers	Industries with 'moderate to low' entry barriers	Industries with 'very high' entry barriers	Industries with 'substantial' entry barriers	Industries with moderate to low entry barriers
25–25·9	1					
24–24·9						
23–23·9				1		
22–22·9						
21–21·9	1			1		
20–20·9						
19–19·9						
18–18·9	1					1
17–17·9						
16–16·9						
15–15·9	2				2	
14–14·9					1	
13–13·9		1	1		1	
12–12·9						
11–11·9		1				
10–10·9					1	
9– 9·9		1				
8– 8·9		2				
7– 7·9			1			

a. Industry average rates are simple averages of the profit rates of dominant firms, as identified above [Not included here. Ed.]

tion of the condition of entry to profits among the eight industries with moderate to low seller concentration is examined, no clear relationship is found. Since all of these industries have either 'substantial' or 'moderate to low' entry barriers (none have 'very high' barriers), and since an impact of the condition of entry on profits within this range was not found in Table 4, this finding was to be anticipated.

The preceding findings are of course based on data so incomplete and on a sample so small that no conclusive confirmation or disconfirmation of our theoretical hypotheses has been possible.

Two tentative judgements, however, emerge. First, dominant firms in industries with very high entry barriers tend systematically to earn higher profit rates than those in industries with lower barriers, even after the separate influence of seller concentration is allowed for. Second, dominant firms in industries with 'substantial' entry barriers do not appear to earn higher profit rates than those in industries with 'moderate to low' barriers. This is potentially consistent with our hypothesis, if in fact the entry barriers in the 'moderate to low' category are low enough so that the dominant firms find entry-forestalling price policies unattractive. Whether or not this crucial condition is fulfilled cannot be adequately demonstrated from available data.

Selling costs and the condition of entry

One seemingly obvious hypothesis developed from our analysis is that there should generally tend to be a positive association between the height of the product-differentiation barrier to entry to an industry and the size (measured probably as a percentage of sales) of its costs of sales promotion. This association would presumably rest on the suppositions that stronger product differentiation is ordinarily accompanied by or rests upon larger selling costs; and that higher product-differentiation barriers to entry are generally erected and maintained by higher selling costs.

Testing of this hypothesis is made difficult by the inadequacy of available data. As regards advertising, we have data for about three-quarters of our twenty industries from the Federal Trade Commission (1944), but these in general refer to a single prewar year and the basis of their calculation is not always apparent. In addition, we have been able to develop, again for about three-quarters of the industries, data on *traceable* advertising costs (periodicals, newspapers, radio and television) for the period around 1950. But these 'traceable' costs are, because of the basis of compilation and counting, short of actual advertising costs by varying and unpredictable margins, so that they do not lend themselves well to analyses involving inter-industry comparisons of advertising costs. In addition, there is the problem of sales-promotional costs other than advertising, which may be quite important in some industries. Here we have mainly the FTC estimates (from the source just mentioned) of 'selling and delivery' costs other than advertising, or alternatively of 'selling and general administrative costs' for about three-quarters of our industries. The difficulty with these data is that it is impossible to determine what proportion of the designated costs are properly classifiable as 'sales promotional', and what proportion ascribable to routine physical distribution. In consequence, only the roughest sorts of judgements can be made concerning the relation of actual sales promotion costs to the height of the product-differentiation barrier to entry.

The general findings of our analysis of this matter are as follows:

1. Industries previously classified as having slight product-differentiation barriers to entry generally have the lowest advertising costs. These include the copper, rayon, commercial flour, gypsum products, meat packing, cement, steel, low-priced men's and women's shoe, and standard canned goods industries. Nearly all of these have apparent actual advertising costs under 1·5 per cent of sales; in no case do the costs apparently run above 2·5 per cent of sales.

2. Industries classified as having moderate product-differentiation barriers to entry on the average have somewhat higher advertising costs in most cases, but generally not very large ones. These include the speciality canned good, high-priced men's shoe, metal container, tire and tube, petroleum refining, soap, and consumer-brand flour industries. Generally, actual advertising costs would appear to run from 2 to 5 per cent of sales in these industries. They are higher, however, for the soap industry (6 to 10 per cent of sales) and lower for metal containers and petroleum refining, although in the last case non-advertising promotional costs appear to be fairly important.

3. Among six industries with great product-differentiation barriers to entry, there are three for which apparent actual advertising costs are high – running from 5 to 8 per cent of sales. These are the cigarette, liquor, and quality fountain-pen industries. In three others, however – autos, tractors and farm machinery and typewriters – apparent actual advertising costs run only from 1·5 to 3 or 4 per cent of sales, although in each of these cases qualitative evidence suggests that non-advertising sales-promotion costs are quite substantial. If this is so, all indus-

tries in this category have selling costs in the highest range.[4] Unfortunately, data on non-advertising sales-promotion costs are so sketchy that no more precise judgements are possible. These tentative findings are not inconsistent with our hypothesis, but they could scarecely be said to verify it in detail.

The condition of entry and the workability of competition

Because of the incomplete nature of the check on our predictions of the association of performance to the condition of entry, as well as the limited scope of these predictions, it is not possible to state any definite conclusions on how the condition of entry affects the workability of competition. A few extremely tentative indications are apparent, however.

First, industries with very high barriers to entry tend more toward high excess profits and monopolistic output restriction than others. If in addition they have great product-differentiation barriers to entry (they do in five of six cases), they probably tend toward high and possibly excessive costs of sales promotion. In their favor it may be said that wastes of inefficiently small scale and excess capacity are not beyond the normal limit among them.

Second, industries with somewhat lower though still substantial barriers to entry tend toward smaller excess profits, smaller selling costs and a lesser degree of monopolistic output restriction. In addition, they generally have a reasonably efficient adjustment of plant and firm scales and of total capacity relative to demand. Some 'degree of monopoly' is usually apparent in the performance of these industries, but it is clearly moderated in comparison with those in the first group. Competition seems, on the basis of the limited range of criteria here applied, 'more

4. A possible qualifying argument is that by incurring these large advertising costs, and concurrently exploiting advantages of large-scale promotion, firms in these industries attain lower physical costs of nationwide distribution than they otherwise might. This is not impossible in one sense – namely that there are conceivable alternatives, retaining product differentiation and nationwide promotion but restricting the promotional budgets of individual firms, which would possibly elevate distribution costs. But it could hardly be argued – theoretically or from the evidence – that distribution costs would be higher in the substantial absence of product differentiation and sales promotion, or under every conceivable alternative pattern of product differentiation and promotion. This distinction is clearly relevant to regulatory problems.

workable' than in the first group – apparently or possibly because of the greater force of potential competition.

Third, industries with 'moderate to low' barriers to entry do not appear to score significantly better in the matter of excess profits and output restriction than those with 'substantial' barriers, though they do no worse and perhaps better in the matter of selling costs. Some of them at least, however, are apparently plagued with the inefficiency of chronic or recurrent excess capacity, the possible origin of which has been rationalized above. It is not generally clear that the lower barriers to entry in this category are associated with a more workable competition than is found in the middle category, and the reverse is possibly true.

Fourth, seller concentration may tend to affect the workability of competition within given categories of industries as identified according to the height of the barrier to entry. In particular, performance may be generally more satisfactory among industries with 'substantial' or 'moderate to low' entry barriers if seller concentration is moderate or low rather than high. But seller concentration alone does not appear to be an adequate criterion of the workability of competition, since high seller concentration seems to be connected with significantly different sorts of performance, depending on the height of the barrier to entry.

Finally, as indicated above, the main culprit in establishing excessive or very high barriers to entry would appear to be product differentiation. It is a strong contributing factor in two cases where such barriers are found (automobiles and typewriters) and the dominant factor in the other three (cigarettes, liquor, quality fountain pens). Extremes in differentiation between established and potential-entrant products spell difficulty with respect to the barrier to entry. On the other hand, moderate product-differentiation barriers to entry may be relatively innocuous. Extreme scale economies pose a serious problem in perhaps only two of the twenty industries studied.

References

BAIN, J. S. (1954), 'Conditions of entry and emergence of monopoly', in E. H. Chamberlin (ed.), *Monopoly and Competition and Their Regulation*, Macmillan.
FEDERAL TRADE COMMISSION (1944), *Distribution Methods and Costs*, pt 5.

9 E. H. Chamberlin

Product Heterogeneity and Public Policy

Excerpt from E. H. Chamberlin, *Towards A More General Theory of Value*, Oxford University Press, 1957, chapter 5.

It has been remarked by Mr Triffin that 'for the historian of economic thought, the most revolutionary feature of monopolistic competition theories will probably be the unprecedented pace at which they conquered their audience' (1940). Interpreting this as he does, mainly in terms of the appearance in textbooks for the first time of chapters on oligopoly, product differentiation and selling costs, he may be right. But I must again lament the widespread misunderstanding of the subject; so that what has 'conquered' appears often to be something quite foreign to the theory, at least as I understand it. Nowhere is this more true than in that part of the whole subject which is taken up in this paper, the reorientation of our ideas as to public policy in view of the fact of product heterogeneity.

Public policy must be presumed to seek in some sense the general welfare, and hence in the economic sphere it implies a welfare economics. The supremacy of pure competition with its corollary of price equal to marginal costs as the economic welfare ideal is well known. Lerner's 'Rule' is a quick and familiar reference (1944, p. 64). What is perhaps not so well appreciated is how explicitly monopolistic competition has been interpreted as merely indicating the nature of the departures from the ideal which need to be corrected. Thus, although it may have reoriented in some degree our ideas as to how the economic system actually works, its impact upon our conception of the model towards which we would move appears to me to have been virtually nil. I say 'towards which' in recognition of the fact that pure competition is evidently a theoretical concept, and that the practical-minded economist is often ready enough to point out that 'no one has ever advocated that it be established'. What we want, to be sure, is some kind of 'workable' competition. But ordinary (purely) competitive theory remains the chief source of our criteria as to what should be done if possible, and of the direction in which we should move so far as we can. A striking instance is the subtitle of this part of the program of these meetings: 'Can the American economy be made more competitive?' The implication is evident that if it can be it should.

Now if pure competition is the ideal, the direction in which we should move is very clear. For it is easy enough to show that the actual economy is shot full of monopoly elements, and hence that any move to get rid of them or to diminish their importance is in the right direction. The main point I want to make is that the welfare ideal itself (as well as the description of reality) involves a blend of monopoly and competition and is therefore correctly described as one of monopolistic competition. If this is true, it is no longer self-evident which way we should move, for it is no longer self-evident on which side of the ideal lies the actuality for which a policy is sought. It is possible that the economy should be made 'more competitive'; but it is also quite possible that it should be made 'more monopolistic' instead. Or perhaps, if there are faults to be found with it, it should simply be changed, towards something else which again involves both monopoly and competition, with the frank admission that, since we cannot measure monopoly and competition quantitatively, there is no way of comparing the actual with the ideal on any yardstick involving these concepts.

Let us proceed at once to the proposition that monopoly is necessarily a part of the welfare norm. In abstract terms it seems to follow very directly from the recognition that human beings are individuals, diverse in their tastes and desires, and moreover widely dispersed spatially. In so far as demand has any force as a guide to production, one would expect entrepreneurs to appeal to them in diverse ways, and thus to render the output of the economy correspondingly heterogeneous, using this term in its broadest sense to embrace not only the qualitative aspects of the product itself, but also the conditions surrounding its sale, including spatial location.[1] And since what people want – an elaborate

1. Apart from the influence of demand, output will also be heterogeneous because of the diversity of nature on the side of production; as illustrated by human services, both directly and as reflected in the products they create; and by the fact that sellers are separated spatially.

system of consumers' preferences – is the starting point in welfare economics, their wants for a heterogeneous product would seem to be as fundamental as anything could be. Heterogeneity as between producers is synonymous with the presence of monopoly; therefore monopoly is necessarily a part of the welfare ideal.

It must be emphasized that any and all monopoly is included within the general concept of heterogeneity or differentiation (although there is no implication of an identity between the actual and the ideal). A monopoly is simply a product under a single control and significantly different from others on the infinite chain of substitutes. This holds equally for a patent, a cement producer separated in space from others, a local gas utility, a toll bridge or the A & P. And they are, of course, all without exception engaged in competition with others near by on the chain of substitutes and with others generally in the system. 'Industry' or 'commodity' boundaries are a snare and a delusion – in the highest degree arbitrarily drawn and, wherever drawn, establishing at once wholly false implications both as to competition of substitutes within their limits, which supposedly stops at their borders, and as to the possibility of ruling on the presence or absence of oligopolistic forces by the simple device of counting the number of producers included. As for the *conventional* categories of industries, it seems increasingly evident to me that they have their origin, not primarily in substitution at all, but in similarity of raw materials or other inputs or of technical methods used. Glass, leather goods, drugs and medicines are obvious examples. Apart from the wide diversity of products embraced by almost any so-called 'industry', spatial separation of producers within it is an added prime obstacle to substitution in most cases. But the main point is that, even if lines were arbitrarily to be drawn, they would have literally nothing to do with the extent and character of the heterogeneity, either within such an industry or beyond it, which would be defensible from the point of view of welfare or of public policy.

All this is in striking contrast with prevailing notions of the significance of product heterogeneity for public policy. The reason is, I believe, mainly a difference in the implications of monopolistic competition on the one hand and of imperfect competition on the other; and the fact that the prevailing notions on public policy have been derived largely from an interpretation which follows the latter. It is worth noting that the terms product and market are used consistently in *The Theory of Monopolistic Competition*, not in their usual broad sense, but with reference only to the individual firm. There are no 'commodities', such as shoes, sheets or shaving brushes, but only groupings of individual products. The term industry was carefully avoided, and does not appear at all (except where its limitations are being pointed out). By contrast, Mrs Robinson (1933, p. 17), followed the tradition of competitive theory, not only in identifying a commodity (albeit elastically defined) with an industry, but in expressly assuming such a commodity to be homogeneous. Such a theory involves no break whatever with the competitive tradition. The very terminology of 'imperfect competition' is heavy with implications that the objective is to move towards 'perfection'.

Even within the terminology of monopolistic competition, the same tendencies have appeared in the connotation which the term differentiation has taken on to many as of something superficial. (Hence the term heterogeneous in this paper.) It is often conceived as describing the reprehensible creation by businessmen of purely factitious differences between products which are by nature fundamentally uniform. In this vein, some have even gone so far as to attribute differentiation, and monopolistic competition generally, to 'imperfect knowledge' (Knight, 1946, p. 104; Stigler, 1946, pp. 214–15, 329), as though the individuality of particular products could be dismissed as an optical illusion based upon ignorance – a purely psychic phenomenon. There seems, on the contrary, to be as much reason for people to lack knowledge of the differences between products as for them to lack knowledge of their similarities; and there is a good prima facie case for believing that 'perfect knowledge' (while causing major shifts in individual preferences) would leave a system in which there were more and stronger preferences than ever. Certainly the consumer research organizations, which are engaged in perfecting the knowledge of their subscribers as to the goods they contemplate purchasing, are as much concerned with differences as with similarities.

Another device for leveling off the heterogeneous output of the economy into a series of purely competitive industries is the distinction between 'rational' and 'irrational' preferences, with its heavy implication that a substantial part of actual preferences are of the latter category. The distinction is not without its complications; but the test is supposedly simple: 'If a consumer were *forced* to have B's goods instead of A's goods, would he feel worse off after the change had taken place? If, in fact, he would consider himself to be worse off, the buyers' preference is rational; if not, it is irrational' (Meade, 1937, p. 155).[2] The conclusion is, of course, that if irrational buyers' preference exists, 'then the community clearly gains by the concentration of the industry's output on a smaller number of firms'. It need only be commented that the argument, for whatever validity it may have, should not be limited in its application to an arbitrarily defined industry, but should be applied generally. On the one hand, it may be said that if Palmolive were abolished, people might be no 'worse off' after they had got used to using Lux and Lifebuoy instead. But on the other hand, it is equally true that if baseball were abolished and bull fights substituted, people might be equally well or better satisfied after they were adjusted to the change, in which case their preferences for baseball should be classified as irrational. Similarly, many people have stopped smoking and, after they got used to it, were no more unhappy than before. There is a case, of course, for improving knowledge in all these matters, but no reason to think that improved knowledge would leave us with fewer or weaker preferences. In some cases it seems clear that increased standardization of certain products by public authority is indicated, as when oligopolistic forces are supporting an unduly large number of producers (Chamberlin, 1933, pp. 100–109), or when the gain in efficiency is judged by proper authorities to be more important than the losses in consumers' surplus through abandoning certain products. But the labeling of most preferences within an arbitrarily defined industry as irrational seems to me to indicate mainly a preference for the purely competitive ideal, and an attempt, perhaps largely unconscious, to salvage it. The alternative is not necessarily to assume that all preferences are rational, but only that they are on the same footing – in other words, to make no invidious distinctions between them as to

2. I believe the distinction was first made by Kahn (1935). It is criticized by Galbraith (1938).

rationality on the basis of the relative proximity of substitutes.

It might be added that no invidious distinctions are indicated either on the basis of whether or not the demands for particular products are influenced by selling expenditures. Here again, stress on irrational preferences makes an easy transition to the labeling of those established by advertising as irrational, and to the conventional sweeping condemnation of advertising as a 'competitive waste' (Meade, 1937, pp. 165–6). Granted that the techniques of modern advertising are often a shocking affront to good taste, or objectionable on other grounds, it remains true, so far as I can see, that the question of whether advertising is wasteful or not, in the sense of being a misallocation of resources, simply cannot be answered by any criteria derived from market demand and cost curves – or from indifference curves either. Here is a major aspect of 'welfare' which appears to lie quite outside the conventional analysis of the subject. The general condemnation of advertising as a waste surely has its primary explanation in the irrelevancy that it could not exist under the perfectly competitive ideal.

The fact that equilibrium for the firm when products are heterogeneous normally takes place under conditions of falling average costs of production has generally been regarded as a departure from ideal conditions, these latter being associated with the minimum point on the curve; and various corrective measures have been proposed. However, if heterogeneity is part of the welfare ideal, there is no prima facie case for doing anything at all. It is true that the same total resources (either within some arbitrarily defined industry or within the whole economy) may be made to yield more units of product by being concentrated on fewer firms. The issue might be put as efficiency versus diversity – more of either one means less of the other. But unless it can be shown that the loss of satisfaction from a more standardized product (again, either within an 'industry' or for the economy as a whole) is less than the gain through producing more units, there is no 'waste' at all, even though every firm is producing to the left of the its minimum point.

How are the two to be compared – a larger, less heterogeneous output as against a smaller, more heterogeneous one? The price system, especially in view of its all-pervasive oligopolistic forces and the omnipresence of selling costs whose welfare status is uncertain, appears to afford no test. If we may allow the individual producer his optimum selling expenditure, included as a lump sum in his fixed costs, and conceive a system in which every producer determines the equilibrium of his firm with reference to a demand curve which measures demand for his product at different prices while all other prices, products and selling costs do not change, we have in the elasticity of demand one index of the strength of buyers' preferences for each product.[3] If adjustment of prices along demand curves of this type could be enforced, many firms whose profits (perhaps nominal) are protected by the absence of vigorous price competition (Chamberlin, 1933, pp. 100–109) would certainly be involved in losses and would be obliged to go out of business before a general equilibrium for the whole economy were realized. There would be less heterogeneity than we find at present, and it would seem that something like what I have described elsewhere as a 'sort of ideal' (Chamberlin, 1933, p. 94)[4] would be established.

Another approach to the same problem is to test old products individually for survival and new products for admission to the economy by a consideration of the surpluses of satisfaction over cost which are sacrificed in one place and generated in another by the transfer of resources involved. Much of what has been written in this connection (Kahn, 1935; Meade, 1937) seems to me to be vitiated by entanglement with the standard theory of 'exploitation' which has evolved out of 'imperfect' competition and which I have elsewhere (Chamberlin, 1953, pp. 182–4, 215–18) shown to be fallacious – a theory in which hired factors are held to be exploited by entrepreneurs. But the theoretical criterion involved can be adapted to an analysis from which this objectionable feature is absent. Of course the old bogey of interpersonal comparisons appears at once; also the familiar problem of subsidy to the expanded firms which, if they had no extra profits before, are now, at the lower prices necessary to sell the larger output, losing

3. The curves of Mrs Robinson (1933, p. 21) cannot be used for this purpose because they are defined as including oligopolistic reactions.

4. With allowance made for the 'diversity of conditions surrounding each producer' (pp. 110–13) the ideal would evidently involve diverse outputs and prices for the individual producers in the system.

money. Unfortunately the matter is too complex to be developed in this short paper. Let us only observe that, for whatever it may be worth, the final welfare equilibrium which emerges from this analysis, as from the preceding one, would inevitably involve product heterogeneity; and that it would be characterized neither by the equation of price and marginal cost nor by production at minimum average cost for the firms involved. Indeed, by this procedure, the adjustment required from any starting point might as easily be to increase the supposedly excess number of firms as to diminish it. As an indication of what is involved, one might under this principle even revive that good old newspaper, the *Boston Transcript*, under public subsidy, since many 'proper Bostonians' were strangely attached to it and no doubt lost heavily in consumers' surplus when it finally folded up.

Let us leave this question of how many products there should be, or of diversity, to say a word about the other major type of adjustment which has been analysed in relation to product heterogeneity and welfare – that of the distribution of resources among a given number of products or among a given number of industries.

It has been proposed that resources be transferred from purely competitive industries, where price equals marginal cost, to 'imperfectly competitive industries', where price is greater than marginal cost, and similarly from less imperfectly competitive to more imperfectly competitive industries, until the ratio of price to marginal cost is the same everywhere. Such a proposal may be dismissed at once on two grounds, either one of which alone is sufficient: the boundaries of an industry being arbitrary, it is quite meaningless, and the demand and cost curves of different firms within any industry are highly diverse as to elasticity and shape. For these two reasons we must abandon altogether the idea of transferring resources in some vague way to an industry, and face the question of the firms to which they are to be attached.[5]

What, then, of equalizing the price-marginal cost ratio as between firms in the economy? Apart from other difficulties, I believe there is a fatal objection to such a conception: the

5. Kahn's analysis explicitly assumes industries in which competition is 'uniformly imperfect' (1935, p. 21), and thus lays down principles for a wholly imaginary problem.

generally prevalent oligopolistic relationships between firms. The logic by which this proposition is usually developed envisages each firm as an isolated monopoly, isolated in the sense that its output and price may be adjusted without appreciable effect on any other single firm. But where oligopolistic influences are present, there are two points to be made. First, the demand curve for any one firm, which would indicate the effect on its price of adding resources to it, cannot be known without knowing which of the many possible patterns of behavior under oligopoly will govern the case at hand. In fact, since adding resources to any one firm would, by lowering its price, inevitably shift the demand curves of others economically near it (since every curve is drawn on the assumption of given prices for other firms), there seems to be no escape from abandoning the conception of transfers between firms considered to be independent, and reconceiving it in terms of groups of some kind. Second, the effect on welfare of adding resources to one firm, where oligopolistic interdependence is involved, is a function of whether or not, and in what quantity, resources are being added at the same time to others economically near. Even assuming that the price behavior could be directed according to some socially enforced rule, the major problem would still remain of finding the rule in welfare terms. I very much fear that, because of oligopolistic interrelationships between the welfare contributions of firms, we are reduced to asserting merely that resources should be transferred from one place to another in the system whenever the net effect will be to increase welfare. This is not very illuminating.

In conclusion, the consequences of product heterogeneity for welfare economics have been either ignored or seriously misunderstood. Monopoly elements are built into the economic system and the ideal necessarily involves them. Thus wherever there is a demand for diversity of product, pure competition turns out to be not the ideal but a departure from it. Marginal cost pricing no longer holds as a principle of welfare economics (not even for toll bridges); nor is the minimum point on the cost curve for the firm to be associated with the ideal. Selling costs may no longer be excluded from the problem or dismissed as an obvious waste; yet the impossibility of discovering from the standard welfare techniques what is the socially ideal expenditure on selling suggests that the techniques are unduly narrow. It has been impossible to discuss in this paper whole families of new problems which put in their appearance with a recognition of the fact that products themselves are variables and that there must be norms for them as well as for prices, costs and outputs. What has been called the 'new welfare economics', instead of being on a 'secure basis' as suggested by Professor Hicks (1939), has quite misconceived a whole set of major problems. It is badly in need of a general overhauling.

References

CHAMBERLIN, E. H. (1933), *The Theory of Monopolistic Competition*, Oxford University Press.

GALBRAITH, J. K. (1938), 'Rational and irrational consumer preferences', *Econ. J.*, vol. 48., pp. 336–42.

HICKS, J. R. (1939), 'The foundations of welfare economics', *Econ. J.*, vol. 48, pp. 696–712.

KAHN, R. F. (1935), 'Some notes on ideal output', *Econ. J.*, vol. 45, pp. 25–6.

KNIGHT, F. H. (1946), 'Immutable law in economics: its reality and limitations', *Amer. econ. Rev.*, vol. 36, pp. 93–111.

LERNER, A. P. (1944), *The Economics of Control*, Kelley.

MEADE, J. E. (1937), *Economic Analysis and Policy*, Oxford University Press.

ROBINSON, J. (1933), *The Economics of Imperfect Competition*, Macmillan.

STIGLER, G. J. (1946), *Theory of Price*, Macmillan.

TRIFFIN, R. (1940), *Monopolistic Competition and General Equilibrium Theory*, Harvard University Press.

10 Arnold C. Harberger

Monopoly and Resource Allocation

A. C. Harberger, 'Monopoly and resource allocation', *American Economic Review Papers and Proceedings*, vol. 64, 1954, pp. 77–87.

One of the first things we learn when we begin to study price theory is that the main effects of monopoly are to misallocate resources, to reduce aggregate welfare, and to redistribute income in favor of monopolists. In the light of this fact, it is a little curious that our empirical efforts at studying monopoly have so largely concentrated on other things. We have studied particular industries and have come up with a formidable list of monopolistic practices: identical pricing, price leadership, market sharing, patent suppression, basing points, and so on. And we have also studied the whole economy, using the concentration of production in the hands of a small number of firms as the measure of monopoly. On this basis we have obtained the impression that some 20 or 30 or 40 per cent of our economy is effectively monopolized.

In this paper I propose to look at the American economy, and in particular at American manufacturing industry, and try to get some quantitative notion of the allocative and welfare effects of monopoly. It should be clear from the outset that this is not the kind of job one can do with great precision. The best we can hope for is to get a feeling for the general orders of magnitude that are involved.

I take it as an operating hypothesis that, in the long run, resources can be allocated among our manufacturing industries in such a way as to yield roughly constant returns. That is, long-run average costs are close to constant in the relevant range, for both the firm and the industry. This hypothesis gives us the wedge we need to get something from the data. For as is well known, the malallocative effects of monopoly stem from the difference between marginal cost and price, and marginal costs are at first glance terribly difficult to pin down empirically for a wide range of firms and industries. But once we are ready to proceed on the basis of constant average costs, we can utilize the fact that under such circumstances marginal and average costs are the same, and we can easily get some idea of average costs.

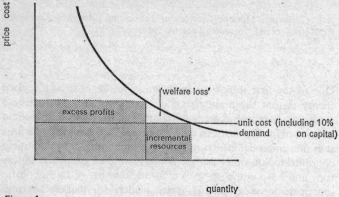

Figure 1

But that does not solve all the problems, for cost and profit to the economist are not the same things as cost and profit to the accountant, and the accountants make our data. To move into this question, I should like to conjure up an idealized picture of an economy in equilibrium. In this picture all firms are operating on their long-run cost curves, the cost curves are so defined as to yield each firm an equal return on its invested capital, and markets are cleared. I think it is fair to say that this is a picture of optimal resource allocation. Now, we never see this idyllic picture in the real world, but if long-run costs are in fact close to constant and markets are cleared, we can pick out the places where resources are misallocated by looking at the rates of return on capital. Those industries which are returning higher than average rates have too few resources; and those yielding lower than average rates have too many resources. To get an idea of how big a shift of resources it would take to equalize profit rates in all industries, we have to know something about the elasticities of demand for the goods in question. In Figure 1, I illustrate a hypothetical case. The industry in question is earning 20 per cent on a capital of ten million dollars, while the average return to capital is only 10 per cent. We therefore build a 10 per cent return into the cost curve, which leaves the industry with one million in excess profits. If the elasticity of demand for the industry's product is unity, it will take a shift of one million in resources in order to expand supply enough to wipe out the excess profits.

The above argument gives a general picture of what I have done empirically. The first empirical job was to find a period which met two conditions. First, it had to be reasonably close to a long-run equilibrium period; that is, no violent shifts in demand or economic structure were to be in process. And second, it had to be a period for which accounting values of capital could be supposed to be pretty close to actual values. In particular, because of the disastrous effect of inflation and deflation on book values of capital, it had to be a period of fairly stable prices, which in turn had been preceded by a period of stable prices. It seemed to me that the late twenties came as close as one could hope to meeting both these requirements.

The late twenties had an additional advantage for me – because my choice of this period enabled me to use Epstein's excellent study (1934) as a source of data. Epstein there gives, for the years 1924–8, the rates of total profit to total capital for seventy-three manufacturing industries, with total capital defined as book capital plus bonded indebtedness and total profit defined as book profit plus interest on the indebtedness. To get rid of factors producing short-period variations in these rates of return, I average the rates, for each industry, for the five-year period. The results are given in column 1 of Table 1. The differences among these profit rates, as between industries, give a broad indication of the extent of resource malallocation in American manufacturing in the late twenties.

Column 2 presents the amount by which the profits in each industry diverged from what that industry would have obtained if it had gotten the average rate of profit for all manufacturing industry. In column 3, these excesses and shortages of profit are expressed as a per cent of sales in the industry. By analogy with Figure 1, you can see that this column really tells by what percentage prices in each industry were 'too high' or 'too low' when compared with those that would generate an optimal resource allocation.

Table 1

Industry	Rate of profit on capital as percentage (1924–8)	Amount by which profits diverged from 'average' (millions)	Column 2 as percentage of sales	Welfare cost of divergence in column 2 (millions of dollars)
Bakery products	17·5	$17	5·3	0·452
Flour	11·9	1	0·4	0·002
Confectionery	17·0	7	6·1	0·215
Package foods	17·9	7	3·3	0·116
Dairying	11·8	3	0·7	0·010
Canned goods	12·4	1	0·6	0·003
Meat packing	4·4	−69	−1·7	0·596
Beverages	5·8	−2	−4·0	0·080
Tobacco	14·1	27	0·3	0·373
Miscellaneous foods	8·1	−13	−2·4	0·164
Cotton spinning	10·0	−0	0	0
Cotton converting	8·0	−1	−0·6	0·008
Cotton weaving	4·7	−15	−5·5	0·415
Weaving woolens	2·6	−16	−9·5	0·762
Silk weaving	7·9	−3	−2·3	0·035
Carpets	9·8	−1	−1·3	0·006
Men's clothing	11·4	1	0·5	0·002
Knit goods	12·9	3	1·9	0·028
Miscellaneous clothing	13·1	1	1·1	0·006
Miscellaneous textiles	9·2	−2	−0·9	0·008
Boots and shoes	15·8	9	3·8	0·172
Miscellaneous leather products	7·7	−3	−2·1	0·032
Rubber	7·6	−23	−2·5	0·283
Lumber manufacturing	7·8	−6	−3·9	0·118
Planing mills	13·1	1	3·2	0·016
Millwork	7·3	−1	−2·9	0·014
Furniture	13·4	2	2·2	0·022
Miscellaneous lumber	12·9	4	1·7	0·034
Blank paper	6·6	−17	−6·2	0·524
Cardboard boxes	13·6	2	3·1	0·031
Stationery	7·5	−2	−3·0	0·030
Miscellaneous paper	9·3	−1	−1·1	0·005
Newspapers	20·1	37	8·5	1·570
Books and music	14·6	2	4·3	0·042
Miscellaneous printing and publishing	18·6	1	5·6	0·028
Crude chemicals	10·2	−0	0	0
Paints	14·6	5	3·3	0·082
Petroleum refining	8·4	−114	−3·6	2·032
Proprietary preparations	20·9	25	11·7	1·460
Toilet preparations	30·4	3	15·0	0·225
Cleaning preparations	20·8	15	5·5	0·413
Miscellaneous chemicals	15·6	45	8·8	0·197
Ceramics	10·8	1	1·0	0·005

Table 1—cont.

Industry	Rate of profit on capital as percentage (1924–8)	Amount by which profits diverged from 'average' (millions)	Column 2 as percentage of sales	Welfare cost of divergence in column 2 (millions of dollars)
Glass	13·5	4	2·6	0·052
Portland cement	14·3	10	8·4	0·420
Miscellaneous clay and stone	17·6	14	8·0	0·560
Castings and forgings	5·6	−234	−7·7	8·994
Sheet metal	10·5	0	0	0
Wire and nails	11·6	1	1·2	0·006
Heating machinery	13·3	3	1·6	0·024
Electrical machinery	15·7	48	5·3	1·281
Textile machinery	13·6	3	6·1	0·092
Printing machinery	9·7	−0	0	0
Road machinery	17·3	10	6·8	0·374
Engines	13·7	2	5·9	0·059
Mining machinery	11·0	1	0·7	0·004
Factory machinery	11·7	33	3·0	0·045
Office machinery	16·1	7	5·6	0·194
Railway equipment	6·0	−24	−9·6	1·148
Motor vehicles	18·5	161	4·4	3·878
Firearms	12·9	1	2·0	0·010
Hardware	12·8	8	2·3	0·092
Tools	11·6	1	1·1	0·006
Bolts and nuts	15·4	1	3·1	0·016
Miscellaneous machinery	12·6	3	2·2	0·032
Non-ferrous metals	11·9	15	1·4	0·106
Jewelry	10·6	0	0	0
Miscellaneous metals	12·5	14	2·0	0·140
Scientific instruments	21·2	20	11·6	1·163
Toys	15·0	1	3·2	0·016
Pianos	9·9	−0	0	0
Miscellaneous special manufacturing	12·0	4	1·4	0·027
Job printing	13·8	4	2·2	0·044

Column 1. From Epstein (1934, Tables 43*D* through 53*D*). Entries in column 1 are the arithmetic means of the annual entries in the source tables.

Column 2. Divergences in the profit rates given in column 1 from their mean (10·4) are here applied to the 1928 volume of capital in each industry. Total capital is the sum of book capital (Epstein, Appendix Table 6*C*) plus bonded debt (Epstein, Appendix Table 6*D*).

Column 3. 1928 figures were used for sales (Epstein, Appendix Table 6*A*).

Column 4. Measures the amount by which consumer 'welfare' fell short of the level it would have attained if resources had been so allocated as to give each industry an equal return on capital. It assumes that the elasticity of demand for the products of each industry is unity and approximates the area designated as 'welfare loss' in Figure 1.

Now suppose we ask how much reallocation of resources it would take to eliminate the observed divergences in profit rates. This depends, as you can see in Figure 1, on the demand elasticities confronting the industries in question. How high are these elasticities? It seems to me that one need only look at the list of industries in Table 1 in order to get the feeling that the elasticities in question are probably quite low. The presumption of low elasticity is further strengthened by the fact that what we envisage is not the substitution of one industry's product against all other products, but rather the substitution of one great aggregate of products (those yielding high rates of return) for another aggregate (those yielding low rates of return). In the light of these considerations, I think an elasticity of unity is about as high as one can reasonably allow for, though a somewhat higher elasticity would not seriously affect the general tenor of my results.

Returning again to Figure 1, we can see that once the assumption of unit elasticity is made the amount of excess profit measures the amount of resources that must be called into an industry in order to bring its profit rate into line. When I say resources here I mean the services of labor and capital plus the materials bought by the industry from other industries. In many ways it seems preferable to define resources as simply the services of labor and capital. This could be done by applying to the value added in the industry the percentage of excess profits to sales. The trouble here is that adding to the output of industry X calls resources not only into that industry but also into the industries that supply it. And by the time we take all the increments in value added of all these supplying industries that would be generated by the initial increase in output of industry X, we come pretty close to the incremental value of sales in industry X. Of course, the movement to an optimal resource allocation entails some industries expanding their output, like X, and others, say Y, contracting their output. If we really traced through the increments to value added which are required in their supplying industries, say Z, we would often find that there was some cancellation of the required changes in the output of Z. Hence by using sales rather than value added as our measure of resource transfer, we rather overstate the necessary movement.

Keeping this in mind, let us return to the data. If we add up all the pluses and all the minuses in column 2, we find that to obtain equilibrium we would have to transfer about 550 million dollars in resources from low-profit to high-profit industries. But this is not the end. Those of you who are familiar with Epstein's study are aware that it is based on a sample of 2046 corporations, which account for some 45 per cent of the sales and capital in manufacturing industry. Pending a discussion of possible biases in the sample a little later, we can proceed to blow up our 550 million figure to cover total manufacturing. The result is 1·2 billion. Hence we tentatively conclude that the misallocations of resources which existed in United States manufacturing in the period 1924–8 could have been eliminated by a net transfer of roughly 4 per cent of the resources in manufacturing industry, or $1\frac{1}{2}$ per cent of the total resources of the economy.

Now let us suppose that somehow we effected these desired resource transfers. By how much would people be better off? This general question was answered in 1938 for an analogous problem by Harold Hotelling (1938).[1] His general formula would

1. The applicability of Hotelling's proof to the present problem can be seen by referring to p. 252. He there indicates that he hypothecates a transformation locus which is a hyperplane. This is given us by our assumption of constant costs. He then inquires what will be the loss in moving from a point Q on the hyperplane, at which the marginal conditions of competitive equilibrium are met, to a point Q' at which these conditions of competitive equilibrium are not met. At Q' a non-optimal set of prices P' prevails. These are, in our example, actual prices, while the equilibrium price-vector P is given by costs, defined to include normal profits. Hotelling's expression for the welfare loss in shifting from Q to Q' is $\frac{1}{2}\Sigma\, dp_i\, dq_i$ where p_i and q_i are the price and quantity of the i-th commodity. We obtain this by defining our units so that the cost of each commodity is $1·00. The equilibrium quantity of each commodity under the assumption of unit elasticities is then equal to the value of sales of that commodity. If we call r_i the percentage divergence of actual price from cost, we may write the total welfare loss due to monopoly as $\frac{1}{2}\Sigma r_i^2.\, q_i$ if the elasticities of demand are unity, and as $\frac{1}{2}\Sigma r_i^2.q_i.k_i$, if the elasticities of demand are k_i. In column 4 of Table 1, I attribute to each commodity a welfare loss equal to $\frac{1}{2}r_i^2.q_i$. This measure of the welfare loss due to monopoly abstracts from distributional considerations. Essentially it assumes that the marginal utility of money is the same for all individuals. Alternatively, it may be viewed as measuring the welfare gain which would occur if resources were shifted from producing Q' to producing Q_i and at the same time the necessary fiscal adjustments were made to keep everybody's money income the same.

be strictly applicable here if all our industries were producing products for direct consumption. The question thus arises, how to treat industries producing intermediate products. If we neglect them altogether, we would be overlooking the fact that their resource shifts and price changes do ultimately change the prices and amounts of consumer goods. If, on the other hand, we pretend that these intermediate industries face the consumer directly and thus directly affect consumer welfare, we neglect the fact that some of the resource shifts in the intermediate sector will have opposing influences on the prices and quantities of consumer goods. Obviously, this second possibility is the safer of the two, in the sense that it can only overestimate, not underestimate, the improvement in welfare that will take place. We can therefore follow this course in applying the Hotelling formula to our data. The results are shown in column 4 of Table 1. This gives, opposite each industry, the amount by which consumer welfare would increase if that industry either acquired or divested itself of the appropriate amount of resources. The total improvement in consumer welfare which might come from our sample of firms thus turns out to be about 26·5 million dollars. Blowing up this figure to cover the whole economy, we get what we really want: an estimate of by how much consumer welfare would have improved if resources had been optimally allocated throughout American manufacturing in the late twenties. The answer is fifty-nine million dollars – less than one-tenth of 1 per cent of the national income. Translated into today's national income and today's prices, this comes out to 225 million dollars, or less than $1·50 for every man, woman and child in the United States.

Before drawing any lessons from this, I should like to spend a little time evaluating the estimate. First let us look at the basic assumption that long-run costs are constant. My belief is that this is a good assumption, but that if it is wrong, costs in all probability tend to be increasing rather than decreasing in American industry. And the presence of increasing costs would result in a lowering of both our estimates. Less resources would have to be transferred in order to equalize profit rates, and the increase in consumer welfare resulting from the transfer would be correspondingly less.

On the other hand, flaws in the data probably operate to make our estimate of the welfare loss too low. Take for example the question of patents and good will. To the extent that these items are assigned a value on the books of a corporation, monopoly profits are capitalized, and the profit rate which we have used is an understatement of the actual profit rate on real capital. Fortunately for us, Professor Epstein has gone into this question in his study. He finds that excluding intangibles from the capital figures makes a significant difference in the earnings rates of only eight of the seventy-three industries. I have accordingly recomputed my figures for these eight industries.[2] As a result, the estimated amount of resource transfer goes up from about 1½ per cent to about 1¾ per cent of the national total. And the welfare loss due to resource misallocations gets raised to about eighty-one million dollars, just over a tenth of 1 per cent of the national income.

There is also another problem arising out of the data. Epstein's sample of firms had an average profit rate of 10·4 per cent during

2. Following is a breakdown of the adjustment for the eight industries in question.

Industry	Adjusted profit rate*	Adjusted rate of excess profit	Adjusted amount of excess profits (millions)	Adjusted welfare loss (millions)
Confectionery	21·1	10·7	11	0·530
Tobacco	19·0	8·6	66	2·225
Men's clothing	14·9	4·5	5	0·068
Stationery	8·8			
Newspaper publishing	27·9	17·5	67	5·148
Proprietary preparations	27·8	17·4	42	4·121
Toilet preparations	50·8	40·4	6	1·400
Printing machinery	12·9	2·5	2	0·064
			199	13·556
Less previous amount of excess profit or welfare loss			−100	−3·845
Net adjustment			99	9·711

* Epstein (1934, p. 530).

the period I investigated, while in manufacturing as a whole the rate of return was 8 per cent. The reason for this divergence seems to be an overweighting of high-profit industries in Epstein's sample. It can be shown, however, that a correct weighting procedure would raise our estimate of the welfare cost of equalizing profit rates in all industries by no more than ten million dollars.[3]

Finally, there is a problem associated with the aggregation of manufacturing into seventy-three industries. My analysis assumes high substitutability among the products produced by different firms within any industry and relatively low substitutability among the products of different industries. Yet Epstein's industrial classification undoubtedly lumps together in particular industries products which are only remote substitutes and which are produced by quite distinct groups of firms. In short, Epstein's industries are in some instances aggregates of sub-industries, and for our purposes it would have been appropriate to deal with the subindustries directly. It can be shown that the use of aggregates in such cases biases our estimate of the welfare loss downward,

3. Epstein's results in samples from small corporations (not included in his main sample) indicate that their earnings rates tend to be quite close, industry by industry, to the earnings rates of the large corporations in the main sample. This suggests that the average rate of profit in the main sample (10·4 per cent) was higher than the average for all industry (8 per cent) because high-profit industries were overweighted in the sample rather than because the sampled firms tended to be the high-profit firms within each industry. The overweighting of high-profit industries affects our estimate of the welfare cost of resource misallocations in two ways. First, quite obviously, it tends to overstate the cost by pretending that the high-profit industries account for a larger share of the aggregate product of the economy than they actually do. Second, and perhaps not so obviously, it tends to understate the cost by overstating the average rate of profit in all manufacturing, and hence overstating the amount of profit which is 'built in' to the cost curves in the present analysis. The estimated adjustment of ten million dollars presented in the text corrects only for this second effect of overweighting and is obtained by imputing as the normal return to capital in the Epstein sample only 8 per cent rather than 10·4 per cent and recomputing the welfare costs of resource misallocations by the method followed in Table 1. It takes no account of the first effect of overweighting, mentioned above, and thus results in an overstatement of the actual amount of welfare cost.

but experiments with hypothetical examples reveal that the probable extent of the bias is small.[4]

Thus we come to our final conclusion. Elimination of resource misallocations in American manufacturing in the late twenties would bring with it an improvement in consumer welfare of just a little more than a tenth of a per cent. In present values, this welfare gain would amount to about two dollars per capita.

Now we can stop to ask what resource misallocations we have measured. We actually have included in the measurement not only monopoly misallocations but also misallocations coming out of the dynamics of economic growth and development and all the other elements which would cause divergent profit rates to persist for some time even in an effectively competitive economy. I know of no way to get at the precise share of the total welfare loss that is due to monopoly, but I do think I have a reasonable way of pinning our estimate down just a little more tightly. My argument here is based on two props. First of all, I think it only reasonable to roughly identify monopoly power with high rates of profit. And secondly, I think it quite implausible that more than a third of our manufacturing profits should be monopoly profits; that is, profits which are above and beyond the normal return to capital and are obtained by exercise of monopoly power. I doubt that this second premise needs any special defense. After all, we know that capital is a highly productive resource. On the first premise, identifying monopoly power with high profits, I think we need only run down the list of high-profit industries to verify its plausibility. Cosmetics are at the top, with a 30 per cent return on capital. They are followed by scientific instruments, drugs, soaps,

4. The extent of the bias is proportional to the difference between the average of the squares of a set of numbers and the square of the average, the numbers in question being the rates of excess profit in the subindustries. Consider an industry composed of three subindustries, each of equal weight. Assume, for an extreme example, that the rates of excess profit (excess profit expressed as a per cent of sales) are 10 per cent, 20 per cent and 30 per cent in the three subindustries. The average rate of excess profit of the aggregate industry would then be 20 per cent, and, by our procedure, the estimate of the welfare loss due to that industry would be 2 per cent of its sales. If we had been able to deal with the hypothetical subindustry data directly, we would have estimated the welfare loss associated with them at $2\frac{1}{3}$ per cent of the aggregate sales.

newspapers, automobiles, cereals, road machinery, bakery products, tobacco, and so on. But even apart from the fact that it makes sense in terms of other evidence to consider these industries monopolistic, there is a still stronger reason for making this assumption. For given the elasticity of demand for an industry's product, the welfare loss associated with that product increases as the square of its greater-than-normal profits. Thus, granted that we are prepared to say that no more than a third of manufacturing profits were monopoly profits, we get the biggest welfare effect by distributing this monopoly profit first to the highest profit industries, then to the next highest, and so on. When this is done, we come to the conclusion that monopoly misallocations entail a welfare loss of no more than a thirteenth of a per cent of the national income. Or, in present values, no more than about $1·40 per capita.

Before going on, I should like to mention a couple of other possible ways in which this estimate might fail to reflect the actual cost of monopoly misallocations to the American consumer. First, there is the possibility that book capital might be overstated, not because of patents and good will, but as a result of mergers and acquisitions. In testing this possibility I had recourse to Weston's recent study of mergers (1953, pp. 100–102). He found that mergers and acquisitions accounted for only a quarter of the growth of seventy-odd corporations in the last half-century. Even a quite substantial overstatement of the portion of their capital involved in the mergers would thus not seriously affect the profit rates. And furthermore, much of the merger growth that Weston found came in the very early years of the century; so that one can reasonably expect that most of the assets which may have been overvalued in these early mergers were off the books by the period that I investigated.

The second possibility concerns advertising expenditures. These are included as cost in accounting data, but it may be appropriate for our present purpose to include part of them as a sort of quasi-monopoly profit. I was unable to make any systematic adjustment of my data to account for this possibility, but I did make a cursory examination of some recent data on advertising expenditures. They suggest that advertising costs are well under 2 per cent of sales for all of the industries in Table 1.

Adjustment of our results to allow for a maximal distorting effect of advertising expenditures would accordingly make only a slight difference, perhaps raising our estimate of the welfare cost of monopoly in present values to $1·50 per capita, but not significantly higher.[5]

I should like now to review what has been done. In reaching our estimate of the welfare loss due to monopoly misallocations of resources we have assumed constant rather than increasing costs in manufacturing industry and have assumed elasticities of demand which are too high, I believe. On both counts we therefore tend to overstate the loss. Furthermore, we have treated intermediate products in such a way as to overstate the loss. Finally, we have attributed to monopoly an implausibly large

5. I was unable similarly to take account of selling costs other than advertising expenditures, even though some of such costs may be the price paid by firms to enhance market control or monopoly position. In principle, clearly, some share of selling costs should be taken into account, and it is a limitation of the present study that no adjustment for such costs was possible. Scrutinizing Table 1, however, I should suggest that such selling costs are important in only a few of the industries listed, and that an allowance for them would almost certainly not alter the general order of magnitude of the estimates here presented. It should be pointed out, also, that the general conclusions reached in this paper are not closely dependent on the precise data used. Suppose, for example, that we had observed the following situation: industries accounting for half the output of American manufacturing were charging prices which yielded them a 10 per cent 'monopoly profit' on sales, while the remainder of industries earned a constant rate of profit on capital (here called normal profit) but no more. If we were, in this situation, to reallocate resources so as to equalize profit rates in all industries, the prices of competitive products would rise and those of monopolistic products would fall. If demand for the product of each sector were assumed to be of unit elasticity, we would estimate the gain in welfare incident upon the reallocation of resources at 0·125 per cent of total industrial sales. This would be just about a tenth of a per cent of the national income if the ratio of manufacturing sales to national income approximated its 1924–8 figure. The estimated welfare gain is obtained as follows: under our elasticity assumption, prices would rise by 5 per cent in the competitive sector and fall by 5 per cent in the monopolistic sector, and quantities would change inversely by an equal percentage. Taking 100 as the aggregate sales of manufacturing, the change in output in each sector will be 2·5, and taking 1 as the index of initial prices in each sector, the change in price in each sector will be 0·05. According to the Hotelling formula, the welfare gain coming from each sector will be $\frac{1}{2}$ (2·5) (0·05), and when these gains are added together the aggregate gain turns out to be 0·125.

share – 33⅓ per cent – of manufacturing profits, and have distributed this among industries in such a way as to get the biggest possible welfare loss consistent with the idea that monopolies tend to make high profits. In short, we have labored at each stage to get a big estimate of the welfare loss, and we have come out in the end with less than a tenth of a per cent of the national income.

I must confess that I was amazed at this result. I never really tried to quantify my notions of what monopoly misallocations amounted to, and I doubt that many other people have. Still, it seems to me that our literature of the last twenty or so years reflects a general belief that monopoly distortions to our resources structure are much greater than they seem in fact to be.

Let me therefore state the beliefs to which the foregoing analysis has led me. First of all, I do not want to minimize the effects of monopoly. A tenth of a per cent of the national income is still over 300 million dollars, so we dare not pooh-pooh the efforts of those – economists and others – who have dedicated themselves to reducing the losses due to monopoly. But it seems to me that the monopoly problem does take on a rather different perspective in the light of present study. Our economy emphatically does not seem to be monopoly capitalism in big red letters. We can neglect monopoly elements and still gain a very good understanding of how our economic process works and how our resources are allocated. When we are interested in the big picture of our manufacturing economy, we need not apologize for treating it as competitive, for in fact it is awfully close to being so. On the other hand, when we are interested in the doings of particular industries, it may often be wise to take monopoly elements into account. Even though monopoly elements in cosmetics are a drop in the bucket in the big picture of American manufacturing, they still mean a lot when we are studying the behavior of this particular industry.

Finally I should like to point out that I have discussed only the welfare effects of resource misallocations due to monopoly. I have not analysed the redistributions of income that arise when monopoly is present. I originally planned to discuss this redistribution aspect as well, but finally decided against it. All I want to say here is that monopoly does not seem to affect aggregate welfare very seriously through its effect on resource allocation. What it does through its effect on income distribution I leave to my more metaphysically inclined colleagues to decide. I am impelled to add a final note in order to forestall misunderstandings arising out of matters of definition. Resource misallocations may clearly arise from causes other than those considered here: tariffs, excise taxes, subsidies, trade-union practices and the devices of agricultural policy are some obvious examples. Some of these sources of misallocation will be discussed in a forthcoming paper. Suffice it to say here that the present paper is not concerned with them.

References

EPSTEIN, R. C. (1934), *Industrial Profits in the United States*, National Bureau of Economic Research.

HOTELLING, H. (1938), 'The general welfare in relation to problems of taxation and of railway and utility rates', *Econometrica*, vol. 6, pp. 242–69.

WESTON, J. F. (1953), *The Role of Mergers in the Growth of Large Firms*, University of California Press.

Part Four
Income Distribution and Relative Shares

Two points to notice about this Part are that it is about the
functional distribution of income rather than the *occupational* or
personal distribution, and that there is no paper explicity and
ostensibly about 'profit'. Of course, any explanation of
'the share of wages' provides an explanation of 'the share of
capital', but this is not necessarily the same thing as a 'theory of
profit'. A theory of profit, has, however, been implicit in previous
parts: marginal productivity to account for normal returns, and
barriers to entry to account for super-normal, 'pure', profit or
rent. Schumpeter's view of profit as the reward to innovation
(see Further Reading) fits this scheme. Innovation leads to profit,
but imitation (entry) in due course competes the profit away.
Thus we might say that the reward to innovation is quasi-rent.
One view of profit, however, does not fit here. To Knight, profit
was peculiarly the reward to bearing uncertainty. The distinction
between risk and uncertainty on which this view depends, is not,
however, easily understood (whereas his discussion of
risk-sharing devices is unsurpassed: see Further Reading).

Some of the issues raised by Kalecki's approach, and the
alternative perfect-competition-technology approach, were
discussed in the Introduction. Solow asks if economists have
been playing the right game in trying to explain 'constancy', and
reminds us of the importance of human capital. The
occupational and personal distributions of income are subjects
which economists are now equipped to investigate seriously.

Kaldor's important paper, 'Alternative theories of
distribution', is reprinted in McCormick and Smith (1968).
Besides a superb survey, Kaldor introduces his 'Keynesian' or
macro-theory of income distribution, which has been described
as the 'widow's cruse' theory (if the capitalists save and the
workers do not then 'workers spend what they get and capitalists

get what they spend'). A good problem is: try to find a model of firms (and households) consistent with the macro-theory of income distribution!

References
McCormick, B. J., and Smith, E. O. (eds.) (1968), *The Labour Market*, Penguin.

Further Reading

The perfect-competition-technology approach was discussed in Part One on production functions. A simple account of the Cobb-Douglas case appears in
G. C. Archibald and R. G. Lipsey, *An Introduction to a Mathematical Treatment of Economics*, pp. 215–22, Weidenfeld & Nicolson, 1967.

Doubt about the sensitivity of income distribution to the elasticity of substitution between capital and labour (and therefore about the use of data on the former to estimate the latter) is expressed in
M. Bronfenbrenner, 'A note on relative shares and the elasticity of substitution', *Journal of Political Economy*, vol. 68, 1960, pp. 284–7.

Criticism of Kaldor's theory will be found in
M. W. Reder, in M. Abramovitz (ed.), *The Allocation of Economic Resources: Essays in Honor of Bernard Francis Haley*, Stanford University Press, 1959.

There are several detailed studies in
Conference on Reasearch in Income and Wealth,
The Behavior of Income Shares, Princeton University Press, 1964.

The reference to Knight is
F. H. Knight, ch. 8, 'Structures and methods for meeting uncertainty', in *Risk, Uncertainty and Profit*, Houghton Mifflin, 1921.

Schumpeter's discussion of profit and innovation is in
J. A. Schumpeter, *Business Cycles*, vol. 1, particularly pp. 72–108, McGraw-Hill, 1939,
and
J. A. Schumpeter, *Capitalism, Socialism and Democracy*, Harper & Row, 1942; Allen & Unwin, 1943.

A pioneering discussion of the economics of human resources is
G. S. Becker, *Human Capital*, Columbia University Press, 1964.

An amusing case study of the effect of barriers to entry on occupational income is
S. Rottenberg, 'The economics of occupational licensing' in Universities National Bureau Committee for Economic Research, *Aspects of Labor Economics*, Princeton University Press, 1962.

11 M. Kalecki

The Distribution of the National Income

Abridged from M. Kalecki, 'The distribution of the national income', from his *Essays in the Theory of Economic Fluctuations*, George Allen & Unwin, 1939, pp. 13–41.

In this essay we investigate both statistically and analytically the relative share of manual labour in the national income. From the social point of view it would be more interesting to consider the share of labour as a whole: but it is the relative share of *manual* labour which is suitable for theoretical analysis.

For the same reason the national income is here given a slightly unorthodox meaning. First, as we are interested in the *home produced* income alone, we exclude from national income that part which is derived from foreign investments. Further, we shall deal with *gross* income, by which is meant the income before deductions for maintenance and depreciation (gross income = net income+maintenance and depreciation).[1]

It is easy to see that the gross national home-produced income is equal to the value added by all industries of an economy. Usually the Government[2] is treated as an 'industry' producing public services, but we shall not adopt this procedure here. Instead we shall mean by national income *the total value added by private enterprises* which we denote below by A.

[Kalecki then discussed the available data for Great Britain (1911–35) and the USA (1919–34). The discussion is omitted, since more and better data is now available. He concluded that '... the relative share of manual labour in the national income in Great Britain showed a remarkable stability both in the long run and the short period', and similarly for the US. The observation is doubtful, but the explanation is still interesting. Ed.]

1. For the sake of brevity we shall speak throughout the essay of 'depreciation' instead of 'maintenance and depreciation'.

2. We mean here by the Government all public authorities.

The degree of monopoly and the distribution of the product of industry

Let us consider an enterprise with a given capital equipment which produces at a given moment an output x and sells it at a price p.[3]

If we denote the entrepreneurial income (inclusive of dividends) per unit of output by e_a, the average 'overhead' costs (interest, depreciation and salaries) by o_a and the average wage and raw material cost by w_a and r_a respectively, we have

$$p = e_a + o_a + w_a + r_a.$$

Further, the short-period marginal costs m (i.e. the cost of producing an additional unit of product with a given capital equipment) is made up of the sum of the short-period marginal cost of 'overheads' o_m, wages w_m, and raw materials r_m,

$$m = o_m + w_m + r_m.$$

We subtract the second equation from the first and obtain

$$p - m = e_a + (o_a - o_m) + (w_a - w_m) + (r_a - r_m). \qquad \mathbf{1}$$

Following Lerner (1934), we shall call the 'degree of monopoly' of the enterprise, the ratio of the difference between price and marginal cost to price, or

$$\mu = \frac{p - m}{p}.$$

If marginal cost is equal to marginal revenue, μ is equal to the inverse of the elasticity of demand for the product of the enterprise. Substituting μ for $(p-m)/p$ in the equation **1**, and multiplying both sides by the output x we get

$$xp\mu = xe_a + x(o_a - o_m) + x(w_a - w_m) + x(r_a - r_m).$$

Such an equation can be written for each enterprise of an economy. Adding the equations for all enterprises we obtain

$$\sum xp\mu = \sum xe_a + \sum x(o_a - o_m) + \sum x(w_a - w_m) + \sum x(r_a - r_m). \qquad \mathbf{2}$$

The sum $\sum xe_a$ is the aggregate entrepreneurial income (inclusive of dividends). Further, the marginal 'overhead' cost is

3. We mean here by p the 'net price', i.e. the revenue per unit of product after deduction of advertising costs, etc.

in general small in comparison with the average cost; thus $\sum x(o_a - o_m)$ can be represented by $(1-\beta)O$, where O is the aggregate overhead cost (interest, depreciation and salaries), and β a small positive fraction. The average cost of raw materials can be supposed approximately constant and consequently the sum $\sum x(r_a - r_m)$ can be neglected. Most complicated are the problems connected with the member $\sum x(w_a - w_m)$; we must deal with them at some length.

The prevailing type of average wage-cost curve seems to have the following shape. It is more or less horizontal up to a point corresponding to the 'practical capacity' of the plant, but slopes sharply upwards beyond it. This point is seldom reached – factories, e.g. only exceptionally work in more than two shifts. Thus in enterprises of this type $w_a - w_m$ is small in comparison with w_a.

Of course in some industries the situation is different. Those producing basic raw materials (agriculture and mining) are normally subject to diminishing returns, and $w_a - w_m$ is usually negative and not small as compared with w_a in the enterprises concerned. Other industries have, on the other hand, distinctly falling average wage-costs until 'practical capacity' is reached (e.g. railways), and here $w_a - w_m$ is positive and not small in relation to w_a.

It is now easy to see that if wage-cost curves of the first type represent a large part of the aggregate wage bill W the sum $\sum x(w_a - w_m)$ is likely to be small in comparison with W. For then in most enterprises $(w_a - w_m)/w_a$ will be small while the rest will be divided between those in which $(w_a - w_m)/w_a$ is positive and those in which it is negative.

We therefore conclude that $\sum x(w_a - w_m)$ can be represented by γW where γ is likely to be a small (positive or negative) fraction. In other words: conditions of approximately constant returns prevail, in the short period, in the economy as a whole.

On the basis of the above considerations we can now write the equation 2 as follows,

$$\sum xp\mu = E + (1-\beta)O + \gamma W$$

or

$$\sum xp\mu = (E+O)-(\beta O-\gamma W),$$

where β and γ are small fractions.

It is obvious that βO is small in relation to $E+O$; and the same can be said of γW since, as the statistical data quoted above show, W is less than half the gross national income A and thus less than $A-W = E+O$. We can conclude that $\beta O-\gamma W$ is small in comparison with $E+O$, and therefore

$$\sum xp\mu = E+O$$

can be regarded as a good approximation. Now let us divide both sides of this equation by the aggregate turnover $T = \sum xp$.

$$\frac{\sum xp\mu}{\sum xp} = \frac{E+O}{T}.$$

The expression on the left-hand side of this equation is the weighted average of the degrees of monopoly μ, which we shall denote by $\bar{\mu}$. The sum $E+O$ is made up of profits, interest, depreciation, and salaries, and thus it is equal to gross capitalist income plus salaries.

We have thus the following proposition: *The relative share of gross capitalist income and salaries in the aggregate turnover is with great approximation equal to the average degree of monopoly*

$$\bar{\mu} = \frac{E+O}{T}. \qquad\qquad 3$$

Some remarks are still necessary on the notion of the turnover T. In our above argument by 'enterprise' was really meant not the firm but a unit producing marketable goods, e.g. a spinning and weaving mill which belong to the same firm must be considered separate 'enterprises'. Indeed, such a weaving mill in its pricing would account the yarn from its 'own' spinning mill at the market price, and consequently the formation of prices is here much as it would be if the two factories belonged to distinct firms.

Now it is important to stress that with this definition of an 'enterprise' the turnover T is *not* dependent on the degree of integration of industry so long as markets for intermediate products are in existence. T is equal to the gross national income plus the aggregate cost of marketable raw materials.

How is it possible for the degree of monopoly to determine the distribution of the product of industry?

The results obtained in the last section may seem paradoxical. In the case of free competition the average degree of monopoly $\bar{\mu}$ is equal to zero; thus equation 3 seems to show that free competition makes it impossible not only to earn profits and interest, but even to cover depreciation and salaries – all gross income being absorbed by wages. This paradox is, however, only apparent. The formula 3 can be correct only when the assumptions on which it is based are fulfilled. According to these assumptions:

1. The short-period marginal-cost curve does not differ considerably in the majority of enterprises from the short-period average-cost curve of manual labour and raw materials up to a certain point corresponding to 'practical capacity'.

2. The output in these enterprises is usually below this point.

These assumptions are quite realistic, but such a state of affairs is possible only with the existence of monopoly or imperfect competition. If free competition prevails, the second condition cannot be fulfilled; enterprises must close down or maintain such a degree of employment that the marginal cost is higher than the average cost of manual labour and raw materials.

In the real world an enterprise is seldom employed beyond the 'practical capacity', a fact which is therefore a demonstration of general market imperfection and widespread monopolies or oligopolies. Our formula though quite realistic is not applicable in the case of free competition.

The second question which may be raised is of a more complex character. According to our formula, the distribution of the product of industry is at every moment determined by the degree of monopoly. Our formula therefore holds both for the short period and in the long run, even though it was deduced on the basis of, so to speak, pure short-period considerations. And contrary to the usual view neither inventions nor the elasticity of substitution between capital and labour have any influence on the distribution of income.

The source of the conflict between our theory and the orthodox view may be explained thus:

1. The long-period analysis of distribution is generally conducted

on the basis of oversimplified representation of output as a function of only two variables – capital (taken *in abstracto*) and labour. In this way, the short-period cost curves are, as we shall see at once, excluded artificially from this analysis.

2. On the basis of our assumptions these curves have a special shape which makes for the elimination of factors other than the degree of monopoly from the mechanism of distribution. To clarify the problems concerned we shall now consider the dependence of the long-run distribution of the product of industry on the shape of the short-period cost curves.

A particular commodity can be produced with various types of equipment requiring more or less labour and raw materials per unit of product. (A change in the scale of plant is also considered a variation in the type of equipment.) The conditions of production are, however, determined not only by the choice of the type of equipment, but also by the intensity with which it is used. Not only may the kind of machinery be varied, but it is also possible, for example, to work with the same machinery in either one or two shifts.

Let us assume for a moment free competition and draw for each alternative type of equipment which can be applied in the production of the commodity considered a short-period marginal-cost curve and a short-period average-cost curve of manual labour and raw materials (Figure 1). The shaded area then represents the value of net capitalist's income, depreciation and salaries, while the unshaded area LMNO represents the cost of manual labour and raw materials.

To determine the position of long-period equilibrium we define first for each type of equipment the level of prices at which the shaded area covers salaries, depreciation, interest, and normal profit (i.e. the rate of profit at which the industry in question neither expands nor contracts). We shall call this price the normal price attached to a given type of equipment, and the corresponding use of this equipment, its normal use.[4] We choose of all types of equipment that to which the lowest normal price is attached. It is easy to see that the normal use of this type of equipment repre-

4. It is easy to see that with free competition the normal use coincides with the so-called 'optimum' use.

sents the long-run equilibrium. It is clear now that the shape of the short-period marginal-cost curves corresponding to various types of equipment influences the formation of long-run equilibrium.

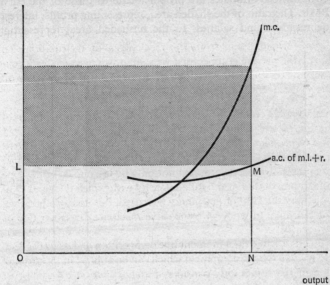

Figure 1

If some change in basic data takes place, e.g. the rate of interest alters or a new invention occurs, the long-run equilibrium is shifted; a new type of equipment is used in a 'normal' way, and in general the relation of the shaded and unshaded areas will be different from that in the initial position. This is quite in accordance with the prevailing long-run theory of distribution. We shall see, however, that such is not the case with the peculiar shape of marginal-cost curves assumed in the deduction of formula 3, and if we admit, instead of free competition, a certain given degree of monopoly.

We take for granted that the short-period marginal-cost curve does not differ appreciably from the average-cost curve of manual labour and raw materials, below the point A (Figure 2). We represent them therefore by the same thick curve PMB.

With a given degree of monopoly the relation of price to marginal cost is a constant $1/(1-\mu)$. Thus if output remains below OA the price corresponding to it is represented by the curve QRC, whose ordinates are proportionate to those of the curve PMB. The ratio of the shaded area, representing profits, interest, depreciation and salaries, to the unshaded area, representing

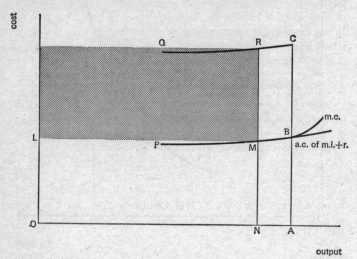

Figure 2

wages and the cost of raw materials, is equal to $1/(1-\mu)$. We define in exactly the same way as before the normal use for each type of equipment as that at which normal profit is earned. The long-run equilibrium is again represented by the normal use of such a type of equipment that, with a given degree of monopoly, it is impossible to earn profits higher than normal by employing a different type. If the basic data alter the new long-run equilibrium is represented by the normal use of a different type of equipment. The long-run equilibrium price of the product alters too, but not its relation to the average cost of manual labour and raw materials, because for all types of equipment the marginal-cost curve coincides with the average-cost curve of manual labour and raw materials, and the degree of monopoly is supposed to be given.

In this way the distribution of the product among factors, as expressed by the relation of the shaded to the unshaded area, remains unaffected by changes of basic data so long as the degree of monopoly is unaltered and the use of equipment in the long-run equilibrium does not reach the point A.[5]

The change of basic data may of course influence the degree of monopoly. For instance, technical progress by affecting the size of enterprises influences the degree of monopoly in an industry. In this case such changes influence the distribution of income, but this is not in contradiction with our results, because it is via the degree of monopoly that the influence operates.

The distribution of the national income

Our aim in this essay is to investigate the changes of the relative share of the wage bill W in the national income A. The difference $A - W$ is of course equal to the sum of gross capitalist's income and salaries. Thus the equation 3 can be written as

$$\frac{A - W}{T} = \bar{\mu}. \qquad \qquad 3a$$

In multiplying both sides by T/W we obtain

$$\frac{A - W}{W} = \bar{\mu} \cdot \frac{T}{W}.$$

From this it follows that the relative share of manual labour in the national income is:

$$\frac{W}{A} = \frac{1}{1 + \bar{\mu}\, T/W}. \qquad \qquad 4$$

This formula shows at once that the increase in the degree of monopoly reduces the relative share of manual labour. The expression increases not only because of the rise in $\bar{\mu}$, but also

5. It may be asked how is it possible for surplus capacity to exist in the long-run equilibrium without inducing firms to curtail their plant. The answer is that large-scale economies prevent the firms from reducing their plant below a certain limit, a state of affairs described by those writers who have shown that imperfect competition must cause equipment in the long run to be used below the 'optimum point' (see, e.g. Harrod, 1934a).

because T/W is increased by a rise in the degree of monopoly since this raises prices in relation to wages.

Changes in T/W can, of course, be caused by influences other than changes in the degree of monopoly. A change in the price of 'basic raw materials', i.e. of the products of agriculture and mining, in relation to wage-costs in other industries, will clearly also have an important influence. It is easy to see that a rise in the prices of 'basic raw materials' in relation to wage-cost must result in an increase of *all* prices in relation to wage-cost and consequently in an increase of T/W. On the other hand, T/W increases in a much lesser proportion than do 'basic raw materials' prices relative to wage-costs. For in each stage of production prices increase (with a given degree of monopoly) proportionately to the sum of raw material- *and wage-costs*.

It is obvious from the formula **4** that with a given degree of monopoly the relative share of manual labour falls when T/W increases, consequently a rise in the prices of 'basic raw materials' as compared with wage-costs by raising T/W must lower the relative share of manual labour. (This may be seen also directly from formula **3a** according to which non-wage earners' income $A - W$ changes with a given degree of monopoly proportionately to the turnover T. Thus if the ratio of turnover to wage-bill T/W increases owing to a rise in the prices of basic raw materials as compared with wage-costs, $(A-W)/W$ must also increase.)

It has been noticed already that a rise in the prices of 'basic raw materials' relative to wage-costs causes an increase of T/W in a *much lesser* proportion. It is easy to see from formula 4 that the proportionate fall in the relative share of manual labour in the national income is even smaller.

We have seen that:

1. A rise of the degree of monopoly causes a decrease in the relative share of manual labour W/A.

2. A rise of prices in 'basic raw materials' in relation to wage-cost causes a fall in W/A but in a much lesser proportion.

We thus have here some reasons for the tendency of the relative share of manual labour in the national income towards stability.

For the degree of monopoly does not undergo violent changes either in the long run or in the short period. The fluctuations in the prices of 'basic raw materials' in relation to wage-costs, though strong, are as stated above only slightly reflected by changes in manual labour's relative share. But of course if the most unfavourable case of joint action of these factors occurs, the change in manual labour's relative share may be appreciable. We shall see below that the remarkable stability of the relative share of manual labour which we notice in statistics is the result of these determinants working in opposite directions. This phenomenon occurred only by chance during the long period considered, and may cease in the future; but in the business cycle there seems to be a steady tendency for the conflict of these two forces to keep the fluctuations in relative share of manual labour within narrow limits.

Changes in the distribution of the national income in the long run

The increasing concentration of industry tends undoubtedly to raise the degree of monopoly in the long run. Many branches of industry become 'oligopolistic', and oligopolies are often transformed into cartels.

This tendency for the degree of monopoly to increase in the long run may, however, be offset by the diminishing imperfection of the market caused by the fall of transport costs in relation to prices, the standardization of goods, the organization of commodity exchanges, etc. In the *Spaetkapitalismus*, however, the first tendency has the upper hand, and the degree of monopoly tends to increase.

As concerns the secular trend of the relation of the prices of 'basic raw materials' to wage-cost, it is difficult to say anything definite *a priori*.

As we have seen in the first section the relative share of manual labour in the national income in Great Britain did not change appreciably between 1880 and 1913. It can be shown that the relation of the prices of 'basic raw materials' to wage-costs also did not alter in this period. For this purpose we shall compare Sauerbeck's index of wholesale prices with Clark's index for the deflation of national income (1938, p. 231). It is clear that the influence of raw material prices as compared with that of wage-costs is much greater upon the first index than upon the second. Now between 1880 and 1913 both of these indices changes in the same proportion (increased by 6 per cent), so that we can conclude that the prices of 'basic raw materials' relative to wage-cost did not change. Obviously, then, the degree of monopoly could not have undergone a substantial change between 1880 and 1913 since with raw material prices unaltered as compared with wage-costs such a change would have been reflected in the relative share of manual labour in the national income.

Turning to the period 1913 to 1935, Sauerbeck's index fell during that time by 2 per cent while 'income prices' rose by about 60 per cent (Clark, 1938, pp. 204, 235), which shows that there was a considerable fall in the prices of raw materials in relation to wage-costs. Thus since the relative share of manual labour was stationary between 1913 and 1935, this means that the degree of monopoly must have substantially increased in this period. Had a fall in the prices of basic raw materials not occurred in the last twenty-five years the relative share of manual labour would have tended to fall appreciably and the recent economic and political development of Great Britain would have been quite different.

The course of events in the USA between 1909 and 1925 was similar. The relative share of manual labour was approximately stable. The wholesale all-commodity index increased in this period by about 50 per cent; King's index of 'income prices' by about 80 per cent (1930, pp. 74, 77). Thus here again the degree of monopoly must have risen considerably, but its influence on the relative share of manual labour was counterbalanced by the fall of the prices of 'basic raw materials' in relation to wage-cost. It is, of course, not at all certain that in the future the rise in the degree of monopoly will continue to be compensated by a fall in the prices of 'basic raw materials'. If it is not, the relative share of manual labour will tend to decline.

Changes in the distribution of the national income during the business cycle

We shall here examine first the cyclical changes in the prices of 'basic raw materials' in relation to wage-cost.

The prices of the produce of agriculture and mining fluctuate much more violently than does the cost of labour in other industries. This is due to the fact that marginal-cost curves in agriculture and mining, as distinct from other sectors of the economy, slope steeply upwards. In addition, wages fluctuate much more in agriculture than in other industries during the business cycle. Consequently 'basic raw material' prices rise relative to wage-cost in the boom and fall in the slump.

Much more complicated is the question of the change of degree of monopoly during the trade cycle. It has recently been argued by Harrod that the degree of monopoly increases in the boom and falls in the slump. In the slump consumers 'resent and resist the curtailment of their wonted pleasures. . . . Their efforts to find cheapness become strenuous and eager. Nor are commercial firms exempt from this influence upon their purchase policy; they, too, have received a nasty jolt and must strain every nerve to reduce costs' (1934b, pp. 86–7). Thus the imperfection of the market is reduced and the degree of monopoly diminished.

Harrod was rightly criticized in that there exist other factors which influence the degree of monopoly in the opposite direction. For instance, in the slump, cartels are created to save profits (Robinson, 1936), and this, of course, increases the degree of monopoly, but when trade revives they are dissolved because of improving prospects of independent activity and the emergence of outsiders.

More important still is the fact that in spite of the fall of prices of raw materials and wages some prices of finished goods tend to be relatively 'sticky' in the slump; this for various reasons: entrepreneurs avoid price cuts because it may induce their competitors to do likewise; cartels are not afraid that outsiders will appear, etc. It can be stated on the basis of data quoted above that the influence of these factors in raising the degree of monopoly during the slump is stronger than that of the diminishing imperfection of the market.

Indeed, if we look at our data on the relative share of manual labour in the national income we see that in general it does not change much during the business cycle. But the prices of basic raw materials fall in the slump and rise in the boom as compared with wages, and this tends to raise the relative share of manual labour in the slump and reduce it in the boom. If the relative share of manual labour remains more or less constant it can be concluded that the degree of monopoly tends to increase in the depression and decline in the boom.

We now see that, as has already been mentioned, the apparent stability of manual labour's relative share during the cycle is in reality the effect of the opposite changes in the degree of monopoly and in the relation of the prices of basic raw materials to wages.

References

CLARK, C. (1938), *National Income and Outlay*, Macmillan.

HARROD, R. F. (1934a), 'Doctrines of imperfect competition', *Q.J. Econ.*, vol. 48, pp. 442–50.

HARROD, R. F. (1934b), *The Trade Cycle*, Kelley.

KING, W. I. (1930), *The National Income and its Purchasing Power*, National Bureau of Economic Research, New York.

LERNER, A. P. (1934), 'The concept of monopoly and the measurement of monopoly power', *Rev. econ. Stud.* vol. 1, pp. 157–75.

ROBINSON, J. (1936), 'A review of *The Trade Cycle*', *Econ. J.*, vol. 46, pp. 391–5.

12 R. M. Solow

A Skeptical Note on the Constancy of Relative Shares

R. M. Solow, 'A skeptical note on the constancy of relative shares',
American Economic Review, vol. 48, 1958, pp. 618–31.

Ever since the investigations of Bowley and Douglas it has been
widely believed that the share of the national income accruing
to labor is one of the great constants of nature, like the velocity
of light or the incest taboo. Keynes (1939, p. 48) called it 'a bit
of a miracle'. Even if it is sometimes observed that the pattern of
distributive shares shows long-run shifts or short-run fluctuations,
the former can be explained away and the latter neglected on
principle. The residual belief remains that, apart from a slight
(and questionable) upward trend and a countercyclical movement, the share of wages in the privately produced national
income is unexpectedly stable. Much effort is devoted to exploiting and explaining this fact.

The object of this paper is to suggest that, like most miracles,
this one may be an optical illusion. It is not clear what exactly
is meant by the phrase: 'The wage share in national income is
relatively stable' or 'historically almost constant'. The literature
does not abound in precise definitions, but obviously literal
constancy is not in question. In any case, what I want to show is
that for one internally consistent definition of 'relatively stable',
the wage share in the United States for the period 1929–54 (or
perhaps longer) has not been relatively stable.

If this contention is accepted, it is not without some general
implications for economic theory. Beginning with Ricardo there
have been sporadic revivals of interest in macroeconomic theories
of distribution.[1] Now it is possible to have an aggregative distribution theory without believing in the historical constancy of

1. I suppose the main contributors since Douglas (1934) have been
M. Kalecki (1938; 1954, ch. 2); Boulding (1950, ch. 14); Kaldor (1956);
Kaldor's main argument was anticipated five years earlier by Hahn (1951).

relative shares, but the belief certainly reinforces the desire for such a theory. After all, a powerful macroeconomic fact seems to call for a macroeconomic explanation. It need not have one, but that is beside the point. As Kaldor says

No hypothesis as regards the forces determining distributive shares could be intellectually satisfying unless it succeeds in accounting for the relative stability of these shares in the advanced capitalist economies over the last hundred years or so, despite the phenomenal changes in the techniques of production, in the accumulation of capital relative to labor and in real income per head (1956, p. 84).

But if, in fact, relative stability of distributive shares is at least partially a mirage, one may feel freer to seek intellectual satisfaction elsewhere. There is still a lot to be explained.

How to be constant though variable

Table 1 shows the share of compensation of employees in a number of different aggregate income totals, so that the reader can see what kind of variability occurs, over the business cycle and over longer periods.

What does an economist mean when he says that the wage share has been relatively stable? Since he does not mean that it has been absolutely constant, he must mean that in some sense or other it has been more nearly constant than one would ordinarily expect.[2] The sentence already quoted from Kaldor suggests that since technique, real capital and real income per head have all changed 'phenomenally', you would normally expect distributive shares to have changed 'a lot', but they have only changed 'a little' and this requires a special explanation. Not to split verbal hairs, it is evident that this is no definition at all. One must have some standard by which to judge whether some particular series of observations has fluctuated widely or narrowly.

Such standards of comparison can arise in a variety of ways. A tight theory may itself provide a benchmark. For example, the fraction of males among live births in a well-defined animal population is subject to statistical fluctuations from year to year. But the theory of sex determination, although perhaps not com-

2. A sporting colleague of mine once offered to bet that Vincent Impellitteri would get more votes for Mayor of New York City than most people expected.

plete, gives some indication of how variable one ought normally expect the series to be. To say that the series is relatively stable could then simply mean that the observed variance is significantly less than the variance expected from the theory. Something like this does appear to be in the back of some authors' minds when

Table 1 Share of Compensation of Employees in Various Income Totals, 1929–55

Year	As per cent of national income	As per cent of privately produced income	As per cent of income originating in corporate business	As per cent of income originating in manufacturing
1929	58·2	55·6	74·6	74·2
1930	61·8	57·3	78·7	76·7
1931	66·5	63·2	87·9	88·0
1932	73·2	69·3	101·0	108·0
1933	73·4	69·5	101·6	104·7
1934	70·0	69·6	88·3	89·4
1935	65·3	60·8	83·8	82·6
1936	66·1	61·3	80·0	78·3
1937	65·1	61·0	79·9	78·7
1938	66·6	61·8	83·0	83·3
1939	66·1	61·6	80·9	79·9
1940	63·8	59·5	76·2	73·4
1941	61·9	57·6	72·7	69·0
1942	61·9	56·8	71·7	71·1
1943	64·4	57·6	72·2	73·4
1944	66·4	58·8	73·8	74·8
1945	68·0	59·8	77·0	77·3
1946	65·5	60·6	79·9	78·8
1947	65·3	61·7	77·5	75·9
1948	63·6	60·0	74·8	72·9
1949	65·2	61·2	75·7	73·5
1950	64·3	60·4	73·6	70·8
1951	65·1	60·8	74·0	71·1
1952	67·2	62·8	76·7	75·4
1953	68·9	64·5	78·5	77·5
1954	64·4	65·0	79·6	79·3
1955	68·9	64·7	77·4	76·5

Source: Department of Commerce, *Survey of Current Business, National Income* Supplement, 1954, and July 1956.

they refer to the stability of the wage share. Take as a starting-point the neoclassical general-equilibrium theory of distribution, which is formulated in terms of production functions, input-ratios, and the like. These quantities fluctuate over time. Ought not the pattern of distributive shares show comparable variability, according to the theory?

But there is a world of difference between this case and the genetic illustration. The general-equilibrium theory is in the first instance a microeconomic one. Between production functions and factor-ratios on the one hand, and aggregate distributive shares on the other lies a whole string of intermediate variables: elasticities of substitution, commodity-demand and factor-supply conditions, markets of different degrees of competitiveness and monopoly, far-from-neutral taxes. It is hard to believe that the theory offers any grip at all on the variability of relative shares as the data change – in fact this may be viewed by some as a symptom of its emptiness. A license to speculate, maybe, but hardly a firm standard. As a matter of speculation, the theory might be taken to imply that the aggregate shares come about through a kind of averaging process, in which many approximately independently changing parameters intervene. From this view would follow an expectation of 'relative stability', if anything.

A second possible source of a standard of variability is suggested by the analogy of statistical quality control. There the problem is also one of detecting 'excessive' variability (or sometimes even deficient variability). But in the absence of some outside specification, the standard is usually given by the past behavior of the process itself. Clearly if the wage share had once oscillated between 50 and 80 per cent and now moved only in the range from 60 to 70 per cent, we could speak of relative stability. But it is not claimed that this is the case.

Third, the contrast between micro- and macroeconomic theories suggests that it might be possible to formulate an *internal* standard of variability. A hint in that direction is contained in a remark of Phelps Brown and Hart (1952): 'Yet it still remains true that the changes in the share of wages in national incomes are not so great as we should expect when we look at the often wide swings of the corresponding shares within particular industries, and this relative stability also calls for explanation.' Indeed it does; if the calorie contents of breakfast, lunch and supper each varies widely, while the twenty-four-hour total remains constant, we at once suspect a master hand at the controls. Similarly if wide swings within industries yield only narrow swings in the aggregate, this points to some specifically interindustrial or macroeconomic force.

But relative shares have denominators as well as numerators. However we subdivide the economy, the over-all share will be a weighted average, not a sum, of the respective shares for the subdivisions. This does not automatically entail that the over-all share will have a smaller variance than the sector shares. That all depends on the intersector correlations, i.e. on the macroeconomic forces. Note an interesting consequence: it is *negative* correlations between sectors which reduce the variance of the weighted average.

Here we have something empirically testable. Suppose, to take the simplest possible case, the economy is divided into k equal-sized sectors, in each of which the wage share is equally variable through time. Then if the sector shares fluctuate independently, the aggregate wage share will have a variance only $1/k$ times the common sector variance. If this were in fact the picture, it would be hard to claim that the relative stability of the aggregate shares required a specifically macroeconomic explanation. It might still be claimed that the aggregate share is more stable than it ought to be on this hypothesis, but now the explanation would have to be sought in the excessive stability of the individual sector shares. I suppose it could be plausibly argued that there are macroeconomic reasons for such microeconomic stability, but this is not the form that current theories take.

The more general case is no more complicated. Suppose there are k sectors, with shares $S_1, \ldots, S_k$ and weights in the aggregate $w_1, \ldots, w_k$. If the S_i represent the share of wages in the sector value-added, the w_i will represent the share of the sector value-added in the total. Let σ_i^2 be the variance of S_i through time, and let symbols without subscripts represent the aggregate share and its variance. Then in the null case of independence among sectors we would find:

$$\sigma^2 = \sum_1^k w_i^2 \, \sigma_i^2, \qquad \qquad 1$$

and in any case we would have

$$S = \sum_{1}^{k} w_i S_i. \qquad \qquad \mathbf{2}$$

Predominantly positive correlations among sectors will yield a larger σ^2 and negative correlations a smaller σ^2.

The value-added weights, however, are not constant from year to year. And on the face of it changes in the weights might be expected to be the main intersectoral force accounting for the relative stability of the aggregate share. If in fact the aggregate share fluctuated less than the sector shares would suggest, this might come about through countershifts in the weights: low-share sectors gaining in weight at the expense of high-share sectors when sector shares rise, and vice versa. There are good theoretical reasons why this might occur, but the fact is that it does not.

This subsidiary proposition is easily testable. It is only necessary to recompute the over-all shares using the observed sector shares but some fixed set of base-year weights. This has been done by Kalecki (1954, p. 32) for US manufacturing, 1879–1937, and by Denison (1954, p. 258) for the 'ordinary business sector', 1929–52. In both cases the fixed-weight series showed approximately the same amplitude of fluctuation as the observed series. The same conclusion can be read from the data to be analysed below. Short- and long-run changes in the importance of the various sectors are important economic facts,[3] but they are not what accounts for the variance or lack of variance of the over-all shares. Thus in making use of formulas **1** and **2** I have in each case recalculated the averages using the value-added weights of a fixed base-year, usually somewhere in the middle of the period.

Empirical results

The sector shares in Table 2 were calculated from the 1954 *National Income* Supplement to the *Survey of Current Business* (pp. 176–9). In each case they represent the ratio of 'compensa-

3. Beck (1958) explicitly investigates short-run changes in over-all shares during the three periods 1930–32, 1941–3, 1950–53. Only in the second of these were weight-shifts a predominant factor. One wonders whether commodity substitution would not prove to be more important in a finer industry classification. Dunlop, in his pioneering study (1950, esp. pp. 163–91), also found weight-shifts to be a significant factor for the period 1929–34.

tion of employees' to 'national income originating'.[4] The original data are reported for eleven sectors, not the seven used here. The four disappearing sectors are: Rest of the World; Government; Finance, Insurance and Real Estate; and Services. The Rest of

Table 2 Share of Compensation of Employees in Income Originating in Selected Sectors of the Economy for Selected Years, 1929–53

Sector	Wt	1929	1935	1937	1939	1941	1947	1951	1953	Variance
Agriculture, etc.	0·113	0·170	0·134	0·153	0·185	0·162	0·170	0·162	0·206	0·0004
Mining	0·031	0·751	0·813	0·715	0·761	0·705	0·733	0·704	0·740	0·0013
Contract Construction	0·056	0·667	0·709	0·704	0·710	0·733	0·727	0·759	0·766	0·0010
Manufacturing	0·441	0·742	0·826	0·787	0·799	0·690	0·759	0·711	0·711	0·0021
Wholesale and Retail Trade	0·230	0·702	0·726	0·691	0·701	0·624	0·633	0·650	0·670	0·0013
Transportation	0·084	0·725	0·800	0·812	0·785	0·717	0·840	0·805	0·815	0·0018
Communications and Public Utilities	0·044	0·541	0·540	0·560	0·550	0·543	0·697	0·619	0·604	0·0030
Total (Current Weights)		0·647	0·658	0·656	0·675	0·613	0·653	0·631	0·696	0·0007
Fixed-Weight Total		0·652	0·702	0·677	0.688	0·613	0·666	0·642	0·678	0·0008

the World is a horse of a wholly different color. Government had to be dropped because our quaint accounting practices measure the value of its product by the compensation of its employees, so that by assumption no income is ever imputed to government-owned capital assets. I dropped the other two non-commodity-producing sectors on the grounds that the value-added concept is rather vague for them, and in many cases probably bears no

4. National income originating is a slightly more net concept than value added, since it excludes depreciation charges, indirect business taxes and business transfers. Compensation of employees is the sum of wages, salaries and the usual supplements. The figures no doubt exclude certain payments which logically ought to be imputed to labor, particularly part of the earnings of unincorporated enterprise (cf. Denison, 1954, p. 256). Probably the salary data also catch certain payments which function more like profits. I doubt that these 'errors of observation' can influence the broad results substantially.

remotely technological relation to conventional inputs. One could make a similar (but weaker) case for not including Trade, and one could argue that the imputation to wages in Agriculture may depend heavily on shifts between family and hired labor; but I have kept both in an effort to widen the coverage. The sector shares are shown for a selection of eight years between 1929 and 1953 but not for all. This was a perhaps unwise attempt to avoid the deep depression years and the war period.

The table shows both the current-weighted over-all labor share and a fixed-weight series using the weights of 1941. In only one year does the use of fixed weights result in a change in the aggregate share of more than two percentage points, and the variability, as measured by the variance, is affected hardly at all. In part this is because the weights do not change radically, the main shift being a decrease in the relative weights of Agriculture and Transportation between 1929 and 1953, with Manufacturing gaining.

The last column shows the variance of each sector share and of the two aggregate-share series. The fixed-weight aggregate has a variance of 0·0008. If formula 1 is used to calculate a theoretical variance on the assumption that the sector shares moved independently in a statistical sense, it turns out to be 0·0005. This difference is almost certainly not statistically significant. We would have to conclude that the aggregate share varied just about as much as it would vary if the individual sector shares fluctuated independently, with positive and negative intercorrelations approximately offsetting each other. If anything, the aggregate share fluctuated a bit *more* than the hypothesis of independence would indicate. Anyone who believes that the aggregate share over this period was unexpectedly stable must believe the same of the sector shares and presumably seek the explanation there.

In Table 3, data from the Census of Manufacturing are analysed in the same way. With the exception of 1941 and the substitution of 1954 for 1953, the same years are represented. Now the ratios give the share of wages only ('production workers' wages') in value added.[5] The fixed-weight average is calculated with weights

5. There are plenty of anomalies as between Table 2 and Table 3. Presumably they reflect the differences in concept between Census and Commerce data, as well as sheer observational error.

equal to the 1947 fraction of each industry group in the aggregate value added. Once again the use of fixed weights makes only a negligible difference. In no year do the shares with fixed and current weights differ by as much as 1 per cent. The seven-year variance of the observed aggregate shares is 0·00028, and for the fixed-weight aggregate it is slightly increased to 0·00036.

But there is a striking difference between the behavior of the Manufacturing data and the wider Commerce figures. When a theoretical variance is calculated from formula 1, i.e. on the assumption that industry shares are statistically independent, it turns out to be only 0·00007. This is one-quarter of the observed share variance and one-fifth of the variance of the fixed-weight over-all share. And this substantial difference is in the 'wrong' direction. The share of wages in manufacturing value-added fluctuates noticeably *more* than it would if the industry shares were mutually uncorrelated. This implies that there is predominantly positive intercorrelation among the wage shares in the separate industries. Instead of a special explanation of the relative stability of the over-all wage share in manufacturing, we appear to need just the reverse: an accounting for its tendency to fluctuate too much.

There are various ways of explaining the facts. Perhaps it is a fair idealization that the several industries buy their labor and capital inputs in the same or similar markets, so they can be imagined to face the same factor prices. If it is further assumed that each industry produces a single commodity with a technology describable by a smooth production function, then everything will depend on the distribution of elasticities of substitution among industries. If nearly all elasticities of substitution are on the same side of unity, then the wage shares will go up and down together in nearly all industries and there will be strong positive correlation. If elasticities of substitution are evenly divided on both sides of unity, there will be two groups of industries whose wage shares will move in opposed phase. Whether the net result is to increase or reduce the variance of the aggregate wage share as compared with the hypothetical zero-correlation value will depend in a complicated way on the arrangement of weights and elasticities.

A special case occurs if each industry is imagined to produce a single commodity with a single fixed-proportions technique. Then every elasticity of substitution is zero and all wage shares move together. It is more interesting to recognize that each 'industry' in Table 3 produces many commodities, some of which are complementary with each other in consumption and some of which are rival. Even if each commodity within an industry is produced by a single technique, it is no longer certain that the industry's wage share will rise and fall with the wage rate. The wage share for each commodity will rise with the wage rate, but those commodities whose production is labor-intensive will rise in price relative to others (assuming some degree of competition) and the intra-industry commodity-mix may shift in favor of capital-intensive commodities enough to decrease the wage share. The outcome depends in an easily calculable way on the factor

Table 3 Share of Production Workers' Wages in Value Added, Selected Manufacturing Industry Groups, Selected Years, 1929–54

Industry group	Wt	1929	1935	1937	1939	1947	1951	1954	Vari-ance
Food	0·121	0·268	0·287	0·291	0·257	0·285	0·297	0·281	0·00019
Tobacco	0·009	0·238	0·208	0·215	0·194	0·273	0·224	0·222	0·00064
Textile Mill	0·072	0·475	0·575	0·545	0·499	0·459	0·540	0·532	0·00173
Apparel, etc.	0·060	0·355	0·483	0·483	0·474	0·454	0·488	0·490	0·00233
Lumber	0·034	0·483	0·541	0·536	0·502	0·473	0·493	0·503	0·00065
Furniture, etc.	0·019	0·422	0·466	0·470	0·438	0·475	0·453	0·454	0·00020
Paper	0·039	0·359	0·370	0·360	0·356	0·352	0·332	0·362	0·00014
Printing and Publishing	0·057	0·284	0·287	0·297	0·279	0·309	0·339	0·338	0·00063
Chemicals	0·072	0·199	0·206	0·212	0·189	0·232	0·212	0·212	0·00018
Petroleum and Coal	0·027	0·207	0·237	0·300	0·256	0·276	0·265	0·301	0·00114
Rubber	0·018	0·385	0·432	0·465	0·397	0·472	0·425	0·407	0·00109
Leather	0·021	0·464	0·526	0·528	0·504	0·473	0·521	0·509	0·00066
Stone, Clay, Glass	0·031	0·417	0·380	0·389	0·361	0·431	0·410	0·392	0·00056
Metals and Products	0·158	0·414	0·450	0·462	0·427	0·479	0·424	0·415	0·00045
Non-electrical Machinery	0·105	0·392	0·446	0·410	0·380	0·460	0·438	0·404	0·00081
Electrical Machinery	0·052	0·341	0·350	0·369	0·335	0·423	0·396	0·357	0·00109
Transportation Equipment	0·079	0·399	0·497	0·518	0·494	0·501	0·477	0·431	0·00185
Miscellaneous	0·028	0·243	0·370	0·410	0·372	0·441	0·434	0·416	0·00461
Total (Current Weights)		0·358	0·395	0·402	0·383	0·407	0·398	0·382	0·00028
Fixed-Weight Total		0·357	0·403	0·406	0·376	0·408	0·401	0·389	0·00036

proportions required by each technique and on the elasticities of substitution in consumption. If in addition commodities are producible with varying factor proportions, then once again the elasticities of substitution in production will play a role along with the other parameters (Hicks, 1936, p. 8).

It must be admitted that none of this is very informative. It is all too static, too inattentive to technical change, too free with unknown and unknowable parameters – in a word, too neoclassical. It would be nice to have a single aggregative bulldozer principle with which to crash through the hedge of microeconomic interconnections and analogies. It is not inconceivable that the bulldozer may yet clank into view; but it is by no means inevitable either.

It is not clear how the newly popular widow's cruse theories (according to which the share of profits in income depends, given full employment, essentially on the rate of investment) can be made to apply on the somewhat disaggregative level to which my empirical results seem to force me. The stickiness of money wages, which forms the short-run side of Kaldor's theory (1956, p. 95), may indeed have something to do with the results of Table 3, although that can hardly be the whole story. [The data next to be presented confirm the suggestion that Table 3's peculiarities are short-run in character.]

There are still other short-run facts that might help to explain the tendency of Table 3's industry shares to move together. An inclination to hoard skilled labor when output declines is one; the longer duration of collective bargaining agreements is another. In Table 4 the attempt is made to wash out some of the short-run effects by using decennial census data over a longer period of time. The layout is the same as that of Table 3, but the coverage is necessarily poorer and the industrial breakdown cruder, because of changes in classification over the years. Broadly speaking, expectations are confirmed.

Once again, the use of fixed (1929) value-added weights results in only a slight increase in the variance of the aggregate wage share as compared with the observed totals. The variance of the observed totals is 0·0003, that of the fixed-weight totals is 0·0004. (Note that the difference between standard deviations, in natural units, is only the difference between 0·017 and 0·020.) Moreover,

Table 4 Share of Production Workers' Wages in Value Added, Selected Manufacturing Industry Groups, Selected Years, 1899–1951

Industry group	Wt	1899	1909	1919	1929	1939	1951	Variance
Food	0·121	0·223	0·212	0·291	0·268	0·257	0·297	0·001
Textiles	0·150	0·462	0·449	0·368	0·420	0·488	0·515	0·002
Metals, etc.	0·320	0·453	0·456	0·476	0·395	0·400	0·424	0·001
Lumber	0·073	0·452	0·488	0·495	0·465	0·470	0·480	0·0002
Leather	0·027	0·532	0·480	0·405	0·464	0·504	0·521	0·002
Paper and Printing	0·109	0·357	0·332	0·331	0·304	0·304	0·336	0·0004
Chemicals	0·064	0·223	0·216	0·265	0·119	0·189	0·212	0·001
Stone, Clay, Glass	0·038	0·548	0·543	0·486	0·417	0·361	0·410	0·006
Tobacco	0·014	0·284	0·288	0·234	0·238	0·194	0·224	0·001
Transportation Equipment	0·086	0·671	0·474	0·440	0·399	0·494	0·477	0·009
Total (Current Weights)		0·412	0·389	0·395	0·368	0·370	0·400	0·0003
Fixed-Weight Total		0.424	0·404	0·404	0·367	0·384	0·409	0·0004

a good part of this small increase is due to the single very high observed wage share in transportation equipment in 1899, together with the fact that the weight of this industry increased from 1899 to 1929. It seems just possible that the character of the output of the industry was changing around the turn of the century. Although this effect does not appear to be very strong in the data here analysed, I suspect that analysis on a finer commodity classification might well show that shifts in the composition of output do have an effect in reducing fluctuations in aggregate shares.

The theoretical variance, calculated from formula 1 on the assumption of the independence of industry shares, is 0·00025. This is less than the observed figure of 0·00040, but probably not significantly so. (The standard deviations are 0·016 and 0·020.) In any case the wide discrepancy found in Table 3 has all but disappeared. This confirms the belief that the positive association of industry shares in Table 3 was essentially short-run in nature. For long periods in manufacturing, and even for short periods in the grosser section breakdown of Table 2, the data are compatible with the hypothesis that subgroup shares fluctuate approximately independently through time; or, more accurately, that positive and negative intercorrelations approximately cancel out.

In general, the data we have examined suggest the following: if by the 'historical constancy' of labor's share it is meant that the share of the total social product imputed to wages has shown a marked absence of fluctuation as compared with the fluctuations of its industrial components, then this belief is probably wrong. Whatever exceptional stability there has been in the pattern of relative shares appears attributable to the components. This in turn suggests that there is no need for a special theory to explain how a number of unruly microeconomic markets are willy-nilly squeezed into a tight-fitting size 0·65 strait-jacket. A theory which wishes to produce the magic number among its consequences may have to say something about the component sectors among its premises.

The character of trends

There are still some interesting problems to be found among the sectors and in the aggregates. One such – and some economists would no doubt prefer to phrase the whole 'historical constancy' question in these terms – is the mildness of the observable trends in the sector shares and in the aggregate relative shares. The history of western capitalism is supposed to be characterized by a long-run accumulation of capital relative to labor. We expect this trend to result in *some* trend in the distribution of the product. Why do we not observe a stronger one?

First, let us look at the orders of magnitude involved. No great accuracy is possible because of the difficulty of finding a reasonable measure of capital stock, because no two available time series are conceptually identical, and finally because of the imputation problem involved. Roughly speaking, during the first half of this century the capital/labor ratio for the private non-farm sector rose by about 60 per cent. But most or all of the increase took place before 1929. Between 1929 and 1949 there was little change, possibly even a decline. In manufacturing the contours were broadly similar, although the initial increase in the capital/labor ratio during the period 1909–29 was considerably greater.[6]

So far as distributive shares are concerned, it is generally accepted that there has been a slight tendency for the labor share to increase secularly. But before 1929 the trend was approximately

6. I am leaving aside the period since 1949, which saw a new burst of net capital formation together with an approximately normal growth of the labor force.

horizontal[7] (with some short-run movements); between 1929 and 1949 there is a more pronounced upward tilt in the wage and salary share as Table 1 shows.

What lends mystery to this picture is that in the first quarter-century, when capital accumulates much more rapidly than the labor force grows, the distributive share picture shows little or no trend. But in the second quarter-century, when the growth of capital relative to labor slows down or ceases, the wage share begins to rise. It seems likely that the difference between the two periods may be tied up with a slightly higher rate of technical progress in the years since 1929.

But let us accept the notion that economic history shows us a strong tendency for capital to grow relative to labor. We are then led to expect a strong trend in relative shares. But which way? The neoclassical answer is that this depends on 'the' elasticity of substitution, or rather on the distribution of elasticities of substitution on either side of unity.[8]

Here we run up against the same kind of verbal question that occupied us earlier. What is a 'strong' trend in relative shares? And what constitutes an elasticity of substitution 'substantially' different from unity in terms of common-sense expectations? And how different from unity need the elasticity of substitution be in order that it convert a strong trend in the capital/labor ratio into a strong trend in relative shares? For the case of a two-factor, constant-returns-to-scale production function, it is not hard to calculate that the elasticity of the labor share with respect to the capital/labor ratio is $-S_K(1-1/\tau)$ where S_K is the share of property in income and τ is the elasticity of substitution.

7. See for instance Kuznets (1952, p. 86). Johnson's calculations (1954, p. 178) show the labor share rising from 69·4 per cent in the decade 1900–1909 to 75·2 per cent for 1940–49, with nearly all the change coming after 1915–24. Johnson's figures are for the whole economy and include, besides the direct compensation of employees, an allowance for the labor content of entrepreneurial earnings. The corresponding figures for compensation of employees are 55 per cent and 64·3 per cent. When restricted to the private sector, compensation of employees amounts to 53 per cent of privately produced income in 1900–1909, and 59 per cent in 1940–49. When the allowance for entrepreneurial earnings is made on the private sector basis the figures are 68 per cent and 71·5 per cent.

8. Remember that shifts in the weights of different sectors in the total appear not to count for very much.

Is an elasticity of substitution of $\frac{2}{3}$ substantially different from unity? It means that a 10 per cent change in the relative costs of capital and labor services will induce a 6·7 per cent change in the capital/labor ratio. If $\tau = \frac{2}{3}$ and $S_K = 0·30$, the elasticity of the labor share with respect to the capital/labor ratio is 0·15. Thus if the capital/labor ratio rises by 60 per cent (with $\tau = \frac{2}{3}$) the labor share should rise by 9 per cent. And since the labor share hovers around 0·70, this means a rise of about 6 or 7 percentage points. But this is just the order of magnitude observed!

I don't mean to conclude from this example that yet another problem evaporates. But before deciding that observation contradicts expectation, there is some point in deciding what it is we expect. In this case what needs precision is the notion of substitutability, and the problem is complicated further by the need to consider changes occurring over varying periods of time.

There are even more fundamental obstacles to a clear evaluation of the argument about trends. An unknown fraction of society's capital takes the form of the improvement of human abilities and skills. Casual observation suggests that this fraction has been increasing over time. Correspondingly an unknown fraction of what we call wages, even 'production workers' wages', no doubt constitutes a rent on that human capital. So the true quantitative picture is far from clear. If it were possible to separate out the part of nominal wages and salaries which is really a return on investment, the share of property income in the total might be found to be steadily increasing. An alternative way of looking at it is to say that investment in education, training, public health, etc., has the effect of increasing the efficiency of the human agent, so that a measurement in man-hours underestimates the rate at which the labor force grows as properly measured in efficiency units. In this case it might be found that the accumulation of non-human capital does not proceed at a faster rate than the labor force grows. These are intrinsically difficult distinctions to draw empirically, but they hold much theoretical and practical importance.

There are of course still other discrepancies between the data we have and the analytical concepts to which we pretend they correspond. The problem of imputing to labor a proper share of the income of unincorporated enterprises has received some attention. But even in the corporate sector possibilities exist for converting what is 'really' property income into nominal labor income, and vice versa, and there are often tax reasons for doing so. If this were a random effect in time it would do no great harm, but in fact it may behave more systematically than that.[9]

To complete the catalog of uncertainties about trends, I ought to mention the intrusion of technical change between the simple facts of factor ratios and factor rewards. About the incidence of historical changes in techniques little is known, and without this it is difficult to know what residual remains to be accounted for.

9. Johnson (1954, pp. 180–82) shows that some part of the apparent increase in the labor share is to be attributed to such statistical artifacts as the growing importance of government-produced income, all of which is conventionally imputed to labor, and the declining importance of agriculture and therewith of home-produced and home-consumed goods.

References

BECK, J. W. (1958), 'An interindustry analysis of labor's share', *Indust. Lab. Rel. Rev.*, vol. 11, pp. 231–46.

BOULDING, K. E. (1950), *A Reconstruction of Economics*, Wiley.

DENISON, E. F. (1954), 'Income types and the size distribution', *Amer. Econ. Rev. Proc.*, vol. 44, pp. 254–69.

DOUGLAS, P. (1934), *The Theory of Wages*, Kelley.

DUNLOP, J. T. (1950), *Wage Determination Under Trade Unions*, Oxford University Press.

HAHN, F. H. (1951), 'The share of wages in the national income', *Oxford econ. Papers*, vol. 3, pp. 147–57.

HICKS, J. R. (1936), 'Distribution and economic progress: a revised version', *Rev. econ. Stud.*, vol. 4, pp. 1–12.

JOHNSON, D. G. (1954), 'The functional distribution of income in the United States, 1850–1952', *Rev. econ. Stats.*, vol. 36, pp. 175–82.

KALDOR, N. (1956), 'Alternative theories of distribution', *Rev. econ. Stud.*, vol. 23, pp. 83–100.

KALECKI, M. (1938), 'The determinants of distribution of the national income', *Econometrica*, vol. 6, pp. 97–112.

KALECKI, M. (1954), *Theory of Economic Dynamics*, Allen & Unwin.

KEYNES, J. M. (1939), 'Relative movements of real wages and output', *econ. J.*, vol. 49, pp. 34–49.

KUZNETS, S. (1952), 'Long-term changes in the national income of the United States of America since 1870', in S. Kuznets and R. Goldsmith (eds.), *Income and Wealth of the United States: Trends and Structure*, Income and Wealth, Series II.

PHELPS BROWN, E. H., and HART, P. E. (1952), 'The share of wages in national income', *Econ. J.*, vol. 62, pp. 253–77.

Part Five
Static Alternatives to Profit Maximization

Several alternative hypotheses have been, or are still being, explored. In the Introduction, we classified them somewhat summarily into non-maximizing models and maximizing models with alternative objective functions. We may now classify them a little more finely, giving the names of the principal innovators as an aid to identification, into the following groups:

1. Full Cost or Mark-up Pricing (Hall and Hitch, Andrews).

2. Behavioural theories (the Carnegie School: Simon; Cyert and March).

3. Sales Maximization (Baumol).

4. Maximization of a utility function containing other arguments besides profit: the static case (Scitovsky, Peston, O. E. Williamson).

5. Maximization of a managerial utility function with growth as at least one argument: the dynamic case (Marris, Baumol, J. H. Williamson).

It is not easy to discover the *theory* of full-cost or mark-up pricing. From a theory, one expects to derive predictions: what happens if demand changes, taxes change, factor prices change? Too often, the advocates of this theory appear to have said 'the mark-up is constant except when it varies', which is no help. It is not too easy to discover what the Behavioural Theory is in this sense, either. References will be found in Further Reading.

(The reader might try the following analytical experiment. It is easy to see that there is a mark-up corresponding to any profit-maximizing price. Under what conditions would the profit-maximizing price be obtained from a constant mark-up as demand shifted? If marginal costs were constant, and demand shifts iso-elastic, what observation, if any, would allow us to discriminate between the short-run profit-maximizing and full-cost hypotheses?)

In this Part, we confine ourselves to the static maximizing alternatives to profit maximization: Baumol, 3, and an example of group 4 above, applied to the Soviet Union. In the next Part, on the Size and Growth of Firms, we shall present the group 5 papers.

Readers of Baumol (and Ames) should notice two points. The first is that both models presuppose the existence of rent, in the sense of the availability of super-normal profit which may either be taken or traded in for other benefits. (The rent is due in one case to private monopoly power, in the other to government intervention.) The other is that both are vague about the general equilibrium setting. What determines the required profit rate in Baumol's case? What happens when prices are set so that *all* firms could make super-normal profit, but expand output instead? Writers on the growth of firms (group 5 above) are investigating some of these problems. This material appears in the next Part.

Readers of Baumol should also notice how easy it is to generalize, and make his rather odd utility function continuous. This was pointed out by Peston (see Further Reading), and is taken for granted by Ames, Baumol himself on growth, Marris, and both Williamsons.

Further Reading
The classic sources for full-cost pricing are
P. W. S. Andrews, *Manufacturing Business*, Macmillan, 1949
and
R. L. Hall and C. J. Hitch, 'Price theory and business behaviour', *Oxford Economic Papers*, vol. 2, 1939, pp. 12–45.
(See Stigler's paper in Part Two for some criticisms of Hall and Hitch.)

There are good discussions in
R. B. Heflebower, 'Full costs, cost changes and prices' in
Universities National Bureau Committee for
Economic Research, *Business Concentration and Price Policy*,
Princeton University Press, 1955; Oxford University Press, 1955,

and
B. Fog, *Industrial Pricing Policies*, trans. I. E. Bailey, North-Holland Publishing Co., 1960.
(Fog, by the way, appears to be unaware of the ideas of a 'testable implication' or comparative statistics. Some of his reported results are, however, extremely funny and very relevant.)

These references, and those for group 2, are Further Reading to the Introduction. They are repeated here for convenience.

H. A. Simon, *Models of Man: Social and Rational*, Wiley, 1957; Chapman & Hall, 1965.

K. J. Cohen and R. M. Cyert, *Theory of the Firm: Resource Allocation in a Market Economy*, Prentice-Hall, 1965.

R. M. Cyert and J. G. March, *A Behavioral Theory of the Firm*, Prentice-Hall, 1963.

Sales maximization and related ideas are discussed in

W. J. Baumol, *Economic Theory and Operations Analysis*, Prentice-Hall, 1961.

W. J. Baumol, *Business Behaviour, Value and Growth*, Harcourt, Brace & World, 1959.

M. H. Peston, 'On the sales maximization hypothesis', *Economica*, n.s. vol. 26, 1959, pp. 128–36.

O. E. Williamson, 'Managerial discretion and business behaviour', *American Economic Review*, vol. 53, 1963, pp. 1032–57.

T. Scitovsky, 'A note on profit maximization and its implications', *Review of Economic Studies*, vol. 11, 1943, pp. 57–60.

13 W. J. Baumol

On the Theory of Oligopoly

W. J. Baumol, 'On the theory of oligopoly', *Economica*, new series, vol. 25, 1958, pp. 187–98.[1]

The oligopoly model which is described in this paper does not pretend to generality. It is meant only to describe approximately the current behaviour of a class of firms and there is no doubt that in other times and circumstances the analysis may become totally inapplicable. Nor does it say anything about the strategic give and take which plays so important a part in the theory of games. And in some respects it breaks sharply with received oligopoly theory. But the model seems to accord fairly well with my own rather spotty observation of the behaviour of a number of American business firms. Moreover, it seems to explain several well-known features of business behaviour which have been puzzling, and to carry some concrete implications for welfare economics, taxation theory, development theory and the theory of monetary and fiscal policy in which the place of oligopoly has been somewhat obscure. A few of these applications are described below.

The sales maximization hypothesis

On grounds which I shall only hint at here, I believe that the typical large corporation in the United States seeks to maximize not its profits but its total revenues which the businessman calls his sales. That is, *once his profits exceed some vaguely defined minimum level*, he is prepared to sacrifice further increases in profits if he can thereby obtain larger revenues. This is suggested by his readiness to use sales as a criterion of the state of his

1. This paper is also published in Baumol (1959). I must express my gratitude to the Guggenheim Foundation for the generous grant which enabled me to complete the manuscript. The paper was delivered as a public lecture at the London School of Economics.

enterprise (e.g. familiar statements such as 'Business is good – sales are increasing'). More important, it is confirmed by a number of cases where businessmen have rejected opportunities (pointed out to them by consultants) to increase their profits at the expense of sales. If they accepted the consultants' analysis of the facts of the situation, as appears to have been the case, this is the acid test. For them the additional profits (and they were not just short-run profits) were not worth the loss in sales.

My hypothesis, then, is that oligopolists typically seek to maximize their *sales* subject to a minimum profit constraint. The determination of the minimum just acceptable profit level[2] is a major analytical problem and I shall only suggest here that it is determined by long-run considerations. Profits must be high enough to provide the retained earnings needed to finance current expansion plans and dividends sufficient to make future issues of stocks attractive to potential purchasers. In other words, the firm will aim for that stream of profits which allows for the financing of maximum long-run sales. The business jargon for this is that management seeks to retain earnings in sufficient magnitude to take advantage of all reasonably safe opportunities for growth and to provide a fair return to stockholders.

Let us see how the businessman, as a good marginalist, will proceed to set his price and hence his output in order to maximize his sales under the profit constraint.

Price–output determination: partial analysis

Sales maximization under a profit contraint does not mean an attempt to obtain the largest possible physical volume (which is hardly easy to define in the modern multi-product firm). Rather it refers to maximization of total revenue (dollar sales) which, to the businessman, is the obvious measure of the amount he has sold.[3] Maximum sales in this sense need not require very large

2. More often the profit constraint probably specifies a minimum rate of return on sales or on investment rather than a minimum total profit level. However, it is easily shown that these alternative forms of the profit constraint make no difference to any of the conclusions which follow.

3. We may be tempted to say then that he suffers from money illusion. But this can hardly be taken as a criticism of his rationality – his objectives simply are what they are and there is nothing inherently rational or irrational about them.

physical outputs. To take an extreme case, at a zero price physical volume may be high but dollar sales volume will be zero. There will normally be a well determined output level which maximizes dollar sales. This level can ordinarily be fixed with the aid of the well-known rule that maximum revenue will be attained only at an output at which the elasticity of demand is unity, i.e. at which marginal revenue is zero.

But this rule does not take into account the profit constraint. That is, if at the revenue maximizing output the firm does in fact earn enough or more than enough profits to meet the competitive requirements, then it will want to produce the sales maximizing quantity. But if at this output profits are too low the firm's output must be changed to a level which, though it fails to maximize sales, does meet the profit requirement.

We see, then, that two types of equilibria appear to be possible: one in which the profit constraint provides no effective barrier to sales maximization and one in which it does. This is illustrated in Figure 1, which shows the firm's total revenue, cost and profit curves as indicated.

The profit and sales maximizing outputs are, respectively, OQ_p and OQ_s. Now if, for example, the minimum required profit level is OP_1 then the sales maximizing output OQ_s will provide plenty of profit and that is the amount it will pay the sales maximizer to produce. His selling price will then be set at $Q_s R_s / OQ_s$. But if the producer's required profit level is OP_2, output OQ_s which yields only profit $Q_s P_s$ clearly will not do. Instead, his output will be reduced to level OQ_c which is just compatible with his profit constraint.

I shall argue presently that in fact only equilibrium points in which the constraint is effective (OQ_c rather than OQ_s) can normally be expected to occur when other decisions of the firm are taken into account.

The profit maximizing output OQ_p will usually be smaller than the one which yields either type of sales maximum OQ_s or OQ_c. For if at the point of maximum profit the firm's marginal costs are positive an increase in output will increase total sales revenue since marginal revenue must at that point be equal to marginal cost and hence it too must be positive. Therefore, if at the point of maximum profit the firm earns more profit than the required minimum,[4] it will pay the sales maximizer to lower his price and increase his physical output.

Suppose now that the total profit curve has a single peak, as in Figure 1, rather than being composed of several hills and valleys.

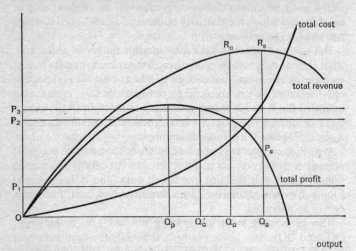

Figure 1

Then a rise in required minimum profits, if it affects output at all, will cause a rise in price and a decrease in the quantity produced. For starting from a sales maximizing output of either variety, an output level which was just shown to be larger than the profit maximizing quantity, any increase in output will only lower profits. Hence if the required minimum profit rises, say from OP_2 to OP_3, so that at the initial output OQ_c the profit level is no longer acceptable, the higher required profit level can only be attained by a cut in physical sales (to OQ'_c), i.e. by a rise in price.

Choice of input and output combinations

The typical oligopolistic firm is a multi-product enterprise (frequently the number of distinct items runs easily into the hundreds) and, of course, it employs a large variety of inputs. In

4. If it earns less than the required minimum at this output there is obviously no output which will satisfy the profit constraint.

this section I examine briefly the effect of sales (rather than profit) maximization on the amounts and allocation of the firm's various inputs and outputs.

We obtain the following result which may at first appear rather surprising: given the level of expenditure the sales maximizing firm will produce the same quantity of each output, and market it in the same ways as does the profit maximizer. Similarly, given the level of their total revenues, the two types of firm will optimally use the same inputs in identical quantities and will allocate them in exactly the same way. This result may be somewhat implausible because one is tempted to think of some products or some markets as higher profit–lower revenue producers than others and one would expect the profit maximizing firm to concentrate more on the one variety and the sales maximizing firm to specialize more in the other. But we shall see in a moment why this is not so, though later I shall show that this view contains an element of truth.

It is easy to illustrate our result geometrically. In Figure 2 let x and y represent the quantities sold of two different products (or sales of one product in two different markets) or the quantities bought of two different inputs. The curves labelled R_1, R_2, etc. are iso-revenue curves, i.e. any such curve is the locus of all combinations of x and y yielding some fixed amount of revenue. Where x and y represent quantities sold if their prices were fixed the R curves would be ordinary straight price lines. Their convexity to the origin represents the diminishing marginal revenues from the sale of x and y as their quantities increase which is the result of their falling prices (negatively sloping demand curves).[5] Similarly, curve CC' represents all combinations of x and y which can be produced with a fixed outlay (total cost). The standard

5. The absolute value of the slope of such a line equals the ratio of the marginal revenue of x to that of y. For points A and C represent the same total revenue. Hence the move from A to B represents a loss in revenue ΔR equal to the gain from moving from B to C., i.e. we have

$$\Delta R = \Delta y \times \text{marginal revenue of } y$$
$$= \text{the marginal revenue of } x \times \Delta x \text{ (approximately)}$$

so that $\Delta y/\Delta x = MRx/MRy$. Therefore the falling slope of an R curve as x increases implies a falling marginal revenue of x relative to that of y. A similar discussion applies to the input analysis.

analysis tells us that the point of tangency T, between CC' and one of the R curves is the point of profit maximization. But it is also the point of revenue maximization because it lies on the highest revenue curve attainable with this outlay. This demonstrates our result.

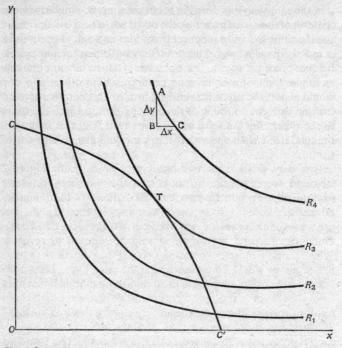

Figure 2

A little reflection should now render the result quite plausible. The point is simply that, *given the level of costs*, since profit equals revenue minus costs, whatever maximizes profits must maximize revenues. Hence differences between the profit and the sales maximizer's output composition or resource allocation must be attributed not to a reallocation of a given level of costs (or revenues) but to the larger outputs (and hence total costs and

258 Static Alternatives to Profit Maximization

revenues) which, we have seen, are to be expected to accompany sales maximization.[6]

Explained in the way we have just done our theorem is completely trivial. But when the sales maximizer's profit constraint is taken into account a more interesting but closely related conclusion can be drawn.

We may view the difference between maximum attainable profits and the minimum profit level expected by the sales maximizer as a fund of sacrificeable profits which is to be devoted to increasing revenues as much as possible.[7] Since each output is produced beyond the point of maximum profits its marginal profit yield will, of course, be negative. In other words, each time it increases the output of some product in order to increase its total revenue the firm must use up more of its fund of sacrificeable profits. This fund of sacrificeable profits must be allocated among the different outputs, markets, inputs, etc. in a way which maximizes total dollar sales. The usual reasoning indicates that this requires the marginal revenue yield of a dollar of profit sacrificed, e.g. by product x, to be the same as that obtained from a dollar of profit lost to any other product, y. In other words, we must have

$$\frac{\text{Marginal revenue product of } x}{\text{Marginal profit yield of } x} = \frac{\text{marginal revenue product of } y}{\text{marginal profit yield of } y}$$

This relationship indicates that, even in the sales maximizing firm, relatively unprofitable inputs and outputs are to be avoided, whatever the level of outlay and total revenue.

Advertising and service competition

As Chamberlin and Brems have emphasized, firms characteristically compete not only in terms of price. In fact, more typically

6. We conclude that when the operations researcher encounters the problem of allocating optimally some *fixed* quantity of a firm's resources, the values of all other decision variables being given, his answer will be exactly the same whether he is dealing with a sales or a profit maximizing firm.

7. Provided that sales maximization does not permit a surplus of profits over the required minimum as would be the case (Figure 1) when required minimum profit is OP_1 so that the sale maximizing output OQ_s is optimal. But as already noted, I shall argue in a later section that this will not normally occur, i.e. that the profit constraint will ordinarily be effective.

the oligopolist's competitive strategy is planned in terms of advertising outlay, product modification and special services offered to the buyer. The decision as to how far to carry each of these activities can be influenced profoundly by the firm's choice of objectives – whether it chooses to maximize sales or profits.

I shall discuss explicitly only the decision on the magnitude of the advertising budget because it is so easily quantifiable. However, the analogy with service and product characteristic planning is fairly clear and certainly suggestive.

The relevant diagram for the advertising decision is completely elementary. On the horizontal axis in Figure 3, I represent the magnitude of advertising expenditure and on the vertical axis total sales (revenue) and total profit. In drawing the total revenue curve I assume, as most businessmen seem to do, that increased advertising expenditure can always increase physical volume, though after a point sharply diminishing returns may be expected to set in.[8] This means that total revenue must vary with advertising expenditure in precisely the same manner. For unlike a price reduction a *ceteris paribus* rise in advertising expenditure involves no change in the market value of the items sold. Hence, while an increase in physical volume produced by a price reduction may or may not increase dollar sales, depending on whether demand is elastic or inelastic, an increase in volume brought about by added advertising outlay must always be accompanied by a proportionate increase in total revenue.

The 45° line, as usual, is able to transfer data on advertising expenditure from the horizontal to the vertical axis – i.e. advertising outlay OA is equal to AK. The other costs of the firm (OC) are taken to be independent of the level of advertisement, since it simplifies but does not affect the argument.[9] If these other costs are added (vertically) to the advertising cost curve (45° line) we obtain the line which depicts the firm's total (production, distri-

8. Of course this is not necessarily true – potential customers may perhaps be repelled by excessive advertising.

9. In fact, this assumption is virtually certain to be false for if advertising increases physical sales volume it must surely increase total production and distribution costs. We may prefer to interpret the diagram as a cross section of three-dimensional revenue and cost functions taken perpendicular to the output axis so that advertising is permitted to increase revenue only by allowing a rise in the price at which the given output is sold.

bution and selling) costs as a function of advertising outlay. Finally, subtracting these total costs from the level of dollar sales at each level of advertising outlay we obtain a total profits curve PP'.

We see that the profit maximizing expenditure is OA_p at which PP' attains its maximum M. If, on the other hand, the sales maximizer's minimum acceptable profit level is OP_1 the constrained sales maximizing advertising budget level is OA_c. It is to be noted that there is no possibility of an unconstrained sales

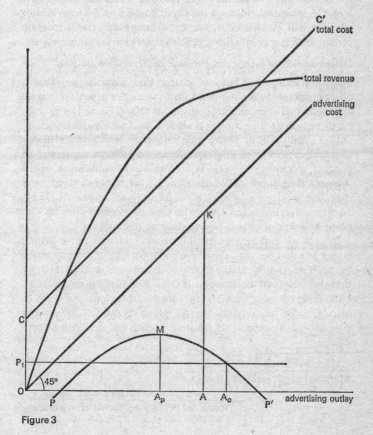

Figure 3

maximum which is analogous to output OQ_s in Figure 1. For by assumption, unlike a price reduction, increased advertising always increases total revenue. As a result it will always pay the sales maximizer to increase his advertising outlay until he is stopped by the profit constraint – until profits have been reduced to the minimum acceptable level. This means that sales maximizers will normally advertise no less than, and usually more than, do profit maximizers. For unless the maximum profit level A_pM is no greater than the required minimum OP_1, it will be possible to increase advertising somewhat beyond the profit maximizing level OA_p without violating the profit constraint. Moreover, this increase will be desired since, by assumption, it will increase physical sales, and with them, dollar sales will rise proportionately.

Determination of prices and outputs: multivariable analysis

The interrelationship between output and advertising decisions now permits us to see the reason for my earlier assertion that an unconstrained sales maximizing output OQ_s (Figure 1) will ordinarily not occur. For if price is set at a level which yields such an output profits will be above their minimum level and it will pay to increase sales by raising expenditure on advertising, service or product specifications. This is an immediate implication of the theorem that there will ordinarily be no unconstrained sales maximizing advertising level. Since its marginal revenue is always positive advertising can always be used to increase sales up to a point where profits are driven to their minimum level.

In fact we can strengthen this result and rule out even the possibility that by coincidence the profit constraint will happen to be satisfied exactly at the point of maximum revenue OQ_s so that this point will coincide with OQ_c. For at the point of maximum total revenue the marginal revenue of each output must be zero. On the other hand, the marginal revenue of advertising expenditure is presumably positive. Hence the equilibrium condition

$$\frac{\text{Marginal revenue of product } x}{\text{Marginal profit yield of product } x} = \frac{\text{marginal revenue of advertising}}{\text{marginal profit yield (cost) of advertising}}$$

can never be satisfied at such a point since the *marginal* profit yield of (or loss from) advertising is always finite.

Examining further the multivariable (many products, many types of advertising expenditure) case we shall see that some overall validity remains to two basic results of the earlier part of this article: that the sales maximizing outputs will exceed those which maximize profits and that a reduction in the minimum acceptable profit level will increase both outputs and advertising expenditures. However, these conclusions do require some modification in detail – for there may be some exceptional products or types of advertising expenditure for which they do not hold.

To see the sense in which the results retain their overall validity we note that as the profit requirement is reduced, production, distribution and selling expenditure must be increased in total, so that at least some outputs or some types of advertising activity must have risen. The reason these costs must grow is almost a matter of arithmetic – as the profit constraint is weakened total revenue is permitted to increase. But if revenue grows and profits fall it follows by subtraction that total costs must become larger.[10]

But while there is necessarily an inverse relationship between the minimum profit requirement and the overall levels of output and advertising this need not be true of every type of product and promotion outlay. For it can be shown that there may be some commodities which are fairly profitable but are inferior revenue producers. These play a role completely analogous with that of inferior goods in the theory of consumer behaviour. When

10. In particular we can conclude that there will be an overall growth in output and advertising in a move from profit to (unconstrained) sales maximization. For profit maximization is equivalent to constrained sales maximization where nothing less than maximum profit is acceptable while pure sales maximization is tantamount to an appropriately low (possibly negative) profit requirement. Of course there may be no finite amount of advertisement which yields (unconstrained) maximum sales although here we must probably give up our assumption that advertisement always yields positive marginal revenues. A simple alternative form of the argument employs the notation $P\text{max} = Rp - Cp$ for the profit maximizer's total profits, revenues and costs and $Ps = R\text{max} - Cs$ for those of the sales maximizer. Since $P\text{max} \geqslant Ps$ and $R\text{max} \geqslant Rp$, then $Cs = R\text{max} - Ps \geqslant Rp - P\text{max} = Cp$ so that the sales maximizer's production and advertising outlays will never fall short of those of the profit maximizer.

revenues and overall outputs are reduced by stricter profit requirements these inferior outputs and perhaps the funds to be spent advertising them will rise.

Some applications: pricing and changes in overhead costs

The foregoing analysis has a number of implications for various areas in economic theory, most of which I did not foresee when I first began to work with the sales maximization hypothesis. First, I shall argue that it can be used to explain some types of business behaviour which have often been observed in practice but which are difficult to rationalize in terms of a profit maximization objective.

Students consistently find one of the most surprising conclusions of the theory of the firm to be the assertion that overhead costs do not matter. So long as these costs really do not vary with the level of output, and provided that it does not lead the firm to close down altogether, no change in the level of its overhead costs should lead the profit maximizing firm to change either its prices or its outputs. This piece of received doctrine is certainly at variance with business practice where an increase in fixed costs[11] is usually the occasion for serious consideration of a price increase.

It is easy to show, however, that this is precisely the sort of response one would expect of the firm which seeks to maximize sales and treats its profits as a constraint rather than as an ultimate objective. For if, in equilibrium, the firm always earns only enough to satisfy its profit constraint, as I argued in the previous section, then a rise in overhead cost must mean that earnings fall below the acceptable minimum. The result is precisely the same as that of an increase in the minimum profit level; outputs and/or advertising expenditures must be reduced in order to make up the required profits. The purpose of any such decrease in production is, of course, to permit an increase in selling price.

This is very easily restated in terms of Figure 4. An increase in overhead costs means, geometrically, a uniform downward shift in the total profit curve by the amount of the overhead expenses. Hence if overheads rise by amount CD output will fall

11. I use the terms 'fixed costs' and 'overheads' loosely, treating them as synonyms, although this is not standard practice.

from OQ_c to OQ'_c, for at OQ_c profits will now be Q_cR which is less than the minimum acceptable level OP_m. By contrast, the change in overhead costs will leave the profit maximizing output unchanged at OQ'_p.

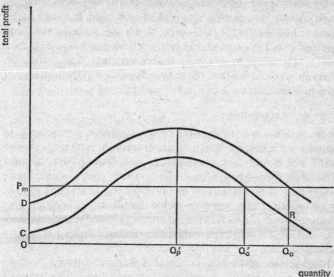

Figure 4

Again, inferior outputs and types of advertising constitute an exception. Sales of these relatively ineffective revenue earners will be increased when increased overheads force the firm to husband its profits more carefully. However, I doubt whether this exception is likely to be very important. Certainly, one would not expect it to loom large in the actual behaviour of business firms whose rough and ready decision-making processes are likely to by-pass the more subtle adjustments called for by optimization analysis.

In line with this last remark I do not wish to go too far in rationalizing the businessman's behaviour with respect to overhead costs. Doubtless, prices are sometimes raised in response to an increase in fixed cost simply because executives are making their pricing decisions in accord with a crude average cost pricing

W. J. Baumol 265

rule of thumb – if costs rise so must prices. And doubtless average cost pricing is sometimes misused to serve the businessman's interests badly. High prices are charged because costs are high at current low output levels – without consideration of the possibility that lower prices can increase volume and so may reduce unit costs. I have come across several such cases. But we must be careful not to sell the businessman short – he is often shrewd and well educated by experience. I really believe that it is not much of an exaggeration to say that the constrained sales maximum hypothesis often is a fairly close approximation to the rationale of the businessman's use of average cost pricing.

Non–price competition

Economists have often noted the oligopolist's reluctance to employ price cutting as a competitive weapon. But this cannot be explained entirely as a manifestation of a desire to live the quiet life. For even when competitive activity does become more vigorous it is notorious that this is very likely to take the form of more advertising expenditure or the introduction of new product features some of which are sometimes considered to be little more than frills. It would appear then that the large firm's competitive effort has been channelled away from price policy and into advertising, service and product characteristic modification.

This phenomenon is not a necessary consequence of sales maximization any more than of profit maximization. But the sales maximization hypothesis can certainly help to account for the psychology behind these practices.

To see why this is so we must remember that to the businessman 'sales' mean total revenue, not physical volume. Now a dollar spent on advertising, if it increases physical volume, must necessarily increase total revenue. But a price reduction is a double-edged sword which, while it serves as an influence to increase total revenue in that it usually adds to the number of units which can be sold, simultaneously works in the opposite direction by reducing the revenue on each unit sold. In other words, as the economist knows so well, depending on whether demand is or is not elastic, price cutting is an uncertain means for increasing dollar sales.

True, price cutting is equally undependable as a method of increasing profits – indeed more so, for if it fails to increase total revenue it must almost certainly reduce profits because the resulting increase in outputs must also add to total costs. But, on the other hand, the effect of advertising, improved service, etc. on sales is fairly sure while, very often, their profitability may be quite doubtful. Thus sales maximization makes far greater the presumption that the businessman will consider non-price competition to be the more advantageous alternative.

Implications for ideal output analysis

Because of the theorist's failure to formulate a well defined theory of oligopoly pricing (even the kinked demand-curve analysis indicates why price may tend to stay what is it, and not how it was set in the first place) oligopolistic output has never been subjected to much explicit analysis by welfare economists in their discussions of ideal output. One comes away only with a rather vague general feeling that after all the oligopolist is practically a monopolist and so he is very likely to fall under the same cloud as an output restricter. One suspects that his outputs are smaller than they would be under the full reign of consumer (or rather, public) sovereignty.

The sales maximization hypothesis does provide us with an analysis of oligopolistic pricing and output determination. Unfortunately it does not seem to open the way to any firm and simple welfare judgements (though what market form *can* be evaluated categorically?). However, some impressionistic conclusions can be drawn.

We recall first that under sales maximization outputs will tend to be larger, overall, than they would be under profit maximization. Nevertheless, they may be smaller than those which would result in zero profits, i.e. smaller than the output levels which are often misleadingly called competitive. This means that in a world where competition was everywhere else perfect, the allocation of resources to an oligopolistic industry would probably be too small – though less so than one would expect of a profit maximization hypothesis.

But approximations to perfect competition are rare and marginal cost pricing, if it is to be found at all, is the exception rather than the rule even in governmentally operated enterprises. Even this weak condemnation of the oligopolistic resource allocation must therefore be considered suspect. Since other industries also fail to bid for resources with energy as great as that which is to be expected of perfect competition, there is no reason to feel that the oligopolistic firm gets less than its appropriate share. Indeed, if it is true (as is suggested in my book) that competition sets the level of the minimum profit rate so that in all firms costs bear a somewhat similar relation to prices we may surmise that some sort of rough parity is established and that oligopolistic pricing leads to an allocation of resources which is as close to the optimum as can reasonably be expected.[12] That is, the distortions may tend roughly to cancel out.[13]

So much for the judgement of oligopoly in a static context. When we include in our evaluation the contribution of oligopoly to economic growth it will be even clearer that the sales maximization hypothesis sheds a favourable light on the effects of oligopolistic organizations on the social welfare. Lest this be taken as apologetics pure and simple, let me add that the discussion provides no grounds for us to dispense with the services of a vigorous authority charged with enforcement of the anti-trust laws in order to prevent the corruption and abuse which can be and often have been, the fruits of great concentration of economic power.

The sales maximization hypothesis has another, rather disturbing, implication for welfare theory. It means that prefixed lump sum ('poll') taxes must lose their convenience for discussions of income redistribution. For even these taxes, like other overheads, can and will be shifted, and their imposition will affect incentives and the allocation of resources. They will be shifted because, when they are levied on him, the oligopolist will raise his prices and reduce his selling costs to a point where his profit constraint is once again satisfied. The explanation of the shiftability of this apparently unshiftable tax is simple – the profit non-maximizer has a reserve of unclaimed profits to fall back on when he is driven to do so by what he considers to be an unsupportable

12. We must be careful, however, and heed Professor McKenzie's warning that *proportionality* of prices and marginal costs will not ordinarily produce an optimal resource allocation. This accounts, in part, for the vague terms in which my present discussion is couched (McKenzie, 1951).

13. In fact, it is tempting to argue that if oligopolistic profits are kept just high enough to yield a normal return on stockholders' investment these firms will actually produce competitive outputs.

increase in his costs, though he can do so only at the sacrifice of sales which mean so much to him. Since no one seems to deny that businessmen do in fact often raise prices when their overheads increase, this point must be accepted even by someone who questions the sales maximization hypothesis.

In describing the workings and implications of the sales maximization hypothesis I have given only the barest indications of the grounds on which it is advanced. At best it is just an approximation to a set of complex and variegated facts and there seems to be no way for it to be tested by statistical or other standard techniques of empirical investigation. Nevertheless on the basis of careful examination of a number of cases it appears to represent the facts somewhat better than do some of the more usual models. In addition, as I have just shown, it helps to explain a number of otherwise puzzling features of oligopolistic behaviour. These are surely standard grounds of scientific method for permitting tentatively one hypothesis to supersede another.

References

BAUMOL, W. J. (1959), *Business Behavior, Value and Growth*, Harcourt, Brace & World.
MCKENZIE, L. (1951), 'Ideal output and interdependence of firms', *Econ. J.*, vol. 61, pp. 785–803.

14 E. Ames

The Economic Theory of Output-Maximizing Enterprises

Excerpt from E. Ames, *Soviet Economic Processes*, Richard D. Irwin, 1965, pp. 50–65.

This chapter presents a microeconomic theory of the behavior of Soviet enterprises. This theory is different from the analysis of private firms, because it assumes the Soviet enterprise seeks to maximize output. Private firms are normally assumed to maximize profit. In this chapter, it is assumed that enterprises are confronted with fixed prices, but plans play no role in the analysis. Thus this chapter is only a first approximation to reality. To present an economic theory of planning, it is necessary to specify how plans affect the terms on which enterprises buy and sell.

Any simple hypothesis about the behavior of an economic organization is suspect. Private firms certainly do not always seek to maximize profits on a day-by-day basis; and it is often said of very large private corporations that the sales department tries to maximize sales, the production department tries to minimize average cost, the personnel department to maximize average labor productivity, and the accounting department to minimize reported profits. Nevertheless, the profit-maximization hypothesis introduces an important ordering and simplification into economic analysis. It is justified if the simplifications it makes are consistent with experience, and if it suggests an approach to the analysis of real situations. In particular, it can only be rejected if a precisely stated hypothesis of a different nature turns out to be a significantly better explanation of an important body of economic data.

When it is assumed that Soviet enterprises seek to maximize output, the assumption plays the same simplifying role in the analysis of Soviet enterprises that the profit-maximization hypothesis plays for private firms. From this hypothesis there will be derived propositions about how Soviet enterprises may be expected to react, and it may be shown that these expected reactions are different from (although not altogether unrelated to) the reactions of private firms. The advantages which this particular hypothesis has at the present time are three. First, it has no theoretical competitors, for the only accounts of Soviet enterprise are institutional or sociological in nature, and do not provide the basis for an analysis comparable in any sense to that possible for private enterprise economies using a profit-maximization hypothesis. Second, it is intuitively plausible in the same sense that the profit-maximization hypothesis is acceptable. Private firms say that they are in business to make profits. Soviet enterprises and the Soviet press say that enterprises exist in order to produce at least as much (and if possible more) than state plans call for. Third, the hypothesis is a simple one. It is easy to make a theory complicated; but until a simple theory clearly breaks down, it is preferable to a complicated one.

There have been cases reported, of course, where Soviet-type enterprises did not try to maximize output. In some of the European satellites there are enterprises which produce solely for export. They do not maximize output, but only seek to meet foreign demand. These do not fit into the present analysis. It is also true that the Enterprise Fund, from which bonuses are paid to management and workers, is calculated on the basis of a scale which depends not only on whether output is at least as great as planned, but also on whether profits are at least as great as planned. A management which sought to maximize bonuses in the short run might well give up some output to achieve some profit. And so on.

The most important simplification introduced by this analysis is that conditions of certainty are assumed. All economic theory (including this) becomes unpleasantly difficult if uncertainty is present. In a first approach, it is prudent to pretend that there is no uncertainty. But it is well to illustrate how uncertainty may affect the output-maximization hypothesis.

Suppose the monthly output plan is one hundred units in January. The enterprise managers feel that they could produce one hundred and twenty units in January. However, they may feel that if they do, they may receive real and psychological reward in early February, but the March plan may be increased to one hundred and thirty. If they make one hundred and five units in January, they will receive some rewards, and be less likely to have a sudden increase in their plans. In this case, their problem is to keep output slightly above plan, even if it is below capabilities. Our theory will not take account of this possible behavior pattern, which is suggested by some circumstantial evidence. We cannot do everything at once.

Output and profits are not the only possible indices of plant performance. For example, average labor productivity is a gauge often used to measure the performance of enterprises. Generally speaking, the question in controlling managerial efficiency proceeds in this sequence: is output at planned levels; if not, is the enterprise holding its costs and profits at planned levels; if not, is labor productivity at planned levels? Generally, investigation of management does not go beyond these points. Only in special circumstances are there clean-cut investigations of waste of materials, of pile-up of work in process, and so on. But management may be called to task for violations of dozens of instructions. There is no difficulty if we wish to complicate our hypothesis.

Let us introduce the ways in which Soviet enterprises may be expected to differ from private enterprises by imagining an economic organization to which both profits and output are important; in particular, suppose that the welfare of the managers is a 'weighted average' of the two. That is, $U = ax + (1-a)y$, where x is output, y profits, and U a reward.[1] This is a simple sort of utility function, but most administrative systems of bonuses must be simple. Suppose now that $C(x)$ is the total cost of producing x units of production; that the price of the finished goods is p; and hence, that $y = px - C(x)$. We now observe that:

$$U = ax + (1-a)\,y$$
$$= ax + (1-a)\,\{px - C(x)\} = ax + (1-a)\,px - (1-a)\,C(x).$$

1. Mathematicians will recognize that I am here using a special case: in a system satisfying

$$dU = U_x\,dx + U_y\,dy$$

the partial derivatives U_x and U_y are constants, and $U_y = 1 - U_x$. This special case illustrates sufficiently the point.

We select the optimum level of U

$$\frac{\partial U}{\partial x} = 0 = a + (1-a)\,p - (1-a)\frac{\partial C}{\partial x}$$

$$\frac{\partial C}{\partial x} = \frac{a + (1-a)\,p}{1-a} = \frac{a}{1-a} + p,$$

so that marginal cost equals price if and only if $a = 0$. (This is the case where profit is maximized.)

Note that if $0 \leqslant a \leqslant 1$, then

$$\frac{\partial C}{\partial x} - p = \frac{a}{1-a} \geqslant 0.$$

(If $a = 1$, marginal cost will be infinite. This is to be expected. Since no constraint on costs has been introduced, producers will produce an infinite amount!) Thus, if $a \neq 0$ (output counts for something in the utility function), marginal cost will exceed price. This consideration suggests that the more output-oriented the firm, the greater will be its marginal cost at equilibrium. Let us see what happens to marginal cost as a increases. The last result, rewritten in the form

$$\frac{a}{1-a} = \frac{\partial C}{\partial x} - p$$

may be differentiated with respect to a:

$$\frac{\partial}{\partial a}\left(\frac{a}{1-a}\right) = \frac{\partial^2 C}{\partial x \partial a}.$$

Since $a/(1-a)$ necessarily increases as a increases, the left side of this expression is positive. The right side must therefore be positive also. An increase in the utility of output, relative to that of profits, means an increase in marginal costs.

This result suggests that if marginal costs are an increasing function of output, the less important profits are in the utility function, the greater output will be. This proposition can be demonstrated graphically. Let us assume provisionally the U-shaped average cost function used in ordinary theory (see Figure 1). As is familiar to us all, profit is maximized at output q_1; but the firm can expand output beyond q_1. In fact it *may* expand output as far as q_2; even if it wished, it could not expand output beyond

q_2, because it would be unable to pay for the cost of producing.[2]

If the enterprise, then, maximizes output (profit being of no consequence) the average cost curve of the enterprise represents its supply curve. This is obviously true if we allow the average revenue function (AR) to rise and fall and if we observe that maximum output traces out the line AC for levels of output at least as great as q_0.

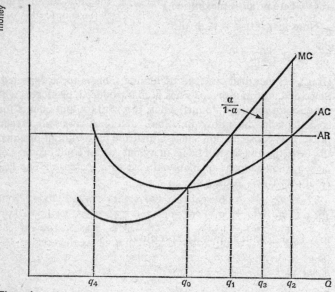

Figure 1

Moreover, if price falls below the lowest point on the average cost function (corresponding to output q_0), the enterprise will produce nothing, so that a 'reservation price' is assumed, even under conditions of maximized output. If price should be at the reservation level (and only then), the enterprise will behave as if it were purely competitive.

For the output-maximizing enterprise, the condition that aver-

2. We disregard, of course, the possibility of the enterprise's drawing large cash reserves, that of its receiving an unlimited subsidy, and other unenlightening possibilities.

age cost equals price is necessary but not sufficient. This condition is satisfied for two levels of output, q_4 and q_2, in Figure 1. The first, however, is a point of *minimum* output. In order that output be maximized, it is thus necessary that average cost be increasing. It is more convenient, perhaps, to say that marginal cost exceeds average cost, which is implied by increasing average cost.[3]

The case in which the firm maximizes some weighted average of prices and output is obviously 'between' the profit-maximizing and the output-maximizing cases. In this case, the supply function is given by the rule (which was derived above)

$$\frac{\partial C}{\partial x} - p = \frac{a}{1-a}.$$

That is, in Figure 1, output is at q_3, where the (vertical) distance between marginal cost (MC) and price (AR) is equal to $a/(1-a)$. If price changes, the quantity supplied will trace out a curve which falls $a/(1-a)$ units below the marginal cost curve, provided that this curve is above average cost. There is thus a reservation price in this case too, but it is higher than that in the case in which output is maximized. (This is true because average cost is rising at all levels of output greater than q_0.)

The graphical equivalent to the evaluation of $\partial^2 C/\partial x \partial a$ given above is the following: if the importance of output to the welfare of the enterprise (a) increases, so does $a/(1-a)$. Consequently, at any given price, output will rise to a point where the vertical distance between marginal cost and average revenue is equal to $a'/(1-a')$. Supply depends both on price and on a; given a supply is a function of price.

The foregoing discussion now enables us to provide a rationale for having drawn a U-shaped average cost function. If prices are fixed, the average cost function must rise beyond some finite level of output. If it did not, enterprises, whether they maximized output or profits, would never have any bounds to the amounts

3. $\dfrac{d}{dx}\left[\dfrac{C(x)}{x}\right] = \dfrac{1}{x}\dfrac{dC}{dx} - \dfrac{1}{x^2}\,C(x) > 0,$

$\dfrac{dC}{dx} - \dfrac{1}{x}\,C(x) > 0,$

$\dfrac{dC}{dx} > \dfrac{C(x)}{x}.$

they produced. On the other hand, we all think we know that there are economies of scale at some point in the production process, regardless of the objective of managers. We are left with a U-shaped cost function.

Reasoning of this sort tells us something about the connection between wages and productivity, and from this we can make some statements about the demand for inputs in enterprises having welfare functions of this sort. Thus, if

$$U = ax + (1-a)y,$$

where x = output, y = profits, and $0 \leqslant a \leqslant 1$, there is a production function relating output to inputs $v_1, \ldots, v_n$:

$$x = x(v_1, \ldots, v_n).$$

If the inputs sell at prices $w_1, \ldots, w_n$, and the price of output is p,

$$y = px - \sum w_i v_i.$$

If optimum amounts of the inputs are used, then for every $i = 1, \ldots, n$,

$$\frac{\partial U}{\partial v_i} = 0 = a \frac{\partial x}{\partial v_i} + (1-a) \left[p \frac{\partial x}{\partial v_i} - w_i \right];$$

so that
$$w_i = \frac{a + p(1-a)}{(1-a)} \frac{\partial x}{\partial v_i} = \left[\frac{a}{1-a} + p \right] \frac{\partial x}{\partial v_i}.$$

If only profit is maximized, so that $a = 0$, then the familiar result follows,

$$w_i = p \frac{\partial x}{\partial v_i} \quad \text{(wages equal the value of the marginal product).}$$

We may also, by a simple rearrangement of terms, find that

$$\frac{a}{1-a} = \frac{w_i}{\partial x / \partial v_i} - p.$$

This condition holds, however, for all inputs. For inputs i and j, then,

$$\frac{w_i}{\partial x / \partial v_i} = \frac{w_j}{\partial x / \partial v_j}$$

$$\frac{w_i}{w_j} = \frac{\partial x / \partial v_i}{\partial x / \partial v_j}.$$

This statement, that the marginal productivities of different factors are proportional to their prices, is familiar to students of private enterprise. It is interesting that so far there is no difference between the two sets of results; however, the general condition

$$\frac{a}{1-a} = \frac{w_i}{\partial x/\partial v_i} - p$$

means that

$$-\frac{a}{1-a}\frac{\partial x}{\partial v_i} = p\frac{\partial x}{\partial v_i} - w_i.$$

The right-hand side is a measure of the profit obtained from selling the output of the marginal unit of the ith input. If $a = 0$, profit maximization occurs, with the familiar result that wages equal the value of the marginal product. In other cases, however, this result would not be valid. If $a > 0$, the marginal unit of output will be sold at a loss.

Proceeding as before, let us consider what happens if output becomes more important, and profits less important as a determinant of enterprise behavior. That is, we consider the effect of increasing a. First, we make some rearrangements of terms

$$\frac{a}{1-a} = \frac{w_i}{\partial x/\partial v_i} - p.$$

Then $\dfrac{\partial}{\partial a}\dfrac{a}{(1-a)} = -\dfrac{w_i}{(\partial x/\partial v_i)^2}\dfrac{\partial^2 x}{\partial v_i\,\partial a}.$

The left side is positive, and $w_i \div (\partial x/\partial v_i)^2$ is positive. Therefore, $\partial^2 x/\partial v_i\,\partial a < 0$. Hence, as output becomes more important (and profits less important) to the enterprise, the marginal productivity of inputs will fall.

This result suggests that firms which try to maximize output will use more inputs under given conditions, and use them less productively than firms which seek to maximize profits. This is an interesting conclusion, if true. Let us see if it is defensible. We start from a 'Marshallian–Hicksian' sort of analysis. Then ordinary theory about productivity says that there will be average and marginal productivity curves of the general form shown in Figure 2.

We shall see later the rationale for this conformation. If the firm is selling at a fixed price, then average revenue product curves and marginal revenue product curves may be obtained by changing the vertical scale of measure: units are multiplied by product price to give values (Figure 3). On the other hand, if the wage rate is given, then the average (variable) cost is shown by a horizontal line. In this case, we assume (as in Soviet practice) that enterprises pay no interest on their capital. If fixed costs are present, 'average cost' becomes 'average variable cost' and 'average total cost' will be the 'sum' of this line and a suitable rectangular hyperbola. The results are quite comparable, but make for messier diagrams.

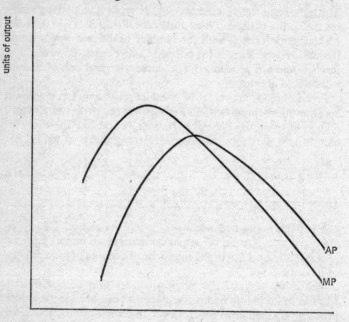

Figure 2

It is well known, of course, that an enterprise maximizing profits will select employment level δ_1, at which marginal cost equals marginal revenue. The demand for labor is the marginal

278 Static Alternatives to Profit Maximization

revenue curve in this diagram and thus (apart from a change in scale) the marginal productivity curve of the preceding diagram; but if the enterprise maximizes output, subject to the condition that average revenue equals average cost, then the enterprise will employ δ_2 units of labor. The average revenue product curve is thus the demand curve for the input. If δ_2 units are employed, total output will be greater, and average productivity and marginal productivity will be less.

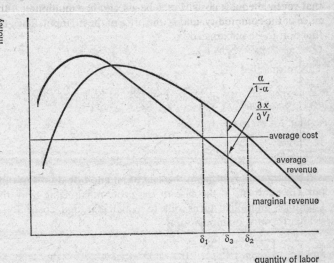

Figure 3

When both output and profits are taken into account, we make use of the equation

$$p = \frac{a}{1-a} + \frac{w_i}{\partial x/\partial v_i},$$

derived above, to obtain the relation

$$\frac{p(\partial x/\partial v_i) - w_i}{\partial x/\partial v_i} = \frac{a}{1-a}.$$

This asserts that the marginal profit from hiring additional labor is equal to the quantity $a/(1-a)$. Consequently, a demand curve for the input is obtained by a vertical displacement of the marginal revenue curve. Average and marginal output, then, are in this case intermediate between the two extreme cases.

These results suggest that it should be worth making a formal statement of what the equilibrium conditions are for enterprises which maximize output, subject to the constraint that revenue must equal cost. Let output be x; x is a function of inputs $1,\dots,n$, so that $x \equiv x(v_1,\dots,v_n)$. Maximization is subject to the constraint that revenue equals costs. Let λ be a Lagrange multiplier, p the price of the commodity, and w_i the price of the ith input. Then the function to be maximized is

$$G \equiv x - \lambda(px - \sum w_i\, v_i).$$

This means that

$$\frac{\partial G}{\partial v_i} = 0 = \frac{\partial x}{\partial v_i} - \lambda\left(p\frac{\partial x}{\partial v_i} - w_i\right) = \frac{\partial x}{\partial v_i} - \lambda\frac{\partial y}{\partial v_i},$$

so that, for every $i = 1,\dots,n$,

$$\frac{1}{\lambda} = \frac{\partial y/\partial v_i}{\partial x/\partial v_i} = \frac{\partial y}{\partial x}$$

is the marginal profit from the sale of an additional unit of output. (In contrast, in the case of the profit-maximizing firm, the Lagrange multiplier turns out to equal marginal cost.) By a straightforward manipulation,

$$\frac{\lambda p - 1}{\lambda} = \frac{\left[\dfrac{\partial x/\partial v_i}{\partial y/\partial v_i}\right]p - 1}{\dfrac{\partial x/\partial v_i}{\partial y/\partial v_i}} = \frac{(\partial x/\partial v_i)p - \partial y/\partial v_i}{\partial x/\partial v_i} = p - \frac{\partial y}{\partial x},$$

which, of course is marginal cost; but

$$0 = \frac{\partial x}{\partial v_i} - \lambda\left[p\,\frac{\partial x}{\partial v_i} - w_i\right] = (1-\lambda p)\,\frac{\partial x}{\partial v_i} - \lambda w_i,$$

so that $\dfrac{\lambda p - 1}{\lambda} = \dfrac{w_i}{\partial x/\partial v_i}.$

The left side is independent of i. Consequently, for any pair of inputs, i, j,

$$\frac{w_i}{w_j} = \frac{\partial x/\partial v_i}{\partial x/\partial v_j}.$$

That is, marginal products are proportional to wages in the output-maximizing enterprise, as they are in competitive firms.

The relation between price and marginal cost may now be derived:

$$\frac{\lambda p - 1}{\lambda} = \frac{w_i}{\partial x / \partial v_i} = \frac{w_i v_i}{x} \frac{1}{(\partial x / \partial v_i)(v_i / x)} = \frac{w_i v_i}{x} \frac{1}{\eta_i}.$$

The quantity η_i is the partial elasticity of output with respect to changes in the ith input. The left side, as we have seen, is marginal cost. Denoting this as M, we have

$$M \eta_i = \frac{w_i v_i}{x}.$$

Summing over all inputs, we obtain average cost A:

$$M \sum_1^n \eta_i = \frac{\sum_1^n w_i v_i}{x} = A.$$

This result is purely formal; however, the condition that output is maximized means that price equals average cost. Making this substitution, then, we find that

$$\frac{A}{M} = \frac{p}{M} = \sum \eta_i.$$

The importance of this proposition is that marginal cost represents the change in the value of resources resulting from a unit change in output. If an industry has several enterprises, each of which has its own production function, then each enterprise will have a different set of output elasticities η_i. Consequently, for any given price, the different enterprises will have different marginal costs. The total amount of resources used by the industry can be made to change if a given total output is reallocated among the producing enterprises. Suppose that factor prices are fixed and that for each firm the η_i are given numbers (i.e. are independent of output levels and of the amounts of inputs used). Let there be n firms, such that for the jth firm $\sum \eta_i$ is a number K_j. Then there will be n different ratios $p / M_j = K_j$, if the firms all sell at the same price.

On the other hand, if it be desired that each firm have the same marginal cost, M, it will be necessary to select n distinct prices, so as to equalize the n different ratios

$$\frac{p_j}{K_j} = M.$$

It is for this reason that planning for output-maximizing enterprises requires a good deal of information. If prices are the same for all enterprises selling a given product, then, in general, it would be possible to reduce the social cost of a given level of output by reallocating output differently among the different enterprises. On the other hand, if the marginal costs of all enterprises are the same (as is necessary for minimizing the total cost of a given level of output), then the price charged by each enterprise must (in principle) be different. It is not possible, however, to set such prices without information concerning the production function of each enterprise, since without such information the quantities K_j cannot be determined.

In a purely competitive economy, prices are equal to marginal costs. The effect of a reallocation of resources among firms or industries can therefore be calculated if prices are known. But in an economy where enterprises maximize output, prices do not have this meaning. The central regulatory or planning authority must have information about each firm to judge the effects of resource changes. The next point is to show that output-maximizing enterprises will respond in a definite fashion to changes in product or input prices.

If an enterprise sells at a fixed price p, then it will maximize its output x, if, and only if, it maximizes its total revenue px. It is formally simpler, and of no practical importance, to present the problem in terms of revenue maximization. That is, the firm maximizes the function

$$G = px - \lambda(px - \sum w_i v_i)$$

subject to $\quad 0 = px - \sum w_i v_i.$

The equilibrium conditions are that

$$\frac{\partial G}{\partial x_i} = p\frac{\partial x}{\partial v_i} - \lambda\left[p\frac{\partial x}{\partial v_i} - w_i\right] = 0 \quad (i = 1,...,n).$$

This may be rewritten

$$0 = (1-\lambda)p\frac{\partial x_i}{\partial v_i}+\lambda w_i$$

and if a new variable μ is defined such that

$$\mu = \frac{\lambda}{\lambda-1},$$

the equilibrium conditions and constraint take the form

$$0 = p\frac{\partial x}{\partial v_i}-\mu w_i \quad (i = 1,\dots, n),$$

$$0 = px - \sum w_i v_i.$$

If a single input price, say the jth, changes, the effect on the equilibrium is given by the system

$$0 = p\sum_k \frac{\partial^2 x}{\partial v_i\partial v_k}\frac{dv_k}{dw_j}-w_i\frac{d\mu}{dw_j}-\mu\delta_{ij} \quad (i = 1,\dots n),$$

$$0 = p\sum \frac{\partial x}{\partial v_k}\frac{dv_k}{dw_j} - \sum w_k\frac{dv_k}{dw_k}-v_j,$$

$$0 = \sum (p\frac{\partial x}{\partial v_k}-w_k)\frac{dv_k}{dw_j}-v_j$$

$$= -(1-\mu)\sum w_k\frac{dv_k}{dw_j}-v_j$$

$$= -\sum w_k\frac{dv_k}{dw_j}-\frac{v_j}{1-\mu}.$$

The solution, in the variables $dv_1/dw_j,\dots,dv_n/dw_j$, $d\mu/dw_j$ thus is the solution of the augmented matrix system, written in block form

$$\begin{bmatrix} p\dfrac{\partial^2 x}{\partial v_i\partial v_j} & -w_i & \mu\delta_{ij} \\ \hline -w_j & 0 & \dfrac{v_j}{1-\mu} \end{bmatrix}.$$

If the price of the product changes, the effect on the equilibrium is given by the system

$$0 = \frac{\partial x}{\partial v_i} + p \sum \frac{\partial^2 x}{\partial v_i \partial v_k} \frac{dv_k}{dp} - w_i \frac{d\mu}{dp} \quad (i = 1,\ldots,n),$$

$$0 = x + p \frac{\partial x}{\partial v_k} \frac{dv_k}{dp} - \sum w_k \frac{dv_k}{dp}$$

$$= x + \sum \left(p \frac{\partial x}{\partial v_k} - w_k \right) \frac{dv_k}{dp}$$

$$= x - (1-\mu) \sum w_k \frac{dv_k}{dp}$$

$$= \frac{x}{1-\mu} - \sum w_k \frac{dv_k}{dp}.$$

The solution, in the variables $dv_1/dp,\ldots,dv_n/dp$, $d\mu/dp$ thus is the solution of the augmented matrix system, written in block form

$$
\begin{bmatrix}
p\dfrac{\partial^2 x}{\partial v_i \partial v_j} & \vdots & -w_i & \vdots & -\dfrac{\partial x}{\partial v_i} \\
\cdots\cdots\cdots & & \cdots & & \cdots\cdots \\
-w_j & \vdots & 0 & \vdots & -\dfrac{x}{1-\mu}
\end{bmatrix}.
$$

The matrices of these systems (omitting the last column) are bordered symmetric matrices of second-order partial derivatives of the production function. They thus have points of resemblance to the matrices discussed in the literature on firms in purely competitive industries. We do not have occasion to make much use of these systems. It is sufficient to point to the fact that the behavior of Soviet enterprises confronted by changes in input and output prices is determinate in the same sense that the behavior of such firms is determinate.

Having established that the inputs $v_1,\ldots,v_n$ depend upon the prices of inputs and of output, we may outline the derivation of the supply function of the output of the enterprise. Since G is output plus a Lagrangian term,

$$G = x - \lambda(px - \sum w_i v_i) = x(1-\lambda p) + \lambda \sum w_i v_i = x.$$

So that $\quad x\lambda p = \lambda \sum w_i v_i.$

Therefore also

$$x = \frac{\sum w_i v_i}{p}.$$

If this last expression is differentiated with respect to p

$$\frac{dx}{dp} = \frac{\sum w_i (\partial v_i / \partial x)(dx/dp)}{p} - \frac{\sum w_i v_i}{p^2}$$

$$0 = \left[\frac{\sum w_i (\partial v_i / \partial x)}{p} - 1 \right] \frac{dx}{dp} - \frac{\sum w_i v_i}{p^2}$$

$$= \left[\sum w_i \frac{\partial v_i}{\partial x} - p \right] \frac{dx}{dp} - \frac{\sum w_i v_i}{p}$$

$$= -\frac{\partial y}{\partial x} \frac{dx}{dp} - \frac{\sum w_i v_i}{p}$$

$$dx = \left[-\frac{\sum w_i v_i / p}{\partial y / \partial x} \right] dp.$$

Since v_i and $\partial y / \partial x$ are functions of p, x may be expressed as a function of price by integration:

$$x(p) = \int_o^p C(z)\, dz,$$

where C is the contents of the square brackets, p having been replaced by the variable of integration z. The contents of the brackets are certainly positive, since $\sum w_i v_i$ is positive, and $\partial y / \partial x$ is negative. Hence $x(p)$ is positive for all positive p.

It might be objected that if rewards to management are not strictly proportional to output, then management should wish to maximize a function of output, rather than output itself. If, however, this function is non-decreasing, then the results here should hold. It might also be objected that Soviet enterprises have a profits plan, which in general is positive. This situation, however, is equivalent to treating planned profits as a cost, so that only above-plan profits are 'true' profits, just as only 'above normal' returns are profits in the theory of pure competition.

There is a more important objection to be raised, however. It has been assumed that enterprises were rewarded solely on the basis of output. This is only a simplification of the true situation, in which profits are of some importance in determining the reward of management. To grant the practical qualification does not diminish the theoretical interest of these results; but a more important objection is that in the analysis so far, it has been shown only that if enterprises seek to maximize output, a determinate outcome obtains (under conditions of certainty) whenever input and output prices are fixed; if these prices change in continuous fashion, output and input levels will also vary continuously, and no importance is assigned to any plans (in the sense in which the word has been used). That is, the enterprise will do what prices and the production function enable it to do, and price regulation alone determines how the system will operate.

There is one sense in which plans can enter this analysis. We assume the production function to be given, in such a way that given prices p, $w_1,\ldots,w_n$, the enterprise will produce quantity x' and use input quantities $v'_1,\ldots,v_n$. Imagine, however, that the enterprise is given also some other 'plan' quantities $x'' > x'$, $v''_1 < v'_1,\ldots,v''_n < v'_n$, and these other quantities are called plans. Then, in effect the plan constitutes an order to develop a different production function. Such a theory would state that the incentive scheme depends upon a special 'profit' function of the form

$$y(x'-x'') - \sum \Omega_i(v'_i-v''_i),$$

where y and the Ω_i are rewards which vary with the extent to which production is above plan and inputs below plan. This function (rather than output) is to be maximized subject to the budget constraint. To the extent, however, that output was the main consideration, y would have large absolute value and the Ω_i small absolute values, and the problem would tend to return to that already described.

Part Six
The Growth and Size of Firms

Knowledge of long-run cost functions should tell us what size
we expect firms to be, but, as Simon and Bonini pointed out in
1958, no one had succeeded in deriving from existing theory and
knowledge of costs any explanation for the observed
size-distributions of firms. It is frequently observed that the
frequency distribution of the size of firms in an industry is not
normal, but roughly log-normal. This means that the distributions
of the sizes measured in natural numbers are highly skewed,
whereas if we take the *logarithms* of the sizes, we find at least a
reasonable approximation to a normal distribution. (The same
thing is true of other size distributions, such as personal income or
trade unions: see Further Reading.) It turns out that a purely
statistical hypothesis about the growth of firms provides an
'explanation' for this phenomenon: 'explanation' in inverted
commas rather than theory, since the statistical assumptions are
not very clearly related to any comprehensible causation. The
papers by Adelman and Hart reprinted here present this approach.

It might be expected that the new theories of the growth of
firms (listed as group 5 in the Introduction to Part Five above)
might do better than the old static theories in explaining the
observed size distributions. At present, they do not, and it is not
easy to bridge the gap. In some of the statistical explanations it is
assumed that the probability of a firm's growing by some
absolute amount at any time t depends only on its size at time $t-1$
(i.e. the probability of a given *proportional* growth is independent
of size). This means that the system has a very limited memory:
earlier periods are irrelevant, initial conditions 'wash out'
(assuming stability). Current developments of growth theories,
however, are directed to explaining the 'steady state', or constant

rate of growth, *g*. Then the size of the firm at any time *t* depends on *g and* on its initial size, which is not explained.

A central assumption of the growth theories (as of the static theories of types 3 and 4) is that they presuppose the possibility of super-normal profit; indeed, in some hands, they go further, and assume that an able management, by repeated innovation, can keep generating new sources of quasi-rents. In this sense, they are 'neo-Schumpeterian'. Schumpeter, as we have seen, viewed profit as the reward to innovation. He also thought that an individual or firm would typically pull-off one *coup* and then rest on its laurels; he did not imagine groups of people or corporations making a habit of it. The bolder view is taken for granted, with little discussion, by some modern growth theorists. They then point to the division between ownership and managerial control in the modern corporation, and attribute to the managers a utility function containing other arguments (principally growth) besides profit (or perhaps omitting profit altogether, which then appears as a 'minimum profit constraint' or 'take-over constraint'). In these models, the managers then forego some monopoly profit to obtain other goods. That monopolists could take out their profit in the form of a quiet life is an ancient observation: the new suggestion is that managers take it out in the form of faster growth than would be consistent with profit maximization. The question then is how shareholders, or the stock-market, let them get away with it. This is the general equilibrium question we already raised in connection with Baumol's static model. It thus turns out that the theory of stock-market valuation, and of take-over, is central to the new growth theories. (References will be found in Further Reading.) Effectively, the interest of the neo-Schumpeterians has switched from imperfections in product markets, which they take for granted, to imperfections in capital markets such as will allow non-owning managements to conduct corporations at non-profit-maximizing levels.

Further Reading

The major works on the 'new growth theories' are reprinted here: there is little else to follow up. What is important is stock-market valuation. The important articles are

M. H. Miller, and F. Modigliani, 'Dividend policy, growth and the
valuation of shares', *Journal of Business*, vol. 34, 1961, pp. 411–33,
J. Lintner, 'Optimal dividends and corporate growth under uncertainty',
Quarterly Journal of Economics, vol. 78, 1964, pp. 49–95,
and
J. Lintner, 'The cost of capital and optimal financing of corporate
growth' *Journal of Finance*, vol. 18, 1963, pp. 292–310.

A model fairly closely related to those of Baumol and Marris appears
in
O. E. Williamson, 'Managerial discretion and business behavior',
American Economic Review, vol. 53, 1963, pp. 1032–57.

The discussion of stochastic processes introduced by two of the
papers in this part is technically advanced. Simpler explanations of
some of the principles involved, together with applications to other
fields, will be found in
S. J. Prais, 'The formal theory of social mobility', *Population Studies*,
vol. 9, 1955, pp. 72–81,

E. H. Phelps. Brown and P. E. Hart, 'The size of trade unions: a study
in the laws of aggregation', *Economic Journal*, vol. 67, 1957, pp. 1–15,

A. D. Roy, 'Some thoughts on the distribution of earnings', *Oxford
Economic Papers*, N.S., vol. 3, 1951, pp. 135–46.

A classic but difficult paper is
H. A. Simon and C. P. Bonini, 'The size distribution of business
firms', *American Economic Review*, vol. 48, 1958, pp. 607–17.

The mathematics required for handling Markov chains is beautifully
laid out in
S. Goldberg, *Introduction to Difference Equations*, Wiley, 1958;
Chapman & Hall, 1958,
and
J. G. Kemeny, J. L. Snell and G. L. Thompson, *Introduction to Finite
Mathematics*, Prentice-Hall, 1957; Bailey & Swinfen, 1957.

As for understanding the distributions (Pareto, Log-Normal, Yule)
referred to, there is no real short-cut: a course in mathematical
statistics is required.

A serious attempt to relate the stochastic approach to received
(Marshallian) value theory is
P. K. Newman and J. N. Wolfe, 'A model for the long-run theory of
value', *Review of Economic Studies*, vol. 29, 1961, pp. 51–61.

Some empirical evidence on profitability, growth, and related matters will be found in

K. D. George, 'Concentration, barriers to entry and rates of return', *Review of Economics and Statistics*, vol. 50, 1968, pp. 273–5, and

A. Singh and G. Whittington, *Growth, Profitability and Valuation*, Cambridge University Press, 1968.

The latter extends tests of the law of proportionate effect discussed by Hart.

15 R. Marris

The Economic Theory of 'Managerial' Capitalism

R. Marris, *The Economic Theory of 'Managerial' Capitalism*, Macmillan, 1964, pp. 1–40, abridged and revised by the author for this volume.

The disappearance of the entrepreneur

'Managerial' capitalism is a name for the economic system of North America and Western Europe in the mid-twentieth century, a system in which production is concentrated in the hands of large joint-stock companies. In many sectors of economic activity the classical entrepreneur has virtually disappeared. His role was essentially active and unitary; once dismembered, no device of collective abstraction could put him together again. As a result (a substantial body of writers have suggested[1]), entrepreneurship in the modern corporation has been taken over by transcendent management, whose functions differ in kind from those of the traditional subordinate or 'mere manager'. These, it is argued, can wield considerable power without necessarily holding equity, sharing profits or carrying risks.

Of course, there never was a managerial revolution. Like the industrial revolution, the development from traditional capitalism to the contemporary form represented the slow replacement of one type of economic organization by another, a process which has not yet ended. Human societies rarely arrange their institutions of production with the rules of behaviour, as seen from the economist's view-point, fully specified. In traditional capitalism, the decision-taker has private-property rights over his instruments. He has the rights of exclusive use and enjoyment subject only to certain limited restraints on his freedom to

1. We refer to the writings of Thorstein Veblen, A. A. Berle, Gardner Means, Chester Barnard, R. A. Gordon, George Hurff, Sargent Florence, Carl Kaysen, J. K. Galbraith, Mrs Edith Penrose (listed in approximate historical order of publication). For a good general survey the reader is referred to Mason (1960), the notes to which may be used as a bibliography.

damage others. (He may burn the factory, but must ensure that the workers have left, and must not negligently allow the fire to spread to his neighbour's property.) There is also the implicit 'rule' that a capitalist who makes continuing losses will eventually cease to be a capitalist: both financially and morally he is encouraged to aim for profit. But how much profit is not stated.

A similar ambiguity applies to the directors of the modern corporation: in law they owe a duty to the shareholders, but its extent is not defined. Directors who refuse to *maximize* profits because, for example, they pay attention to competing social interests, cannot legally be penalized: and may well be popular. The position is not very different in the socialist forms of managerial society. The manager of an industrial plant under Communism is given specific instructions, usually consisting of quantitative production targets which it may literally cost him his life to ignore, but the rules as a whole, when examined, commonly prove quite inadequate to define the implied system of national resource allocation.

Because they are rudimentary, the rules tell us little about the game. Implicitly, they define a field (the economy), some players (producers and consumers) and some balls (goods and money). Violence to other players (theft) is illegal; certain coalitions (companies) are permitted if approved by the referee, others (combinations in restraint of trade) are not. But as to goals we know strangely little. If coalitions are formed, we do not know how these will behave – what goals, if any, they will set themselves, how they will determine the interior distribution of any utility they may acquire. To date, most economic theories have proceeded on particular simplifying assumptions about these questions, many of which now appear doubtful when applied to the special type of coalition represented in the modern corporation. In order to see why this is so, it is necessary to begin by re-examining the traditional system.

The essence of the traditional method of economic organization is the unification of the functions of risk-carrying, reward-receiving and operational decision-taking in one individual. By combining ownership with management, the person who carries much of the risk also makes most of the decisions determining its extent. As owner he receives the rewards of success, and is therefore motivated to optimize the balance between boldness and prudence. By combining risk-taking with decision-taking, traditional capitalism reduces the cost of the former while increasing the efficiency of the latter. That is why there is still quite an amount of it about.

The offsetting disadvantage, of course, is that owner-management imposes severe restraints on scale, restraints deriving not only from difficulties of delegation but also from the inevitable emphasis on internal financing and consequent restriction on the firm's rate of growth. Important economies may therefore remain unexploited. It was to overcome these disadvantages that the social architects of the nineteenth century invented the public, joint-stock, limited liability company, and thus invented modern capitalism: the managerial restraint on scale was overcome by resort to collective ownership and delegated control, while the financial restraint was handled by the issue of marketable shares carrying limited liability.

In England, where the invention occurred, it was greeted by considerable public criticism, so effective for a time that the necessary legislation was delayed for several decades. The critics realized that a major change was involved. They saw the advantages of owner-management being lost; they could not see the advantages to be gained because they distrusted large-scale organization.[2] Nevertheless, as everyone knows, the public joint-stock company arrived, prospered and multiplied, until, by the mid-twentieth century, not only was an overwhelming proportion of the national income in Britain and North America produced by companies, but the greater part came from firms of the type in which shareholders were numerous and their holding dispersed.

In effect, then, we now have an economic system in which the traditional and the corporate methods are legally and economically permitted to co-exist, and in which each may predominate where its relative advantages are greatest. But it is by no means necessary that in order to survive both types of firm must adopt the same internal rules of behaviour; either or both, for example, may well dispense with profit maximization. This is not only because the relative advantages of the one or the other are in

2. See for example the *Economist*, 27 January 1855, pp. 84–5.

some areas so overwhelming that differences in behaviour are easily offset, but also because the competitive environment has been made highly imperfect. Once large-scale organizations appear the prevailing condition is oligopoly.

Economic theory struggled manfully with the 'external' conditions of oligopoly, but failed to penetrate inside the firm. Until recently almost all 'micro' analysis implicitly regarded the corporation as a form of collective entrepreneurship, to be treated in much the same way as the one-man business, and nearly twenty years elapsed between the discovery of the managerial evolution and the appearance of related theories of the firm.[3] As a consequence there has been a failure to consider whether the assumed behaviour of *organizations*, such as companies, could logically be expected to arise from rational behaviour by their members, even when rational behaviour is confined to more or less orthodox utility maximization. A man's preference system is the result of his social situation, of the society around him and of the way it has moulded his psyche. But his social situation depends in turn on economic organization. For example, it is by no means obvious that action intended to maximize the utility of a company's stockholders is consistent with maximizing the utility of the action-takers, i.e. of the management.

The traditional pre-history of a corporation

Most large companies have grown out of smaller businesses of a more or less traditional type. For the moment, however, let us postulate a situation in which, when new economic activities are to be organized, there is a straight choice between the one or the other form only. Given that a man has noticed an opportunity for profit, how should he decide between a traditional business and floating a company? If he proceeds traditionally, he must have access to initial capital, and he must be prepared to carry a high proportion of the risk.[4] He will receive the whole income from both management and risk-taking, will have absolute right to

3. We refer to the theories of Downie (1958) and Baumol (1959).

4. The private limited company, or closed corporation, provides an apparent exception, but is essentially a form of traditional capitalism of which it can be said that risk avoided by the owners is largely thrown on to creditors (see Gower, 1957, p. 65).

dispose of that income, and will have absolute and unquestioned control. But the income, the wealth and the empire of power will be constrained by the scale limitations of traditional organization. If on the other hand a company is floated, some of the constraints are lifted, while the founder is yet able to secure for himself an important position as manager, chairman or president. This may provide him with prospects of both financial and 'psychological' rewards. But unless he has put up more than half the capital (in which case the organization can be regarded as effectively more or less traditional) none of these positions is absolutely guaranteed. Each depends on the consent of others and also, in principle, on the service he has to sell, as, for example, special knowledge of the trade. His income will be a salary determined by complex factors by no means entirely under his control. But to the extent that the larger-scale organization is more efficient, the income prospects may be better than the profit prospects of the traditional organization; in some ways more risky, in some ways more secure. Total satisfaction will depend also on non-financial considerations, such as personal evaluation of the relative merits of the two types of role. A manager is a different type of person from an entrepreneur, with different ideals and different personal values. A man might prefer flotation then, if he liked a salaried status, if he had little capital to invest, and if the advantages of large-scale organization were considerable. In other words, taking all things into account, in some circumstances pure flotation might mean greater utility.

But in practice, whatever might be preferred, wherever exploitation of the economic opportunity requires the development of a significant amount of organization, as is usual, for example, in manufacturing industry, pure flotation is rarely practicable. Investors are not readily induced to subscribe to the shares of an as yet non-existent organization. The overwhelming proportion of operations involving the formation of new public companies represents re-organization of traditional enterprises sufficiently successful to command confidence and now attempting to break through their constraints. Let us re-consider the process of growth which occurred before this point was reached.

Suppose, for the sake of argument, that previous growth has not been limited by demand: either demand exceeds capacity or the entrepreneur knows how to develop new markets when old ones are saturated. His constraints are thus mainly managerial and financial. The management problem has been widely discussed in orthodox literature, and arises essentially from the difficulties of delegation and coordination in an organization originally designed for one-man control. This has usually been regarded as a limit on absolute size rather than on the rate of growth. The financial constraint, on the other hand (which has been less discussed) apparently limits only the rate of growth. For finance to limit ultimate size, special assumptions are required.

If a traditional capitalist firm does not borrow, its compound-interest growth-rate cannot exceed the rate of net profit (after tax, depreciation and 'subsistence' for the entrepreneur) earned on capital employed, and the growth of the owner's wealth and of the firm's assets are synonymous. If, however, borrowing is allowed and is practised, the rate of growth of the size of the firm, measured by capital employed, is no longer necessarily the same as the growth rate of the entrepreneurial property. But provided the profit rate exceeds the interest rate, both can grow faster than the maximum possible when borrowing is not allowed, because the annual difference between profit and interest may be used as a source of capital for further reinvestment. Therefore, whether he derives utility from his own wealth, from the size of the firm or from both, it appears at first sight that rational behaviour requires the traditional capitalist to borrow as much as he can. At second glance, the answer is not so simple.

For if at each round of growth more is borrowed than is re-invested from the previous period's profits, the ratio of borrowed to re-invested money in the capital structure will steadily rise; in effect the firm will become increasingly 'levered', or, in British terminology, 'geared'. Leverage or gearing increases the risks of both lenders and borrower. Lenders know that as the leverage ratio rises the margin of assets covering their loan must be proportionately reduced: there is increasing danger that in the event of an unexpected decline in earning power the value of assets would become less than liabilities. The borrower (the entrepreneur), on the other hand, is more likely to see the problem in terms of the burden of interest charges against his profits: if profits fall, he is liable to default on payments, and may be forced into liquidation in circumstances where, were it not for the leverage, he would have been able to continue in business. Put more generally, the effect of leverage (for both borrower and lender) is to increase the risk of insolvency for any given probability-distribution of earnings.

If, therefore, it is desired to increase the rate of growth nevertheless, 'non-contractual' borrowing will be necessary. But lenders with no contractual rights to interest nor security for their capital inevitably require a share in ownership and control. They otherwise have no protection from wilful withholding of dividends, refusal to earn profits or negligent inefficiency. *It follows that a traditional enterprise cannot grow rapidly by means of indefinitely increasing leverage and still remain traditional.*

If for convenience we define a maximum-leverage point (i.e. maximum consistent with retaining the traditional organization) by reference to some ratio of outstanding debt to book value of total assets, the financial constraint on the growth rate of a traditional firm can be made precise. Once the maximum-leverage ratio has been reached, growth is constrained by the need to ensure that at each subsequent round of expansion, the proportionate increase in debt does not exceed the proportionate increase in total capital: if debt is permitted to expand faster, the leverage ratio will again begin to rise. So unless there are sons, sons-in-law or other relatives able to succeed the founder and maintain the rate of profit, the maximum financial size can be determined quite easily if we know the initial capital, know the working life of the founder, and can apply these factors to the maximum growth rate. If the maximum financial size is smaller than the managerial maximum, the typical history of a firm without a successor (in the absence of the possibility of corporate reorganization) would be to grow to some size no greater than the financial maximum, and then to die. If, however, we assume either that the founder's life is very long or that he can always find efficient successors, there is no maximum financial size. The firm will grow until it reaches its managerial limit; finance will merely have determined the length of time taken to get there. This is probably the more typical case.

The limits on size can be penetrated by changing the structure of the firm. By corporate reorganization the autocratic figure of the founder is replaced by a management team and the financing problem is eased by acquiring shareholders (although, as we shall see, the financial growth rate of a company is by no means without limit). Thus by 'going public' – a British expression for the conversion of a closed corporation into an open one – traditional enterprises can continue to grow in a new form, and this has been the origin of an overwhelming proportion of established public corporations. The advantages to the *firm* are obvious; less obvious are the advantages to the owner-founder. Before the change, the growth of the enterprise was closely associated with the growth of his personal wealth; after the change, the connection is considerably weakened. Why then does he agree? He may be approaching retirement and seeking a convenient method of realizing his gains, a motive which is particularly powerful where taxation discriminates against income. Or he may have concluded that the economies of scale are so considerable that cooperation with other people and other capital would on balance increase the growth of the value of his own equity, despite the fact that he would no longer be sole owner. Finally, he may in truth be more interested in promoting the continued growth of the organization he has founded, for its own sake, even though his personal financial position is not to be significantly improved. The organization may have become an expression of his ego, and its growth as such may provide direct utility. There is nothing in the rules of traditional capitalism to require an owner-manager to exclude all satisfaction but money. Where the founder can make arrangements to guarantee him an important continuing role until he chooses to retire, this motive of continuity is particularly likely to be effective, but even where he cannot make such arrangements, the founder may nevertheless obtain pleasure from watching the further development of his 'baby' long after he has ceased to direct it.

Under the 'Protestant Ethic' the profits earned by a man in his business were regarded as manifestations not of a stochastic process but of the hand of God. Business success could be interpreted as a sign of grace and if, therefore, God showed one of His elect a good investment opportunity, the beneficiary was duty bound to take it. Combined with the Puritan moral injunction against consumption, the resulting morality implied a continual attempt to maximize profits and to re-invest most of the proceeds. The 'Puritan' was thus a man with an almost unlimited appetite for future wealth; a negative rate of time discount (Tawney, 1926; Weber, 1930). His utility function contained only one variable, and this Divine index was the logarithm of net assets. Of course, if one was not of the elect, nothing was of any use anyway, but, fortunately for economic progress, one did not discover the truth until one died.

In psychoanalytic language the business drive is sublimated libido, and perhaps the business itself represents a castrated son. The position is more complicated, however, when actual (un-castrated) sons are employed in the enterprise, and intended to inherit it. The psychological conflicts set up in these situations are familiar, and it is often unclear what the father really wants. The usual conclusion of observers is that he would rather his son succeeded in an organization of his own – the father's – making, than that he made his way in the world, thus demonstrating man-liness. *En tout cas,* whether as a sign of grace or to satisfy his ego, the founder attaches utility to the continuity of the organiza-tion he founded, as such, irrespective of the direct financial advantage.

As a matter of fact, most organizations have inherent tendencies to attempt to perpetuate themselves (see Samuelson, 1948, p. 131). Though a traditional capitalist might wish his firm to express no more than himself, the firm itself contains individuals who may feel differently. Thus the baby cannot always be prevented from growing and showing signs of independence, whatever the parent may desire. If the baby succeeds, it is almost certain, sooner or or later, to be transformed into a modern corporation, an institution of considerable ambiguity, to which we now turn.

The corporate collective

Unlike many human institutions, a joint-stock company has a rather specific legal constitution. The law, however, is mainly concerned to protect creditors and investors from obvious fraud, and has done little to push these great productive institutions in any particular economic or social direction. Thus company law represents no more than a special aspect of the general protection of property in the ordinary legal framework of capitalism. But however 'non-economic' the purposes of the corporate constitution, it is the framework within which the game is played and must therefore be taken seriously. A joint-stock company is a legal person intended to engage in trade or business, although it is not compelled to trade and may, in practice, undertake almost any known human activity. This person, which is really a specially defined collective, may sue and be sued, prosecute and be prosecuted, employ labour, own assets, incur debts, and be subjected to taxation. Its management is vested in a board of directors who sign documents, bind the company and generally behave as its agents. None of the directors, however, need necessarily hold a significant equity in the company, nor must the directors necessarily be employees of the company in any other capacity. But directors *may* be substantial equity holders and *may* be full-time managerial employees.

The company, then, is a legal institution owning productive assets as if it were an individual. Who then owns the company? The law provides for a body of shareholders, or more precisely for a body of shares. These are the property of individual holders and, like other property, are transferable to other real persons either as gifts or for consideration. They can also be owned by other legal persons. They entitle the owner to a bundle of rights in the company, and generally, but not always, they are originally issued in return for some specific consideration such as the subscription of capital. Usually the resulting rights attaching to the share are *equitable* relatively to the consideration, e.g. if the consideration is capital, capital dividend and voting rights are awarded in proportion to the amount of capital supplied (Gower, 1957, p. 319). Thus the *company* issues the shares, but the rights inherent in the shares give real persons some aspects of part-owners of the company. Strictly, however, all that a shareholder owns is his bundle of rights. His shares are his property, the company is not. The shareholders are not the legal owners of the assets of the company, nor even, in many countries, of the current profits before distribution.

The directors, on the other hand, are servants of the company, not apparently, of the shareholders. But do not the rights inherent in the shares provide the holders with virtual *de facto* ownership and control? Many people believe this to be the case (and indeed many believe, erroneously, that shareholders are proprietors *de jure*), and it is certainly true that if a company is not owned by its members, it is owned by no one. Almost universally, the company meeting appoints the directors; therefore the right to vote at the meeting apparently provides definite indirect collective control. Similarly, the rights to dividend and capital imply a position which, if a long way from that of sole owner, is by no means that of a true *rentier*. This, however, is far from the end of the matter. For it is the directors who determine the dividend, and they have gradually acquired discretion to withhold considerable proportions of current profits, which then, either as fixed or liquid assets, become the property of the company. This capital accumulated from retained profits 'belongs' to the shareholders only to the extent provided by their specific rights. The increased capital behind each share should lead to increased earnings, from which shareholders will benefit provided these are distributed. Shareholders also benefit if the directors decide on a capital distribution or if the business is sold. But the shareholders cannot in general directly initiate a capital distribution except by enforcing total liquidation, i.e. by causing the assets to be sold at break-up value.

In social accounting terms, company law creates concepts of corporate income and corporate capital, distinct from and by no means identical with the more familiar concepts of personal income and personal capital: the value of company assets is not necessarily equal to the market value of corresponding stocks. It has been suggested, in fact, that the existence of corporate income is the essence of managerial capitalism (Wiles, 1961, p. 186). Through gradual development of the practice of substantial dividend retentions, corporate assets, created from corporate income, have become a partly autonomous factor in the economic system, and the industrial capital of western democracies is no longer divided into two classes, 'public' and 'private', but rather into three, 'public', 'private', and 'corporate'. The corporate sector likes to be described as 'private', but this may represent no more than a desire to conceal, and thus protect, the underlying independence.

Corresponding to the third concept of capital, we may identify a third body of persons, rivalling the shareholders for its control. These are 'the managers' – a term of art which, since Burnham (1941), has been generally applied to people who control and operate, but do not substantially 'own' productive institutions. To Veblen (1923) and Burnham they were technicians, and Veblen thought they were not powerful. Berle and Means (1932) saw them as neither technicians nor capitalists, but rather as disembodied entrepreneurs enjoying many of the fruits of capitalism without themselves providing much capital or taking proportionnate risks. More recent writers, notably Gordon (1961; see also Latham in Mason, 1960, pp. 228–31), have emphasized their role as organizers and administrators. This is surely correct. It was by providing virtually a new factor of production – the capacity for large-scale organization – that the new system broke the restraints on traditional capitalist production. Large-scale production depends uniquely on large-scale organization. The profits and dividends of large companies are derived from the professional abilities of people who know how to flatten the U-shaped cost curve. This ability gives them considerable influence and bargaining power.

It is sometimes suggested that in the corporate sector boards of directors may be regarded as trustees for shareholders, that they are, in fact, like watchdog committees set up to keep management in its place. This view, however, is not supported by legal authorities (Gower, 1957, pp. 471–2; Katz, 1958, p. 172; Hurff, 1950, p. 113), and in any case the managers have themselves considerably assimilated the directorial system. Legally the function of the board is to operate the company. For the purpose, it employs executives who may, as we have seen, themselves be directors. But board members who are also full-time employees command the power of organization and hence must in general dominate (Gordon, 1961, ch. 6). In the US the majority of all directors are in this position (Gordon, 1961, p. 119). Thus, by combining the functions of employee and employer, the management body is considerably freed from direct external restraints, a condition which is emphasized by the fact that the great majority of board nominations are proposed by existing directors. In practice, in many firms, the board itself recedes into the background and operations are taken over by committees of senior executives, not all of whom are necessarily directors (Gordon, 1961, ch. 5).

For these reasons, the distinction between 'management' and stockholders is a valid one, and the two groups may properly be regarded as separate elements in the corporate structure. More precisely, we define 'the management' as the particular in-group, consisting of directors and others, which effectively carries out the functions legally vested in the board. This does not mean that shareholders and management are necessarily opposed, or that policy will necessarily differ from that which might be pursued in a system where managers were immanent. *All we are saying is that the two groups are sufficiently distinct, and the managers sufficiently autonomous, that the existence of a harmony of interests cannot be regarded as axiomatic.* Therefore, in order to understand the economic system of the corporations, it is essential to assess the factors determining the relative influence of, or balance of power between, these two forces operating within them.

No empirical investigation is required to assert that the behaviour of an organization will represent the outcome of the interactions of the desires, ideals, ethics and constraints of the individuals or groups of which it is composed. Individuals may attach utility in varying degrees to what the organization does for them, to what it does for other members, to what it does for outsiders and to what it does for itself. At one extreme, they may regard the organization as little more than a vehicle for satisfying personal economic needs, at the other they may identify it with their own egos to such an extent that its collective prosperity takes precedence over all ordinary personal considerations. But whatever the utility function associated with his participation, the individual's influence over policy will depend not only on this, but also on his bargaining position. Neither the most junior office girl nor the owner of a single share is likely to have much influence, unless the one is the managing director's mistress or the other his wife. But even a virtuous office girl will have some influence, because if the organization does not provide her with sufficient utility to induce her continued participation she will cease to participate. This, of course, is recognized in the orthodox theory of the firm, but only on the assumption that the utility functions of all participants are of the relatively simple kind postulated in the post-classical theory of net advantages. If participants attach utility to other aspects of company policy – for example, if they prefer to work in an organization which does not aim for large profits – the results, even at the present stage of the argument, could be quite far-reaching. However, it is evident that the influence of individual participants may often exceed many times the inducement minimum, particularly, of course, in the case of high management.

The pull of the management in an individual company greatly exceeds the sum of the values of the individuals' qualifications on the open market. The management is a team which has been built up over a period of time and has acquired unique ability to operate a particular business (Penrose, 1959, p. 46). The profits earned by the assets depend on the management; they by no means reside entirely in the character of the assets themselves. Indeed, to a considerable extent, the physical assets are notably subordinate to the human assets in the general economic picture of the firm: an investor can far more realistically be said to be buying a share in (i.e. interest in) the organization than a share in a particular set of physical assets. In truth, he is buying a compound of the assets and the organization. The organization has special knowledge and ability in managing the assets and the assets have been built up to match the special talents of the organization. This is what is meant by a 'going concern'. Hence the value of the team is very much greater than the sum of the salaries the members could earn if disbanded.

Of course, management can always be replaced. But the new team will not be familiar with the firm's particular operation, even if it has considerable experience of the particular trade. A complete change of management is likely to increase the rate of return on the company's capital only if the existing management is very inefficient. This point is of crucial importance because, as we have seen, in cases where a concentration of shareholders is in a position to impose sanctions on the board, their legal weapon essentially resolves into the threat of dismissal. Shareholders cannot legally interfere directly with any other aspect of management. In order to remove a senior manager not on the board against the wishes of the existing board, they must at least threaten to replace a majority of the existing directors with their own nominees. Both sides, therefore, possess a 'deterrent' of sorts, and the outcome is uncertain. Therefore, even in a fairly closely-held company, the management has considerable autonomy through economic influence, because its members represent an organization capable of operating the assets, while the shareholders in general do not. It follows as a corollary that the relative strength of a management's position depends *inter alia* on its relative commercial efficiency.

The factor of commercial efficiency, however, is specific to individual firms. More general factors in the balance of power are the procedural facility with which the directors can be dismissed, the distribution of holdings and the various economic consequences of shares being saleable. The right to elect is of little influence if the procedure for dismissal is cumbersome, and the votes themselves are of little influence if they are statistically dispersed and their holders unorganized. *But dispersed votes regain their potency if the firm can be threatened with take-over or if selling activity 'punishes' management in any other way, for example, by affecting future supplies of finance or by damaging managerial prestige.*

In England, since the Second World War, all the directors in any public company can be removed by simple majority at a properly constituted meeting. In the US, where the law varies from state to state, the position is sometimes more circumscribed. In England, shareholders are also restrained by the effect of the law relating to contracts between directors and their companies (Gower, 1957, pp. 124–7). And in general, both in the UK and the US, dismissal of directors is in practice rare, except where an individual or small organized group has acquired a majority holding and is engaged, in fact, in a take-over raid.

As to the statistical distribution of holdings, the familiar facts are that the proportion of British and North American manufacturing output produced by companies of the type where a single person or family holds impregnable control has been small for sometime past; that by the late nineteen-thirties, in two-thirds of large and medium-size English companies and in four-fifths of large US companies, in each case not even the top twenty shareholders had between them sufficient stock to command an absolute majority; and that since then dispersion has continued to increase, and in England, at least, the trend appears to have been accelerating. It follows that only by organizing could shareholders, in the majority of cases, make effective use of their votes. But typical shareholders are unorganized almost by definition. They spread their holdings in order to avoid, among other risks, the risk of finding themselves locked into a firm with whose policies they are dissatisfied, and if in fact dissatisfied, they generally prefer to sell rather than go to the trouble and expense of organizing opposition. The directors, on the other hand, have usually a small collective holding sufficient to dominate meetings in the absence of concentrated or resolute opposition. Typically, boards hold from one to two per cent of the total equity, a fact which has often been adduced to demonstrate separation of control from ownership. The reinforcing effect on control has received less emphasis. It is particularly significant that while managements do not usually hold large blocks of shares, their holdings are rarely negligible. They are not owner-managers, because their holdings represent small proportions of their total wealth, and associated dividends small proportions of their total incomes. Perhaps they could be described as 'controller-managers'. We are forced inevitably to the conclusion that if shareholders in general possess countervailing power, it must be found mainly in the factors we have yet to discuss, i.e. in the transferability of shares and in the existence of an organized stock-market.

Because shares are bought and sold in an organized market, management policies must affect their prices. But these, in turn, react on management in several ways. Firstly, it is by no means unlikely that the market valuation of a company directly enters the managerial utility function. They may feel prestige associated with healthy prices – a sign of approbation from the investing class – they may feel loyalty to their shareholders, or they may have a sense of conscience towards the shares as such: under modern conditions, the share *holders*, as a body of persons, are changing every day, but the shares, though abstract, are constant, and their market price well known. The shares may be thought to represent a collective super-ego, enforcing 'good' (i.e. traditional) management behaviour. Note, however, that we are concerned with the influence of the stock-market as a whole, including potential buyers and actual sellers, i.e. we are not merely concerned with the particular individuals who happen to be holding the company's shares at a particular moment. The price of a company's shares may change substantially without any significant change in membership (turnover of stock), and the membership may change substantially without any significant change in price. We are concerned only with the price, with the way it is affected by management policy and with the way policy may be affected by it. This is the impersonal logic of the corporate system.

Secondly, share prices may also affect supplies of finance, not only new-issue finance but also, by permeation, borrowing-power in the bond market. Here our concern is with new issues alone. There is a double implication. Managers may desire expansion, in which case their utility is affected directly, or, alternatively, if firms pursuing certain policies are unable to expand, in the long run others will predominate: in other words, financial policies inimical to growth do not have a survival value.

Thirdly, share prices may favour a radical change in the voting distribution, i.e. a take-over raid. Some policies may depress prices so far that the aggregate market value of the equity becomes significantly less than the value, to a single outsider, of the assets behind the equity. The 'outsider' would be a person or organized group who could value the assets on the assumption that sufficient stock was obtained to guarantee easy dismissal of the present directors and a suitable change of policy. Take-over raids are difficult and risky, but if the prospective gain is large enough, the attempt will seem worth while. Therefore potential raids are, and always have been, a real factor to any management wishing to stay in office. Investors value voting rights not so much because they expect to use them, but because they can be sold to someone who might. The balance of power between investor and manager involves two institutions: on the one hand the stock-market, essentially an exchange for *rentier* paper; on the other, the voting share, something of a pre-managerial phenomenon. Take-overs, as against voluntary mergers, are feared because typically, after a successful raid, the whole top management is dismissed, losing job, prestige and perquisites of office. Thus policies likely to induce raids also lack survival value.

The effects of potential take-over raids and of the long-run supply of finance are intimately connected, because the take-over danger can be affected by dividend policy, and retentions are a source of finance. Both are also affected by investment policy, i.e. by the attempted rate of expansion and profits expected. A take-over raider is a person or company aiming for virtual ownership. He or they intend to acquire sufficient stock to be able to dismiss and appoint directors at will, to distribute capital, to amalgamate with other firms controlled, perhaps, by themselves, to appoint executives at salaries of their own choosing – to appoint, perhaps, themselves, their relatives or their friends. They may plan to re-organize the firm, sell the assets, distribute capital and realize quick capital gains. Alternatively, they may intend to continue the business on existing lines, but managed with greater efficiency or with a different pay-out policy. *En tout cas* they require at least 51 per cent of the voting stock and probably more; the precise requirement will depend on the existing distribution of holdings, on the terms of the charter and on the laws of the country.

Two methods are typically available. Either the raider may attempt to buy the necessary shares on the open market, or he may publicly announce that he will buy all the existing stock at a stated price provided sufficient acceptances are received to ensure the desired degree of control – the so-called conditional offer in a procedure known as a take-over 'bid'. The open-market method suffers from the disadvantage that, unless the market is perfect and the operations perfectly secret, the price is almost certain to rise as the purchases develop. The 'bid' method, on the other hand, suffers because, the announcement being public, the offer price will almost certainly have to be higher than the pre-existing market price, and part of the benefits of the raid will necessarily be shared with the old stockholders. Often the announcement will also bring other bidders into the field, as the raider's commercial competitors strive to prevent him increasing his domination of their industry. In practice the cheapest method is usually some combination of the two, but the average price paid for stock will still almost always exceed the price ruling in the market before the operation began or was rumoured.

For the moment, however, let us assume most of these tiresome details away. The raider can acquire all the stock he needs by secret open-market purchases without affecting the price at all: the average price he pays for stock is the price quoted by dealers the day before he began buying. There are no substantial blocks of votes held by persons or groups who value them above the ruling market price, and the raid is not discovered by the existing management until it is too late; they cannot defend themselves by announcing policy changes. The purchase price therefore reflects the market valuation ratio based on the expected results of existing managerial policies.

We then ask how the existing management's policies must be constrained if they desire to avoid creating market conditions in which a raid (on our assumptions, necessarily successful) would be likely to occur. Policies lying within the constraints will be called 'safe'. In real life, because markets are imperfect and raiders unable to maintain secrecy, managements will be fairly secure if they pursue policies considerably more dangerous than the most dangerous of those which are safe on this definition; but we can validly assume that the economic characteristics of 'reasonably' safe policies are determined by and vary with the characteristics of those defined as theoretically safe; therefore by analysing the latter we may also roughly delineate the former (for obvious reasons, the 'limiting case' method is more convenient).

When one takes over a large company, one acquires a particular set of assets associated with a partly specific labour force and a rather more specific body of middle and junior managers; one also acquires various other ingredients known as 'goodwill'. But whatever or whoever one is, if the assets are to continue to earn, one will have to be able to provide a more or less complete new high management. This is evidently a considerable restriction, for circumstances where the assets can be realized in a quick capital gain involving no continuing management are rare, though lucrative. In this book we are concerned with the large companies which produce the bulk of industrial output, and he who wishes to raid these must be able to provide at least the rudiments of the high management needed for large-scale organization. Alternatively, he must accept a lower level of efficiency. If 'he' is some kind of traditional capitalist he should not, in principle, be so well-equipped for the purpose as the typical professional managerial team, and must therefore set his organizational disadvantage against the possible benefits of changes of policy.[5]

However, the 'pure' traditional capitalist is by no means the only species of wolf in the forest. Some raiders combine traditional characteristics with modern; incorporated, but closely held; concerned mainly with getting rich, but nevertheless capable of considerable organization. Some with apparently traditional motivation are, in fact, akin to management specialists. Finally, of course, powerful raids are frequently made by other purely managerial organizations. The successful among those represent involuntary mergers imposed by one professional team on another, for motives which at least in principle may differ considerably from the traditional.

One requirement, however, is common to all raiders: they must have the means of payment. They must either possess or be able to borrow large sums in cash, or, if incorporated, they must either have large reserves or mortgageable assets or be able to offer to issue new shares in their own company, in payment for the shares of the raided company at a rate of exchange which is both acceptable to the recipients and does not dilute the raider's own old stock to a greater extent than is considered desirable or safe. This last method is not compatible with our assumption of secrecy, but the fact that it is widely used in conditional offers only serves to emphasize that, unlike us, real raiders assume real stock markets to be highly imperfect. On our assumptions, raiders must have cash.

If the social accounting essence of managerial capitalism lies in the existence of corporate capital, its economico-institutional essence lies in the widespread separation, not so much of ownership from control as of organization from finance. In the course

5. For example, Florence (1953), noted two English companies, Dunlop Rubber and Harrods Stores, as presenting outstanding examples of dispersed shareholding, the largest holder in neither having more than one half of 1 per cent of the stock. Holdings dispersed in this degree imply 'managerial control', but also facilitate the task of the raider. Harrods, as the name implies, are not manufacturers but a large West End department store, world famous for both the variety and costliness of their wares. In 1960, against violent opposition from the existing management, the business was successfully raided by a traditional capitalist from Scotland. By contrast, Dunlop, at the time of writing, remains inviolate.

of the managerial evolution the quantity of organizational talent in society has been vastly increased, but in the process it has become professionalized, bureaucratized and largely separated from finance. The majority of professional top managers spend a large part of their working lives in a single firm, and at any one time only a small proportion of them are seeking to move. When they do move, their method of transfer is professional rather than capitalistic; that is, they do not take capital with them. In the small business sector, conditions are reversed, and lying between the small- and large-scale sectors there is a significant penumbra where traditional and modern methods are mixed. Some of these businesses have large turnovers and yield large profits, but it is noticeable that they are rarely found in industries typically requiring genuine large-scale organization. It follows that in the modern world take-over raiders, wherever they occur, are scarce, and being scarce, in order to function, must be appropriately rewarded.

But although scarce, they exist, and, if sufficiently tempted, pounce. In measuring the temptation represented by a particular firm, a 'traditional' raider can value the assets on the basis of any pay-out ratio he chooses (because, if successful, the choice will be his), on his own, rather than the market's, rate of discount and on the rate of return he expects to obtain with the management he intends to install and the investment policy he intends to pursue. Because he is scarce, his discount rate (reflecting the next most profitable use for his capital) will be high, and because he is traditional we may assume that, although of no great managerial efficiency, he will attempt to pursue the investment policy expected to yield the maximum rate of return, given the nature of the business, the character of the assets and his actual organizational capacity.

Because we are not yet ready to discuss theories of managerial motivation, the case of the 'managerial' raider is rather vaguer. We shall, however, be reasonably consistent with our own later arguments if we assume that he or they apply a rate of discount equivalent to the rate of return obtainable with unchanged policies within 'their' own firm and a rate of return no lower than the rate expected from the highest-yielding policy, in the merged organization, consistent with a rate of expansion at least as fast as the rate associated with the existing policy in the raider's present organization. If the managerial raider pays cash, he will also assume a zero retention ratio. (If, violating our assumptions, he uses the exchange-of-share method, he must take account of the fact that any newly created stock will rank equally for dividend with his own old stock, and the result is therefore affected by the terms of the offer and his own expected retention ratio.) We may then say that a successful managerial raid requires that the return in the merged organization exceed not only the average of the two 'old' rates, but also the rate expected by the market were the unified firm itself to be taken over by the defending management (if not, the defenders could successfully form a company to retake captor and prize). In other words the market must believe, not only that the merger would be profitable, but that the new combine would be better managed by the aggressor management than by the defendant. Here again, however, we are wandering into a world which violates the analytical assumptions, because, on these, the market never has an opportunity of assessing the raider.

Clearly, therefore, a 'managerial' raid is less amenable to formal analysis and, although it is in practice the most common type, we shall attempt first to develop a 'traditional' theory, in the hope that this will throw some light on the other. If raiders in general were abundant relatively to their efficiency no existing management could then survive unless it had available at least one policy yielding at least the market rate of discount, if not better. Managements with such policies available would be forced to pursue them, and all other managements would eventually be eliminated by raiders. No firm would survive pursuing any policy yielding less than the market discount rate.

Such a world could properly be described as 'neo-classical', an imaginary world, that is, of institutional assumptions appropriate to modern capitalism, behaviour assumptions appropriate to traditional capitalism, and theorems similar to those of the nineteenth century. It is a world, of course, which could never exist; or, more precisely, if created, could never persist, because the assumptions are internally contradictory. The institutions of modern capitalism are impossible to reconcile with the assumption that raiders are not scarce. The problem with neo-classical economics is not so much that it does not apply to the world in which we live as that it could not apply to any viable capitalist system at all. If we repealed the Company Acts, banned large-scale organizations, and/or provided professional managers with almost unlimited supplies of finance at a constant rate of interest, we might conceivably resurrect some kind of traditional capitalism (and thus, no doubt, succeed in making ourselves considerably poorer). But if we did, the results would be 'classical', period. Alternatively, we could pass a series of laws requiring managements to follow decision-rules designed to produce the neo-classical results directly. Then we should have not capitalism but socialism. To put the point another way: the productive units of modern capitalism are not only large, but their size distribution is extremely skewed, and the risk of take-over diminishes with the size of the firm: therefore, even in a system in which firms of average size were subject to considerable take-over 'discipline', the giants who produce the bulk of the output would remain relatively immune.

In the subsequent chapters of this book the author developed a theory intended to systematize the basic concepts but which in some respects now seems to have been unnecessarily complicated. The basic idea was that the modern capitalist corporation should be seen as an institution of indefinite life capable of continuous growth. Growth itself was likely to be a major objective of the managers, but the threat of take-over or 'classical' loyalties to shareholders' welfare might prevent this objective from being pursued at all costs, especially if the costs were reflected in a reduced stock-market value. The underlying task of a theory, therefore, was to determine the connection between desired and/or expected growth-rate on the one hand and the likely demand-price for the shares on the other. This was achieved by means of a 'steady-state' model in which assumptions were made such that once the main lines of the firm's policy have been laid down, and the 'instrumental' variable available to management quantitatively determined, its sales, profits, assets and dividends would grow at a common, constant annual percentage rate until such time as either the policy was changed, the environment changed, or both changed. Thus on a steady-state path, sales, profits and assets, etc. all remain constant in relation to one another (so that, e.g. the rate of profit on capital is constant), but, of course, it may be possible to choose from alternative steady-state paths, each with a different (but constant) growth-rate and different values of the constant ratios such as rate of profit. By assuming that it is the expected path of dividends which ultimately determines current stock-market value, it is thus possible to postulate that in choosing a growth-rate the firm, in effect, chooses the stock-market value as well. It will not always be the case that accelerated growth means a higher valuation ratio,[6] so a conflict between growth and shareholders' welfare may need to be resolved, as suggested above.

The simpler version of the theory, as it has subsequently developed (Marris and Wood, 1971), takes advantage of a theorem which implies that on certain not unreasonable assumptions the stock-market should be indifferent as to whether a given growth-rate is financed mainly by new share issues (with or without dilution), or mainly by retained profits or by a combination of both. In effect, therefore, a model which assumes that *all* growth is internally financed will probably be as satisfactory for most purposes as a model which permits a mixture of internal and external finance.

We can assume that the stock-market is concerned essentially with two basic elements in the prospects of a share, namely the current dividend and its expected long-run growth-rate, the latter indicating both expected future dividends and prospects of capital gain. Just exactly how investors trade off between present and expected future dividends is a complicated matter involving theories of time-preference, risk-aversion and asset holding (Marris and Wood, 1971).[7] It is clear, however, that any *given* current dividend whose future is subject to a given degree of risk must be valued more highly the greater its expected future growth-rate – unless the higher growth-rate in some way increases risk by an offsetting amount. It is in fact a well-known proposition that under conditions of certainty (including the certain belief that the firm will last for ever), the positive effect of the expected dividend growth-rate itself increases and must eventually, theoretically, become infinite in the sense that at some finite positive

6. Stock-market value expressed as a ratio of total net assets.
7. For the complete theory see Lintner in Marris and Wood (1971).

(certain) expected growth-rate, the demand price of the share tends to infinity. In practice, because the future is uncertain and because the degree of uncertainty is likely in fact to increase the further we look ahead into the future, this effect is damped and we may, in fact, reasonably assume that the relationship between share price (or more precisely, the price-dividend ratio) is well behaved and perhaps approximately linear. For example, suppose a firm is expected with certainty to continue for ever and is currently paying a dividend of one dollar per share; suppose expectations regarding this dividend in the future are uncertain but the most likely outcome (mathematical expectation) is thought to be that it will neither tend to grow nor to diminish, because the firm is believed to be pursuing a policy of zero growth, the demand price for such a share might be ten dollars. If, however, the policy and circumstances of the firm were believed to be such that the most probable future development would be that the dividend of one dollar would grow in the future at an average annual compound-interest rate of 5 per cent per annum, then the share might sell for fourteen dollars, and with an expected growth-rate of 10 per cent, perhaps for eighteen dollars,[8] and so on. If we can specify this kind of relationship, we can theoretically determine the stock-market value provided we know only the current dividend and the expected steady-state growth-rate.

The growth-rate and the dividend, however, are themselves directly linked by another type of relationship which forms a further fundamental element in the basic theory of the growing corporation. This derives from the idea that the large corporation usually has a considerable influence over its own growth destiny. It cannot grow indefinitely by reducing prices on existing products because this reduces profitability, cuts off finance and

8. In the absence of all uncertainty, a non-growing dividend of one dollar would be worth ten dollars if the investors' pure rate of time discount were 10 per cent. Growing at 5 per cent per annum this share is worth twenty dollars because the capitalization factor for a perpetual annuity discounted at i growing at g is $1/(i-g)$, the growth-rate being perfectly analogous to negative interest. Consequently, with a time-discount rate of 10 per cent and a growth-rate of 10 per cent, as above, under conditions of certainty the capitalization factor is $1/(10-10)$, i.e. it is infinite. The examples above differ from this because of the effects of risk. For a further discussion again see Lintner in Marris and Wood (1971).

generally invalidates the 'steady-state' assumptions. It can, however, actively search out new markets by developing new products or by entering already established markets where profit possibilities are as high or higher than in its own existing markets. It may also promote the growth of demand for its existing products by advertising. All these activities cost time, effort and money. In the first place cash must be diverted from profits earned in existing markets to finance the process of search, research and development. In the second place, the more successful the search, the more demand is created, the more capacity is needed to meet the demand and the greater the proportion of profits (after deducting sums diverted to search and development) which must be retained to finance tangible investment in expanded productive capacity. Consequently, given the profitability of the existing activities (which in this model is taken as 'exogenous'), the faster the *desired* growth of the firm the less the amount of cash available for dividends. The current dividend associated with any expected growth-rate must therefore be lower, the higher that growth-rate, a relationship which may conveniently be normalized by expressing the current dividend as a ratio of existing assets. On the steady-state assumptions, the dividend itself, of course, grows at the common rate, therefore this relationship implies that an increase in growth-effort twists the time path of dividends, reducing the immediate prospects but increasing the longer run prospects.

So, an increase in the desired growth-rate of the firm affects the two basic elements in the demand-price for a share in opposite ways; by increasing the expected growth-rate of the dividend, we increase the value of a given current dividend, but by devoting more resources to growth, the current dividend is itself depressed. It is possible that the latter effect may outweigh the former through the whole range of positive growth-rates. Alternatively, at the low end of the range the opposite condition is equally possible, but the assumptions imply that it is mathematically inevitable that in due course, as the assumed growth-rate progressively increases, the net effect eventually must again become negative.

It follows that the model (or, more correctly, the class of models) defines a *valuation curve*, indicating a theoretically predicted valuation ratio for any given desired and expected growth-rate. This curve must have a positive intercept (the valuation ratio must be positive for a zero growth-rate) and may either slope downwards throughout its length until reaching zero, where the cash resources required for growth absorb all profits and preclude all dividends, or it will rise to a positive maximum and then decline correspondingly. If we ignore the possibility of negative growth-rates, the first case can be thought of as one where the growth-rate for maximizing the valuation ratio happens to be zero. The growth-rate of the individual firm is necessarily faster than the 'classical' growth-rate, and the growth-rate of the whole economy may also be faster if it happens that increased striving for growth on the part of managers has the effect of increasing the national rate of technical progress and innovation.

References

BAUMOL, W. J. (1959), *Business Behavior, Value and Growth*, Harcourt, Brace & World.
BERLE, A. A., and MEANS, G. (1932), *The Modern Corporation and Private Property*, Macmillan.
BURNHAM, J. (1941), *The Managerial Revolution*, Indiana University Press.
DOWNIE, J. (1958), *The Competitive Process*, Duckworth.
FLORENCE, P. S. (1953), *The Logic of British and American Industry*, University of North Carolina Press.
GORDON, R. A. (1961), *Business Leadership in the Large Corporation*, University of California Press.
GOWER, L. C. B. (1957), *Modern English Company Law*, Stevens.
HURFF, G. (1950), *Social Aspects of Enterprise in the Large Corporation*, University of Pennsylvania Press.
KATZ, W. G. (1958), 'The philosophy of mid-twentieth century corporation statutes', *Law and Contemporary Problems*.
MARRIS, R., and WOOD, A. (eds.) (1971), *The Corporate Economy*, Macmillan.
MASON, E. (ed.) (1960), *The Corporation in Modern Society*, Harvard University Press.
PENROSE, E. (1959), *The Theory and Growth of the Firm*, Oxford University Press.
SAMUELSON, P. (1948), *Economics*, McGraw-Hill.
TAWNEY, R. H. (1926), *Religion and the Rise of Capitalism*, Murray; Penguin, 1938.
VEBLEN, T. (1923), *Absentee Ownership*, Beacon Press.
WEBER, M. (1930), *The Protestant Ethic and the Spirit of Capitalism*, trans. T. Parsons, Allen & Unwin.
WILES, P. J. (1961), *Price, Cost and Output*, Oxford University Press.

R. Marris 317

16 W. J. Baumol

On the Theory of Expansion of the Firm [1]

Excerpt from W. J. Baumol, 'On the theory of expansion of the firm', *American Economic Review*, vol. 52, 1962, pp. 1078–87.

Economists who have spent time observing the operations of business enterprises come away impressed with the extent of management's occupation with growth. Expansion is a theme which (with some variations) is dinned into the ears of stockholders, is constantly reported in the financial pages and in the journals devoted to business affairs. Indeed, in talking to business executives one may easily come to believe that growth of the firm is the main preoccupation of top management. A stationary optimum would doubtless be abhorrent to the captains of industry, whose main concern is surely not at what size their enterprises should finally settle down (except where sheer size endangers their standing with the administrators of the antitrust laws) but rather, how rapidly to grow.[2]

Although the static theory of the firm is a helpful snapshot description of a system in motion,[3] it is useful also to have an alternative construction of the kind which is described in this

1. This paper owes much to the growing literature of the dynamics of the firm. Particularly, I am indebted to Robin Marris for permitting me to read his unpublished manuscript (*The Microeconomics of Managerial Capitalism*) and to Herbert Frazer who wrote his doctoral dissertation on the subject. Highly relevant and stimulating is Penrose (1959). In addition I owe much to the work of Quandt (Knorr and Baumol, 1961, pp.156-66).

2. This view is not unrelated to one of Kaldor's well-known arguments (see Kaldor, 1934). Here the author reminded us that equilibrium of the competitive firm requires some sort of increasing costs to make it unprofitable for the company to expand indefinitely. But under pure competition there seems to be no obvious source of diminishing returns, and hence little reason for *any* scale of operations of the competitive firm to constitute a long-run stationary equilibrium situation.

3. Thus I am emphatically *not* proposing that the conventional theory of the firm be relegated to the garbage heap or the museum of curious anti-

paper – another equilibrium analysis in which the *rate of growth* of output, rather than its *level*, is the variable whose value is determined by optimality considerations.

A simple growth equilibrium model

For simplicity the first model is confined to a case in which input and output prices are fixed (pure competition), and where the production function is linear and homogeneous. Thus I am either dealing only with the period of time before the firm grows so large that the prices become variables which are subject to the influence of the firm, or we must assume that all firms grow together and that in this process no one of them outgrows the others sufficiently to constitute it a significant force in the market. This premise permits me to evade the problem of demand for the expanding outputs of the firm. So long as it operates under conditions of pure competition its demand curves will be perfectly elastic and no marketing problems will affect its plans.[4]

It is assumed that management considers only a very simple growth pattern – a fixed percentage rate of growth, to be continued into the indefinite future. This heroic assumption is adopted to permit a simple characterization of the optimal growth path by means of a single variable, the permanent percentage rate of growth, g.[5]

---

quities. Static analysis of a nonstationary phenomenon can be immensely illuminating, and the received theory of the firm contains many very helpful results, both from the point of view of the understanding of the workings of the economy and the applied work of the operations researcher. It would be folly to deny ourselves the use of this body of analysis just because its domain of applicability is somewhat limited.

4. However, if all firms expand simultaneously in this way they may encounter secularly declining prices and problems of Keynesian excess supply. This macroeconomic problem is not discussed here since it merits being considered by itself in some considerable detail. I have elsewhere taken the optimistic position that if all firms expand rapidly enough they will usually create sufficient purchasing power to constitute a market for their products. No doubt many readers will question this hypothesis which appears to be a distant relative of the Say's Law family.

5. If this premise is not employed and the optimal rate of growth at every future moment of time is left to be determined, we are forced in to the morass of the theory of functionals and we cannot escape without at least some recourse to the calculus of variations.

Finally, it is assumed, at least for the moment, that the company's objective (which determines the optimal rate of growth of its output) is conventional profit maximization.

It is posited that costs can be divided into two categories: ordinary production and operating costs, and costs which arise only as a result of the expansion process. That is, any costs which would be associated with a given level of output if the output rate were not changing may be classed under output costs; any additional outlays above and beyond the output costs are called expansion costs. Output costs will only be taken into account implicitly, in the net revenue figures. That is, in discussing revenues, net revenue figures, from which output costs have already been deducted, will be employed.

Let R represent the initial net revenue of our firm, g be the rate of growth (which is to be determined), and i be the rate of interest relevant in discounting future revenues. Then, because of the constancy of the prices of all of the firm's inputs and outputs and the linear homogeneity of the production function, net revenues will grow precisely in the same proportion as inputs. Thus, in t periods, the firm's net revenue will be $R(1+g)^t$, and the discounted present value of that net revenue will be

$$R \left[\frac{1+g}{1+i} \right]^t.$$

The present value of the expected stream of revenues will therefore be

$$P = \sum_{t=0}^{\infty} R \left[\frac{1+g}{1+i} \right]^t = R \frac{1}{1-(1+g)/(1+i)} = R \frac{1+i}{i-g}, \qquad \mathbf{1}$$

provided only[6] that $g < i$ so that $(1+g)/(1+i) < 1$ as is required for convergence of the geometric series **1**.

6. The problems caused for such a model if the rate of growth exceeds the rate of interest are well known. Specifically, the geometric series **1** will then not converge and the present value of the firm's profit stream will no longer be finite (see, e.g. Durand, 1957). However, as Miller and Modigliani have shown, the case $g > i$ is not a serious possibility. They write: 'Although the case of (perpetual) growth rates greater than the discount factor is the much-discussed "growth stock paradox" . . . it has no real economic significance. . . . This will be apparent when one recalls that the discount rate, . . . though treated as a constant in partial equilibrium (relative price) analysis

It is perfectly obvious in this situation that we have

$$\frac{\partial P}{\partial g} > 0, \qquad\qquad\qquad 2$$

that is, the present value of the net revenue stream will grow indefinitely with the rate of expansion g. In fact, P will grow at an increasing rate with g, and its value will exceed any preassigned number as g approaches i, as shown in the net revenue curve, RR′ in Figure 1. There is clearly nothing here to place a limit on the rate of expansion of the firm.

The firm will only be constrained from accelerating its activities without limit by its expansion costs, the present value of which we designate as $C(g)$. The literature is replete with discussions of the administrative costs of growth and there is no point in recapitulating these materials here. It is enough to point out that growth is what strains the firm's entrepreneurial resources and adds to the company's risks, and it may be expected that after some point the resulting increases in costs will catch up with the marginal revenues derived from more rapid expansion.[7] That is,

---

of the kind presented here, is actually a variable from the standpoint of the system as a whole. That is, if the assumption of finite value for all shares did not hold, because for some shares g was (perpetually) greater than i, then i would necessarily rise until an over-all equilibrium in the capital markets had been restored' (1961). (The notation has been changed from the original to that employed in this paper.)

An alternative way of avoiding this problem is to drop the (unrealistic) premise that the horizon is infinite. However, a finite horizon (say one involving five periods) will yield an expression for total revenue which is somewhat more messy than 1. Though it will be a fifth-degree polynomial, it will have only positive coefficients and so any equilibrium will still be unique. Indeed, the results of the infinite horizon model all seem to continue to hold in the finite horizon case.

7. This view of the shape of the cost function can also be defended with the aid of the usual (somewhat shaky) appeal to the second-order maximum conditions. For, given the shape of our revenue function, the cost curve must behave in the manner shown in Figure 1 or there would be no profit-maximizing growth rate.

Note also that C is likely to be a function of other variables in addition to g, i.e. it is apt to depend on the initial absolute level of output – a small firm is likely to find it less costly to expand 10 per cent than does a large company. However, since $C(g)$ is the present value of all expected future costs taken together, initial cost differences may not play a very important role.

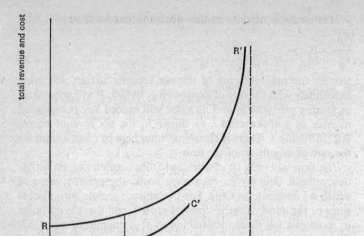

Figure 1

it may be assumed that the slope of the cost curve CC′, which is the graph of the function $C(g)$, will normally be less than that of RR′ near the horizontal axis, but that eventually the slope of the former will catch up with and finally exceed that of the latter. (It may be, however, that in some cases the slope of the cost curve will exceed that of the revenue curve throughout the positive quadrant so that the optimal growth rate will be zero negative.)

Specifically, we obtain the growth-profit function:

$$\Pi = P - C(g) = R\frac{1+i}{i-g} - C(g). \qquad 3$$

The profit-maximizing conditions are then (using the notation Π_g for $\partial\Pi/\partial_g$, etc.),

$$\Pi_g = P_g - C'(g) = R\frac{1+i}{(i-g)^2} - C'(g) = 0, \qquad 4$$

(the first-order marginal revenue equals marginal cost condition), and

$$\Pi_{gg} = 2R\frac{1+i}{(i-g)^3} - C''(g) < 0, \qquad 5$$

the second-order condition.

Graphically, the equilibrium rate of growth is given by Og_e in Figure 1, the value of g at which the slope of the expansion cost curve CC′ and that of RR′ are equal.[8]

Comparative statics in the analysis of the model

This simple growth model can easily be made to yield some results in terms of comparative statics. While some of these are not particularly surprising, they may offer some reassurance that the model does not possess particularly perverse properties, and that it can serve as an instrument of analysis much like the standard stationary equilibrium model.

First, a rise in the interest rate will reduce the present value of the stream of expected revenues, for we have[9] by 1

$$P_i = R\frac{(i-g)-(1+i)}{(i-g)^2} = -R\frac{1+g}{(i-g)^2} < 0. \qquad 6$$

Moreover, a rise in the interest rate will reduce the *marginal* revenue yield of increased economic growth, P_g, for we have, differentiating 6 partially with respect to g,

$$P_{ig} = P_{gi} = -R\frac{(i-g)^2 + 2(i-g)(1+g)}{(i-g)^4} < 0 \qquad 7$$

by our basic assumption $g < i$.

It is now rather simple to prove that (at least in a perfect

8. We might even envision a long-run zero-profit competitive growth equilibrium in which entry has caused shifting of the curves and produced a zero-profit tangency position at which growth level has settled. There is some question in my mind whether, in a growth model such as this, much relevance can be ascribed to that type of long-run adjustment.

9. A complication is introduced by the fact that interest payments are among the output costs which have been subtracted from our net revenue figure, R, so that R should no longer be treated as a constant when differentiating with respect to i. This can be taken care of by noting that our assumptions of linear homogeneity and constant price imply that the quantity of money capital employed by the firm should be strictly proportionate

capital market where some market rate of interest determines the relevant discount factor) a rise in the interest rate will reduce the equilibrium rate of growth of the firm. For differentiating the first-order maximum condition 4 totally and setting $d\Pi_g = 0$ (so that the equilibrium condition continues to hold) we obtain:

$$d\Pi_g = P_{gi}\, di + \Pi_{gg}\, dg = 0$$

or

$$\frac{dg}{di} = -\frac{P_{gi}}{\Pi_{gg}} < 0 \qquad\qquad 8$$

by 5 and 7.

Geometrically, this obvious result is a consequence of the fact that a rise in i reduces the slope of the RR′ curve in Figure 1 throughout its length, as indicated by 7, so that the equilibrium growth level, Og_e, must move to the left. [Other comparative static results were also obtained from the model. Ed.]

Profit versus growth maximization

The discussion so far has been confined to the case of pure competition and has assumed that the firm's objective is to maximize profit. But larger *oligopolistic* firms may well have a different set of objectives (Baumol, 1959, chs. 6–8). Specifically, I have suggested that management's goal may well be to maximize 'sales' (total revenue) subject to a profit constraint. Though I remain firmly convinced of the merit of the hypothesis as a static characterization of the current facts of oligopolistic business operation, in the present context – a growth equilibrium analysis – it is desirable to modify the hypothesis in two respects.

First, maximization of *rate of growth* of sales revenue seems a somewhat better approximation to the goals of many management groups in large firms than is maximization of the current *level* of sales. For example, most company publicity materials

---

with $R(1+g)^t$. Say it will equal $kR(1+g)^t$ and therefore incur an annual interest payment, $ikR(1+g)^t$. In that case we need merely write

$$R = R^*(1-ik)$$

and make this substitution in our revenue function 1. It may then easily be verified by direct differentiation that the resulting expression for P_i will be slightly more complicated than 6 but that it will still be negative. A similar remark holds for 7 and 8.

seem to emphasize the extent to which the firm has 'progressed' rather than the sheer magnitude of its current operations. In my earlier static model I was forced to employ a sales-revenue-level objective as an approximation to a measure of the rate of growth of the firm's scale of operations. A growth equilibrium model now frees me from this necessity.

The second modification deals with the nature of the profit constraint, which in a static model may have seemed to be arbitrarily imposed from the outside – perhaps even a device to avoid explaining what had to be explained, very much like the fixed mark-up of doubtful origin which lies at the heart of the full-cost pricing discussions. A growth analysis enables me to give an explanation of the profit constraint which, I hope, is somewhat less superficial and rather more convincing.

From the point of view of a long-run growth (or sales) maximizer, profit no longer acts as a constraint. Rather, it is an instrumental variable – a means whereby management works towards its goals. Specifically, profits are a means for obtaining capital needed to finance expansion plans. Capital is raised both by direct retention of profits and by the payment of dividends to induce outside investors to provide funds to the company. But, beyond some point, profits compete with sales. For the lower prices and higher marketing outlays which are necessary to promote sales also cut into net earnings. Hence, too high a level of profits will reduce the magnitude of the firm's current operations, while too low a profit level will prevent future growth. The optimal profit stream will be that intermediate stream which is consistent with the largest flow of output (or rate of growth of output) over the firm's lifetime.

Specifically, this optimal profit rate can be described with the aid of a simple model such as the following:[10]

Let

g represent our firm's growth rate,

I be its level of investment as a per cent of the value of current capital assets (the percentage rate of growth of the firm's money capital),

10. For present purposes there is no need to take explicit account of such decision variables as prices, advertising outlay, etc.; but the model can easily be expanded to do so.

Π be the profit rate as a per cent of present equity[11]

D be the dividend as a per cent of present equity, and

E be the retained earnings as a per cent of present equity per unit of time.

The objective then is to maximize

$$g = f(I, \Pi)$$

subject to[12]

$$I = \phi(\Pi, D) + E$$

$$\Pi \equiv D + E.$$

The first of these equations, the objective function, expresses the competitive relationship between growth and profit rates, and states that the rate of growth of the firm's operations varies (directly) with investment, and (after a point) inversely with the profit rate (as indicated in Figure 1). The next equation, however, shows that the profit rate indirectly assists growth by providing capital through retained earnings, and by attracting funds from outside sources at a rate, $\phi(\Pi, D)$, which depends both on the dividend rate and the company's profit rate. From this system we can then determine the optimal profit rate, Π, which from our long-run point of view enters into the constraints just as one of the variables in the system. Only in a static sales-maximization model, then, does profit appear as an independent datum arbitrarily given from the outside – a fixed minimal profit requirement which has somehow to be met by the firm.

11. In practice, of course, different profit rates may be optimal at different points in the company's history. But in the fixed-price constant-returns-to-scale model which is employed here there is no reason to depart from a single optimal profit level.

12. Perhaps, in accord with the Miller-Modigliani view (1961) that dividends do not matter, D should be omitted from the ø function. Other possible variables that have been suggested to supply funds to the firm are $d\Pi/dt$ – the rate of growth of the firm's profit rate, and g, the rate of growth of its output.

It has been suggested that other, partly conventional, constraints are imposed by the capital market and should be incorporated in a more elaborate version of the model. These include restrictions on the debt-equity ratio, on the ratio between current assets and sales, and on the extent of reliance on non-internal financing.

Substantive theorems for a (sales) growth maximization model may be developed which contrast its consequences with those of profit maximization.[13] However, these propositions are completely analogous with those which I have already developed elsewhere for the case of sales maximization. For example, the growth maximizer's sales, advertising outlay, and (trivially) his growth rate will be larger than those of the profit maximizer and the pricing and output decisions of only the former may be expected to vary in response to changes in fixed costs. Since the logic of these results in our present analysis is exactly the same as it was in the sales maximization model there is no point in repeating the argument here.

I will only suggest what appears to be the most important point, that our discussion has shown the standard apparatus of marginal analysis and mathematical programming to be fully applicable to decision problems even when management's objective is not the venerable profit maximization of economic theory.

13. It is sometimes stated or implied that long-run growth and profit max-imization must lead to identical decisions and results (Penrose, 1959, p. 29). But if, as in our model, it is rates rather than assets whose growth is being maximized, or if, even in the long run, investment in the firm can fall short of or exceed profit earnings, it is extremely easy to find counter-examples. In fact, only in the most unusual circumstances would sales revenue/growth maximization be achieved by the maximization of profits.

References

BAUMOL, W. J. (1959), *Business Behavior, Value and Growth*, Harcourt, Brace & World.

DURAND, D. (1957), 'Growth, stocks and the Petersburgh paradox', *J. Finance*, vol. 12, pp. 348–63.

KALDOR, N. (1934), 'The equilibrium of the firm', *Econ. J.*, vol. 44, pp. 60–76.

KNORR, K., and BAUMOL, W. J. (eds.) (1961), *What Price Economic Growth?*, Prentice-Hall.

MILLER, M. H., and MODIGLIANI, F. (1961), 'Dividend policy growth and the valuation of shares', *J. Bus.*, vol. 34, pp. 411–33.

PENROSE, E. (1959), *The Theory of the Growth of the Firm*, Oxford University Press.

17 J. H. Williamson

Profit, Growth and Sales Maximization

J. H. Williamson, 'Profit, growth and sales maximization', *Economica*, vol. 33, 1966, pp. 1–16, with a new appendix written for this volume.

Introduction

One of the more discredited concepts in the theory of the firm is that of an 'optimum size' of firm. Empirical evidence has provided no substantiation for the thesis of a long-run U-shaped cost curve and, since firms are not restricted to the sale of a single product or even a particular range of products, there is no more reason to expect profitability to decline with size than there is evidence to suggest that it does. This raises the question as to what does limit the size of a firm. The answer that has been given is that there are important costs entailed in *expanding* the size of a firm and that these expansion costs tend to increase with the firm's rate of growth. This view was first advanced by Penrose (1959), has been most fully developed by Marris (1964), and has received its most elegant formulation in a paper by Baumol (1962).

The development of a theory of growth of the firm was a necessary prerequisite to another feature of the last two analyses just cited – the consideration of alternative assumptions about managerial objectives. Only static profit maximization and Baumol's static sales maximization hypothesis (1959) (with its seemingly arbitrary minimum profit constraint) can be analysed other than in a growth context. Many economists, the author included, would judge that these are less realistic assumptions than that management wishes to maximize growth or a discounted sum of future sales. Whether they in fact are is an empirical question whose resolution demands a technique for elucidating the alternative implications of different objectives. The principal purpose of this paper is to construct a model which will permit one to derive the differences in behaviour that would follow from the objectives of maximizing profits, maximizing growth and maximizing (discounted) sales.

The framework in which this is accomplished is that of a permanent growth model of the firm. The model is based upon that presented by Baumol (1962), but has been considerably extended. It is developed in the second section, simplified in the third, and solved in the fourth. The basic assumption of a permanent growth model is that unit costs and revenues are independent of the absolute scale involved, although they depend in the traditional ways on the level of the firm's operations relative to its present size. It therefore follows that, if prices and technology are unchanging or altering in appropriately offsetting ways, management is able to make a once-for-all selection of the values of its policy variables. (Where these are not expressed in ratio form, the appropriate value of the variable will increase at a constant proportionate rate over time.) Of course, if at some future date (contrary to the expectations presently held with certainty) there were a change in external circumstances, or a change in management's objectives, or a change in management (perhaps as a result of take-over) with a consequential change in objectives, then the values of these variables would change to new 'permanent' levels.

The (economic) policy variables on which any firm has to reach decisions may conveniently be classified into four categories, though the firm actually has only three degrees of freedom in selecting them. First, there are the decisions on input levels required to satisfy the efficiency conditions – the selection of least-cost input combinations, the optimal distribution of given investment funds among alternative projects, and the optimal distribution of sales effort.[1] Second, there is the other decision that is analysed in traditional price theory, that of the output, price or sales[2] level in the current period; this will be referred to as the output decision. Third, there are the financial decisions embracing the division of profits between dividends and retained

1. This is intended to include the decision as to whether to raise price in order to finance, say, extra advertising, given whatever constraint is imposed by the 'output decision'.
2. The existence of a demand curve implies that these are equivalent.

earnings, the flotation of new equity and the raising of new capital by bond finance. Fourth, there is the decision as to how much should be spent on expanding the size of the firm – the investment decision.

The present paper is largely confined to a consideration of the output decision, the retention ratio and the flotation of new equity. The reasons for this restriction are as follows. The efficiency conditions are irrelevant to our aims since they will be satisfied by a firm successfully pursuing any of the objectives under investigation (or, for that matter, virtually any other consistent aim apart from an easy life). If the firm sells bonds, it will not be able to increase the ratio of debt to assets (i.e. its 'gearing' or 'leverage') indefinitely because of the added risk involved (Marris, 1964, p. 206). The extra investment funds that accrue from this source will therefore bear a constant ratio to the funds obtainable from the other two sources, so that inclusion of this complication would not add any qualitatively different conclusions. Finally, the investment decision need not be considered explicitly as it is implied by the net revenue and the financial decisions of the firm – this is the missing degree of freedom.

Given the framework outlined, and in particular the basic assumption of rather stationary external circumstances that is necessary to construct a permanent growth model, only weak additional assumptions are necessary to prove the following results:

1. The growth rate of the firm cannot be increased by resort to additional equity finance.

2. Growth is never limited by lack of finance as such, as postulated by Baumol (1962) and Downie (1958), but by the fear of takeover, as postulated by Marris (1964).

3. A profit- or growth-maximizer will grow at a positive rate if it is a profitable firm; a sales maximizer need not.

4. It is not possible, as Baumol has claimed (1962), to derive the static sales maximization model from the assumption of growth maximization. (It can, however, be derived from a long-run sales maximization assumption.)

5. A profit and growth maximizer would reach the same output

decision, but a sales maximizer would, except in a limiting case, produce more.

6. A profit-maximizer would, except in a limiting case, distribute more of its profits than a growth-maximizer.

Development of the model

We define the following variables, where lower-case letters denote ratios and capitals denote other variables. Where no time subscript appears, that variable is to be interpreted as applying to time zero. (The time subscript for period zero is included in those equations where variables for other periods appear as well.) Since the rate of interest is assumed constant and the permanent growth context implies that retention ratio and rate of new issue are maintained constant, the variables i, r and f never carry a time subscript.

(a) Policy variables:

S = value of sales or total revenue; r = retention ratio; f = (permanent) growth rate of equity.

(b) Exogenous variables:

$$k = \frac{\text{value of firm at which it would be taken over}}{\text{potential maximum value of firm}};$$

i = rate of interest.

(c) Variables which are exogenous at time zero but endogenous thereafter:

K = capital; F = equity.

(d) Endogenous variables:

R = net revenue (profits), which consists of total revenue less those costs which the firm would incur to maintain current output if it were not growing; $X \equiv C + I =$ expansion costs (i.e., all other costs incurred by the firm); $I =$ (net) investment, i.e. addition to capital; $C =$ non-investment expansion costs; $M =$ market value of firm; $g =$ future (permanent) growth rate of S_t, R_t, K_t, X_t I_t, C_t; $m \equiv M/F =$ value of share.

Most of these definitions are self-explanatory. The exceptions are k, which will be explained, and g, the future permanent growth rate of the firm. This, it should be noted, is an endogenous variable whose value is determined by the particular decisions made regarding the firm's policy variables. In order to assess the generality of the model, it is necessary to investigate briefly the plausibility of the assumption that the six variables listed will all grow at the same rate.

Consider a perfectly competitive firm with an unchanging linear homogenous production function facing constant prices, and assume that the increasing costs of growth arise because the process of expanding management requires existing managers to spend some of their time training new managers and integrating them into the managerial team. Then increasing output by a certain proportion, g, over its present level would increase total revenue, costs and hence net revenue in this same proportion. Moreover, the output expansion would require an equal proportionate increase in the capital stock, since with unchanging technology the firm would wish to maintain the ratio of capital to output found optimal in the present period. A growth of g in the present period requires a certain level of spending on management training, C; an equal proportionate increase in the next period requires an expenditure of $(1+g)C$, since the unit cost of training managers is maintained constant by the increased stock of existing managers to do the training, but the number needing to be trained increases by the proportion g. In this simple case, therefore, it is easy to show that total revenue, net revenue, the capital stock and the various forms of expansion costs all increase at the same rate g.

Although it cannot be demonstrated in an equally rigorous manner, the implication of recent discussion is that much the same conclusion is likely to apply to a diversified, oligopolistic firm. Suppose that the general level of output prices is constant; then total revenue will expand at the same rate as output provided that the firm is not forced to cut its prices in order to move down existing demand curves. But the virtually unlimited opportunities for diversification remove any such necessity. Net revenue will also expand at this rate, not only if factor prices and technology are constant, but also if they offset one another; this would occur if wages increased at the same rate as productivity rose due to neutral technical progress. It is well known that with neutral technical progress the capital-output ratio is constant, so that the capital stock and therefore investment will also increase at the same rate. No modification of the argument in the previous paragraph is required so far as C is concerned. Consequently, it is not unreasonable to postulate that S, R, K, X, I and C will all increase at the same rate as output if the price level is constant. (If prices were increasing at a constant rate, these variables would all increase at the same rate in real terms but an appropriately magnified rate in money terms.)

The first relationship we shall derive, that between sales and net revenue, comes from the standard theory of the firm. As output expands (in the current period), net and total revenue both increase initially but eventually both reach maxima. Net revenue reaches a maximum first due to positive marginal costs, and the position of maximum total revenue marks the end of the economically interesting output range. The relationship may therefore be summarized as

$$R = R(S), \qquad R'' < 0. \tag{1}$$

Second, let us analyse expansion costs. By definition, these consist of the cost of adding to the capital stock to keep it in line with the planned greater sales in the following period plus such other costs as the firm must incur in the process of expansion. Assuming a constant capital-output ratio and constant prices, it is evident that $I = gK$. More interesting are the other expansion costs, which were the principal interest in Penrose's inquiry (1959) and have been extensively discussed by Marris (1964). They consist largely of the managerial diseconomies involved in growing fast and the costs of research, development and sales promotion entailed in diversification. The literature on this point may conveniently be summarized for our purposes by the assumptions made about $C(g)$ below, although the last one – that the marginal cost of growth is negligible for very small growth rates – is less firmly founded than the others.

$$X \equiv I + C = gK + C(g), \qquad \begin{aligned} C' &> 0, \\ C'' &> 0, \\ C(0) &\equiv 0, \\ C'(0) &\approx 0. \end{aligned} \tag{2}$$

Taking the inverse function of equation 2, one derives

$$g = g(X), \qquad g' > 0, \quad g'' < 0. \qquad\qquad 3$$

The statement that growth depends on the amount spent on expansion, but that there are decreasing returns to such expenditure, is actually weaker than the assumptions from which it was derived. As a matter of fact, the latter are needed only in the proof of result 3.

The sources from which expansion funds may be obtained are retained earnings and the proceeds of new equity issues. Retained earnings are defined as the product of the retention ratio and net revenue. (Of course, insofar as the tax laws permit some expansion costs to be counted as current costs, the conceptual retention ratio differs from the published ratio of a firm.) The amount raised by floating new equity is the product of the price for which the shares are sold and the number that are sold. The number sold in period 0 is the product of the proportionate increase in the number of shares and the number outstanding at the start of the period, or fF. Their price is computed on the assumption that dividends are paid on existing shares prior to selling the new shares, so that the amount that investors will be willing to pay for the new shares is the price of a share in period 1, m_1, discounted to the present period. It follows that

$$X_0 = rR_0 + \frac{m_1}{1+i} fF_0 = rR_0 + \frac{fM_1}{(1+i)(1+f)}. \qquad\qquad 4$$

The market value of the firm is given by the discounted future earnings of the shares at present outstanding.[3] In period t, the firm will earn a net revenue of $(1+g)^t R$, but it will only pay out $(1-r)(1+g)^t R$. Moreover, some of this will accrue to those who purchase new securities issued between time zero and t; only $F/(1+f)^t F$ will accrue to those who own shares at the beginning.

3. This is only one of several possible ways in which the stock-market value of the firm may be computed. It is what Miller and Modigliani (1961) term the 'stream of dividends approach' to valuation, and is the simplest one to apply in the present model. The other approaches are logically equivalent since we are implicitly assuming absence of transactions costs, taxes and uncertainty. It may be noted that the permanent growth context permits one to dispense with consideration of undistributed profits or capital stocks.

Discounting these future earnings and summing yields the market value of the firm as

$$M = \sum_{t=0}^{\infty} \left[\frac{1+g}{(1+f)(1+i)} \right]^t (1-r)R \qquad \qquad 5$$

$$= \left[\frac{1}{1-(1+g)/(1+f)(1+i)} \right] (1-r)R = \frac{(l-r)(1+f)(1+i)R}{i-g+f+if}$$

provided that $(1+f)(1+i) > 1+g$ so that the geometric series converges. A sufficient condition for this is $i > g$. Although we have listed i as an exogenous variable, there is an overwhelming economic reason for believing that $i > g(R)$; since otherwise a firm which invested slightly less than R would have an infinite valuation by the stock market, the interest rate would be revised upwards by the stock market till this ceased to be true. And it will be shown below that $i > g(R)$ is a sufficient condition to ensure that $i > g$. It may also be noted that, since $R_1 = (1+g)R_0$ and all other factors in equation 5 are invariant over time, one has

$$M_1 = (1+g)M_0. \qquad \qquad 6$$

Simplification of the model

It is interesting to analyse a frequent assumption to the effect that there is an absolute limit to the amount of finance a firm can obtain for expenditure on expansion (see Baumol, 1962, pp. 1085–6; Downie, 1958, p. 66). The reasoning is that with low pay-out rates any increase in dividends is so effective in raising share prices as to permit a greater augmentation of external finance than the loss of internal finance; and vice versa when pay-out rates are high. Consequently there is a trade-off between external and internal finance and some optimum financial policy which maximizes access to total funds. At this point expansion funds reach an absolute maximum.

To investigate this proposition, one substitutes equations 5 and 6 into 4 to yield

$$X = rR + \frac{(1-r)(1+g)fR}{i-g+f+if}. \qquad \qquad 7$$

To find that combination of the firm's financial policy variables which maximizes the finance available for expansion (and therefore its growth rate), one differentiates **7** with respect to r and f, remembering that g is a function of r and f.

$$\frac{\partial X}{\partial r} = R + \frac{fR}{(i-g+f+if)^2} \times$$
$$\times \left[(1-r)(1+i)(1+f)\frac{\partial g}{\partial r} - (1+g)(i-g+f+if) \right]. \qquad \textbf{8}$$

At $r = 1$, this simplifies to

$$\frac{\partial X}{\partial r} = \frac{(1+f)(i-g)R}{i-g+f+if} > 0,$$

provided that $i > g$. Since the first term in the square brackets in **8** is positive when $r < 1$, it follows that $\partial X/\partial r > 0$ throughout the feasible range of r and irrespective of the value of f.

$$\frac{\partial X}{\partial f} = \frac{(1-r)R}{(i-g+f+if)^2} \left[(1+g)(i-g) + f(1+i)(1+f)\frac{\partial g}{\partial f} \right] > 0.$$

Assuming that as $f \to \infty$ the growth rate approaches a finite limiting value g_0, one has, however,

$$\lim_{f \to \infty} X = rR + \frac{(1-r)(1+g_0)R}{1+i}. \qquad \textbf{9}$$

One concludes that there is no optimum retention ratio and rate of equity creation which maximize the availability of new finance. An increase in the rate of selling shares will always increase the funds available, though these funds will approach a finite limiting value. Similarly, any increase in the retention ratio will increase the availability of funds.

The maximum funds that would be available through retentions are R. This exceeds the maximum available if new equity is issued, since the value of equation **7** is always less than R provided $r < 1$; and if $r = 1$ then $X = R$ and all funds are raised internally. But when the retention ratio is unity the value of the firm is zero by equation **5**. Marris has argued that this is not an economically significant solution (1964, ch. 1), since when a potentially profitable firm is depressed to a low market value it creates the risk of provoking a take-over raid.[4] This indeed seems

4. Analytically, take-over means that new values of the policy variables are selected, presumably with the aim of raising M. The raiders will make a profit provided that the new value of M exceeds that which existed under the policies of the previous management. (We assume a perfect capital market.)

by far the most powerful reason for believing that firms will be constrained at some determinate point in their desire to grow.

Result 1 of the first part was proved in the last paragraph; growth can never be increased by resort to additional equity finance. The significance of this conclusion may be assessed by supposing that the firm has made its investment decision, so that X and therefore g are determined, and its output decision, so that R is specified. Then from equation 7 the rate of equity creation, f, needed to finance X will depend on r by the formula

$$f = \frac{(i-g)(X/R-r)}{(i-g)r+(1+g)-X/R(1+i)}.$$

Substituting in 5 and simplifying yields[5]

$$M = \frac{(1+i)(R-X)}{i-g}.$$

In other words, we are living in a Miller and Modigliani (1961) type of world where, because there are no transactions costs, taxes or uncertainty, the purely financial decisions of the firm have no impact on its value or on the rate of return enjoyed by investors. There is therefore no compelling reason for a firm to choose any particular method of raising finance. However, it is a familiar fact that management prefers to raise finance internally and that new equity issues are comparatively unusual occurrences, and this is presumably explicable in terms of the frictions involved in equity flotation that are ignored in our model. The analysis therefore suggests that the essential role of new issues is to finance occasional bursts of abnormal expansion where increasing returns are present rather than permanent, steady growth. In view of the above, it is possible to simplify the analysis in the fourth section very considerably by assuming that all finance is raised internally with no loss of generality.

5. It may be noted that this bears a close similarity to Baumol's equation 3 (1962, p. 1081), except that we have provided, by breaking down his $C(g)$ into

$$\sum \left(\frac{1+g}{1+i}\right)^t X,$$

a rather convincing reason for expecting his second-order conditions to be fulfilled.

Result 2 was that the restraint on growth always consists of a fear of take-over rather than that there exists some absolute maximum on the amount of funds the firm could obtain; this proposition was also established above. Although not immediately obvious, this conclusion is intuitively plausible. Essentially, a firm could always increase its expansion funds at the cost of its present shareholders, either by reducing its dividends or by promising a higher proportion of future dividends to new shareholders, were it not for the power of present shareholders to sell out to a new management which would engage in fewer expansion activities which are so costly as to earn a return below the current rate of interest.

Finally, it may be noted that we have also established that $i > g(R)$ is sufficient to ensure $i > g$. By definition, X cannot exceed R when $f = 0$. And we also established that $r < 1$ implies $X < R$. Consequently, expansion funds cannot exceed net revenue,[6] so that the assumption that the stock market behaves in such a way as to give the firm a finite value ensures that no firm can ever (i.e. even with the aid of new issues) achieve a permanent growth rate as large as the interest rate.

A comparison of profit, growth and sales maximization

Profit maximization is, of course, interpreted as the desire to maximize the present value of the firm, M. Neither is there any difficulty in interpreting the meaning of growth maximization in the context of a permanent growth model, since total revenue, net revenue, and assets all expand permanently at the same rate g. Slightly less obvious is the appropriate definition of sales maximization, since the total sales of a firm between now and infinity are obviously infinite. But so, of course, are total profits over this period: they are reduced to a well-defined value by the technique of discounting. It seems quite plausible to suppose that managements which derive utility from the size of the undertaking they control will similarly discount future sales. After all, most managers must anticipate retirement or coronory thrombosis in the less than infinitely far distant future, so that it is reasonable to

6. It should be noted that, if we were to take account of bond finance, the maximum funds available to the firm could exceed R. Consequently, the condition $i > g(R)$ would require strengthening.

suppose that they will prefer an increase in sales in the present to an equal increase in the future. We therefore assume that management applies a discount rate s to future sales, and therefore seeks to maximize a function H of the form

$$H = \sum_{t=0}^{\infty} \left(\frac{1+g}{1+s}\right)^t S = \frac{1+s}{s-g} S, \qquad \qquad 10$$

provided that $s > g$ so that the geometric series converges. It must be admitted that there is no particularly convincing reason for believing that $s > g$ analogous to that for assuming $i > g$; if the condition does not hold, presumably management is in a state of bliss. Or perhaps it just satisfices.

Profit maximization

It was shown in the third section that it is possible to assume that all finance is raised internally without loss of generality. One may therefore set $f = 0$ in equation 5, so that the problem of the profit-maximizing firm is to select S and r so as to maximize

$$M = \frac{(1-r)(1+i)R}{i-g}, \qquad \qquad 11$$

subject to $\quad g = g(rR), \qquad g' > 0, \quad g'' < 0,$
$\qquad \qquad \quad R = R(S), \qquad R'' < 0.$

Now $\quad \dfrac{\partial M}{\partial R} = \dfrac{(i-g)(1-r)(1+i)+(1-r)(1+i)R\partial g/\partial R}{(i-g)^2} > 0$

so that the profit-maximizing firm will select that output level S^* that maximizes net revenue (R^*).

One also has

$$\frac{\partial M}{\partial r} = \frac{-(i-g)(1+i)R+(1-r)(1+i)R\partial g/\partial r}{(i-g)^2} = 0,$$

or $\quad 1-r = \dfrac{i-g}{\partial g/\partial r} \qquad \qquad 12$

as the first-order condition for a profit-maximizing retention ratio.

This result is most easily interpreted diagrammatically. By substituting R^* into $g = g(rR)$, one obtains a unique relationship between the retention ratio and the growth rate that this permits, and from the signs on the derivatives of g this has the shape shown by $g(rR^*)$ in Figure 1. Intuitively, for a given level of net revenue – which happens to be the maximum possible level since the firm desires to maximize profits – the amount of finance available for expansion is a linear function of the retention ratio, but the assumption of increasing costs of expansion leads to a situation in which the permitted rate of growth increases less than in proportion to the retention ratio.

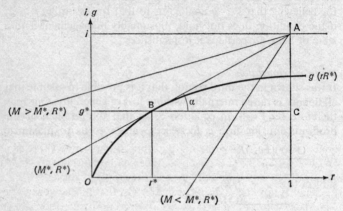

Figure 1

One may also plot on this diagram a series of curves which reflect the extent to which the objective function of the firm is met, i.e. a set of curves which show all those combinations of r and g at which the value of the firm would be equal to some particular level of M. We shall borrow the term 'iso-valuation line' from Marris (1964, p. 252) to describe these loci of points at which the value of M is constant. Each one is labelled with the value of M that it represents when R has the value specified after M. The iso-valuation lines show a relationship between g and r and may therefore be derived by rearranging equation **11** to yield

$$g = i - \frac{(1+i)R}{M} + \frac{(1+i)R}{M}r.$$

340 The Growth and Size of Firms

Hence all of the iso-valuation lines converge on the point A at which $r = 1$ and $g = i$, although they do not do anything quite as embarrassing as meet at this point since M is undefined when $g = i$. They are all upward-sloping straight lines: higher growth is needed to compensate for reduced dividends if the value of the firm is to remain unchanged. Finally, the less steep is the line – i.e. the higher it appears – the greater is the value of M that it represents.

The object of the profit-maximizing firm is therefore to reach the highest possible iso-valuation line. This occurs in the diagram at B, the point of tangency to $g(rR^*)$. We shall denote the value of the firm at this point by M^*. At B it is evident that

$$BC = \frac{AC}{\tan a},$$

i.e. $$1 - r = \frac{i - g}{\partial g / \partial r},$$

which is the first-order condition **12** for a profit-maximizing retention ratio. It is apparent that the assumption of decreasing returns to expansion expenditure reflected in the shape of $g(rR^*)$ ensures that the second-order condition will be satisfied.

There is nothing in the diagram to show that this tangency condition need occur at a positive g. However, the assumptions made about $C(g)$ in equation **2** imply that in the neighbourhood of $g = 0$, we have $gK \approx X = Rr$, so that $\partial g / \partial r \approx R/K$. Now the definition of a profitable firm is one that earns a rate of return on capital employed greater than the rate of interest, so that, if the firm is profitable, $R/K > i$, which implies $\partial g / \partial r > i$ at $g = 0$. At this point, therefore, the left-hand side of **12** exceeds the right-hand side, and reducing this inequality requires a higher r and g. Since it is by definition true that a growth-maximizing firm will grow at least as fast as a profit-maximizing one, this establishes that (profitable) profit- and growth-maximizers will grow at a positive rate, which was the first part of Proposition 3.

Growth maximization
It was shown in the last section that the constraint on a growth-maximizer arises from the danger of being taken over. A firm is

likely to be taken over when its market value sinks to a low level in comparison with what the new owners could expect to make out of it.[7] The measure that Marris adopts as an indicator of the value of the firm to a take-over raider is the value of its net assets which, in our model, are represented by K. However, a more appropriate norm would seem to be M^*, since it is in general reasonable to expect that a new management would not change the total nature of the trading activities in which the firm engages. It will therefore be assumed that management wishes to prevent the stock-market value of the firm falling below a specified proportion, k, of its potential maximum value, in order to safeguard its job security. This proportion k will vary inversely with the efficiency of existing management relative to that which would be provided by the potential raiders; it will tend to vary directly with the extent to which these raiders are themselves 'profit-motivated'. Without some sort of general equilibrium analysis beyond the scope of the present paper, it is necessary to take k as exogenous.

The problem of the growth-maximizer is therefore to select S and r so as to maximize

$$g = g(rR)$$

subject to $\quad M \geqslant kM^*, \quad 0 < k \leqslant 1,$
$\qquad\qquad R = R(S).$

Since $\partial g/\partial R > 0$, the growth maximizer will select the same output level S^* as the profit maximizer; both will seek the highest possible level of current net revenue.[8] This is the first part of result 5; it has the (happy?) consequence that the voluminous literature on pricing policy may be applied without modification to growth-maximizing firms. It also establishes that it is not possible to derive the static sales maximization model from the

7. For his development of a theory of take-over, on which the present remarks are largely based, see Marris (1964, ch. 1).

8. Intuitively, one might have expected a growth-maximizer to keep his initial sales down so as to 'keep the base small'. While this factor would operate in any finite period model (and this constitutes an additional reason for believing that the sales-maximization hypothesis may be fruitful), it is inoperative in a permanent growth context since it would involve keeping subsequent sales down correspondingly as well.

postulate of growth maximization, as was stated in proposition 4.[9]

Since $\partial g/\partial r > 0$ and $\partial M/\partial r < 0$ for values of $r > r^*$, it is obvious that the constraint will be exactly satisfied and r_g, the growth-maximizing retention ratio, will be given by a corner solution. The diagrammatic solution to the problem is shown in Figure 2. If one draws any horizontal from AB to the iso-valuation line (M^*, R^*), and then divides this horizontal in the ratio $1-k:k$, the iso-valuation line passing through the resulting point

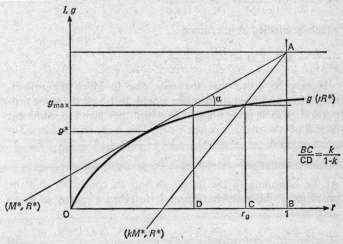

Figure 2

9. Baumol's error arose from a confusion between the firm's current net revenue, R, and what one may term its profitability (the excess of revenue over *all* costs), $R-X$. Specifically, he argued that since faster growth involves lower profits (meaning profitability), the sales level needed to maximize growth would be determined as a compromise between the desire to earn profits to finance expansion and the reduction in profits (here equated to net revenue) caused by this faster growth. But it is clear that a growth-maximizer will never be prepared to forego current net revenue, unless one introduces some quite different postulate such as that future expansion costs will be less if sales are pushed further in the present. (A rationale for this might be the creation of consumer goodwill.) In other words, the unprofitable activities that a growth-maximizer engages in are those involved in pushing g beyond g^* and not those arising from pushing S beyond S^* (see Baumol, 1962).

J. H. Williamson 343

is (kM^*, R^*). The intersection of this iso-valuation line with $g(rR^*)$ yields the maximum possible growth rate, g_{max} which is clearly greater than the profit-maximizing growth rate g^* unless $k = 1$.

Formally, one derives

$$M = \frac{(1-r)(1+i)R^*}{i-g} = \frac{k(1-r^*)(1+i)R^*}{i-g^*} = kM^*,$$

or $\quad \dfrac{1-r}{k} = \dfrac{1-r^*}{i-g^*}(i-g) = \dfrac{i-g}{\tan a}$

which is satisfied at g_{max} since

$$\frac{i-g}{\tan a} = BC+CD = \frac{BC}{k} = \frac{1-r}{k}.$$

It may be noted that the only case in which the growth-maximizer and profit-maximizer would distribute the same proportion of their profits is that in which they stand in imminent danger of take-over, i.e. when $k = 1$. This is the result asserted in proposition 6.

Sales maximization

At the beginning of the fourth section we concluded that the problem of the sales-maximizer is to select r and S so as to maximize

$$H = \frac{1+s}{s-g}S \quad \text{(provided } s > g\text{)} \qquad\qquad \mathbf{10}$$

subject to $\quad M \geqslant kM^*, \qquad g = g(rR), \qquad R = R(S).$

Now $\partial H/\partial g > 0$, $\partial g/\partial r > 0$ and $\partial M/\partial r < 0$ imply that the sales-maximizer will also exhaust such slack as may be provided by $k < 1$ and exactly satisfy the constraint. It follows that

$$1-r = \frac{kR^*}{R}\frac{1-r^*}{i-g^*}(i-g),$$

so that one could construct the relevant iso-valuation line on Figure 2 by making

$$\frac{BC}{CD} = \frac{kR^*/R_s}{1-kR^*/R_s}$$

if one knew R_s, the sales-maximizing value of R. There is, however, no way of determining R_s from this diagram. If we assume
that R_s is known and is less than R^*, then the optimal iso-
valuation line (kM^*, R_s) would lie between (kM^*, R^*) and $(M^*,
R^*)$. The equilibrium r would occur at the highest intersection
of this line with $g(rR_s)$, which would lie to the right of $g(rR^*)$.
However, this diagram does not yield any very interesting information for the sales-maximizing case.

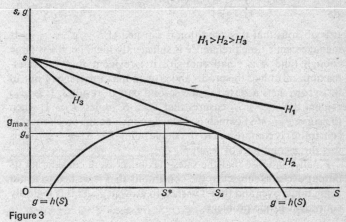

Figure 3

Consider instead the way in which g will vary with S, given that
the constraint is exactly satisfied. As sales increase to S^*, g will
rise to reach a maximum of g_{max} and then start to decline as the
'surplus' is used to finance unprofitable sales rather than
unprofitable growth. One therefore obtains a curve with the
properties of $g = h(S)$ in Figure 3. An increase in k would reduce
the height of this curve throughout its length.

One may also derive a series of iso-H curves by rearranging 10
to read

$$g = s - \frac{1+s}{H}S.$$

The iso-H curves therefore all approach the point $(S = 0, g = s)$,
though they do not actually reach it since H is undefined at this
point. They are all downward-sloping straight lines. Higher curves
represent larger values of H.

It is obvious that the highest attainable value of H is H_2, where the iso-H curve is tangential to $h(S)$. It is easy to confirm that that is the maximum by differentiating 10 with respect to S to get the first-order condition for the sales-maximizing level of sales S_s, and it is apparent from the diagram that the second-order condition will also be satisfied provided the demand curve is monotonic:

$$\frac{\partial H}{\partial S} = \frac{(s-g)(1+s)+(1+s)S\partial g/\partial S}{(s-g)^2} = 0, \quad \text{or} \quad s-g+S\frac{\partial g}{\partial S} = 0.$$

It is obvious that this condition is satisfied at $S = S_s$, $g = g_s$. If management's time preference is sufficiently high, i.e. if s is large enough (and k is small enough), it is evident that the sales-maximizer, unlike the profit- and growth-maximizers, will not in fact grow, as is asserted in the second part of result 3. It is also evident that $s > g_{max}$ ensures that $S_s > S^*$ unless $k = 1$, when the curve $g = h(S)$ (which is defined to include the stock-market constraint) is compressed to the single point $S = S^*$, $g = g^*$. This was the second part of result 5.

Finally, suppose that the sales-maximizer were considering its output decision subject to the constraints that it wished to avoid being taken over and that it wished to grow at g_s. This is logically equivalent to the problem

maximize S, subject to $R \geqslant R_s$.

This demonstrates that Baumol's static hypothesis, that firms try to maximize sales subject to a minimum profit constraint, can be derived from the long-run sales-maximization hypothesis, as asserted in result 4.

Conclusion

In a paper such as this one cannot delve into the vast body of theory underlying many of the relationships assumed. For example, a large part of the books by Penrose and Marris are devoted to investigating the theory behind the restrictions that we have placed on the shape of $g(X)$. Similarly, we have joined Robinson (1933) in sweeping aside all the complications of oligopolistic interdependence by assuming that the output decision is taken on the basis of well-defined demand curves. What a permanent growth model of the type developed in this paper is capable of providing, however, is a means of linking such problems as these together in a simple and systematic way.

We have demonstrated that doing this enables one to establish a number of interesting results, some of which are far from trivial. The most interesting were listed in the Introduction, so that there is no point in repeating them here. The most general conclusion is one that one would hesitate to state explicitly were it not for the suspicion it still seems to engender in certain quarters: that in all cases except where profitability is at best the minimum sum necessary to prevent take-over,[10] the policies the firm pursues will depend on the form of its objectives. Profit-, growth- and sales-maximizers will act differently.

One could easily extend the above analysis to include more general managerial utility functions such as $U(g, M)$ or $U(g, S)$. The former would yield indifference curves tangential to $g(rR^*)$ above r^* in Figure 1, the latter indifference curves tangential to some point on the downward-sloping part of $h(S)$ in Figure 3. But no very interesting insights seem to emerge from such a generalization.

Of more interest is the observation that any one of the three objectives is capable of yielding a set of comparative-statics theorems. For example, inspection of Figures 1 and 2 makes it clear that an increase in the rate of interest would reduce the growth rate and the retention ratio for both profit- and growth-maximizing firms. Changes in the efficiency of the firm or the prices of its factors would have straightforward implications for the position of such curves as $g(rR^*)$ and $h(S)$, which could similarly lead to comparative-statics predictions. It does not seem to be possible to predict the effect of a proportional profits tax on the retention ratio without making assumptions additional to those contained in the paper; I suspect that one requires some condition such as $g''' =$ constant to get a definite solution.

Finally, it is interesting to draw attention to an empirical finding which has caused a certain amount of discomfort in the past

10. Baumol's conclusion in (1959) that a sales-maximizer who could only just satisfy his minimum profit constraint would act in the same way as a profit maximizer is, of course, a special case of this result.

but for which we are able to offer a superior explanation to 'systematic irrationality on the part of the investing public' (Miller and Modigliani, 1961, p. 432), or discount rates that vary with the futurity of the return (Marris, 1964, p. 221). This is the finding that 'when stock prices are related to current dividends and retained earnings, higher dividend payout is usually associated with higher price-earnings ratios' (Friend and Puckett, 1964, p. 657). The reason that this has caused dismay is that 'investors should be indifferent if the present value of the additional future returns resulting from earnings retention equals the amount of dividends foregone', whereas apparently they are not. But, of course, investors are irrational in preferring dividends only if the present value of the additional future returns actually *does* equal the amount of dividends foregone, and if the firm is a growth- (or for that matter a sales-) maximizer then it is obvious from Figure 2 that they do not, for the retention ratio is pushed beyond the point at which the value of the firm is maximized. With a great deal of ingenuity Friend and Puckett manage to cast a certain amount of doubt on the conventional findings, but the bulk of the empirical evidence would still seem to indicate that dividends are more highly valued. Since this is consistent with the view that shareholders are rational in seeking to maximize their wealth, and that management rationally seeks objectives other than profit maximization, while any other interpretation assumes that at least one of these parties acts irrationally, one may conclude that there is substantial empirical evidence favouring abandonment of the time-honoured profit-maximization assumption.

Appendix (1969)

When this article was written I was ignorant of the calculus of variations and analogous techniques of inter-temporal optimization. I was therefore obliged to assume that, irrespective of initial conditions, the firm's choice was restricted to steady-state growth paths, so that the policy that would maximize a particular objective function could be found by the calculus.

Since 1965 my education has been extended. I have not had the time to undertake the mathematics involved in extending the model to non-steady state conditions, but I have done enough work with similar models to gain some intuitive grasp on their behaviour, and it therefore seems worthwhile venturing some comments on the subject. So far as I can see, any analytically-tractable model must postulate conditions in which steady-state solutions are possible; the generalization envisaged consists merely in dropping the assumption that one will start off on a steady-state path from arbitrary initial conditions.

One definitional problem that arises as soon as the assumption of steady-state growth is dropped is the appropriate interpretation of 'growth maximization', since the growth rate of different variables is not the same at a particular point in time and the growth rate of any particular variable changes over time. If steady-state solutions are possible, however, it seems natural to require that the firm tends ultimately to approach a balanced, steady-state expansion. There will clearly be some growth rate that is the maximum permanently sustainable, and a growth-maximizer will clearly endeavour to end up growing at this rate. But this is not a sufficient restriction to impose, for one would not wish to describe as a growth-maximizer a firm that ultimately achieved this growth rate but did so at a lower size than was possible. A growth-maximizer is, therefore, a firm that seeks to grow asymptotically at the maximum feasible steady-state rate with as large a size as possible. (Any measure of firm size will suffice, since the firm's activities will be in a particular balance when its growth settles down to steady state.)

One of the central features of the paper is the assumption of 'dynamic diminishing returns' ($C'' > 0$); the costs of expansion increase more than proportionately as the rate of expansion increases. One might reasonably define a fixed factor as one whose input is subject to this effect, since its presence precludes instantaneous adjustment of the input to the optimal level. In technical terms, a fixed factor is a pre-determined variable whose rate of change is described by a differential equation.

It is implicitly assumed in the paper (equation 2) that capital is a variable factor, since its supply can be increased or decreased indefinitely in a single period without supply costs increasing more than proportionately. The idea of a pre-determined variable is incorporated through the $C(g)$ function, for which the alternative rationales of management as a fixed factor and the level of demand are offered. Suppose that one were to consider the problem of maximizing managerial-utility functionals appropriate to profit-, growth- and sales-maximizers subject to the constraints enumerated in the paper and also to an initial capital stock and an initial level of the single composite fixed factor. The optimal policies would differ from those indicated in the paper in only one respect. In general the initial capital stock will differ from the level that would be optimal at time zero, so that there will be a need to instantaneously adjust the capital stock to an appropriate level. (This level will be larger for a sales-maximizer than for a profit- or growth-maximizer.) Having made this initial adjustment to a 'balanced' state, the firm will expand in steady-state on a trajectory whose slope is determined by the factors analysed in the paper and whose height is dependent solely on the initial stock of the fixed factor. (A model essentially similar to this has been analysed by Solow, in a seminar delivered at L S E on 5 November 1968.)

A more adequate model would recognize the existence of at least two pre-determined variables, representing management and the level of demand. (In addition, one might argue that conventional factors such as labour and capital are to some extent fixed factors in the sense used here. Their inclusion would further complicate the model, but would not add anything qualitatively new.) In such a model, the two pre-determined variables will only be brought into balance gradually, with the one whose initial value is above the asymptotic path growing less rapidly in the early stages.

It seems to me that it is this model which is of the greatest interest, and that it justifies a full and rigorous analysis. This would preferably be undertaken in terms of the basic demand and production functions, rather than being content with such proxy functions as my R(S), so as to permit the derivation of a full range of comparative dynamics theorems. In the meantime, the foregoing paper can provide a useful framework provided that it is interpreted as describing developments if the firm starts off in a balanced state. Its principal deficiency is that the initial state *cannot* be balanced for both profit/growth and sales-maximizers if the firm inherits a capital stock, as well as its managerial and demand conditions, from the past. The six propositions listed at the end of the introduction appear to remain valid in the generalized model.

References

BAUMOL, W. J. (1959), *Business Behavior, Value and Growth*, Harcourt, Brace & World.

BAUMOL, W. J. (1962), 'On the theory of expansion of the firm', *Amer. econ. Rev.*, vol. 52, pp. 1078–87.

DOWNIE, J. (1958), *The Competitive Process*, Duckworth.

FRIEND, I., and PUCKETT, M. (1964), 'Dividends and stock prices', *Amer. econ. Rev.*, vol. 54, pp. 656–82.

MARRIS, R. (1964), *The Economic Theory of 'Managerial' Capitalism*, Macmillan.

MILLER, M. H., and MODIGLIANI, F. (1961), 'Dividend policy, growth and the valuation of shares', *J. Bus.* vol. 34, pp. 411–33.

PENROSE, E. (1959), *The Theory of the Growth of the Firm*, Oxford University Press.

ROBINSON, J. (1933), *The Economics of Imperfect Competition*, Macmillan.

18 Irma G. Adelman

A Stochastic Analysis of the Size Distribution of Firms

I. G. Adelman, 'A stochastic analysis of the size distribution of firms',
Journal of the American Statistical Association, vol. 53, 1958, pp. 893–904.

The forces determining the distribution of firm sizes within a particular industry are so varied and so complex that any theoretical attempt to portray the effects of their interactions must of necessity be either drastically simplified or else hopelessly complicated. On the other hand, since a major portion of the literature in industrial organization is devoted to a study of the relationship between market structure and firm behavior, even a simplified model for predicting the equilibrium composition of an industry may not be without interest.

Our primary purpose in this paper is to adapt the probabilistic method which is due to Markov (see Feller, 1950; Kemeny, Snell and Thompson, 1957) to the analysis of the structure which a given industry would eventually reach if certain current trends were to continue. This probabilistic approach was first applied in economics to the analysis of income and wage distributions (Solow, 1951; Champernowne, 1953). More recently, the same technique was also employed by Hart and Prais (1956) in an investigation of business concentration. In their article, Hart and Prais presented matrices of transition probabilities for firms in British industry. But, they did not proceed to derive an equilibrium market structure for manufacturing because, as they stated (1956), of the difficulty of realistically handling the phenomena of entry and exit of firms from the industry. However, this obstacle can be overcome. As a result, it becomes possible to investigate what shape the equilibrium size distribution of firms would assume were past tendencies to persist. In this process, a different, dynamic concept of equilibrium is introduced. Also, in addition to the derivation of the implications for concentration, a measure of firm mobility is constructed along the lines suggested by Prais (1955) in a paper on social mobility.

In view of the inherent importance of steel in the economy of the United States, as well as the preponderance of its oligopolistic form of organization within our society, we shall use the suggested technique in order to describe the ultimate size composition and concentration of the steel industry in this country. It will be seen that the configuration we find for this case is not at all unreasonable and is indeed in accord with the opinions of experts in the field.

The derivation of the equilibrium structure for an industry

We shall assume that the firms which comprise an industry are grouped according to some criterion of size into a number of classes. We then regard the evolution of a corporation through these classes as a stochastic process, in which the probability per unit time of movement from one group to another is a function only of the two groups involved. That is to say, the likelihood that a corporate entity will advance a given number of steps during a period depends solely upon its size at the beginning of the period and the number of steps involved, and is independent of the previous history of the firm. In our approach, then, the growth of an enterprise is statistical in nature, with absolute size as the determinant of development.

Obviously, this model constitutes a considerable simplification. For we represent all those economic forces which determine the growth pattern of business organisms within a given industry by a single portmanteau variable – corporate size. This is tantamount to the assumption that such economic factors as entrepreneurship, financial structure and position, proneness to introduce technological change, economies of scale, and profits are all strongly correlated with size. Or, perhaps, that the magnitudes and behavior of the growth-promoting variables are more nearly homogeneous within a specified size group than they are from stratum to stratum.

Another simplifying assumption is that the effects of the interactions among all these variables, which are summarized in our model by several size-dependent transition probabilities, are taken to remain invariant throughout the evolutionary process. While this is a strong restriction, it is analogous to that used in long-run comparative statics: that the forces which operate during the sample period will continue unchanged until equilibrium is reached. Actually, if the time period over which the transition probabilities are evaluated is sufficiently long and includes at least one complete business cycle, the use of this approximation may be expected to lead to qualitatively correct conclusions.

Under these conditions, the historical development of the distribution of firm sizes in a given industry can be described by a process which is due to Markov. Basically (and in mathematical terms, for a moment), one arranges the transition probabilities into a square matrix. By operating with this matrix upon a vector which represents the structure of the industry at the beginning of one period, one derives the structure for the next time interval. Repeating the process indefinitely leads (under one further restriction) to a vector which describes the equilibrium state.

There is, however, one modification which must be made in the Markov process before we can use it profitably in our work – we must provide for entry into and departure from the industry. To do this, we add to our m size classes a large additional group which acts as a reservoir of potential entrants into the system. We then assign as the probability of moving from this zeroth group to, say, the jth group a value just sufficient to make the average number of firms entering the jth class per year correspond to the actual number of new firms started annually in the appropriate size range. Similarly, the failure of a firm will be represented as a movement into the zeroth class.

We now let p_{ij} denote the probability that a firm in size class i will, during the next period, enter group j. Thus, for example, p_{13} will represent the likelihood that, in one time period, an enterprise of magnitude 1 will grow sufficiently to be included in class 3; similarly, p_{20} will stand for the probability that, during a unit of time, a firm in size range 2 will go out of business for any reason whatever.

Using this notation, we arrange the transition probabilities p_{ij} into a matrix which may be written as

$$P = \begin{bmatrix} p_{00} & p_{01} & p_{02} & \cdots & p_{0m} \\ p_{10} & p_{11} & p_{12} & \cdots & p_{1m} \\ \cdot & \cdot & \cdot & & \cdot \\ \cdot & \cdot & \cdot & & \cdot \\ \cdot & \cdot & \cdot & & \cdot \\ p_{m0} & p_{m1} & p_{m2} & \cdots & p_{mm} \end{bmatrix}.$$

Since each element of this matrix is non-negative, and since

$$\sum_{j=0}^{m} p_{ij} = 1 \qquad\qquad\qquad\qquad\qquad \mathbf{1}$$

for each i, the matrix P is a *stochastic* matrix (Kemeny, Snell and Thompson, 1957, p. 217). But we must place on additional restriction upon the shape of P before we can determine the ultimate size distribution of firms in an industry: we require that all states be accessible. In other words, a firm starting in any class i must have a non-zero probability of moving into any other group j in a *finite* number of periods. In this event, P will be a *regular* stochastic matrix (p. 220), and we may use directly a number of theorems which have been proved elsewhere concerning such matrices.

One such theorem states that there exists an equilibrium solution to the Markov process (p. 220). Furthermore, it has been shown that this equilibrium is unique and independent of the initial configuration (p. 221). That is, the repeated application of the set of transition probabilities represented by P will cause *any* initial distribution of firm sizes to approach this unique equilibrium state. Under the above assumptions, then, an industry – regardless of whether it was originally in a purely competitive state or in an oligopolistic one – will, given the same transition probabilities, assume the same ultimate type of organization. This result is, of course, merely the logical implication of the economic assumption that the subsequent development of a firm is independent of its past history.

Before we derive the form of this equilibrium solution, however, we must examine in more detail the meaning of equilibrium in a Markov process. An equilibrium structure in this model may be defined as that distribution for which the average number of corporations entering a given stratum per period equals the average number of businesses leaving it. Our concept of equilibrium is thus statistical in nature for the industry, and dynamic for the individual firm. In other words, equilibrium in this paper does not imply that there is no movement of enterprises between strata. On the contrary, the stochastic conception of equilibrium explicitly requires that firms move in and out of each class. But on the average, the forces acting to increase the number of enterprises in a given size range are exactly counterbalanced by those tending to decrease it.

As stated above, the equilibrium solution may be derived, at least in principle, by the repeated application of P to any initial distribution vector. Symbolically, if the structure described by a row vector

$$(s_j^n) = (s_0^n, s_1^n, \ldots, s_m^n), \qquad\qquad 2$$

the components of which represent the proportion of firms in each class at that time, the configuration after the next time step may be found from

$$(s_j^n)P = (s_j^{n+1}). \qquad\qquad 3$$

By successive substitutions, one may write

$$(s_j^n)P^{n+1} = (s_j^{n+1}). \qquad\qquad 4$$

But to find the equilibrium vector by multiplying P by itself a large number of times is, in the general case, a tedious process. A simpler approach is to make use of the fact that, in equilibrium, the distribution of enterprises among strata must be invariant. That is, for the equilibrium vector (t_j), we may rewrite 3 as

$$(t_j)P = (t_j). \qquad\qquad 5$$

Since (t_j) is an $m+1$ component vector, and P is a square matrix, 5 provides us with a set of $m+1$ equations, from which it would appear that we can derive the $m+1$ components of the vector (t_j). However, since (t_j) represents a *relative* distribution, we must also have

$$\sum_{j=0}^{m} t_j = 1. \qquad\qquad 6$$

We now have $m+2$ equations 5 and 6 in $m+1$ unknowns. But it can be shown that (any) one of the equations 5 is not linearly independent of the others and therefore that any one of these equations may be dropped from the system. Thus we are left with a set of $m+1$ linearly independent equations (if our assumption about accessibility is satisfied) in $m+1$ unknowns, from which we can evaluate the equilibrium structure of the industry.

An index of industrial mobility

The stochastic matrix P may be utilized further in order to construct an index of corporate mobility analogous to the index of social mobility of Prais (1955). Intuitively, it would appear reasonable to express the concept of mobility in terms of the average period a representative firm remains in the same size interval. For the more fluid the structure of an industry, the shorter will be the time before a typical corporation will move from one stratum to another. But the specification of an index requires also a reference situation to which a given industrial complex can be compared. We therefore take as our measure of corporate mobility the *ratio* of the average number of years spent in a class in a perfectly mobile industry (to be defined below) to the corresponding quantity for the industry in question.

The mean life time L_j of a corporation in the jth stratum may be found by noting that the total time spent in an interval by all the s_j firms originally included therein is given by

$$T_j = s_j^0 + s_j^0 p_{jj} + s_j^0 p_{jj}^2 + \dots . \qquad 7$$

Therefore, the average firm will remain in the jth level for a period

$$L_j = \frac{T_j}{s_j^0} = 1 + p_{jj} + p_{jj}^2 + \dots = \frac{1}{1 - p_{jj}}. \qquad 8$$

Before we can write down our index of corporate mobility, however, it is necessary to evaluate the lifetimes for an industry in which movement is uninhibited. In general (*à la* Prais, 1955) we define a perfectly mobile corporate structure as one for which the probability that a firm will move from class A to class B during a single period is independent of A. With this definition, each column of the transition matrix P for a perfectly mobile industry of m size classes is composed of m identical positive numbers, and as usual, the sum of the elements of each row is unity.

There are, in principle, an infinite number of perfectly mobile industries which may be used for comparison. Of these, there is precisely one whose equilibrium structure is identical to that which will be reached by our particular group of firms. This perfectly mobile industry, which we choose for our standard of mobility, has the transition matrix

$$T_1 = \begin{bmatrix} t_0 & t_1 & \cdots & t_m \\ \cdot & \cdot & & \cdot \\ \cdot & \cdot & & \cdot \\ \cdot & \cdot & & \cdot \\ t_0 & t_1 & \cdots & t_m \end{bmatrix}. \qquad\qquad 9$$

The index for industrial mobility for time n may be written as

$$I^n = \frac{\sum\limits_{j=0}^{m} t_j/(1-t_j)}{\sum\limits_{j=0}^{m} s_j^n/(1-p_{jj})}. \qquad\qquad 10$$

The steel industry

We shall now illustrate the procedure of the preceding sections by applying the assumptions and tools developed there to the derivation of the consequent equilibrium structure of the steel industry in the United States. For the purposes of this study, this industry was defined as that group of enterprises with assets exceeding one million dollars, whose major activity consists of the production of pig iron, steel ingots and basic steel shapes; the registry of these firms was compiled from *Moody's Manual of Industrials* (1930–57). Two considerations led us to select this sector for our investigation. First of all, the steel industry is of basic importance to the nation's economy. Secondly, the present market structure within this field of activity is fairly typical of that of industry in general. For, as is well known, the current form of organization of the steel industry is oligopolistic in character, consisting of less than five dominant firms together with a large fringe of smaller enterprises. This latter circumstance suggests, in addition, that the nature of the equilibrium configuration predicted for steel might well be of interest as an indication of equilibrium tendencies for United States manufacturing industry.

We therefore proceeded to derive the shape predicted by our model for the equilibrium size distribution of firms engaged in the manufacturing of iron and steel in the United States. A first step in this direction, was the quantification of the matrix of transition probabilities P.

Before we could accomplish this task, however, we had to select an index of corporate size. Our choice was the dollar value of a firm's total assets, as listed in *Moody's Manual of Industrials*. This indicator was preferred over the obvious alternatives (such as, e.g. the number of employees, the dollar value of sales or net value added) primarily because it was easier to obtain this type of data. However, the choice of index of size is not crucial to the applicability of the technique. Furthermore, it would be reasonable to expect that all indices of size would, in practice, be highly correlated.

The years selected for our study of the steel industry were 1929–39 and 1945–56. These two decades were chosen in order to have a fairly long, cyclically well balanced period, for which reasonably homogeneous and reliable statistical data would be available. The war years were omitted from our investigation in order not to bias our results.

Next, we divided the continuous scale of firm asset sizes into seven discrete ranges. Two problems emerged in fixing these ranges. First, we would expect that a firm's ability to change its (asset) size during a given period would be related to its initial size. Larger firms would be likely to grow by greater absolute amounts than smaller ones. Hence, the class intervals were constructed so that their absolute width was greater for large than for small enterprises. Secondly, we were faced with the problem of statistical deflation. For, it would appear unreasonable to assume *a priori* that a prewar firm with ten million dollars' worth of assets is necessarily equal in magnitude to a ten million dollar post-war enterprise. To achieve greater inter-period comparability, then, we required that the class limits of a given size range represent the same percentage of the industry's total assets in both 1934 and 1950, the midpoints of the two time periods. Therefore, since the ratio of the value of industry assets in 1934 to their value in 1950 was 0·60, we were led by the above considerations to the choice of class intervals given in Table 1.

With this selection of asset ranges, we traced the year to year growth pattern of each domestic steel firm in terms of its movements within the class intervals 0 through 6. In this connection, mergers were treated in a manner analogous to outright sale – i.e. as the disappearance of one enterprise and the aggrandisement

Table 1 Class Intervals

Class name	Class limits 1929–39 (in millions of dollars)	Class limits 1946–56 (in millions of dollars)
0	0 – 0·599	0 – 0·99
1	0·6 – 5·99	1 – 9·99
2	6 – 29·99	10 – 49·99
3	30 – 59·99	50 – 99·99
4	60 – 299·99	100 – 499·99
5	300 – 599·99	500 – 999·99
6	600 – 2999·99	1000 – 4999·99

of another. Generally speaking, it was assumed in this connection that it was the smaller firm who lost its corporate identity. Now, if a_{ij} denotes the number of movements of firms from class i to class j throughout the period under consideration, our transition probabilities p_{ij} become

$$p_{ij} = \frac{a_{ij}}{\sum\limits_{j=0}^{6} a_{ij}}.$$

11

Of course, if a corporation stayed in the same asset class j during two successive years, this event was treated as an observation of type a_{jj} and its probability denoted by p_{jj}. Naturally, expression **11** represents merely an empirical relative frequency approximation to the true probability which is inherently a limiting concept.

The above definition of p_{ij}, however, still leaves the probabilities p_{0j} arbitrary. For, since, by the very nature of the case, no data on the number of businesses retaining the status of potential entrants could be collected, a_{00} could not be evaluated empirically. This deficiency was remedied by assuming that

$$\sum_{i=0}^{6} a_{0j} = 100,000.$$

Our choice of number was guided by the desire to keep the reservoir of incipient enterprises large by comparison with the number of corporations actually within the industry. But this arbitrary selection does not affect the economically relevant portion of our results (see footnote 3 for proof).

The statistics upon which our p_{ij} were based were considerably better than might be inferred from the fact that the average number of firms engaged in steel production was around 100. For, during the period of our investigation, a typical firm experienced twenty-one transitional movements[1] of the type a_{ij}. Consequently, the total number of observations underlying the quantification of the p_{ij} was almost 2100.

Given the computed values of the p_{ij}, the resulting matrix of transition probabilities for the steel industry in the United States becomes

$$[P] = \begin{bmatrix} 0.99942 & 0.00040 & 0.00016 & 0.00001 & 0.00001 & 0 & 0 \\ 0.021 & 0.911 & 0.068 & 0 & 0 & 0 & 0 \\ 0.024 & 0.039 & 0.908 & 0.028 & 0.001 & 0 & 0 \\ 0 & 0 & 0.076 & 0.872 & 0.052 & 0 & 0 \\ 0.008 & 0 & 0 & 0.016 & 0.947 & 0.028 & 0 \\ 0 & 0 & 0 & 0 & 0.037 & 0.926 & 0.037 \\ 0 & 0 & 0 & 0 & 0 & 0.024 & 0.976 \end{bmatrix}. \qquad \textbf{12}$$

An examination of this matrix P reveals several interesting facts. First of all, as might have been expected, the most probable outcome for each firm is that it will remain in the same class interval. For, the diagonal terms p_{jj} are uniformly very much larger than the other p_{ij} (for $j \neq i$). Secondly, our observations bear out Marshall's dictum *natura non facit saltum*. For those firms which survive generally move up or down one asset range at a time. Of course, this conclusion is weakened by the fact that, in view of our selection of class intervals, it would require an extraordinarily high rate of growth for a firm to move from class j to class $j+2$ in a single year. Thirdly, entry occurs predominantly into the lowest two asset ranges. During the entire period of our investigation only one $200 million firm (Kaiser Steel, in 1951) and one $70 million firm (M. K. Porter Co., in 1955) were formed. On the other hand, failure of small firms would appear to be considerably more probable than that of large ones, with the

1. The transitional movements of firms between 1939 and 1946 were not included in our data.

probabilities of failure approximately uniform for firms possessing assets of less than \$50 million. Indeed, no firm of size 3 or larger failed during the twenty-three years of our study, inasmuch as the two firms[2] with assets of approximately \$100 million which disappeared in the pre-war years did so as a result of mergers. This may be due to the fact that large firms merely reorganize.

Finally, we are in a position to find the equilibrium configuration of firm sizes predicted by our model for the steel industry. For, if we substitute our experimentally derived P into relationship 5, and replace the fourth equation of 5 by 6 as explained above, we obtain a set of seven independent simultaneous equations which can be solved for the equilibrium values of the t_j $(j = 0,\ldots,6)$. The latter, of course, represent the relative frequency distribution of firms among our asset strata, in the equilibrium state. With this procedure, our set of simultaneous equations becomes

$$
\begin{bmatrix}
-0.00058 & 0.021 & 0.024 & 0 & 0.008 & 0 & 0 \\
0.00040 & -0.089 & 0.039 & 0 & 0 & 0 & 0 \\
0.00016 & 0.068 & -0.092 & 0.076 & 0 & 0 & 0 \\
0.00001 & 0 & 0.001 & 0.052 & -0.053 & 0.037 & 0 \\
0 & 0 & 0 & 0 & 0.029 & -0.074 & 0.024 \\
0 & 0 & 0 & 0 & 0 & 0.037 & -0.024 \\
1 & 1 & 1 & 1 & 1 & 1 & 1
\end{bmatrix}
\begin{bmatrix}
t_0 \\ t_1 \\ t_2 \\ t_3 \\ t_4 \\ t_5 \\ t_6
\end{bmatrix}
=
\begin{bmatrix}
0 \\ 0 \\ 0 \\ 0 \\ 0 \\ 0 \\ 1
\end{bmatrix}. \quad \mathbf{13}
$$

The first six equations in 13 come from 5 and the last is equation 6. This system can easily be solved to yield the equilibrium vector

$$t = (0.9480, 0.00938, 0.01169, 0.00376, 0.00903, 0.00708, 0.01091).$$

But, since our stratum 0 was entirely arbitrary, the relationship between the proportion of firms in this category and the rest of the industry is uninteresting. A more meaningful picture can be obtained if we consider solely the relative distribution of firms

2. These firms were Central Alloy, which consolidated with Republic Steel in 1930, and Tennessee Coal which was acquired by US Steel in 1935.

actually active in the industry. To do so, we need only normalize our results so that $\sum_{i=1}^{m} t_j = 1$. The consequent equilibrium distribution of firms in the industry is then summarized in the last two columns of Table 2, along with that actually observed in 1929 and

Table 2 Asset Distribution within the Steel Industry

Stratum	1929		1956		Equilibrium	
	% Firms	% Assets[a]	% Firms	% Assets[a]	% Firms	% Assets[b]
1	25·00	1·15	27·68	0·98	18·09	0·11
2	43·47	8·64	39·29	6·79	22·55	0·68
3	16·30	9·49	8·93	4·36	7·25	0·61
4	11·96	24·70	16·96	21·90	17·42	3·92
5	1·09	5·42	5·36	26·86	13·65	12·54
6	2·18	50·60	1·79	39·11	21·04	82·14
	100·00	100·00	100·00	100·00	100·00	100·00

a. Source of data: disaggregated data from *Moody's Manual of Industrials*.

b. This column was computed on the assumption that the mean firm in each stratum will possess the same assets in equilibrium as it did in 1956.

in 1956. Note that this distribution is independent of the choice of the number of firms in the zeroth class.[3] As is evident from this table, our results indicate that considerable growth in the size of the median firm might be expected. For, while both in 1929 and 1956 the median occurred in the second stratum, in equilibrium the median will be at the beginning of the fourth asset range. And,

3. The proof of this statement can be seen readily from the schematic solution of the equations 9 for t_j by determinants. Since each of the elements of the first column of the determinant of coefficients (Δ) except the last is inversely proportional to the number of firms (N) assumed to be in the zeroth group, will be a function of N. But Δt_o will be independent of N, as Δt_o is the determinant obtained by replacing the first column of Δ by a column whose elements are zero except for the last (which is unity) and no other elements of Δt_o depend on N. Thus $t_o = \Delta t_o / \Delta$ will be a function of N. The rest of the quantities $\Delta t_j (j > 0)$ will be all proportional to $1/N$, since the reduction of the 7×7 determinant to a 6×6 determinant by cancelling out the jth column and the seventh row leaves a determinant in which each of the elements of the first column is proportional to $1/N$. Thus, for i, j both greater than zero,

$$\frac{t_i}{t_j} = \frac{\Delta t_i}{\Delta t_j}$$

is independent of N.

if we apply the 1956 class limits to the equilibrium state, our model predicts that the median steel firm existing at that time will possess $150 million worth of assets, as compared to thirty in 1956 and twenty-two in 1929. It should be noted, however, that the figure of $150 million represents a minimal estimate, inasmuch as it was based upon the assumption of no further growth of the industry as a whole after 1956. Qualitatively, at least (and this is all that is hoped from this study) this conclusion would appear to be reasonable. In fact, students of the steel industry have generally been of the opinion that a marked increase in corporate size coupled with an augmented degree of both vertical and horizontal integration might be anticipated on technological grounds. Interestingly enough, the application of our technique to the data reveals the existence of forces operating in this direction, in spite of the fact that, in real terms, no growth in median firm size has actually taken place between 1929 and 1956.

Secondly, while our conclusions with respect to the degree of concentration in steel must be qualified by the fact that our study provided no opportunity for a corporation to expand beyond asset class 6, they point towards a decrease in the degree of concentration prevailing in this industry. For, if we assume that the mean value of assets in each class interval is the same in equilibrium as it was in 1956, the number of firms holding 50 per cent of industry assets predicted for the equilibrium state is thirteen, as compared with two in 1929 and four in 1956. Furthermore, with the same hypothesis, we obtain the dotted Lorenz curve of Figure 1 for the stationary state, as compared to the two lines for 1929 and 1956. Thus, an increase in the degree of competition would appear to be foreshadowed for the steel industry. But our assumptions would tend to lead us to underestimate the equilibrium degree of concentration.

As explained earlier, our data may also be utilized for the investigation of trends in the mobility of firms in the steel industry. The second column of Table 3 presents the average number of years spent by a representative corporation in each asset range; the entries in this column were computed by applying equation **8** to the appropriate probabilities in transition matrix P. Note that the mean lifetime of firms in the zeroth class was omitted from our table. This procedure was adopted in spite of the fact that it

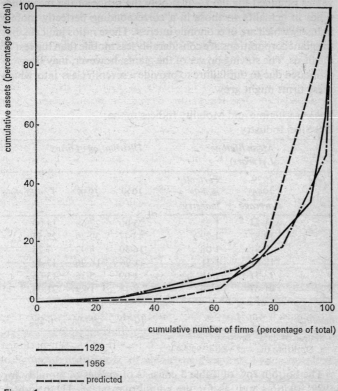

cumulative assets (percentage of total)

cumulative number of firms (percentage of total)

———— 1929
—·—·— 1956
— — — — predicted

Figure 1

would be tempting to interpret such a figure as an indication of barriers to entry, because p_{00} (and hence L_0) is directly dependent upon the arbitrarily selected magnitude of the zeroth asset range. For the same reason, our computations of the L_j for the perfectly mobile industry (see Table 3) were based upon a modified matrix π from which the zeroth class interval was excluded, and the t_j normalized accordingly.

The substantial equality of mean lifetimes for all firm sizes in a perfectly mobile industry is interesting. However, since the width of our class intervals strongly conditions the numerical

Irma G. Adelman 365

values obtained for the L_j, it is only the ratios of the mean lifetimes in actuality to those in a corresponding perfectly mobile industry which are of economic interest. These ratios indicate that the giant corporations are considerably less mobile than the rest of the firms. The staying power of the giants, however, may be overestimated due to our failure to provide a seventh class into which these firms might grow.

Table 3 Lifetime and Mobility Indices in the
U S Steel Industry

	Mean lifetime: L_j (years)		Distribution of firms		
Class	1929–1956[a] average	Perfectly mobile industry	1929	1956	Equilibrium
1	11·24	1·22	25·00	27·68	18·09
2	10·87	1·29	43·47	39·29	22·55
3	7·81	1·08	16·30	8·93	7·25
4	18·87	1·21	11·96	16·96	17·42
5	13·51	1·16	1·09	5·36	13·65
6	41·67	1·26	2·18	1·79	21·04
Index of mobility			10·1%	9·6%	6·5%

Source of data: See text.
a. Omitting the war years 1940–44.

The bottom row of Table 3 consists of indices of mobility for 1929, 1956 as well as for the equilibrium state. These indices were, of course, computed by applying our definition 10 to the data in the table. Generally speaking, the mobility of firms in the steel industry during the sample period was approximately 10 per cent of that in a perfectly mobile corporate structure. Furthermore, these indices would tend to indicate the existence of a consistent trend for a decline in the mobility of steel producers. This tendency would appear to be a consequence of the decrease in concentration. For, the presence of a larger proportion of all firms in the least mobile uppermost class interval entails both some deconcentration and some loss of mobility.

Summary and conclusions

In this paper, we have presented a technique for the derivation of the equilibrium size distribution of corporations within an industry. Our basic postulate is that the growth pattern of firms is a size-dependent stochastic process, with probabilities of transition constant in time. As discussed above, the structure of the industry will generally tend towards a unique equilibrium state which is independent of the initial configuration. Since the assumptions upon which the analysis is based were seen to be reasonable, the results obtained with the Markovian approach are of considerable interest as an indication of equilibrium tendencies in industry.

As a test of this technique, we examined the steel industry in the United States. We found that one might expect a tendency towards deconcentration, as well as a growth in the size of the median firm. Since both of these trends have been forecast on other grounds, it would appear that the application of the technique presented here does not lead to absurd results, and, therefore, that it may prove quite useful in the study of industrial structure.

Furthermore, one might be able to investigate other problems in industrial organization, such as that of plant location, etc., in a similar manner. Indeed, any corporate characteristic which can be quantified can, in principle, be analysed in the same way, provided only that all the conditions stated in the text are satisfied.

References

CHAMPERNOWNE, D. G. (1953), 'A model of income distribution', *Econ. J.*, vol. 63, pp. 318–51.

FELLER, W. (1950), *An Introduction to Probability Theory and Its Applications*, Wiley.

HART, P. E., and PRAIS, S. J. (1956), 'The analysis of business concentration: a statistical approach', *J. Roy. Stats. Soc.*, vol. 119, pt 2, pp. 150–81.

KEMENY, J. G., SNELL, J. L., and THOMPSON, G. L. (1957), *Introduction to Finite Mathematics*, Prentice-Hall.

Moody's Manual of Investments, Industrial Securities (1930–57).

PRAIS, S. J. (1955), 'Measuring social mobility', *J. Roy. Stats. Soc.*, vol. 118, pp. 56–66.

SOLOW, R. M. (1951), 'Some long-run aspects of the distribution of wage incomes', *Econometrica*, vol. 19, pp. 333–9.

19 P. E. Hart

The Size and Growth of Firms

P. E. Hart, 'The size and growth of firms', *Economica*, new series, vol. 24, 1962, pp. 29–39.

In recent years there have been several statistical studies of the relationship between the size and growth of firms, a problem which has long been of interest to economists. Such analyses of this relationship date back at least to Gibrat's *Les inégalités économiques* (1931) in which he formulated his *law of proportionate effect*, arguing that the proportionate change in the size of the firm was independent of its absolute size. Such a law of growth generates a lognormal size-distribution of firms, a distribution which closely resembles distributions of firms observed in practice. This approach was extended by Simon and Bonini, who argued that the simple lognormal is a special case of a family of skew distributions called the Yule distribution (1958). In addition, the dynamic properties of the size-distribution of firms have been investigated, with the aid of a homogeneous Markov chain analysis, by Adelman (1958). This in turn has been generalized by Newman and Wolfe to allow for changing transition probabilities (1960).

The present paper comments on the economic implications of some of these results, notes some inconsistencies, questions whether parts of the analyses make economic sense, and offers some evidence on the rates of growth of large and small firms in the United Kingdom.

The economic implications of the law of proportionate effect

The typical size-distribution of firms is positively skew, with a few large firms and many small firms. In practice this skewness can often be removed by plotting the frequencies against the logarithms of size. The resulting curve often approximates the normal curve, so that the original distribution may be deemed to be lognormal. The widespread occurrence of this type of distribution is interesting because it suggests an equally widespread law of growth of firms which produces this common distribution.

A normal curve is generated when a large number of small, independent, random forces act on a variate in an additive manner; and a lognormal curve can be generated if they act multiplicatively. In the present context this means that the determinants of the growth of firms tend to change the size of firms by randomly distributed *proportions*. Some forces make for an increase, some make for a decrease, but all act randomly in the sense that there is no tendency to favour or disfavour firms of any particular size. Gibrat referred to this process of equi-proportionate growth as the *law of proportionate effect*.

The first implication of this simple model is that large, medium and small firms have the same *average* proportionate growth. The second implication is that the *dispersion* of growth-rates around the common average is also the same for large, medium and small firms. The third implication is that the *distribution* of proportionate growth-rates is also lognormal. Thus if in any period firms on average stay the same size, so that average proportionate growth is unity, just as many firms double as halve their sizes. Not only are the logarithms of proportionate growth symmetrically distributed around the mean growth, but they are distributed in accordance with the normal curve of Gauss. Since this applies to all firms, it follows that if x per cent of large firms *double* their size, x per cent of small firms *halve* their size. Therefore a fourth implication of the simplest lognormal model is that the relative dispersion of the sizes of firms tends to increase over time. In this analysis the disparity of the sizes of firms increases over time in spite of the fact that large firms have the same average proportionate growth as medium and small firms; this is so because the 50 per cent of large firms with above-average growth include firms which were formerly among the smallest in the class of large firms but which enter the ranks of the very largest firms and overtake some of the former leaders.

This economic interpretation of a few lines of algebra may be interesting, not to say fascinating: but to what extent is it true?

Some evidence of size and proportionate growth

The four implications outlined above follow from the generation of a simple lognormal distribution. While it is true that the observed size-distribution of firms often approximates this model, it is also true that some size-distributions of firms do not fit this simple curve, but are merely positively skew. Indeed, Simon and Bonini argue that the lognormal curve is a special case of the Yule distribution. The Yule distribution is generated jointly by Gibrat's law of proportionate effect and an assumed birth process, the latter normally a constant rate of birth of new firms in the smallest size-class. In this respect the Yule distribution is undoubtedly superior to the simple lognormal distribution, because the birth and death of firms imply zero size at one point of time, which cannot readily be incorporated in a model based on a logarithmic curve. Simon and Bonini found that the Yule distribution gives a good fit to the size-distribution of firms in the United States steel industry. This suggests that the law of proportionate effect is present in the growth of United States steel firms, but that some birth process is also at work.

Little is known about the relationship between the birth, death and size of firms in the United Kingdom. However, as noted in a previous article which was concerned with public companies, the chances of death of companies with securities quoted on the Stock Exchange seem to decrease with increases in their size (Hart and Prais, 1956; Ma, 1960). This not very surprising finding also modifies the original statement that the growth-rates are independent of absolute size. A similar modification has to be made to allow for births of firms. But since it is most unlikely that new Stock Exchange quotations will be representative of births into the manufacturing sector as a whole, it is impossible to outline the form of the modification to the law of proportionate effect which is required. One suspects that the chances of birth, like the chances of death, decrease as the larger-size groups are reached, with the difference that, while a large firm is unlikely to die, it is not at all unusual for a new firm to be born large, especially when it is a subsidiary of a foreign enterprise.

Granted that there are changes in the business population which are necessarily beyond the explanatory scope of the law of proportionate effect, to what extent is this single law of growth true of surviving companies? Some evidence which may help to answer this question is provided by calculations of the mean and variance – denoted by m and s^2 – of the logarithms of proportionate changes in the profits of four sets of firms, each sub-divided into 'small' and 'large'. Profits are measured gross of tax and net of depreciation, and are used simply because the figures are readily available as part of a more general investigation of profits. It is true that profits are highly correlated with other measures of size, but their volatility is such that most economists would prefer assets, output, value-added or even employment as a measure of absolute size. In the present case, however, this volatility may be an advantage because it probably weights the tests against the hypothesis of equi-proportionate growth; for example, we should expect the profits of small firms to fluctuate more than those of large firms through the trade cycle.

In the first set of data the logarithms of proportionate changes in profits of forty quoted brewing companies were calculated for 1931–2 and 1936–7 from published company accounts. They were subdivided into twenty-two 'small' companies, with less than one million pounds issued capital in 1930, and the remaining eighteen 'large' companies. In the downswing of 1931–2 the value of m for the twenty-two small companies is 1·8763 in units[1] of logarithms to the base 10. That is, on the (geometric) average, the profits of small brewing companies fell by 24·8 per cent (antilog 1·8763 = 75·2). The standard error of this estimated average is $\pm 0·0260$. The corresponding value of m for the eighteen large companies is 1·8875 ($\pm 0·0169$). A statistical test shows that the difference between these two values of m is not significant at the 5 per cent level of probability.[2] Similarly, the values of m for small and large brewing companies in the upswing of 1936–7 are not significantly different at the 5 per cent level, being 2·0253 ($\pm 0·0121$) for the twenty-two small brewing companies and 2·0290 ($\pm 0·0113$) for the eighteen large brewing companies.

1. In this section all measurements are in units of logarithms to the base 10.
2. Values of m and s^2 in this section were submitted to the normal tests of significance. The assumption of normality may be justified if the distributions of proportionate changes in profits are regarded as samples from lognormal populations. Values of s^2 for small and large firms were submitted to an F-test, and if no significant difference was found at the 5 per cent level of probability, the corresponding values of m were submitted to a t-test. If the values of s^2 differed at the 5 per cent level, the corresponding values of m were submitted to a test proposed by Welch for which tables have been prepared by Aspin (Welch, 1947; Aspin, 1949).

The second set of data relates to the proportionate changes in profits of thirty-six cotton spinning companies for 1937–8 calculated from summaries published in *Tattersall's Cotton Trade Review*. These companies were divided into eighteen 'small' and eighteen 'large' companies, the dividing line being drawn at 100,000 spindles. The values of m are 2·1343 ($\pm$0·063) for small companies and 2·0284 ($\pm$0·045) for large. Once again there is no significant difference between the means of the logarithms of proportionate changes in profits of small and large companies.

The third set of firms consists of 124 business units classified in the drink industry by the National Institute of Economic and Social Research in its standardization of the accounts of all companies quoted on the Stock Exchange.[3] In this group there were fifty-seven 'small' business units and sixty-seven 'large', the dividing line being placed at one million pounds net tangible assets. Calculations relate profits in 1954 to those in 1950. The value of m for small firms is 2·017 ($\pm$0·034), and for large firms 1·9958 ($\pm$0·043). There is no significant difference between these two values of m at the 5 per cent level of probability.

The fourth group of firms consists of 229 unquoted firms, some private companies and some partnerships, for which profits figures for 1953 and 1954 have been collected by the Oxford Institute of Statistics in its survey of small firms. The dividing line between 'small' and 'large' has been drawn at £25,000 net assets, with 116 firms falling below this limit. The value of m for the 116 'small' firms is 1·9934 ($\pm$0·0277) and that for the 113 'large' firms 2·0165 ($\pm$0·021). Once again there is no significant difference at the 5 per cent level between the two values of m.

These results are consistent with that part of the law of proportionate effect which states that on the average the proportionate growth of firms is the same irrespective of whether they are large or small. None of our tests refutes this hypothesis of equi-proportionate growth. While this does not, of course, imply that the theory is correct, it does provide additional support to those who follow Gibrat.

But even if we accept the first part of the law of proportionate effect which refers to average proportionate change in the size of

3. A business unit is a company with all subsidiaries in which it has more than 50 per cent of voting power.

firms, it is difficult to accept the second part which states that the dispersion of proportionate growth around this common average is the same for small as for large firms. One would expect large firms, with more diversified production, to have a lower dispersion of changes in profits simply because they have a better chance of offsetting unsuccessful lines of activity against their more profitable lines. Unfortunately, the estimates of s^2 – measuring the variance of the logarithms of proportionate changes in profits – in our four sets of data do not provide a consistent answer. For the second and fourth groups (of thirty-six cotton spinning companies and 229 unquoted firms) there are no significant differences at the 5 per cent level between the values of s^2 for small and large firms. These results are consistent with Gibrat's law of proportionate effect. On the other hand, the value of s^2 for the twenty-two brewing companies in the first set of data is significantly *larger* than that for the large firms; this is inconsistent with the law of proportionate effect, and agrees with our economic intuition. Finally, for our third group of 124 quoted business units, the value of s^2 for small firms is significantly *smaller* than that for large firms; this conflicts both with Gibrat and with our economic common-sense expectations.

Some evidence on the third and fourth implications

To study the third and fourth implications of Gibrat's law of proportionate effect, we need a bivariate size-distribution of firms showing the sizes of the same set of firms at two points of time. Table 1, which shows the sizes of 1981 business units (with shares quoted on the Stock Exchange) at 1950 and 1955, is an example. This table is a continuation of the tables given in an earlier article by Hart and Prais (1956), in which full details of method are given. Briefly, the size of a business unit is measured by the market valuation of its quoted securities.[4] The relevant business units are

4. The use of stock market valuation as a measure of size is justified when considering measures of business concentration, which depend on the variance of the logarithms of size and are not affected by adjustment to correct for price changes. But this is not true for measures of location, such as the mean of the logarithms of market valuation, which is clearly influenced by price changes; and to this extent the number of firms doubling their size between 1950 and 1955 is clearly less than that suggested by Table 1. This limitation does not affect the use of Table 1 in the present context to illustrate size mobility.

those in the Stock Exchange categories 'Commercial and Industrial' and 'Breweries and Distilleries', with the exception that in Table 1 all 'births' and 'deaths' have been excluded. The choice of size-classes so that each upper limit is double the lower limit is a simple way of performing a logarithmic transformation of the data, and calculations are made easy by the fact that in logarithms to the base 2 each class is equal to unity.[5]

Table 1 Bivariate Size-Distribution of Business Units, 1950–55. Size-Class in 1950.

Upper limits of size-classes: stock market valuations (thousands of pounds)	A	B	C	D	E	F	G	H	K	L	M	N	O	P	Q	R	S	T	Total 1955
3 A			3																3
7 B																			000
15 C				6		3	6	3											18
31 D				3	6	6	9												24
62 E	3			6	12	24	12												57
125 F				12	24	60	84	15											195
250 G			3	3	9	51	117	75	21										279
500 H					3	24	54	144	48	4	3								280
1000 K						15	36	117	156	15									339
2000 L							12	54	93	117	25	1							302
4000 M						3	3	21	45	60	53	21							206
8000 N								3	15	42	70	33	2						165
16000 O										3	22	10	17	2					54
32000 P											1	6	15	7					29
64000 Q													5	8	2				15
128000 R													3	4	1				8
256000 S															2	2	1		5
512000 T																	2		2
Total 1950	3	3	33	54	186	333	432	378	241	174	71	42	21	5	2	3			1981

(Left margin vertical label: Size-Class in 1955)

Source: Hart (1960, pp. 653–72).

The third economic implication mentioned in the first section was that the distribution of proportionate growth-rates of firms tends to be lognormal. This distribution may be obtained from Table 1 by summing diagonally across the table. For example, the sum of elements *AA*, *BB*, *CC*,. . ., *TT* in the leading diagonal gives

5. In this section measurements are in units of logarithms to the base 2.

the total of business units which on average stayed the same size over the period 1950–55. The sum of the elements in the diagonal immediately below this, namely (row) *B* (column) *A*, *CB*, *DC*,. . ., *TS* gives the number of business units which on average *doubled* in size. And so we can proceed to determine the distribution of business units by their proportionate growth with results as follows:

Proportionate growth (size in 1955/size in 1950)	$\frac{1}{32}$	$\frac{1}{16}$	$\frac{1}{8}$	$\frac{1}{4}$	$\frac{1}{2}$	1	2	4	8	16	32
Number of firms	3	6	18	59	308	722	513	261	79	9	3: 1981

It can be seen that some 36·5 per cent of the sample (722 of 1981) stayed in the same size-class over the period. On either side of this central tendency, the distribution appears to tail off fairly symmetrically, when the size-classes of proportionate growth are regarded as equal (as they are on a logarithmic scale).

But is this rough symmetry sufficient to justify the third implication that the distribution of proportionate growth is normal after logarithmic transformation? This question is difficult to answer, because it is not certain whether the usual statistical tests of normality can be applied in the present case.[6] If we use a graphical test, by plotting on logarithmic probability paper the cumulative form of the distribution given in the preceding paragraph, we see that it is not exactly lognormal. However, the slight deviations from lognormality may be small enough to be explained by sampling errors, so that the lognormal hypothesis remains tenable. It may still be true that some other theoretical distribution can provide a better fit to the facts and provide a superior explanation of the generation of the size-distribution of proportionate growth of firms. The lognormal is only one of many theoretical distributions which may be applied to the growth of firms; but because of its simplicity, and because of its many properties related to the familiar normal curve, it can serve as a useful tool of economic analysis until it is displaced by a superior form.

So much for the third implication of the law of proportionate

6. See the criticisms advanced by Kendall and Stuart in the discussion of Hart and Prais (Hart and Prais, 1956, p. 185).

effect. The fourth implication leads us into the more advanced dynamics of the theory of the growth of the firm. This concerns the movement of firms between size-groups over time and implies that the variance of the logarithms of the sizes of firms tends to increase over time. In fact the variance of the 1950 marginal distribution in Table 1 is 4·05 and that for 1955 is 5·51, so that Table 1 is consistent with the theory. But it is important to know why this variance increased between 1950 and 1955 and, in particular, to know whether it was due to any tendency for large firms in 1950 to grow more quickly than small firms.

This question is easily answered. From the data in Table 1 it is possible to calculate the correlation between size in 1955 and size in 1950, and the corresponding regression of 1955 on 1950. In practice we work in terms of deviations from the mean; and the ratio of the variance in 1955 to the variance in 1950 is equal to β^2/ρ^2, where β is the regression coefficient and ρ is the correlation coefficient (Hart and Prais, 1956). For our present purpose it is convenient to express this relationship as follows:

$$\text{Var}_{1955} = \beta^2 \text{ Var}_{1950} + \sigma_{\varepsilon}^2, \qquad \qquad 1$$

where $\rho^2 = 1 - \sigma_{\varepsilon}^2/\text{Var}_{1955}$ in the usual way, with σ_{ε}^2 measuring the scatter about the regression line. The economic interpretation of equation 1 is straightforward. If $\beta = 1$, small and large firms have the same average proportionate growth; if $\beta < 1$, there is a 'regression' of firms towards the mean size and small firms have a larger proportionate growth on the average than do large firms; if $\beta > 1$, then large firms grow more quickly than small firms. The value of β calculated from Table 1 is 0·99 ($\pm 0·02$), which is sufficiently near unity to enable us to say that on the average small and large firms had the same average proportionate growth during the period 1950–55.

This implies that the variance of the size-distribution of firms in Table 1 increased between 1950 and 1955 due to the residual variance, σ_{ε}^2. From an economic point of view σ_{ε}^2 may be regarded as measuring the variance of the multiplicative erratic shocks referred to in the first section. Once again, the data in Table 1 are consistent with the law of proportionate effect.

When β is unity, the residual variance may also be regarded as measuring the variance of the distribution of proportionate growth. This in turn reflects size mobility, or the extent to which firms move from one size-class to another over time. For example, when $\sigma_\varepsilon^2 = 1$, then the standard deviation of the distribution of proportionate change is also 1 (in units of logarithms to the base 2). Since in a normal curve 68 per cent of observations lie within plus or minus one standard deviation of the mean, it follows that 32 per cent of firms have more than double or less than half of the mean proportionate growth. More simply, 32 per cent of firms have substantial changes in size. Similarly, when $\sigma_\varepsilon^2 = 4$, 38 per cent of firms have proportionate growths varying between half and double the mean growth (38 per cent of observations in a normal curve lie within $\pm\frac{1}{2}\sigma$ from the mean), and no less than 62 per cent of firms have substantial changes in size. Clearly, the larger is σ_ε^2, the greater is size mobility, a result which is used later in this section.

The general picture emerging from this analysis is that the relative dispersion of the size-distribution of firms, measured by the variance of the logarithms of their sizes, tends to increase continuously over time because β in equation 1 is generally near unity, and σ_ε^2 is necessarily positive, being a sum of squares.

Mrs Adelman has recently put forward an analysis which conflicts with this fourth implication of the law of proportionate effect and argues that the size-distribution of firms tends towards an equi-librium position after which there will be no tendency for its dis-persion to change (1958). Table 1 is useful in explaining her approach. If each element in the central part of Table 1 is divided by the sum of the column in which it stands, we obtain a matrix showing the proportion of firms moving between size-classes. For example row E would read: —, 3/3, —, 6/33, 12/54,..., —. If we regard these relative frequencies as probabilities, we have a transition matrix showing the probability of firms moving between the various size-classes. When this matrix of transition probabilities is applied to the size-distribution of firms in 1950, there results the size-distribution of firms in 1955. In the simple notation of matrix algebra:

$$\mathbf{y} = \mathbf{A}\mathbf{x} \qquad\qquad 2$$

where $\mathbf{y}$ is a column vector representing the size-distribution of surviving firms in 1955, **A** is the matrix of transition probabilities in Table 1, and **x** is a column vector representing the size-distribution in 1950. This process could be repeated; the matrix **A** could be applied to the 1955 size-distribution to give an estimate of the size-distribution in 1960. Indeed, it can be shown that, if the matrix **A** is constant, an equilibrium size-distribution will be reached eventually, such that the number of firms in each size-class becomes a stable proportion and does not change (Feller, 1950).[7] Moreover, this equilibrium size-distribution will depend solely on **A** and not on the original size-distribution in 1950. The process whereby a size-distribution in any year is linked to size-distributions of previous years by a matrix of transition probabilities is an example of a Markov chain, and when **A** is constant the Markov chain is said to be homogeneous. In fact Adelman was able to apply a homogeneous Markov chain analysis to firms in the United States steel industry from 1929 to 1956, and calculated an equilibrium distribution with which she compared the observed distribution in 1956. She was therefore able to predict future developments in this size-distribution towards the equilibrium size-distribution of firms in the United States steel industry.

In spite of this encouraging result and in spite of the elegance of the argument, her analysis is difficult to accept mainly because there is no reason to suppose that transition probabilities are constant. In fact, we should expect them to vary between slump and boom on the one hand, when the mobility of firms between size-classes can be expected to be high, and periods of war or stagnation, on the other hand, when we should expect size-mobility to be generally lower. It is difficult to obtain a satisfactory measure of size mobility but, as we have seen, a good case can be made for using the residual variance of a regression of the logarithms of size in year 2 on those of year 1. If this is accepted, then it is worth noting that for companies with shares quoted on the Stock Exchange from 1885 to 1950, this indicator fluctuated between a minimum of 1·04 in the period 1907–24 and a maximum of 2·18 in the period 1885–96 (Hart and Prais, 1956). In the relatively depressed years, 1924–39, it was 2·01, compared with only 1·24 in the period 1939–50 covering the Second World War. This

7. An excellent non-mathematical description of Markov chains is given by Prais (1955a; see also Prais, 1955b).

evidence confirms our suspicions that size-mobility varies over time and that it is not safe to assume constant transition probabilities. If this argument is correct, a homogeneous Markov chain analysis of the growth of firms, however strong its aesthetic appeal, cannot be applied to the real world.

In a most stimulating essay, Newman and Wolfe (1960) follow a similar approach to that of Mrs Adelman. Their approach differs from hers in that they treat the relative frequencies of a bivariate size-distribution as referring to the actual proportions of firms which change their size-class and not as a set of constant probabilities. That is, the matrix A is treated by them as deterministic rather than stochastic, and they consider the likely economic forces which would determine A. For example, they argue that prices would be an important influence because an increase in price would be likely to foster the growth of firms and lead to upward size mobility. Though this approach sounds plausible, it is difficult to reconcile with the observed size-distributions, which are generally explained by a stochastic process or which at any rate are likely to have a large random component in addition to their 'economic' determinants. The shape of the observed size-distribution of firms can be explained in many ways. Most explanations, however, include a reference to something like 'a large number of small, independent disturbances acting in a multiplicative manner on the size of the firm' simply because this phenomenon would generate a distribution approximating the observed size-distribution. According to this particular approach, it would be possible to explain only a small proportion of the variance of the growth of firms by the variances of price, managerial ability, techniques, consumers' tastes, government policy and the like. A list of such forces would omit many other forces influencing growth; and while the collective effect of the omitted forces may be assumed to be random, they would be numerous relatively to the determining 'economic' variables specified in any regression analysis of the growth of firms.

It would be exceedingly difficult, but not impossible, to carry out such a regression analysis in an attempt to measure the importance of price, etc., in the determination of the growth of firms. In fact, an analysis of this type has been performed on a size-distribution of incomes, which has a similar shape to the size-distribution of firms and which is presumably generated by a similar process. In his study of the incomes of engineers and scientists in Canada, Professor Rosenbluth (1960) postulated that the inequality of their salaries could be explained by their experience (measured in years since graduation), the industry in which they worked, the particular region in Canada in which they worked, and their particular function (e.g. administration, selling, research, teaching, consulting, etc.). Most economists would regard this list as containing the theoretically important economic determinants of the salaries of scientists. Yet altogether they accounted for only about 30 per cent of the inequality of incomes. The residual variance accounted for the other 70 per cent.

If arguments by analogy are permitted, these results reinforce the view that there is a large stochastic component in the forces determining the growth of firms, which makes it difficult to adopt a deterministic explanation. We should expect the growth or decline of a firm to depend on the quality of its management, on the tastes of its customers, on the development of techniques, on government economic policy, and on many other economic forces. But if the argument of this article is accepted, we should expect these influences to account for a relatively small part of the proportionate growth of firms. There will be a long list of other causes – the weather, the international political situation, the import policy of countries overseas and many more – some making for growth, some making for decline, but together apparently acting randomly on the sizes of firms.

References

ADELMAN, I. G. (1958), 'A stochastic analysis of the size distribution of firms', *J. Amer. Stats. Assoc.*, vol. 53, pp. 893–904.

ASPIN, A. A. (1949), 'Tables for use in comparisons whose accuracy involves two variances, separately estimated', *Biometrika*, vol. 25.

FELLER, W. (1950), *An Introduction to Probability Theory and Its Applications*, Wiley.

GIBRAT, R. (1931), *Les inégalités économiques*, Paris.

HART, P. E. (1960), 'Concentration and its measurement in the United Kingdom', in H. ARNDT, (ed.), *Die Konzentraztion in der Wirtschaft*, Berlin.

HART, P. E., and PRAIS, S. J. (1956), 'The analysis of business concentration: a statistical approach', *J. Roy. Stats. Soc.*, vol. 119, pt 2, pp. 150–75.

MA, R. (1960), 'Births and deaths in the quoted public sector in the United Kingdom, 1949–53', *Yorkshire Bull. econ. soc. Res.*, vol. 12, pp. 90–95.

NEWMAN, P. K., and WOLFE, J. N. (1960), *An Essay on the Theory of Value*, Purdue University.

PRAIS, S. J. (1955a), 'The formal theory of social mobility', *Pop. Stud.*, vol. 9, pp. 72–81.

PRAIS, S. J. (1955b), 'Measuring social mobility', *J. Roy. Stats. Soc.*, vol. 118, pp. 56–66.

ROSENBLUTH, G. (1960), *Salaries of Engineers and Scientists, 1951*, Canadian Political Science Association.

SIMON, H. A., and BONINI, C. P. (1958), 'The size distribution of business firms', *Amer. econ. Rev.*, vol. 48, pp. 607–17.

WELCH, B. L. (1947), 'The generalization of "student's" problem when several different population variances are involved', *Biometrika*, vol. 24.

Part Seven Linear Programming

The appearance of linear programming in its own section at the end of this volume may have a strangely old-fashioned air: after all, it would not be at all fanciful to *start* an intermediate course in microeconomics with programming, and to branch out later! The reason for programming here appearing in a separate section is not that it is an afterthought or appendix, but, on the contrary, that its universality makes alternative classification of introductory articles impossible.

Programming was developed as a technique for finding optimal solutions to problems involving the simultaneous use of many activities. It may thus be regarded as a method for doing something the achievement of which is taken for granted in the usual analysis, namely finding 'efficient points'. Notice that the conventional production function gives the *boundary* of the set of production possibilities: it is thus assumed that firms are not wastefully 'inside' their frontier. In fact, techniques for finding points on the frontier are of great practical use. Programming is thus an important technique in operations research. It might be thought that programming was therefore of limited interest to the economist, but this is an error. Baumol and Quandt bring out the relationship between results in programming and standard competitive theory, and the new insights given by the former.

Programming also provides a technique for economic planning. This involves the supersession of the market by institutional direction – just what Coase pointed out was the nature of the firm (see Further Reading). We thus find many issues – planning versus the price mechanism, the possibility of socialism, the size and efficiency of firms – united: they are problems in efficient decision-taking, and solutions depend upon the costs of available techniques of decision-taking. We are back where we started: economics is about the allocation of scarce resources, which may be determined by the market or within institutions. In no economy is it determined wholly by one or the other. The efficient extent of decentralization depends on the costs of alternative decision methods. Economics gains much in intellectual unity when we realize that the techniques used to improve efficiency in an Indian cotton mill can be used to plan economic development or illuminate problems in regional economic policy.

Further Reading

Two obvious books are

W. J. Baumol, *Economic Theory and Operations Analysis*, Prentice-Hall, 1961,
and
R. Dorfman, P. A. Samuelson and R. M. Solow, *Linear Programming and Economic Analysis*, McGraw-Hill, 1958.

Johansen's paper,
L. Johansen, 'Regional economic problems elucidated by linear programming', *International Economic Papers*, vol. 12, 1967, pp. 63–81, is technically within the reach of anyone who has followed the papers printed here.

The case of the Indian cotton mill is in
G. Morton, 'Linear programming: an application in an Indian textile mill', *Operation Research Quarterly*, vol. 9, 1958, pp. 198–206.

For the relationship between the development of positive economics and developments in techniques of decision taking, see
H. A. Simon, 'Theories of decision making in economics and behavioural science,' *American Economic Review*, 1959, reprinted in his *Models of Man* and in *Managerial Economics*, G. P. E. Clarkson (ed.), Penguin, 1968,
and
T. C. Koopmans, 'Efficient allocation of resources', *Econometrica*, vol. 19, 1951, pp. 455–65.

Two interesting works on 'how to be efficient' are
T. M. Whitin, *The Theory of Inventory Management*, Princeton University Press, 1953; Oxford University Press, 1953 (see particularly the first four chapters),
and

C. C. Holt, F. Modigliani and others, 'Mathematics for production scheduling', *Harvard Business Review*, vol. 36, 1958, pp. 51–8.

The last reference we give is to a classic paper:
R. E. Coase, 'The nature of the firm', *Economica*, n.s., vol. 4, 1937, pp. 386–405, reprinted in *Readings in Price Theory*, American Economic Association, published by Allen & Unwin, 1953.

20 Robert Dorfman

A Non-Mathematical Exposition

R. Dorfman, 'Mathematical or "linear" programming: a non-mathematical exposition', *American Economic Review*, vol. 43, 1953, pp. 797–825.

This paper is intended to set forth the leading ideas of mathematical programming[1] purged of the algebraic apparatus which has impeded their general acceptance and appreciation. This will be done by concentrating on the graphical representation of the method. While it is not possible, in general, to portray mathematical programming problems in two-dimensional graphs, the conclusions which we shall draw from the graphs will be of general validity and, of course, the graphic representation of multi-dimensional problems has a time-honored place in economics.

The central formal problem of economics is the problem of allocating scarce resources so as to maximize the attainment of some predetermined objective. The standard formulation of this problem – the so-called marginal analysis – has led to conclusions of great importance for the understanding of many questions of social and economic policy. But it is a fact of common knowledge that this mode of analysis has not recommended itself to men of affairs for the practical solution of their economic and business problems. Mathematical programming is based on a restatement of this same formal problem in a form which is designed to be useful in making practical decisions in business and economic affairs. That mathematical programming is nothing but a reformulation of the standard economic problem and its solution is the main thesis of this exposition.

1. The terminology of the techniques which we are discussing is in an unsatisfactory state. Most frequently they are called 'linear programming' although the relationships involved are not always linear. Sometimes they are called 'activities analysis', but this is not a very suggestive name. The distinguishing feature of the techniques is that they are concerned with programming rather than with analysis, and, at any rate, 'activities analysis' has not caught on. We now try out 'mathematical programming'; perhaps it will suit.

The motivating idea of mathematical programming is the idea of a 'process' or 'activity'. A process is a specific method for performing an economic task. For example, the manufacture of soap by a specified formula is a process. So also is the weaving of a specific quality of cotton gray goods on a specific type of loom. The conventional production function can be thought of as the formula relating the inputs and outputs of all the processes by which a given task can be accomplished.

For some tasks, e.g. soap production, there are an infinite number of processes available. For others, e.g. weaving, only a finite number of processes exist. In some cases, a plant or industry may have only a single process available.

In terms of processes, choices in the productive sphere are simply decisions as to which processes are to be used and the extent to which each is to be employed. Economists are accustomed to thinking in terms of decisions as to the quantities of various productive factors to be employed. But an industry or firm cannot substitute Factor A for Factor B unless it does some of its work in a different way, that is, unless it substitutes a process which uses A in relatively high proportions for one which uses B. Inputs, therefore, cannot be changed without a change in the way of doing things, and often a fundamental change. Mathematical programming focusses on this aspect of economic choice.

The objective of mathematical programming is to determine the optimal levels of productive processes in given circumstances. This requires a restatement of productive relationships in terms of processes and a reconsideration of the effect of factor scarcities on production choices. As a prelude to this theoretical discussion, however, it will be helpful to consider a simplified production problem from a commonsense point of view.

An example of mathematical programming

Let us consider an hypothetical automobile company equipped for the production of both automobiles and trucks. This company, then, can perform two economic tasks, and we assume that it has a single process for accomplishing each. These two tasks, the manufacture of automobiles and that of trucks, compete for the use of the firm's facilities. Let us assume that the company's plant is organized into four departments: sheet metal stamping, engine assembly, automobile final assembly and truck final assembly – raw materials, labor and all other components being available in virtually unlimited amounts at constant prices in the open market.

The capacity of each department of the plant is, of course, limited. We assume that the metal stamping department can turn out sufficient stampings for 25,000 automobiles or 35,000 trucks per month. We can then calculate the combinations of automobile and truck stampings which this department can produce. Since the department can accommodate 25,000 automobiles per month, each automobile requires 1/25,000 or 0·004 per cent of monthly capacity. Similarly each truck requires 0·00286 per cent of monthly capacity. If, for example, 15,000 automobiles were manufactured they would require 60 per cent of metal stamping capacity and the remaining 40 per cent would be sufficient to produce stampings for 14,000 trucks. Then 15,000 automobiles and 14,000 trucks could be produced by this department at full operation. This is, of course, not the only combination of automobiles and trucks which could be produced by the stamping department at full operation. In Figure 1, the line labeled 'metal stamping' represents all such combinations.

Similarly we assume that the engine assembly department has monthly capacity for 33,333 automobile engines or 16,667 truck engines or, again, some combination of fewer automobile and truck engines. The combinations which would absorb the full capacity of the engine assembly department are shown by the 'engine assembly' line in Figure 1. We assume also that the automobile assembly department can accommodate 22,500 automobiles per month and the truck assembly department 15,000 trucks. These limitations are also represented in Figure 1.

We regard this set of assumptions as defining two processes: the production of automobiles and the production of trucks. The process of producing an automobile yields, as an output, one automobile and absorbs, as inputs, 0·004 per cent of metal-stamping capacity, 0·003 per cent of engine-assembly capacity, and 0·00444 per cent of automobile-assembly capacity. Similarly the process of producing a truck yields, as an output, one truck and absorbs, as inputs, 0·00286 per cent of metal-stamping capacity,

Robert Dorfman 389

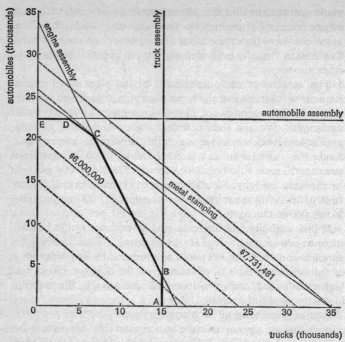

Figure 1 Choices open to an automobile firm

0·006 per cent of engine-assembly capacity, and 0·00667 per cent of truck-assembly capacity.

The economic choice facing this firm is the selection of the numbers of automobiles and trucks to be produced each month, subject to the restriction that no more than 100 per cent of the capacity of any department can be used. Or, in more technical phraseology, the choice consists in deciding at what level to employ each of the two available processes. Clearly, if automobiles alone are produced, at most 22,500 units per month can be made, automobile assembly being the effective limitation. If only trucks are produced, a maximum of 15,000 units per month can be made because of the limitation on truck assembly. Which of these alternatives should be adopted, or whether some combination of

390 Linear Programming

trucks and automobiles should be produced depends on the relative profitability of manufacturing trucks and automobiles. Let us assume, to be concrete, that the sales value of an automobile is $300 greater than the total cost of purchased materials, labor and other direct costs attributable to its manufacture. And, similarly, that the sale value of a truck is $250 more than the direct cost of manufacturing it. Then the net revenue of the plant for any month is 300 times the number of automobiles produced plus 250 times the number of trucks. For example, 15,000 automobiles and 6000 trucks would yield a net revenue of $6,000,000. There are many combinations of automobiles and trucks which would yield this same net revenue; 10,000 automobiles and 12,000 trucks is another one. In terms of Figure 1, all combinations with a net revenue of $6,000,000 lie on a straight line, to be specific, the line labelled $6,000,000 in the figure.

A line analogous to the one which we have just described corresponds to each possible net revenue. All these lines are parallel, since their slope depends only on the relative profitability of the two activities. The greater the net revenue, of course, the higher the line. A few of the net revenue lines are shown in the figure by the dashed parallel lines.

Each conceivable number of automobiles and trucks produced corresponds to a point on the diagram, and through each point there passes one member of the family of net revenue lines. Net revenue is maximized when the point corresponding to the number of automobiles and trucks produced lies on the highest possible net revenue line. Now the effect of the capacity restrictions is to limit the range of choice to outputs which correspond to points lying inside the area bounded by the axes and by the broken line ABCDE. Since net revenue increases as points move out from the origin, only points which lie on the broken line need be considered. Beginning then with Point A and moving along the broken line we see that the boundary of the accessible region intersects higher and higher net revenue lines until point C is reached. From there on, the boundary slides down the scale of net revenue lines. Point C therefore corresponds to the highest attainable net revenue. At point C the output is 20,370 automobiles and 6481 trucks, yielding a net revenue of $7,731,481 per month.

The reader has very likely noticed that this diagram is by no means novel. The broken line, ABCDE, tells the maximum number of automobiles which can be produced in conjunction with any given number of trucks. It is therefore, apart from its angularity, a production opportunity curve or transformation curve of the sort made familiar by Irving Fisher, and the slope of the curve at any point where it has a slope is the ratio of substitution in production between automobiles and trucks. The novel feature is that the production opportunity curve shown here has no defined slope at five points and that one of these five is the critical point. The dashed lines in the diagram are equivalent to conventional price lines.

The standard theory of production teaches that profits are maximized at a point where a price line is tangent to the production opportunity curve. But, as we have just noted, there are five points where our production opportunity curve has no tangent. The tangency criterion therefore fails. Instead we find that profits are maximized at a corner where the slope of the price line is neither less than the slope of the opportunity curve to the left of the corner nor greater than the slope of the opportunity curve to the right.

Diagrammatically, then, mathematical programming uses angles where standard economics uses curves. In economic terms, where does the novelty lie? In standard economic analysis we visualize production relationships in which, if there are two products, one may be substituted for the other with gradually increasing difficulty. In mathematical programming we visualize a regime of production in which, for any output, certain factors will be effectively limiting but other factors will be in ample supply. Thus, in Figure 1, the factors which effectively limit production at each point can be identified by noticing on which limitation lines the point lies. The rate of substitution between products is determined by the limiting factors alone and changes only when the designation of the limiting factors changes. In the diagram a change in the designation of the limiting factors is represented by turning a corner on the production opportunity curve.

We shall come back to this example later, for we have not exhausted its significance. But now we are in a position to develop with more generality some of the concepts used in mathematical programming.

The model of production in mathematical programming

A classical problem in economics is the optimal utilization of two factors of production, conveniently called capital and labor. In the usual analysis, the problem is formulated by conceiving of the two factors as cooperating with each other in accordance with a production function which states the maximum quantity of a product which can be obtained by the use of stated quantities of the two factors. One convenient means of representing such a production function is an 'isoquant diagram', as in Figure 2. In this familiar figure, quantities of labor are plotted along the horizontal axis and quantities of capital along the vertical. Each of the arcs in the body of the diagram corresponds to a definite quantity of output, higher arcs corresponding to greater quantities.

If the prices per unit of capital and labor are known, the combinations of labor and capital which can be purchased for a fixed total expenditure can be shown by a sloping straight line

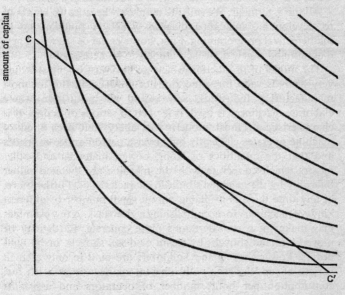

Figure 2 An isoquant diagram

like CC′ in the figure, the slope depending only on the relative prices. Two interpretations follow immediately. First, the minimum unit cost of producing the output represented by any isoquant can be achieved by using the combination of labor and capital which corresponds to the point where that isoquant is tangent to a price line. Second, the greatest output attainable with any given expenditure is represented by the isoquant which is tangent to the price line corresponding to that expenditure.

This diagram and its analysis rest upon the assumption that the two factors are continuously substitutable for each other in such wise that if the amount of labor employed be reduced by a small amount it will be possible to maintain the quantity of output by a *small* increase in the amount of capital employed. Moreover, this analysis assumes that each successive unit decrement in the amount of labor will require a slightly larger increment in the amount of capital if output is to remain constant. Otherwise the isoquants will not have the necessary shape.

All this is familiar. We call it to mind only because we are about to develop an analogous diagram which is fundamental to mathematical programming. First, however, let us see why a new diagram and a new approach are felt to be necessary.

The model of production which we have just briefly sketched very likely is valid for some kinds of production. But for most manufacturing industries, and indeed all production where elaborate machinery is used, it is open to serious objection. It is characteristic of most modern machinery that each kind of machine operates efficiently only over a narrow range of speeds and that the quantities of labor, power, materials and other factors which cooperate with the machine are dictated rather inflexibly by the machine's built-in characteristics. Furthermore, at any time there is available only a small number of different kinds of machinery for accomplishing a given task. A few examples may make these considerations more concrete. Earth may be moved by hand shovels, by steam or diesel shovels, or by bulldozers. Power shovels and bulldozers are built in only a small variety of models, each with inherent characteristics as to fuel consumption per hour, number of operators and assistants required, cubic feet of earth moved per hour, etc. Printing type may be set by using hand-fonts, linotype machines or monotype machines. Again, each machine is available in only a few models and each has its own pace of operation, power and space requirements, and other essentially unalterable characteristics. A moment's reflection will bring to mind dozens of other illustrations: printing presses, power looms, railroad and highway haulage, statistical and accounting calculation, metallic ore reduction, metal fabrication, etc. For many economic tasks the number of processes available is finite, and each process can be regarded as inflexible with regard to the ratios among factor inputs and process outputs. Factors cannot be substituted for each other except by changing the levels at which entire technical processes are used, because each process uses factors in fixed characteristic ratios. In mathematical programming, accordingly, process substitution plays a role analogous to that of factor substitution in conventional analysis.

We now develop an apparatus for the analysis of process substitution. For convenience we shall limit our discussion to processes which consume two factors, to be called capital and labor, and produce a single output. Figure 3 represents such a process. As in Figure 2, the horizontal axis is scaled in units of labor and the vertical axis in units of capital. The process is represented by the ray, OA, which is scaled in units of output. To each output there corresponds a labor requirement found by locating the appropriate mark on the process ray and reading straight down. The capital requirement is found in the same manner by reading straight across from the mark on the process line. Similarly, to each amount of labor there corresponds a quantity of output, found by reading straight up, and a quantity of capital, found by reading straight across from the output mark.

It should be noted that the quantity of capital in this diagram is the quantity used in a process rather than the quantity owned by an economic unit; it is capital-service rather than capital itself. Thus, though more or less labor may be combined with a given machine – by using it more or fewer hours – the ratio of capital to labor inputs, that is, the ratio of machine-hours to labor hours – is regarded as technologically fixed.

Figure 3 incorporates two important assumptions. The fact that the line OA is straight implies that the ratio between the capital input and the labor input is the same for all levels of

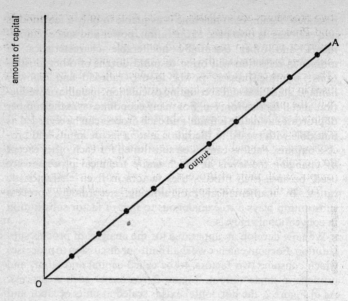

Figure 3 A process

output and is given, indeed, by the slope of the line. The fact that the marks on the output line are evenly spaced indicates that there are neither economies nor diseconomies of scale in the use of the process, i.e. that there will be strict proportionality between the quantity of output and the quality of either input. These assumptions are justified rather simply on the basis of the notion of a process. If a process can be used once, it can be used twice or as many times as the supplies of factors permit. Two linotype machines with equally skilled operators can turn out just twice as much type per hour as one. Two identical mills can turn out just twice as many yards of cotton per month as one. So long as factors are available, a process can be duplicated. Whether it will be economical to do so is, of course, another matter.

If there is only one process available for a given task there is not much scope for economic choice. Frequently, however, there will be several processes. Figure 4 represents a situation in which two procedures are available, Process A indicated by the line OA and Process B indicated by OB. We have already seen how to interpret points on the lines OA and OB. The scales by which output is measured on the two rays are not necessarily the same. The scale on each ray reflects the productivity of the factors when used in the process represented by that ray and has no connection with the output scale on any other process ray. Now suppose that points L and M represent production of the same output by the two processes. Then LM, the straight line between them, will represent an isoquant and each point on this line will correspond to a combination of Processes A and B which produces the same output as OL units of Process A or OM units of Process B.

To see this, consider any point P on the line LM and draw a

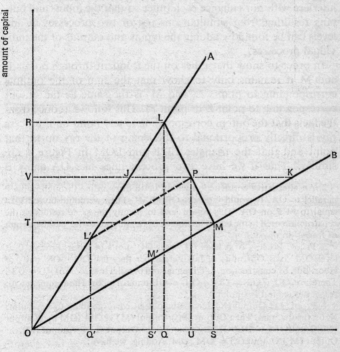

Figure 4 Two processes

line through P parallel to OB. Let L′ be the point where this line intersects OA. Finally mark the point M′ on OB such that OM′ = L′P. Now consider the production plan which consists of using Process A at level OL′ and Process B at level OM′.[2] It is easy to show that this production plan uses OU units of labor, where U is the labor coordinate of point P, and OV units of capital, where V is the capital coordinate of point P.[3]

Since the coordinates of point P correspond to the quantities of factors consumed by OL′ units of Process A and OM′ units of Process B, we interpret P as representing the combined production plan made up of the specified levels of the two processes. This interpretation implies an important economic assumption, namely, that if the two processes are used simultaneously they will neither interfere with nor enhance each other so that the inputs and outputs resulting from simultaneous use of two processes at any levels can be found by adding the inputs and outputs of the individual processes.

In order to show that P lies on the isoquant through points L and M it remains only to show that the sum of the outputs corresponding to points L′ and M′ is the same as the output corresponding to point L or point M. This follows at once from the facts that the output corresponding to any point on a process ray is directly proportional to the length of the ray up to that point and that the triangles LL′P and LOM in Figure 4 are similar.[4] Thus if we have two process lines like OA and OB

2. An alternative construction would be to draw a line through point P parallel to OA. It would intersect OB at M′. Then we could lay off OL′ equal to M′P on OA. This would lead to exactly the same results as the construction used in the text. The situation is analogous to the 'parallelogram of forces' in physics.

3. Proof: Process A at level OL′ uses OQ′ units of labor, Process B at level OM′ uses OS′ units of labor, together they use OQ′+OS′ units of labor. But, by construction, L′P is equal and parallel to OM′. So Q′U = OS′. Therefore, OQ′+OS′ = OQ′+Q′U = OU units of labor. The argument with respect to capital is similar.

4. Proof: Let Output (X) denote the output corresponding to any point, X, on the diagram. Then Output (M′)/Output (M) = OM′/OM and Output (L′)/Output (L) = OL′/OL. By assumption: Output (L) = Output (M). So Output (M′)/Output (L) = OM′/OM. Adding, we have:

$$\frac{\text{Output (M′)}+\text{Output (L′)}}{\text{Output (L)}} = \frac{OM′}{OM}+\frac{OL′}{OL} = \frac{L′P}{OM}+\frac{OL′}{OL} = \frac{L′L}{OL}+\frac{OL′}{OL} = 1.$$

and find points L and M on them which represent producing the same output by means of the two processes then the line segment connecting the two equal-output points will be an isoquant.

We can now draw the mathematical programming analog of the familiar isoquant diagram. Figure 5 is such a diagram with four process lines shown. Point M represents a particular output by use of Process A and points L, K, J represent that same output by means of Processes B, C, D, respectively. The succession of line segments connecting these four points is the isoquant for that same output. It is easy to see that any other succession of line segments respectively parallel to those of MLKJ is also an isoquant. Three such are shown in the figure. It is instructive to compare Figure 5 with Figure 2 and note the strong resemblance in appearance as well as in interpretation.

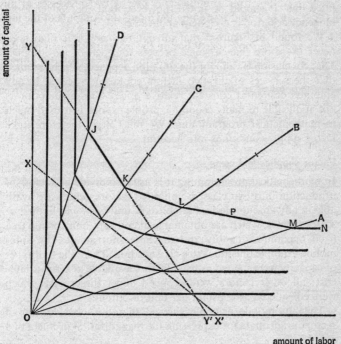

Figure 5 Four processes

We may draw price lines on Figure 5, just as on the conventional kind of isoquant diagram. The dashed lines XX' and YY' represent two possible price lines. Consider XX' first. As that line is drawn, the maximum output for a given expenditure can be obtained by use of Process C alone, and, conversely, the minimum cost for a given output is also obtained by using Process C alone. Thus, for the relative price regime represented by XX', Process C is optimal. The price line YY' is drawn parallel to the isoquant segment JK. In this case Process C is still optimal, but Process D is also optimal and so is any combination of the two.

It is evident from considering these two price lines, and as many others as the reader wishes to visualize, that an optimal production program can always be achieved by means of a single process, which process depending, of course, on the slope of the price line. It should be noted, however, that the conventional tangency criterion is no longer applicable.

We found in Figure 5 that an optimal economic plan need never use more than a single process for each of its outputs.[5] That conclusion is valid for the situation depicted, which assumed that the services of the two factors could be procured in any amounts desired at constant relative prices. This assumption is not applicable to many economic problems, nor is it used much in mathematical programming. We must now, therefore, take factor supply conditions into account.

Factor supplies and costs

In mathematical programming it is usual to divide all factors of production into two classes: unlimited factors, which are available in any amount desired at constant unit cost, and limited or scarce factors, which are obtainable at constant unit cost up to a fixed maximum quantity and thereafter not at all. The automobile example illustrates this classification. There the four types of capacity were treated as fixed factors available at zero variable cost; all other factors were grouped under direct costs which were considered as constant per unit of output.

The automobile example showed that this classification of factors is adequate for expressing the maximization problem of a

5. Recall, however, that we have not taken joint production into account nor have we considered the effects of considerations from the demand side.

firm dealing in competitive markets. In the last section we saw that when all factors are unlimited, this formulation can be used to find a minimum average cost point.

Both of these applications invoked restrictive assumptions and, furthermore, assumptions which conflict with those conventionally made in studying resource allocation. In conventional analysis we conceive that as the level of production of a firm, industry or economy rises, average costs rise also after some point. The increase in average costs is attributable in part to the working of the law of variable proportions (Cassels, 1946), which operates when the inputs of some but not all factors of production are increased. As far as the consequences of increasing some but not all inputs are concerned, the contrast between mathematical programming and the marginal analysis is more verbal than substantive. A reference to Figure 4 will show how such changes are handled in mathematical programming. Point J in Figure 4 represents the production of a certain output by the use of Process A alone. If it is desired to increase output without increasing the use of capital, this can be done by moving to the right along the dotted line JK, since this line cuts successively higher isoquants. Such a movement would correspond to using increasingly more of Process B and increasingly less of Process A and thus, indirectly, to substituting labor for capital. If, further, we assume that unit cost of production is lower for Process A than for Process B this movement would also correspond to increasing average cost of production. Thus both marginal analysis and mathematical programming lead to the same conclusion when factor proportions are changed: if the change starts from a minimum cost point the substitution will lead to gradually increasing unit costs.

But changing input proportions is only one part of the story according to the conventional type of analysis. If output is to be increased, any of three things may happen. First, it may be possible to increase the consumption of all inputs without incurring a change in their unit prices. In this case both mathematical programming and marginal analysis agree that output will be expanded without changing the ratios among the input quantities and average cost of production will not increase (Knight, 1921, p. 98). Second, it may not be possible to increase the use of some of the inputs. This is the case we have just analysed. According to both modes of analysis the input ratios will change in this case and average unit costs will increase. The only difference between the two approaches is that if average cost is to be plotted against output, the marginal analyst will show a picture with a smoothly rising curve while the mathematical programmer will show a broken line made up of increasingly steep line segments. Third, it may be possible to increase the quantities of all inputs but only at the penalty of increasing unit prices or some kind of diseconomies of scale. This third case occurs in the marginal analysis, indeed it is the case which gives long-run cost curves their familiar shape, but mathematical programming has no counterpart for it.

The essential substantive difference we have arrived at is that the marginal analysis conceives of pecuniary and technical diseconomies associated with changes in scale while mathematical programming does not.[6] There are many important economic problems in which factor prices and productivities do not change in response to changes in scale or in which such variations can be disregarded. Most investigations of industrial capacity, for example, are of this nature. In such studies we seek the maximum output of an industry, regarding its inventory of physical equipment as given and assuming that the auxiliary factors needed to cooperate with the equipment can be obtained in the quantities dictated by the characteristics of the equipment. Manpower requirement studies are of the same nature. In such studies we take both output and equipment as given and calculate the manpower needed to operate the equipment at the level which will yield the desired output. Studies of full employment output fall into the same format. In such studies we determine in advance the quantity of each factor which is to be regarded as full employment of that factor. Then we calculate the optimum output obtainable by the use of the factors in those quantities.

These illustrations should suffice to show that the assumptions made in mathematical programming can comprehend a wide

6. Even within the framework of the marginal analysis the concept of diseconomies of scale has been challenged on both theoretical and empirical grounds. For examples of empirical criticism see National Bureau of Economic Research (1943). The most searching theoretical criticism is in Sraffa (1926).

variety of important economic problems. The most useful applications of mathematical programming are probably to problems of the types just described, that is, to problems concerned with finding optimum production plans using specified quantities of some or all of the resources involved.

Analysis of production with limited factors

The diagrams which we have developed are readily adaptable to the analysis of the consequences of limits on the factor supplies. Such limits are, of course, the heart of Figure 1 where the four principal lines represent limitations on the process levels which result from limits on the four factor quantities considered. But Figure 1 cannot be used when more than two processes have to be considered. For such problems diagrams like Figures 3, 4 and 5 have to be used.

Figure 6 reproduces the situation portrayed in Figure 5 with some additional data to be explained below. Let OF represent the maximum amount of capital which can be used and thus show a factor limitation. The horizontal line through F divides the diagram into two sections: all points above the line correspond to programs which require more capital than is available; points on and below the line represent programs which do not have excessive capital requirements. This horizontal line will be called the capital limitation line. Points on or below it are called 'feasible', points above it are called 'infeasible'.

The economic unit portrayed in Figure 6 has the choice of operating at any feasible point. If maximum output is its objective, it will choose a point which lies on the highest possible isoquant, i.e. the highest isoquant which touches the capital limitation line. This is the one labelled J'K'L'M', and the highest possible output is attained by using Process A.

Of course, maximum output may not be the objective. The objective may be, for example, to maximize the excess of the value of output over labor costs. We shall refer to such an excess as a 'net value'. The same kind of diagram can be used to solve for a net value provided that the value of each unit of output is independent of the number of units produced[7] and that the cost of

7. This is a particularly uncomfortable assumption. We use it here to explain the method in its least complicated form.

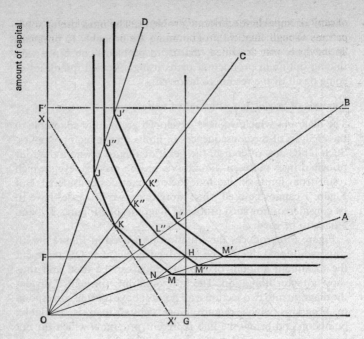

Figure 6 Four processes, with limitations

each unit of labor is similarly constant. If these provisos are
met, each point on a process ray will correspond to a certain
physical output but also to a certain value of output, cost of labor
and net value of output. Further, along any process ray the net
value of output will equal the physical output times the net
value per unit and will therefore be proportional to the physical
output. We may thus use a diagram similar to Figure 6 except
that we think of net value instead of physical output as measured
along the process rays and we show isovalue lines instead of isoquants. This has been done on Figure 7, in which the maximum
net value attainable is the one which corresponds to the isovalue
contour through point P, and is attained by using Process C.

It should be noted in both Figures 6 and 7 that the optimal
program consisted of a single process, that shifts in the quantity

404 Linear Programming

of capital available would not affect the designation of the optimal process though they would change its level, and that the price lines, which were crucial in Figure 5, played no role.

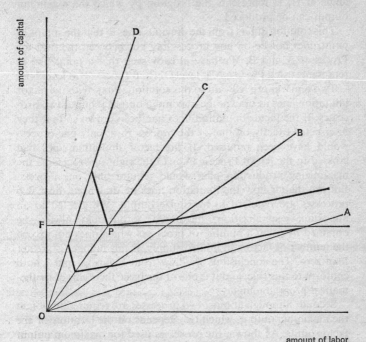

Figure 7 Four processes with isovalue lines

The next complication, and the last one we shall be able to consider, is to assume that both factors are in limited supply. This situation is portrayed in Figure 6 by adding the vertical line through point G to represent a labor limitation. The available quantity of labor is shown, of course, by the length OG. Then the points inside the rectangle OFHG represent programs which can be implemented in the sense that they do not require more than the available supplies of either factor. This is the rectangle of feasible programs. The greatest achievable output is the one which corresponds to the highest isoquant which touches the rectangle of feasible programs. This is the isoquant $J''K''L''M''$, and furthermore, since the maximum isoquant touches the rectangle at H, H represents the program by which the maximum output can be produced.

This solution differs from the previous ones in that the solution-point does not lie on any process ray but between the rays for Processes A and B. We have already seen that a point like H represents using Process A at level ON and Process B at level NH.

Two remarks are relevant to this solution. First: with the factor limitation lines as drawn, the maximum output requires two processes. If the factor limitation lines had been drawn so that they intersected exactly on one of the process rays, only one process would have been required. If the factor limitation lines had crossed to the left of Process D or to the right of Process A, the maximizing production plan would require only one process. But, no matter how the limitation lines be drawn, at most two processes are required to maximize output. We are led to an important generalization: maximum output may always be obtained by using a number of processes which does not exceed the number of factors in limited supply, if this number is greater than zero. The conclusions we drew from Figures 6 and 7 both conform to this rule, and it is one of the basic theorems of mathematical programming.

Second: although at most two processes are required to obtain the maximum output, which two depends on the location of the factor limits. As shown, the processes used for maximum output were Processes A and B. If somewhat more capital, represented by the amount OF', were available, the maximizing processes would have been Processes C and D. If two factors are limited, it is the ratio between their supplies rather than the absolute supplies of either which determines the processes in the optimum program. This contrasts with the case in which only one factor is limited. Just as the considerations which determine the optimum set of processes are more complicated when two factors are limited than when only one is, so with three or more limited factors the optimum conditions become more complicated still and soon pass the reach of intuition. This, indeed, is the *raison d'être* of the formidable apparatus of mathematical programming.

We can make these considerations more concrete by applying them to the automobile example. Referring to Figure 1, we note that the optimum production point, C, lay on the limitation lines for engine assembly and metal stamping, but well below the limits for automobile and truck assembly. The limitations on automobile and truck assembly capacity are, therefore, ineffective and can be disregarded. The situation in terms of the two effectively limiting types of capacity is shown in Figure 8.

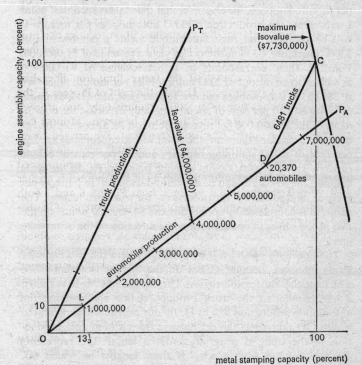

Figure 8 Automobile example, optimal plan

In Figure 8 the ray P_A represents the process of producing automobiles and P_T the process of producing trucks. These two processes can be operated at any combination of levels which does

Robert Dorfman 407

not require the use of more than 100 per cent of either metal-stamping or engine-assembly capacity. Thus the rectangle in the diagram is the region of feasible production programs. The optimal production program is the one in the feasible region which corresponds to the highest possible net revenue.[8] Thus it will be helpful to construct isorevenue lines, as we did in Figure 7. To do this, consider automobile production first. Each point on P_A corresponds to the production of a certain number of automobiles per month. Suppose, for example, that the scale is such that point L represents the production of 3333 automobiles per month. It will be recalled that each automobile yields a net revenue of $300. Therefore, 3333 automobiles yield a revenue of $1,000,000. Point L, then, corresponds to a net revenue of $1,000,000 as well as to an output of 3333 automobiles per month. Since (see p. 389) 3333 automobiles require $13\frac{1}{3}$ per cent of metal-stamping capacity and 10 per cent of engine-assembly capacity, the coordinates of the $1,000,000 net revenue point on P_A are established at once. By a similar argument, the point whose coordinates are $26\frac{2}{3}$ per cent of metal stamping capacity and 20 per cent of engine capacity is the $2,000,000 net revenue point on P_A. In the same manner, the whole ray can be drawn and scaled off in terms of net revenue, and so can P_T, the process ray for truck production. The diagram is completed by connecting the $4,000,000 points on the two process lines in order to show the direction of the isorevenue lines.

The optimum program is at point C, where the two capacity limits intersect, because C lies on the highest isorevenue line which touches the feasible region. Through point C we have drawn a line parallel to the truck production line and meeting the automobile production line at D. By our previous argument, the length OD represents the net revenue from automobile production in the optimal program and the length DC represents the net revenue from trucks. If these lengths be scaled off, the result, of course, will be the same as the solution found previously.

8. Since the objective of the firm is, by assumption, to maximize revenue rather than physical output, we may consider automobile and truck production as two alternative processes for producing revenue instead of as two processes with disparate outputs.

Imputation of factor values

We have just noted that the major field of application of mathematical programming is to problems where the supply of one or more factors of production is absolutely limited. Such scarcities are the genesis of value in ordinary analysis, and they generate values in mathematical programming too. In fact, in ordinary analysis the determination of outputs and the determination of prices are but two aspects of the same problem, the optimal allocation of scarce resources. The same is true in mathematical programming.

Heretofore we have encountered prices only as data for determining the direct costs of processes and the net value of output. But of course the limiting factors of production also have value although we have not assigned prices to them up to now. In this section we shall see that the solution of a mathematical programming problem implicitly assigns values to the limiting factors of production. Furthermore, the implicit pricing problem can be solved directly and, when so solved, constitutes a solution to the optimal allocation problem.

Consider the automobile example and ask: how much is a unit (1 per cent) of each of the types of capacity worth to the firm? The approach to this question is similar in spirit to the familiar marginal analysis. With respect to each type of capacity we calculate how much the maximum revenue would increase if one unit were added, or how much revenue would decrease if one unit were taken away. Since there is a surplus of automobile-assembly capacity, neither the addition nor the subtraction of one unit of this type would affect the optimum program or the maximum net revenue. Hence the value of this type of capacity is nil. The analysis and result for truck assembly are the same.

We find, then, that these two types of capacity are free goods. This does not imply that an automobile assembly line is not worth having, any more than, to take a classic example, the fact that air is a free good means that it can be dispensed with. It means that it would not be worthwhile to increase this type of capacity at any positive price and that some units of these types could be disposed of without loss.

The valuation of the other types of capacity is not so trivial.

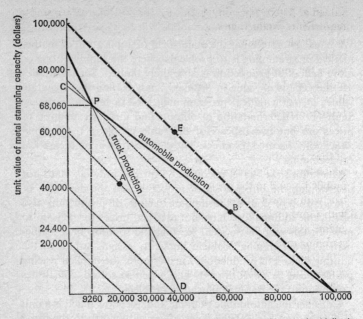

unit value of engine assembly capacity (dollars)

Figure 9 Automobile example, implicit values

In Figure 9 possible values per per cent of engine-assembly capacity are scaled along the horizontal axis and values per per cent of metal-stamping capacity are scaled along the vertical axis. Now consider any possible pair of values, say engine-assembly capacity worth $20,000 per unit and metal stamping worth $40,000. This is represented by point A on the figure. Applying these values to the data on pages 389–90, the values of capacity required for producing an automobile is found to be:

$$(0.004 \times \$40,000) + (0.003 \times \$20,000) = \$220$$

which is well under the value of producing an automobile, or $300.[9] In the same way, if engine-assembly capacity is worth $60,000 per per cent of capacity and metal-stamping capacity is

9. These unit values are also marginal values since costs of production are constant.

410 Linear Programming

valued at $30,000 per unit (point B), the cost of scarce resources required to produce an automobile will be exactly equal to the value of the product. This is clearly not the only combination of resource values which will precisely absorb the value of output when the resources are used to produce automobiles. The automobile production line in the figure, which passes through point B, is the locus of all such value combinations. A similar line has been drawn for truck production to represent those combinations of resource values for which the total value of resources used in producing trucks is equal to the value of output. The intersection of these two lines is obviously the only pair of resource values for which the marginal resource cost of producing an additional automobile is equal to the net value of an automobile and the same is true with respect to trucks. The pair can be found by plotting or, with more precision, by algebra. It is found that 1 per cent of engine-assembly capacity is worth $9259 and 1 per cent of metal-stamping capacity is worth $68,056.

To each pair of values for the two types of capacity, there corresponds a value for the entire plant. Thus to the pair of values represented by point A there corresponds the plant value of $(100 \times \$20,000) + (100 \times \$40,000) = \$6,000,000$. This is not the only pair of resource values which give an aggregate plant value of $6,000,000. Indeed, any pair of resource values on the dotted line through A corresponds to the same aggregate plant value. (By this stage, Figure 9 should become strongly reminiscent of Figure 1.) We have drawn a number of dotted lines parallel to the one just described, each corresponding to a specific aggregate plant value. The dotted line which passes through the intersection of the two production lines is of particular interest. By measurement or otherwise this line can be found to correspond to a plant value of $7,731,500 which, we recall, was found to be the maximum attainable net revenue.

Let us consider the implications of assigning values to the two limiting factors from a slightly different angle. We have seen that as soon as unit values have been assigned to the factors an aggregate value is assigned to the plant. We can make the aggregate plant value as low as we please, simply by assigning sufficiently low values to the various factors. But if the values assigned are too low, we have the unsatisfactory consequence that some of the processes will give rise to unimputed surpluses. We may, therefore, seek the lowest aggregate plant value which can be assigned and still have no process yield an unimputed surplus. In the automobile case, that value is $7,731,500. In the course of finding the lowest acceptable plant value we find specific unit values to be assigned to each of the resources.

In this example there are two processes and four limited resources. It turns out that only two of the resources were effectively limiting, the others being in relatively ample supply. In general, the characteristics of the solution to a programming problem depend on the relationship between the number of limited resources and the number of processes taken into consideration. If, as in the present instance, the number of limited resources exceeds the number of processes it will usually turn out that some of the resources will have imputed values of zero and that the number of resources with positive imputed values will be equal to the number of processes.[10] If the number of limited resources equals the number of processes all resources will have positive imputed values. If, finally, the number of processes exceeds the number of limited resources, some of the processes will not be used in the optimal program. This situation, which is the usual one, was illustrated in Figure 6. In this case the total imputed value of resources absorbed will equal net revenue for some processes and will exceed it for others. The number of processes for which the imputed value of resources absorbed equals the net revenue will be just equal to the number of limited resources and the processes for which the equality holds are the ones which will appear at positive levels in the optimal program. In brief, the determination of the minimum acceptable plant value amounts to the same thing as the determination of the optimal production program. The programming problem and the valuation problem are not only closely related, they are basically the same.

This can be seen graphically by comparing Figures 1 and 9. Each figure contains two axes and two diagonal boundary lines. But the boundary lines in Figure 9 refer to the same processes

10. We say 'usually' in this sentence because in some special circumstances the number of resources with positive imputed values may exceed the number of processes.

as the axes in Figure 1, and the axes in Figure 9 refer to the same resources as the diagonal boundary lines in Figure 1. Furthermore, in using Figure 1 we sought the net revenue corresponding to the highest dashed line touched by the boundary; in using Figure 9 we sought the aggregate value corresponding to the lowest dashed line which has any points on or outside the boundary; and the two results turned out to be the same. Formally stated, these two figures and the problems they represent are *duals* of each other.

The dualism feature is a very useful property in the solution of mathematical programming problems. The simplest way to see this is to note that when confronting a mathematical programming problem we have the choice of solving the problem or its dual, whichever is easier. Either way we can get the same results. We can use this feature now to generalize our discussion somewhat. Up to now when dealing with more than two processes we have had to use relatively complicated diagrams like Figure 6 because straightforward diagrams like Figure 1 did not contain enough axes to represent the levels of the processes. Now we can use diagrams modeled on Figure 9 to depict problems with any number of processes so long as they do not involve more than two scarce factors. Figure 10 illustrates a diagram for four processes and is, indeed, derived from Figure 6. In Figure 10 line A represents all pairs of factor values such that Process A would yield neither a profit nor a loss. Lines B, C and D are similarly interpreted. The dashed line T is a locus along which the aggregate value of the labor and capital available to the firm (or industry) is constant. Its position is not relevant to the analysis; its slope, which is simply the ratio of the quantity of available labor to that of capital, is all that is significant. The broken line JKLMN divides the graph into two regions. All points on or above it represent pairs of resource values such that no process gives rise to an unimputed surplus. Let us call this the acceptable region. For each point below that broken line there is at least one process which does have an unimputed surplus. This is the unacceptable region. We then seek for that point in the acceptable region which corresponds to the lowest aggregate plant value. This point will, of course, give the set of resource values which makes the accounting profit of the firm as great as possible without giving rise to any

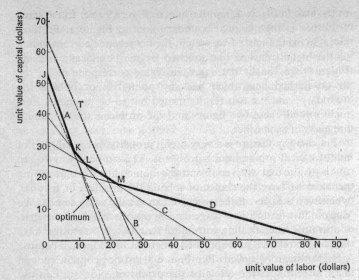

Figure 10 The valuation problem, four processes

unimputed income. The point which meets these requirements is K, and a dotted line parallel to T has been drawn through it to indicate the minimum acceptable aggregate plant value.

At point K Processes A and B yield zero profits, and Processes C and D yield losses. Hence Processes A and B are the ones which should be used, exactly as we found in Figure 6. To be sure, this diagram does not tell the levels at which A and B should be used, any more than Figure 6 tells the valuations to be placed on the two resources. But finding the levels after the processes have been selected is a comparatively trivial matter. All that is necessary is to find the levels which will fully utilize the resources which are not free goods. This may be done algebraically or by means of a diagram like Figure 8.

Applications

In the first section we asserted that the principal motivation of mathematical programming was the need for a method of analysis which lent itself to the practical solution of the day-to-day problems of business and the economy in general. Immediately after making that claim we introduced a highly artificial problem followed by a rather extended discussion of abstract and formal relationships. The time has now come to indicate the basis for saying that mathematical programming is a practical method of analysis.

The essential simplification achieved in mathematical programming is the replacement of the notion of the production function by the notion of the process. The process is a highly observable unit of activity and the empirical constants which characterize it can be estimated without elaborate analysis. Furthermore in many industries the structure of production corresponds to operating a succession of processes, as we have conceived them. Many industrial decisions, like shutting down a bank of machines or operating an extra shift, correspond naturally to our concept of choosing the level of operation of a process. In brief, mathematical programming is modelled after the actual structure of production in the hope that thereby it will involve only observable constants and directly controllable variables.

Has this hope been justified? The literature already contains a report of a successful application to petroleum refining (Charnes, Cooper and Mellon, 1952). I have made a similar application which, perhaps, will bear description. The application was to a moderate-sized refinery which produces premium and regular grades of automotive gasoline. The essential operation studied was blending. In blending, ten chemically distinct kinds of semi-refined oil, called blending stocks, are mixed together. The result is a saleable gasoline whose characteristics are approximately the weighted average of the characteristics of the blending stocks. For example, if 500 gallons of a stock with octane rating of eighty are blended with 1000 gallons of a stock with octane rating of eighty-six the result will be $500+1000 = 1500$ gallons of product with octane rating of $(\frac{1}{3} \times 80) + (\frac{2}{3} \times 86) = 84$.

The significant aspect of gasoline blending for our present purposes is that the major characteristics of the blend – its knock rating, its vapor pressure, its sulphur content, etc. – can be expressed as linear functions of the quantities of the various blending stocks used. So also can the cost of the blend if each of the blending stocks has a definite price per gallon. Thus the problem of finding the minimum cost blend which will meet given quality specifications is a problem in mathematical programming.

Furthermore, in this refinery the quantities of some of the blending stocks are definitely limited by contracts and by refining capacity. The problem then arises: what are the most profitable quantities of output of regular and premium gasoline, and how much of each blending stock should be used for each final product. This problem is analogous to the artificial automobile example, with the added complication of the quality specifications. The problem is too complicated for graphic analysis but was solved easily by arithmetical procedures. As far as is known, mathematical programming provides the only way for solving such problems. Charnes, Cooper and Farr have recently published the solution to a similar problem which arose in the operations of a metal-working firm (1953).

An entirely different kind of problem, also amenable to mathematical programming, arises in newsprint production. Freight is a major element in the cost of newsprint. One large newsprint company has six mills, widely scattered in Canada, and some two hundred customers, widely scattered in the United States. Its problem is to decide how much newsprint to ship from each mill to each customer so as, first, to meet the contract requirements of each customer, second, to stay within the capacity limits of each mill, and third, to keep the aggregate freight bill as small as possible. This problem involves 1200 variables (6 mills × 200 customers), in contrast to the two or four variable problems we have been discussing. In the final solution most of these variables will turn out to be zero – the question is which ones. This problem is solved by mathematical programming and, though formidable, is not really as formidable as the count of variables might indicate.

These few illustrations should suffice to indicate that mathematical programming is a practical tool for business planning. They show, also, that it is a flexible tool because both examples deviated from the format of the example used in our exposition. The petroleum application had the added feature of quality specification. In the newsprint application there were limits on the quantity of output as well as on the quantities of the inputs. Nevertheless mathematical programming handled them both easily.

On the other hand, it should be noted that both of these were small-scale applications, dealing with a single phase of the operation of a single firm. I believe that this has been true of all successful applications to date. Mathematical programmers are still a long way from solving the broad planning problem of entire industries or an entire economy. But many such broad problems are only enlarged versions of problems which have been met and solved in the context of the single firm. It is no longer premature to say that mathematical programming has proved its worth as a practical tool for finding optimal economic programs.

Conclusion

Our objective has been only to introduce the basic notions of mathematical programming and to invest them with plausibility and meaning. The reader who would learn to solve a programming problem – even the simplest – will have to look elsewhere,[11] though this paper may serve as a useful background.

Although methods of solution have been omitted from this exposition, we must emphasize that these methods are fundamental to the whole concept of mathematical programming. Some eighty years ago Walras conceived of production in very much the same manner as mathematical programmers, and more recently Wald and von Neumann used this view of production and methods closely allied to those of mathematical programming to analyse the conditions of general economic equilibrium (Wald and Neumann, 1951; Neumann, 1945). These developments, however, must be regarded merely as precursors of mathematical programming. Programming had no independent existence as a mode of economic analysis until 1947 when Dantzig announced the 'simplex method' of solution which made practical application feasible (Koopmans, 1951). The existence of a method whereby economic optima could be explicitly calculated stimulated research into the economic interpretation of

11. The standard reference is Koopmans (1951). Less advanced treatments may be found in Charnes, Cooper and Henderson (1953); and Dorfman (1951).

mathematical programming and led also to the development of alternative methods of solution. The fact that economic and business problems when formulated in terms of mathematical programming can be solved numerically is the basis of the importance of the method. The omission of methods of solution from this discussion should not, therefore, be taken to indicate that they are of secondary interest.

We have considered only a few of the concepts used in mathematical programming and have dealt with only a single type of programming problem. The few notions we have considered, however, are the basic ones; all the rest of mathematical programming is elaboration and extension of them. It seems advisable to mention two directions of elaboration, for they remove or weaken two of the most restrictive assumptions which have here been imposed.

The first of these extensions is the introduction of time into the analysis. The present treatment has dealt with a single production period in isolation. But in many cases, successive production periods are interrelated. This is so, for example, in the case of a vertically integrated firm where the operation of some processes in one period is limited by the levels of operation in the preceding period of the processes which supply their raw materials. Efficient methods for analysing such 'dynamic' problems are being investigated, particularly by Dantzig (1953). Although the present discussion has been static, the method of analysis can be applied to problems with a time dimension.

The second of these extensions is the allowance for changes in the prices of factors and final products. In our discussion we regarded all prices as unalterable and independent of the actions of the economic unit under consideration. Constant prices are, undeniably, a great convenience to the analyst, but the method can transcend this assumption when necessary. The general mathematical theory of dealing with variable prices has been investigated (Kuhn and Tucker, 1951, pp. 481–92) and practical methods of solution have been developed for problems where the demand and supply curves are linear.[12] The assumption of con-

12. I reported one solution of this problem to a seminar at the Massachusetts Institute of Technology in September 1952. Other solutions may be known.

stant prices, perhaps the most restrictive assumption we have made, is adopted for convenience rather than from necessity.

Mathematical programming has been developed as a tool for economic and business planning and not primarily for the descriptive, and therefore predictive, purposes which gave rise to the marginal analysis. Nevertheless it does have predictive implications. In so far as firms operate under the conditions assumed in mathematical programming it would be unreasonable to assume that they acted as if they operated under the conditions assumed by the marginal analysis. Consider, for example, the automobile firm portrayed in Figure 1. How would it respond if the price of automobiles were to fall, say by $50 a unit? In that case the net revenue per automobile would be $250, the same as the net revenue per truck. Diagrammatically, the result would be to rotate the lines of equal revenue until their slope was 45 degrees. After this rotation, point C would still be optimum and this change in prices would cause no change in optimum output. Mathematical programming gives rise, thus, to a kinked supply curve.

On the other hand, suppose that the price of automobiles were to rise by $50. Diagrammatically this price change would decrease the steepness of the equal revenue lines until they were just parallel to the metal stamping line. The firm would then be in a position like that illustrated by the YY' line in Figure 5. The production plans corresponding to points on the line segment DC in Figure 1 would all yield the same net revenue and all would be optimal. If the prices of automobiles were to rise by more than $50 or if a $50 increase in the price of automobiles were accompanied by any decrease in the price of trucks, the point of optimal production would jump abruptly from point C to point D.

Thus mathematical programming indicates that firms whose choices are limited to distinct processes will respond discontinuously to price variations: they will be insensitive to price changes over a certain range and will change their levels of output sharply as soon as that range is passed. This theoretical deduction surely has real counterparts.

The relationship between mathematical programming and welfare economics is especially close. Welfare economics studies the optimal organization of economic effort; so does mathematical programming. This relationship has been investigated especially by Koopmans (1951) and Samuelson (1949). The finding, generally stated, is that the equilibrium position of a perfectly competitive economy is the same as the optimal solution to the mathematical programming problem embodying the same data.

Mathematical programming is closely allied mathematically to the methods of input-output analysis or interindustry analysis developed largely by W. W. Leontief (1951). The two methods were developed independently, however, and it is important to distinguish them conceptually. Input-output analysis finds its application almost exclusively in the study of general economic equilibrium. It conceives of an economy as divided into a number of industrial sectors each of which is analogous to a process as the term is used in mathematical programming. It then takes either of two forms. In 'open models' an input-output analysis starts with some specified final demand for the products of each of the sectors and calculates the level at which each of the sector-processes must operate in order to meet this schedule of final demands. In 'closed models' final demand does not appear but attention is concentrated on the fact that the inputs required by each sector-process must be supplied as outputs by some other sector-processes. Input-output analysis then calculates a mutually compatible set of output levels for the various sectors. By contrast with mathematical programming the conditions imposed in input-output analysis are sufficient to determine the levels of the processes and there is no scope for finding an optimal solution or a set of 'best' levels. To be sure, input-output analysis can be regarded as a special case of mathematical programming in which the number of products is equal to the number of processes. On the other hand, the limitations on the supplies of resources which play so important a role in mathematical programming are not dealt with explicitly in input-output analysis. On the whole it seems best to regard these two techniques as allied but distinct methods of analysis addressed to different problems.

Mathematical programming, then, is of significance for economic thinking and theory as well as for business and economic planning. We have been able only to allude to this significance. Indeed, apart from the exploration of welfare implications, very little thought has been given to the consequences for economics of mathematical programming because most effort has been devoted to solving the numerous practical problems to which it gives rise. The outlook is for fruitful researches into both the implications and applications of mathematical programming.

References

CASSELS, J. M. (1946), 'On the law of variable proportions', in W. Fellner and B. F. Haley (eds.), *Readings in the Theory of Income Distribution*, Irwin.

CHARNES, A., COOPER, W. W., and FARR, D. (1953), 'Linear programming and profit preference scheduling for a manufacturing firm', *J. Op. Res. Soc. Amer.*, vol. 1, pp. 114–29.

CHARNES, A., COOPER, W. W., and HENDERSON, A. (1953), *An Introduction to Linear Programming*, Wiley.

CHARNES, A., COOPER, W. W., and MELLON, B. (1952), 'Blending aviation gasolines', *Econometrica*, vol. 20, pp. 135–59.

DANTZIG, G. B. (1953), 'A note on a dynamic Leontief model with substitution', *Econometrica*, vol. 21, p. 179.

DORFMAN, R. (1951), *Application of Linear Programming to the Theory of the Firm*, University of California Press.

KNIGHT, F. H. (1921), *Risk, Uncertainty and Profit*, Houghton Mifflin.

KOOPMANS, T. C. (ed.) (1951), *Activity Analysis of Production and Allocation*, Wiley.

KUHN, H. W., and TUCKER, A. W. (1951), 'Non-linear programming', in J. Neyman (ed.), *Proceedings of the Second Berkeley Symposium on Mathematical Statistics and Probability*, University of California Press.

LEONTIEF, W. W. (1951), *The Structure of the American Economy 1919–39*, Oxford University Press.

NATIONAL BUREAU OF ECONOMIC RESEARCH (1943), *Cost Behavior and Price Policy*.

NEUMANN, J. VON (1945), 'A model of general economic equilibrium', *Rev. econ. Stud.*, vol. 13, pp. 1–9.

SAMUELSON, P. A. (1949), 'Market mechanisms and maximization', Rand Corporation.

SRAFFA, P. (1926), 'The laws of returns under competitive conditions', *Econ. J.*, vol. 36, pp. 535–50.

WALD, A., and NEUMANN, J. VON (1951), 'On some systems of equations of mathematical economics', *Econometrica*, vol. 19, pp. 368–493.

21 W. J. Baumol and R. E. Quandt

Dual Prices and Competition

W. J. Baumol and R. E. Quandt, 'Dual prices and competition', from
A. R. Oxenfeldt (ed.) *Models of Markets*, Columbia University Press, 1963,
pp. 237–64.

In their recent work on economic problems mathematicians made a discovery which attracted a great deal of attention. It was found that for every economic problem which can be described as a linear program, and for many problems which can be described as nonlinear programs, there is an associated artificial problem which is known as the dual. That is, corresponding to each such programming problem, one can construct a second artificial problem called the dual of the first. The dual program has properties which are useful for computational purposes and interesting to the mathematician. But more remarkable and surprising is the fact that on closer inspection, the artificiality of the dual problem largely disappears. It becomes one which has a powerful and significant economic interpretation, one which seems to have 'sneaked up' on the inventors of duality, rather than to have been placed there intentionally. To a considerable extent, the significance of the dual is the conservatism of its theoretical implications. Rather than providing a major revolution and a significant departure from neo-classical analysis, it has granted new authority to the mainstream of economic theory and the marginal analysis with which it is associated.

In this paper we shall try to assess the significance of duality for the understanding of pricing and competition, from the point of view of both the analyst and the practitioner. It should be stated in advance, however, that the significance of duality for these areas is not entirely straightforward. This theory has proved more helpful in dealing with competition within the firm, that is, among different segments and divisions of the firm, than it has for the analysis of competition among firms. Moreover, duality, and the pricing analysis which is derived from it, has been more directly relevant to the pricing of inputs than of outputs.

Unfortunately, there is no simple manner in which the structure of the duality analysis can be described. Once it is understood, it does have considerable intuitive appeal; but before that stage can be attained substantial preliminary effort must be invested in comprehension of the structure. For this reason, a substantial portion of our paper will be devoted to exposition, and those readers who are familiar with the general area may therefore wish to skip the first few sections.

Elements of linear programming

Before we can even attempt to explain the workings of the dual program it will be necessary to go into some detail on the linear programming problem itself. For this purpose it is convenient to concentrate on an illustrative economic problem. Consider a firm operating under pure or perfect competition which is selecting the items to be included in its product line; that is, for each potential product, the firm must determine whether it pays to produce that item and, if so, how much it is most profitable to produce. The firm is taken to be operating with a linear, homogeneous production function, that is, one where a doubling of all inputs will permit a doubling of all outputs. More specifically, our assumptions and notation may be described as follows:

1. The firm considers producing a number of products whose respective quantities are $Q_1, Q_2, ..., Q_n$ where Q_1 is the quantity to be produced of commodity 1, and so on. In particular, if the decision is to have $Q_5 = 0$, for example, this means that commodity five will not be produced at all.

2. It is also assumed that the profit per unit of output for each product is a given constant. These profits are respectively represented by $\pi_1, \pi_2, ..., \pi_n$, so that, for example, π_1 is the number of dollars of profit earned by the production of one unit of commodity one.

3. It is also assumed that the firm's production capacity is limited by a number of resource bottlenecks. That is, at least in the short run, there are several inputs, such as workers with specialized skills, certain types of machinery or raw material, each of which

is available to the firm in fixed or limited quantities. The maximum availabilities of each of these scarce resources are represented by the quantities $c_1, c_2, ..., c_m$, where m represents the total number of bottlenecks to which the firm is subject.

4. It is assumed that the production of one unit of any given product uses up a constant number of units of each resource. For example, if commodity seven is shoes, and each pair of shoes uses up $\frac{3}{10}$ of a kilowatt hour of electricity in its production, where electricity is scarce resource number two for the firm, we designate the amount of electricity used per pair of shoes produced by k_{27}. That is, we have in this case $k_{27} = 0.3$. Our linear programming problem may now be written as follows:

maximize profits $\pi = \pi_1 Q_1 + \pi_2 Q_2 + ... + \pi_n Q_n$

subject to $k_{11} Q_1 + k_{12} Q_2 + ... + k_{1n} Q_n \leqq c_1$

$$\cdot \quad \cdot \quad \cdot \quad \cdot \quad \cdot \quad \cdot \quad \cdot \quad \cdot \quad \cdot$$

$k_{m1} Q_1 + k_{m2} Q_2 + ... + k_{mn} Q_n \leqq c_m$

$Q_1 \geqq 0, \quad Q_2 \geqq 0, \quad ..., \quad Q_n \geqq 0.$

The equation for π is the profit function. It tells us that the firm's total profit is equal to the profit per unit of output one produced times the quantity of output one, plus the profit per unit of output two, times the quantity of output two, and so on. The firm's object, then, is taken to be the maximization of this total profit.

However, the circumstances of the firm do not give it complete freedom to make any decisions it wishes. The next set of inequalities, the ones involving the $c_1, ..., c_m$, represent the company's limited resources. For example, since k_{11} tells us the quantity of input one that will be used per unit of output one, $k_{11} Q_1$ then represents the total quantity of the first resource which will be used in producing product number one. Adding to this the quantity of the first resource which will be used in product number two, that is, adding to this $k_{12} Q_2$, and so on, we get the total quantity of resource one which will be needed by the firm. But any production decision which is feasible for the firm must not use up more of resource one than is available. That is, the total requirement of resource one must be less than or equal to the available amount, c_1. That is precisely what is specified by the first of our inequalities. The remaining resource-use inequalities obviously have a similar interpretation.

Finally, we have the non-negativity conditions, $Q_1 \geqq 0$, and so on which tell us that it is impossible to produce negative quantities of any output, a stipulation which turns out to have more significance than at first appears. Specifically, these last inequalities point out one of the most obvious sources of difficulty in a more conventional analysis which uses differential calculus or straightforward marginal analysis to determine optimal product quantities. Specific numeral examples can easily demonstrate that these techniques may sometimes yield the absurd recommendation that negative quantities of various products be manufactured.

Let us turn now to a discussion of the definition and meaning of duality. It should be emphasized that, so far, nothing has been said explicitly about prices. Prices do occur implicitly in the assumption that unit profits for each output are constant. This, in turn, is usually interpreted to mean that the prices themselves are assumed to be invariant with respect to quantity produced and supplied and, indeed, that is precisely what we would expect to result from our premise of perfect competition. Up until this point, then, our linear programming model would appear to have very little to say either about the determination of prices or the operation of the competitive process. And certainly, it would seem to say no more about these subjects than the most elementary of standard models of economic theory.

Definition of the dual problem

Before we turn to the economic interpretation of the dual, it will be desirable to describe the meaning of duality in a purely abstract manner, without any reference to meaning or interpretation. At the end of this section, given any linear programming problem, the reader should be able to recognize and construct its dual.

Suppose a mischievous gremlin were let loose on a linear programming problem, and decided that he would turn everything he possibly could on its head. There are a number of obvious things he would think of. For the word 'maximize' he would substitute 'minimize'. For the symbol $\geqq$ he would substitute $\leqq$. Furthermore, a nice way to add to the resulting confusion might be to put the capacity figures, $c_1, c_2, \ldots, c_m$, where the unit profit figures, $\pi_1, \pi_2, \ldots, \pi_n$, used to be, and vice versa. For good measure, he might reverse the order in which the constants appear in the inequalities, or, better yet, he might rewrite them so that instead of reading across we would now read down. That is, where k_{12} was formerly the second constant in the first inequality, he would now make it the first constant in the second inequality. In other words, by reading across in the first inequality we would formerly have found the constants, k_{11}, k_{12}, k_{13} and so on. Now we would find these same constants not by reading across from left to right but by reading down from the first inequality to the second to the third, and so on. Finally, to cap the confusion, our gremlin would probably decide to get rid of our original variables, Q_1, Q_2,..., Q_n, altogether and substitute for them an entirely new set of variables, v_1, v_2,..., v_m. Having done all this, he would find himself with the linear programming problem which may be written as follows:

$$\text{minimize} \quad v = c_1 v_1 + c_2 v_2 + ... + c_m v_m$$
$$\text{subject to} \quad k_{11} v_1 + k_{21} v_2 + ... + k_{m1} v_m \geqq \pi_1$$
$$\cdot \quad \cdot \quad \cdot \quad \cdot \quad \cdot \quad \cdot \quad \cdot \quad \cdot \quad \cdot \quad \cdot \quad \cdot$$
$$k_{1n} v_1 + k_{2n} v_2 + ... + k_{mn} v_m \geqq \pi_n$$
$$v_1 \geqq 0, \quad v_2 \geqq 0, \quad ..., \quad v_m \geqq 0.$$

This new program is what we call the dual. Let us list its characteristics explicitly.

1. If the primal problem involves maximization the dual involves minimization, and vice versa.

2. If the primal involves $\geqq$ signs the dual involves $\leqq$ signs, and vice versa.

3. The profit constants in the primal problem replace the capacity constants, and vice versa.

4. In the resource-use inequalities the constants which were found by going from left to right are positioned in the dual from top to bottom, and vice versa.

5. A new set of variables appears in the dual.

6. Neglecting the number of non-negativity conditions, if there are n variables and m inequalities in the primal problem, in the dual there will be m variables and n inequalities.

Finally, it should be noted that if we were to let our gremlin loose again and have him do his work on the dual problem, he would again reach the problem with which he started. That is, if he were to take the dual problem and subject it to all the abuses which he had heaped on our original linear program, he would find that, in the end, he would have undone all his mischief. The dual of the dual problem is the original linear programming problem itself. It follows that given such a pair of problems it is entirely arbitrary which of them is referred to as the dual. Each one of them is the dual of the other.

These rules for the construction of the dual are illustrated in the following pair of numerical linear programming problems. The reader should verify that these problems do indeed constitute one another's dual, as follows:

maximize $\pi = 2Q_1 \times 6Q_2$

subject to $\quad 4Q_1 + Q_2 \leqq 5 \quad$ (sky hooks),
$\qquad\qquad 3Q_1 + 2Q_2 \leqq 7 \quad$ (electricity),
$\qquad\qquad Q_1 + Q_2 \leqq 2 \quad$ (wibblers),
$\qquad\qquad Q_1 \geqq 0, \quad Q_2 \geqq 0.$

Minimize $V = 5V_1 + 7V_2 + 2V_3$

subject to $\quad 4V_2 + 3V_2 + 1V_3 \geqq 2$
$\qquad\qquad 1V_1 + 2V_2 + 1V_3 \geqq 6$
$\qquad\qquad V_1 \geqq 0, \quad V_2 \geqq 0, \quad V_3 \geqq 0.$

It will be noted, for example, that in our illustration the maximization problem involves two variables and, not counting the non-negativity conditions, three inequalities, whereas the minimization problem involves three variables and two inequalities. It should also be pointed out that one feature is not tampered with in going from a linear programming problem to its dual – the inequalities of the non-negativity condition retain their directions. That is, both in the primal and in the dual problem each variable is required to be greater than or equal to zero.

Interpretation of the dual

We must now breathe economic life into the scrambled program which our gremlin produced for us. We started with a well-defined and meaningful economic problem which we wrote out mathematically as a linear program and out of that, arbitrarily and capriciously, we produced another program which is related to the first in a peculiar fashion. What possible economic meaning can this dual program have?

We shall show that the variables of the dual program, the V_1, V_2 and V_3 in our numerical examples, can be interpreted as the economic values of the firm's three scarce resources. Let us assume that our three scarce resources are, respectively, sky hooks, electricity and wibblers, so that our original linear programming problem tells us that the firm has available to it 5 sky hooks, 7 units of electric capacity and 2 wibblers. V_1 may then be described as the accounting value to the firm of a sky hook, V_2, as the accounting value of a unit of electrical capacity, and V_3 as the accounting value of a wibbler.

Tentatively accepting the interpretation, let us look at the first inequality in the dual problem and see what meaning it might possibly have. It will be remembered that the coefficient 4 of the variable V_1 in that inequality had a definite meaning in our primal problem. There it represented the number of sky hooks necessary to produce one unit of output 1. Similarly, the second coefficient, 3, in our dual inequality, that is, the coefficient of V_2, represented in the original problem the number of units of electricity needed to produce a unit of output 1. Finally, the coefficient of the V_3 in our dual inequality represented the number of wibblers needed to produce a unit of output 1. In sum, the three coefficients represent the quantities of the three different inputs which go into a unit of commodity one. Now, if each sky hook is worth V_1 dollars, then 4 sky hooks would be worth four times V_1 dollars and, similarly, if each unit of electricity is worth V_2 dollars, the 3 units of electricity would be worth $3V_2$ dollars. Finally, the 1 wibbler would be worth 1 times V_2 dollars if each unit is worth V_3. We see, then, that the expression on the left hand side of our inequality, $4V_1 + 3V_2 + 1V_3$, has a straightforward economic interpretation, given the meaning which has tentatively been assigned to our variables. That sum is the total value of the inputs whch are necessary to produce one unit of output of commodity 1.

Only one more step is needed to complete our interpretation of this inequality. We must now recall what is signified by the number 2 on the right hand side of that inequality. Going back to the original problem once more, we see that the 2 is the unit profit one obtains by producing the first commodity. Each unit of commodity 1 which is manufactured yields $2 to the firm. Our first inequality can now be read to state the following: The value of the inputs used in the production of a unit of commodity one must be greater than or equal to the profit which the firm makes by producing a unit of commodity.

At first glance, this appears to be a curious requirement. It would seem to mean that the firm must always lose money, or at best break even, by producing commodity 1 because the value of the inputs used in its manufacture will always eat up the profits, and possibly, more. Actually, however, this last interpretation is a mistake which one makes all too easily. The number 2 is a profit figure and not a revenue figure. Hence, the fact that the value of inputs exceeds profits does not mean that profits are zero or negative. Profits are $2 per unit of output, as stated, and that is all there is to it. Furthermore, V_1, V_2 and V_3 are not cost figures; they are accounting values which have been assigned to our three inputs. One can assume that the firm has already acquired its sky hooks, electricity and wibblers and that these now represent an overhead or fixed cost, so that their current value to the firm may be totally independent of their historic, sunk costs, incurred when these inputs were obtained. Rather, the Vs should be interpreted as an accounting device designed to divide the profits of the firm among the three scarce inputs. We are saying, in effect, that the firm could not earn its $2 on each unit of output 1 without having any sky hooks, electricity or wibblers available to it. In other words, these profits are ascribable or imputable to these three inputs and the question is, what valuation of each input appropriately imputes these profits. Our first inequality, then, states that we must assign to each of the inputs a value sufficiently great to impute all the profits of output number 1. If the inequality were violated, that is, if the values were so low that the sum of the values of the inputs were less than $2, we would still have some unimputed profits, that is, some profits which had not been ascribed to one of the inputs. Just as the first inequality of the dual program imputes the profit from commodity 1, so the second inequality imputes all the profit from each unit of output 2 to these inputs. It states that

W. J. Baumol and R. E. Quandt 429

the values of the three inputs which are used to make a unit of commodity 2 must account fully for the \$6 of profit which are yielded by a unit of commodity 2.

We will see presently why it is correct to write these as inequalities rather than equations, that is, why we do not require that the values of the inputs be exactly equal to the profits. One simple reason that appears at once follows from the fact that the number of variables and the number of inequalities need not be the same. We have three variables in our dual problem, and two inequalities. We could just as easily have had, say, six variables and fifteen inequalities. If we had attempted to write these as equations rather than equalities, we would have had a system involving fifteen equations in six unknowns and, obviously, this would be likely to run us into difficulties; that is, usually it is impossible to satisfy a system of linear equations containing more equations than unknowns.[1] Since, therefore, in such a situation we may be forced to relinquish equality in part of the system, we have chosen between the two apparently less desirable alternatives, over-imputation and underimputation, and have decided to favor the former. That is, we have said, if it is absolutely necessary to assign values to our inputs which make the imputed value of the inputs used in producing a unit of output either greater than or less than unit profits, let us assign values which are greater than unit profits.

But once we have stated the inequalities in this way, it would appear that there is no problem at all. We need only assign values as capriciously high as we wish to each of the inputs, to be sure that they will more than account for all of the profits. What prevents this sort of arbitrary solution is the fact that V must be minimized in the dual problem. V also has an economic interpretation. It will be recalled that we have 5 sky hooks, so that the total value of the sky hooks available to the firm will be $5V_1$ and similarly, the total value of the electricity available to the firm will be $7V_2$ because there are 7 units of electricity at the firm's command, and so on. Hence, V represents the total value of all the inputs which the firm has under its control. The dual problem then says that we are to find the smallest value for this

1. i.e. unless sufficiently many equations are linear combinations of the remaining equations.

stock of inputs which completely accounts for all the profits of each of the outputs.

So far, one may have the feeling that this interpretation is somewhat strained. We have forced an economic reading on our dual problem but that interpretation seems to have been picked out of the air and we have not indicated any reason why an economist, or anyone else, should really be interested in it. However, mathematicians have proved a number of theorems about the dual problem which add power to the entire construct. Before describing these theorems, we must emphasize that they deal exclusively, unless otherwise stated, with the optimal solutions to the primal and dual problems. That is, they deal with the quantities of the various outputs which maximize profits in the primal problem and the imputed values of the inputs, the $V_1,...,V_n$, which minimize the value expression, V.

Theorem 1. The maximum value of π in the primal problem is equal to the minimum value of V in the dual problem.

The first theorem tells us that the imputation process will turn out to be more effective than we had any right to expect. We had set up our constraints in the dual problem in such a way that overimputation seemed very likely. It seemed entirely possible that for some commodities the value of the inputs used in their production would exceed their profitability. Hence, one might well expect that the accounting value of all the inputs used in the production process will exceed the sum of the profits which are available to the firm. In fact, Theorem 1 tells us that this will never occur – that if our problems are amenable to solution, that is, if the problems have any solutions at all, they will exactly impute away all of the firm's profits, no more and no less. We will return to the logic behind this result presently, for it has an entirely plausible explanation. But first, it will be necessary to examine several other theorems.

Theorem 2. The imputed values of the firm's scarce inputs are exactly equal to their marginal profitabilities.[2]

2. For purposes of this theorem it is assumed that we deal with 'nondegenerate' linear programs. For present purposes this may be considered a technicality which need not concern the nonspecialist reader.

This result is precisely in accord with the traditional notions of economic theory. It is a standard economic proposition that a scarce resource should be used up to the point at which its marginal contribution equals its price. That is to say, we should consider the utility of a scarce resource to be equal to the addition to our returns which would be offered to us by the acquisition of another unit of that item. And it can be proved that this is exactly what is meant by the Vs in our dual problem. V_1, the accounting value which is assigned to a sky hook, is equal to the increase in the profits which would be earned by the firm if the number of sky hooks which it had available were increased from 5 to 6. In other words, an alternative way of finding V_1 might be to solve a second linear programming problem which was the same as our original problem, except that the number on the right hand side of our first constraint was 6 instead of 5. By comparing the profits to be earned in the two situations and finding how much larger is the profit in the second than in the first, we would have a value for our first dual variable, V_1. This is doubtless very reassuring. It shows us that all roads do indeed lead to Rome – that all methods of optimality analysis are, after all, good marginalism. And if this reassurance comes to us in an entirely unexpected way it is no less welcome for it.

Theorem 3. In the inequalities of the dual problem, any excess of the accounting value of the inputs used to produce some item over the profitability of that item can be interpreted as the opportunity cost of producing that item.

This is really a corollary of the preceding theorem. It states that if the accounting value assigned to the inputs needed to produce, say, commodity 1, is $9, then, on every unit of commodity 1 which is produced we suffer an opportunity loss of $7 True, we still obtain $2 in profits by producing that unit of commodity 1, but in so doing we are giving up even higher profits which could be obtained by transferring our resources from the production of commodity 1 to the manufacture of some other commodity. Indeed, the fact that the opportunity cost in this case is $9−2 = $7 means that if we transferred the resources from the production of commodity 1 to the manufacture of the most profitable of the products which the firm can produce, we would obtain an additional $7 for each unit of commodity 1 which we gave up. In particular, an item whose profits are precisely imputed by the values of our dual variables must be one of the goods whose production is most profitable to the firm. To understand this, we note that the value of the inputs of such an item must be precisely equal to the unit profits of that commodity so that the opportunity loss involved in producing that item must be zero. There must be no other way for the firm to use its resources more profitably. We can see intuitively how this opportunity cost interpretation follows from the preceding theorem, that is, from Theorem 2. If V_1 is the marginal profitability of a sky hook, $4V_1$ will be a rough measure of the profits which the firm would hope to earn from the four units of sky hooks which it uses up in the production of a unit of commodity 1. Similarly, $3V_2$ represents the profits which the electricity used in producing in a unit of commodity 1 could potentially earn for the firm, and so on. Thus, $4V_1+3V_2+1V_3$ represents the maximum profits which the firm could hope to earn from the resources used up in the production of a unit of commodity one. If these potential profits are greater than the two dollars which one actually earns from the production of a unit of that commodity, then, clearly, the firm is not doing as well as it could be. It is suffering an opportunity loss by misallocating resources to that particular output. This result should prepare us for the next theorem.

Theorem 4. If the solution of the dual problem involves a positive opportunity loss for some commodity k, then the solution of the primal problem will contain a zero output level for that commodity k.

Going back to our illustrative case, if we have

$$4V_1+3V_2+1V_3>2,$$

the solution associates a positive opportunity cost with commodity 1. In other words, the firm would do better to reallocate resources away from the production of commodity 1 to some other output. Therefore, it is not surprising that in the corresponding primal solution, Q_1 equals zero. And, indeed, it is not too difficult to prove that this will always be the case; that is, that the solution of the primal and dual problems, even though calculated quite independently, will always mesh in such a way as to make good economic sense. Whenever the dual problem solution indicates that a certain commodity is unprofitable in the relative sense, that is, whenever it indicates that despite its possibly high unit profits the item involves an opportunity loss, then an independent calculation of the optimal solution of the primal problem will show that that commodity will not be produced. This, also, is a very comforting result.

Incidentally, this result also gives us some idea as to why Theorem 1 holds. Theorem 4, which we are now discussing, admits the possibility that the Vs will imply a positive opportunity cost for some commodities. But those will be the commodities which are not produced at all. In other words, the output of those items will be zero and the resources going into their production will be zero. Thus, the only items which are produced are those for which the profits are exactly imputed by our dual calculation. Commodity 2 will only be produced if $1V_1 + 2V_2 + 1V_3 = 6$. In sum, when we consider only the commodities which are actually produced, it will be clear that the imputed values will be exactly sufficient to account for their earned profits. Hence, the total imputed values of all resources used must equal the total profits of the firm, which is what Theorem 1 states.

Theorem 4 also has the following interesting consequence. In linear programming, the difficult thing to determine is which outputs it will, and which outputs it will not pay to produce. Once we have determined which items will be turned out it is relatively easy to find out in what quantities they should be manufactured. Theorem 4 tells us that we can learn which commodities it will pay us to produce either by a direct calculation on the basis of the original linear program or by solving the dual problem. We thus have a strategic choice. We can solve one problem or the other, whichever happens to be easier or more convenient. Actually, this statement underemphasizes the degree of connection between the solution of the original problem and that of its dual. Once we have solved either of these problems it is a trivial matter to find the solution to the other. Usually, from the solution of the original problem the solution of the dual can be written out by inspection, or vice versa. Let us now turn to the final theorem.

Theorem 5. Any input which is not fully used will receive an accounting value equal to zero.

Suppose we solve a primal problem and find that the most profitable output program requires the company to leave one wibbler unused. Since wibblers are the third of the scarce inputs, this last theorem tells us that the solution to the dual problem will yield the value $V_3 = 0$. Of course, this also makes good economic sense. Any input which is redundant must have, one would expect, a zero economic value. Or, looked at in terms of the interpretation of Theorem 2, if some input has a positive marginal profitability, clearly, no portion of that resource will remain unused in an optimal solution. Obviously, we could always increase profits by using the unemployed portion of that input.

It may be of interest to note that Theorems 4 and 5 are basically the same, one applying to the original problem and the other to the dual problem. They both state that if a constraint in one of the problems involves an inequality ($<$ or $>$), then the corresponding variable in the other problem will have the value zero. In the case of Theorem 5 we can see this as follows: The left hand side of the first constraint represents the number of sky hooks which will be used up in the production of commodities 1 and 2. If this total adds up to less than 5, it means that there will be an unused quantity of sky hooks. Only if $4Q_1 + Q_2$ is equal to 5 will the company's supply of sky hooks be used up completely, and only in these circumstances can the value of V_1 be unequal to zero, according to the theorem.

There are a number of other interesting and important theorems about duality which have been proved by mathematicians but most of these are of limited interest for present purposes and, in addition, they are much more abstruse and difficult to explain.

Illustrative example

A rather interesting illustration of the workings of the duality relationships is presented by the following linear programming problem:

maximize $pQ_1 + Q_2 + 2Q_3$
subject to $2Q_1 + Q_2 \leqq 100$,
$$Q_1 - Q_2 + Q_3 \leqq 0$$
and $\quad Q_1 \geqq 0, \quad Q_2 \geqq 0, \quad Q_3 \geqq 0.$

Interpretation: Production of the first commodity brings in p dollars of profit (p to be discussed later) and uses 2 units of the first and 1 unit of the second resource. Production of the second commodity brings in \$1, uses 1 unit of the first resource, and yields 1 unit of the second resource as a by-product. The third commodity involves only the sale of the second resource at a price of \$2 per unit. The interpretation of the first constraint is obvious. The second constraint says: the sales of resource 3 must not exceed the output of that resource, minus the amount which is used up: $Q_3 \leqq Q_2 - Q_1$. The dual of our problem is:

minimize $\quad 100V_1 + 0V_2$
subject to $\quad 2V_1 + V_2 \geqq p$,
$$V_1 - V_2 \geqq 1,$$
$$V_2 \geqq 2$$
and $\quad V_1 \geqq 0, \quad V_2 \geqq 0, \quad V_3 \geqq 0.$

We conclude from the last inequality that our accounting price for the second resource (V_2) must not be less than the market price, \$2.

Second, one can prove that if $p < 8$, the first commodity will not be produced[3] and the imputed price, V_2, of the second resource will equal \$2, i.e. it will equal its market price, whatever the actual value of p.

Third, if $p > 8$, none of the second resource will be sold (since it is so valuable in producing output), and its imputed value will increase above 2 and will be higher, the higher is p. If $p = 8$, we are indifferent between selling or not any of the second resource.

All this makes good sense: as long as it is profitable to sell

3. Proof: By the second dual inequality, $V_1 \geqq 1 + V_2$, so that if $V_2 \geqq 2$ then $V_1 \geqq 3$, and hence $2V_1 + V_2 \geqq 8$. Thus, if p is less than 8, we must have $2V_1 + V_2 > p$, and so production of item 1 will involve an opportunity loss.

the second resource, its value to us cannot go above market price. When it is not profitable to sell because some commodity using it gives high profit, its imputed value must rise in accord with the increased marginal revenue product of the second resource.

Remarks on duality and non-linear programming

So far, the discussion has been confined exclusively to the simple case of linear programming. As we have already stated, this implicitly assumes that we are dealing with a situation involving pure or perfect competition. As soon as the firm's selling price becomes a variable whose value is influenced by the quantities of the commodities which it produces, we are automatically faced with a non-linear programming problem. This is so because in the expression for the profit of the firm which is being maximized, we must have a term representing total revenue for each output, that is, price times quantity. But if the price of that commodity is itself a function of quantity, $f(Q)$, then price times quantity is given by $Q \times f(Q)$. In other words, we have an expression which is virtually certain to be non-linear and may involve some complicated function of Q. Non-linear programming involves a variety of computational and conceptual difficulties which lead to a temptation to employ linear approximations wherever this is reasonably justified. Unfortunately, as we have just seen, the absence of perfect competition normally destroys the justification for this sort of approximate calculation.

Happily, theorems very closely analogous to those which we have described for the case of linear programming apply to wide classes of non-linear programming problems. Most of these developments rest on the work of Kuhn and Tucker, as well as on the earlier writings of von Neumann. The analysis runs into serious difficulties only if the economic situation with which we are dealing involves significant discontinuities and important increasing returns. The presence of diminishing returns to scale or of negatively sloping demand curves which may essentially be interpreted as diminishing returns to marketing effort causes no important problems. Thus, with the warning that in dealing with problems of competition, and with most actual firms, one is likely to have to resort to non-linear programming, and warned that the

W. J. Baumol and R. E. Quandt 437

non-linear case is somewhat less simple than the one we have just described, one may nevertheless proceed on the assumption that most of what has been said in this paper about duality is relevant for the subsequent discussion.

Usefulness of duality theory: preliminary

We come now to the heart of this paper, the evaluation of the contribution of duality theory to the understanding of the competitive process and to pricing, in particular. Before we proceed to the details on this discussion several preliminary matters must be considered.

It is well known that linear programming calculations have been exceedingly useful in many industrial contexts and, in some cases, to government, and that the same has been true to a somewhat more limited extent of non-linear programming, though the applicability of the latter is virtually certain to increase in the future, as computational methods improve. A wide variety of practical problems have been rendered far more tractable by the use of these techniques. There are many standard examples, including the selection of advertising media, the blending of animal feeds, the determination of transportation routes, and the scheduling of productive processes. Moreover, the wide variety and ingenuity of non-standardized applications is also impressive. Particularly where there are concrete decisions to be made and specific numbers to be calculated, programming has often proved invaluable. In all of this, duality theory has played a role. By making clear the marginal calculations which lay behind the analysis, it provided better understanding of the problems. Perhaps more important for the practical man is the fact that duality provided for faster, more economical calculations in many cases. For, as we have already seen, in solving any linear programming problem we have the choice between solving either the original problem or its dual, and a somewhat similar situation holds in the case of non-linearity. It happens that in many circumstances it is better strategy to conduct one's numerical calculations in terms of the dual than in terms of the original program, and a number of specialized computational approaches have been developed on this basis.

However, it must be emphasized that all of this is largely beside the point. No one, to our knowledge, has questioned the usefulness of mathematical programming and duality, and documentation of their helpfulness would be as simple as it would be uninteresting. None of the applications which have so far been listed has anything essential to do with either the structure of competition or the nature of the pricing process and, thus, it is outside the range of our present interest. It was suggested as a frame of reference for these papers that the usefulness of a technique might be evaluated in terms of the interests of four different classes of persons. These are the empirical investigator of economic institutions, the economic theorist, the businessman and the maker of government policy. The relevance of duality to the interests of each of these will be discussed in turn, with the exception of the first of the four classes. We believe that duality theory is completely irrelevant for the work of the empirical investigator of economic institutions. The reasons for this are not difficult to determine. Programming is, by its very definition, an instrument for the calculation of optimal decisions, decisions which maximize or minimize the achievement of some objective. As a result, programming analyses and calculations are likely to yield prescriptive rather than descriptive results. They are apt to present advice rather than actuality. Though the economic theorist often finds it convenient and useful to proceed on the assumption that the members of the economy behave optimally, from their own points of view, that consumers maximize utility, and that business firms maximize profits, this is surely no safe premise for the empirical student. Departures from perfectly calculated behavior are his meat and drink. Habits, traditions and psychological quirks which are sufficiently prevalent are of as much or greater interest to him than the degree of approximation to some normative ideals. A programming problem and its dual are empty of this sort of material. A programming calculation can therefore be expected to be of interest to him, only as a matter of contrast, to show him how far what is departs from what might have been; to enable him to evaluate the degree of 'inefficiency' in the rough and ready operations of the actual economy, as compared to what might be achieved if optimal calculations were widely made and followed.

Duality and government operation

There is a fairly considerable body of literature which ties duality theory into the operations of government and the pricing mechanism. The antecedents of this literature are to be found in the writings of Lerner, Lange, and others, who produced a considerable body of work on the application of marginal analysis to the economics of socialism and governmental control of the economy. It will be recalled that these writers maintained, essentially, that socialism could achieve its economic objectives without giving up the independence and initiative of the individual decision maker. Following the standard analysis of welfare economics, they pointed out that competition provided a mechanism which closely circumscribed the decisions of the businessman and the other participants in the economy. In crudest terms, a businessman could not afford to produce anything for which there existed no profitable market and so, in Adam Smith's phrasing, 'by directing . . . industry in such a manner as its produce may be of the greatest value, he intends only his own gain, and he is in this, as in many other cases, led by an invisible hand to promote an end which was no part of his intention'.

The more sophisticated and complex analysis of modern welfare economics had extended these results and made them far more specific and rigorous. It was shown that if businessmen and consumers operated under a regime of perfect competition, then, given certain criteria of efficiency and consumer welfare, the economy would automatically and without any interference produce results which were optimal – in the limited sense of Pareto-optimality – for its members. This is a remarkable result, though, for a variety of reasons, its practical applicability is rather limited. It states that a perfectly competitive system is a giant analogue computer which calculates the decisions necessary to achieve maximal well-being and, indeed, which automatically sees to it that these decisions are made and carried out.

Lerner and Lange argued that where the economy departed from conditions of pure competition, these results could be achieved artificially with a minimum of governmental interference. By forcing managers to behave as though they were operating under perfect competition, by requiring that they produce up to the point where price equals the marginal costs of production, and by insisting that markets be cleared, that is, by lowering the price whenever there is an excess supply and raising the price whenever there is unsatisfied demand, it was suggested that the benefits of socialist planning could be obtained without the details and nuisances involved in the setting and enforcement of quotas, norms, rations and the like. Each manager would be told that he was responsible for his own profitability and for his own decisions, provided only that he followed the simple rules of the game, the rules which called for marginal cost pricing and for clearing of the market. Certain difficulties for this proposal were noted, for example, in the case of economies of large-scale production, but these are not relevant to the present discussion.

The mathematical programming and activity analysis literature has brought about a revival of interest in these ideas. It has been shown that the dual prices or values which are calculated from the dual programming problem can be used as the basis of a profitability requirement whose function would be closely analogous with that of the Lange–Lerner analysis. In allocating the economy's limited resources, the government need not set out specific quotas for the individual firms which constitute the economy. Instead, it need only set a price on each product, and a price on each scarce resource which is given by its dual value. We have already seen that any operation which produces some commodity that is not included in an optimal mix will necessarily suffer an opportunity loss in terms of these dual values. If the businessman is actually charged these dual prices, this opportunity cost is converted into a very real dollars and cents deficit. That is, if management were charged the dual values for all its inputs, it would find that it could break even only by concentrating production on those commodities which are optimal. Thus, we can crudely characterize the conclusion of this analysis as the assertion that one can achieve the advantages of detailed central planning and careful optimality calculation without telling the individual decision makers what they should do. A simple change in bookkeeping practices, together with the businessman's continued dedication to the pursuit of profits, would suffice to produce these ideal results.

There is no doubt that these results and this analysis are of great interest to the economist, but more careful consideration indicates that their practical application is likely to be highly limited, even in an economy in which central planning is an accepted goal. First of all, in the linear programming case there is a particular problem which is worth mentioning. It is true that in these circumstances if product managers pay for resources prices equal to their dual values, they will automatically produce a commodity if and only if its unit profit is equal to the value of the resources necessary to produce it. Thus, dual prices might indeed lead to correct decisions as to which items should be produced and which should not be produced. But dual prices do not, in these circumstances, indicate to management how much of each commodity which is included in the product line should be manufactured. In the linear programming case, since there are constant returns to scale and fixed prices, given that a product is profitable, it will be equally lucrative whether produced on a large scale or on a small. What prevents the indefinite expansion of the production of such a remunerative product is the scarcity of resources. Declining profitability of the production of an item as the market becomes saturated is not what brings production to a halt. Hence, in the linear programming case, dual prices, while they would direct production into the correct channels, would not necessarily yield the optimal relative utilization of these channels.

A second limitation of the use of duality as a device for preserving decentralized decision making is that the method appears to break down in the presence of important economies of large scale and significant discontinuities in production. Since these are important facts of industrial arrangements, one must not be surprised to find a variety of situations where so simple a scheme will run into serious and perhaps insuperable difficulties.

Finally, it must be emphasized that the degree of decentralization and extent of economy in decision making involved in dual pricing is largely illusory. As has been emphasized several times, solution of the original problem and of the dual essentially amount to the same thing; that is, if one is solved the other is automatically also solved. Hence, if the central planning board is to go to the trouble of finding the dual prices, it must, in the process, calculate quotas and norms for individual producers.

The fact that these trappings of direct intervention may be kept in the background by means of dual pricing may be a psychological advantage but it involves no material change in the situation. The central planning board has made the complete calculation and whether it prefers to present it in one form or the other, there has been no economy in calculation, nor is there any real increase in the freedom of the individual decision maker. He is, in effect, given a choice, but for all practical purposes the choice is between following the desires of the central planning board or committing economic suicide. Dual pricing, in effect, tells him that any other action than that which the board desires will necessarily and rapidly lead him to bankruptcy. If this be freedom of choice for the decision maker then so, perhaps, is the choice between following the decisions of the central planning board and the option of a paid vacation in the salt mines of Siberia.

Duality and business decisions

It should now be easy to see why we made the earlier statement that dual pricing is of more relevance for the evaluation of inputs than of final commodities. The values which emerge from the solution of the dual problem have nothing to do with the market price of the commodity which is manufactured. Rather, they give the value to the firm of the input which it employs in its productive process.

This at once suggests an application which may be of use to the businessman. Indeed, it is an application which has been investigated recently. The users of an important agricultural commodity have been experiencing some difficulty in determining which grade or variety of this commodity to purchase for their purposes. Currently, the market prices of these different grades bear a very tenuous relationship to the usefulness of the different grades to the processor.

Moreover, a certain grade may be more useful to one type of manufacturer than to another. How, then, should a businessman decide which one of the available grades to purchase? An approach to this matter which should now be clear to the reader is the calculation of dual values for these different grades. Comparison of actual market prices with these dual values should enable the businessman readily to determine which grades are

W. J. Baumol and R. E. Quandt 443

appropriate for his purpose. This approach is not only obvious, it is also promising. But even here it has its limitations and it is not quite as exciting as it might at first appear. It is not so very exciting, because all we are asserting here is that the firm's decision as to which inputs to purchase should be based on the marginal profitability of the alternatives. Comparison of the marginal profitability of the different items with their prices should tell at once which are desirable and which are not. Stated in this way, the result becomes much more familiar sounding and less impressive. Moreover, it points up the essential difficulty in the procedure, which is the problem of obtaining the data on which to base the calculation. The bulk of the work will be neither the formulation of the relevant programming problem nor the subsequent calculation, but the collection of the marginal profitability statistics in a form which provides sufficient accuracy and relevance to make the calculation useful.

A second application of duality to business decisions is analogous to the decentralized decision-making scheme which was discussed in the government policy section. Many large firms are composed of a considerable number of divisions operating partially or almost entirely independently. Very frequently these divisions compete with one another, either through inadvertence or as a result of direct decree by top management. But there is no reason to believe that even if these divisions were operated optimally from the point of view of the divisions themselves, they would produce results which would aggregate to an ideal situation from the point of view of the firm as a whole. This is the basic problem of suboptimization. The welfare of the whole is not the sum of the welfare of its parts. For example, if the divisions compete with one another, each may force down the profits of its rival and the end result may be a reduction in the total profits of the company. For the same reason that dual values may permit the semblance of decentralized decision making in an economy they may also preserve the same appearances to the division managers in a company. If central management is convinced that it can calculate the optimal programs for its constituent segments, dual values may represent the ideal instruments for their enforcement. Though in industrial applications many of the reservations which were raised in relation to the use of dual pricing in decentralized economic planning for the economy are also applicable, it is plausible that some exceptions will occur.

A suggestive illustration is provided by at least one large retail chain where, in continuation of long-established tradition, reordering for inventory is done entirely by the decision of the store managers. In the past, store managers were the only ones who had a good and up-to-date estimate of inventory levels and, therefore, any attempt to centralize reordering decisions would almost certainly have produced inefficiency and waste. However, with the advent of the electronic computer, inventory record keeping has now been moved to company headquarters. Current information on inventory status is more readily obtained from the computer than from any other source. Today store managers still continue to make up orders, but these delivery requests are based on statistics which are obtained from company headquarters. This illustration is presented for two reasons. First of all, it shows that it has now become possible to centralize decisions where that procedure would formerly have been uneconomical. Second, it has emphasized the need for managerial independence, at least to a degree, as a means for maintaining local initiative and morale. In such circumstances dual pricing may soon be given an effective role, for it possesses the essential requisites of the situation. It maintains the form of decentralized decision making while disposing of its substance.

Duality and economic theory

We turn finally to the topic closest to our own hearts – the relevance of programming and duality to the work of the economic theorist. From his point of view, the entire body of analysis suffers from two important limitations. First, as already stated, it is an instrument of optimality calculation. It is normative rather than descriptive. Thus, it should be more useful in welfare economics than in positive economics. Only to the extent that the behavior of individuals and firms is approximately optimal, will a linear programming calculation give a reasonably close description of actual behavior. Of course, this is a consideration which has always borne relatively little weight with economists. We have usually proceeded on the assumption that reasonably good predictions would be yielded by an optimality analysis. A second limitation of programming analysis is the fact that it is primarily quantitative rather than qualitative. Though the duality theorems which have been described previously have very important qualitative characteristics, most programming calculations can only be made in terms of specific numbers and specific examples. It is difficult to obtain qualitative programming results analogous with the very interesting comparative statics theorems of neo-classical analysis. It is as though we were forced, in the theory of production, to make all our analyses in terms of specific production functions, with specific coefficients and specific forms for the variables. This is a limitation which most theorists would have found intolerable until now. However, there are two things that can be done about it. First, as has been shown in the duality discussion and already mentioned in this section, with some degree of difficulty more general qualitative theorems can indeed be developed for programming problems. More novel, perhaps, is the approach which has been made possible by the availability of high speed electronic computers. These permit sensitivity analyses in which the effects of changes in values of the parameters in a problem can be examined by direct computation. In effect, what is done is shown by our last linear programming illustration, where the value of the price of the first output is permitted to vary. If a succession of different numbers is substituted for p in the profit function, successive calculations will show how the optimal solution will change and how the level of profitability will be affected. Thus we can obtain qualitative results by means of an inductive experimental approach, trying alternative values of the parameters and recording and analysing their effects.

Aside from this, the main function of programming in economic theory and the light which it sheds on the competitive and pricing processes has, as already stated, largely consisted in an extension, further explanation, and confirmation of the standard marginal analysis. Duality has shown us that implicit in every optimality analysis and optimal decision process must be concepts of opportunity costs and marginal yield. It has shown this for a much wider variety of situations than was formerly covered and has offered us many new insights into the logic of the process.

One interesting consequence of all this has been the new position of marginal analysis in the Soviet Union. There, in recent years, the marginal apparatus has quite unexpectedly been restored to respectability and, interestingly enough, this has been the work of the mathematicians rather than of the pure economists. For the Soviet mathematicians have shown that many planning problems require for their analysis the entire apparatus of mathematical programming, and in investigating this apparatus, they independently came upon the structure and theorems of duality. Once it became apparent that programming works, and actually produces results, the rest was accepted more easily. It is interesting that recent writers have made no bones about the matter. In the Soviet publications it is now widely stated that marginal calculations are entirely necessary and appropriate for optimal decision-making. Though there is some effort to interpret these results in a way which reconciles them with Marxian doctrine, those who accept them are in the ascendancy.

It is also noteworthy that the relationship of programming to economic theory is a two-way street. For example, some computational methods for non-linear programming, which are based on some economic models of oligopolistic competition, are currently being explored. Methods somewhat analogous to the Cournot process, whereby the firms finally attain their equilibrium point, are proposed for the solution of programming problems. But, all in all, it must be conceded that duality has given us no brilliant and deep insights into the nature of competition and pricing. Largely, perhaps, this is because, by its very nature, programming theory is empty of empirical content. It makes no pretense at being otherwise. But, surely, without empirical premises we can hope to shed very little light on matters which are essentially empirical.

Acknowledgements

Acknowledgements are due to the following for permission to reproduce the Readings in this volume:

1 Princeton University Press
2 Princeton University Press
3 *American Economic Review* and Joe S. Bain
4 Augustus M. Kelley Publishers
5 *Econometrica* and Sir John R. Hicks
6 *Review of Economic Studies* and G. C. Archibald
7 University of Chicago Press
8 Harvard University Press
9 Oxford University Press Inc.
10 *American Economic Review* and A. C. Harberger
11 Mrs Adela Kalecka
12 *American Economic Review* and R. M. Solow
13 *Economica* and W. J. Baumol
14 Richard D. Irwin Inc.
15 Macmillan and Co and R. Marris
16 *American Economic Review* and W. J. Baumol
17 *Economica* and John Williamson
18 American Statistical Association and Irma G. Adelman
19 *Economica* and P. E. Hart
20 *American Economic Review* and Robert Dorfman
21 Columbia University Press

Author Index

Subject Index

Accounting
  cost, 45
  data, cross-section, 44, 48
Activity or Process *see*
  Mathematical programming
Advertising, 98–124, 176, 187,
  264–7
  as a 'competitive waste', 196
  costs of, 188, 189n, 212, 213n,
  220n
  and an increase in demand, 100
  and service competition, 259–62
  and variations in factor prices,
  100
Allocation, of resources, *see*
  Resources
Assembly costs, 41, 42
Average cost, 27, 42, 44, 111–13,
  279, 281
  curves, 108, 111, 112, 224, 225,
  274
  function, 27, 27n, 34, 36, 41, 42,
  273, 275
  pricing, 265, 266

Barriers to entry *see* Conditions
  of entry
Behavioural theories, 16, 249
Boston Transcript, 198
Bureau of Labor Statistics, 138n,
  141, 142n, 149, 150
Business cycle, 229, 230–32, 234,
  354

Capacity
  excess capacity *see* Excess

individual market, 68
  National Industry, 63–6, 73, 79
Capital
  corporate, 301
  cost, 46
  human, 217, 247
  labour ratio, 245, 247, 395
  market, 324
  return to, 202–3, 211, 341
  stock, 332
Capitalism
  economic theory of 'Managerial'
  291–317
  traditional, 293
Carnegie School, 16, 249
Cartels, 231
Census of manufactures, 58n, 60,
  61, 62, 64, 72, 74, 240
Cobb-Douglas production
  function, 11, 12n, 218
Collective bargaining
  agreements, 243
Collusion, 128–35, 144, 145, 150,
  158
Company
  directors, 306
  flotation of, 295
  joint-stock, 291, 299, 300, 301
  law, 299, 301, 305
  private limited, 294n
  shareholders, 300–306
  shares, 300–307, 315, 334
Comparative static(s), 14, 347
  analysis, 83
  of monopolistic competition, 85,
  97–124

Department of Commerce, 235
Demand
  cross-elasticity of, 130, 145
  elasticity of, 108–12, 127, 128n,
    154, 202–7
  law of, 87, 88
Dimensions of output *see* Output
Diminishing returns, 221
  dynamic, 349
Discount, rate of time, 299, 315n
Distribution
  costs, 41, 42, 72
  general equilibrium theory of, 236
  of income *see* Income, National
    income
  macroeconomic theory of, 233
Duopoly, 91–5
  Cournot model of, 84
  neo-classical theory, 85
  and retaliation, 91

Economies of scale, 21–72, 108,
  115, 276, 298, 396, 402
  concentration and condition of
    entry, 53–81, 170–78
  curves, 53
  defined, 27
  empirical evidence on, 25–42
  'engineering' estimates of, 56
    see also Plant
  and multi-plant firms, 70–77
  pecuniary, 55, 70n, 176
Elasticity
  of demand *see* Demand
  of substitution *see* Substitution
Endowment of resources, 9, 10
Enterprise
  definition of, 222
  fund, 271
  Soviet, 270, 271
  supply function of, 284–5
  theory of output-maximizing,
    270–86

see also Firm
Entrepreneur, disappearance of,
  291–4
Entrepreneurial
  ability, 44
  capacity, 49, 50
  income, 220
Excess capacity, 108, 113–15, 177,
  190
Exploitation, theory of, 197

Factor costs, 41, 42, 400–403
  see also Advertising,
    Wages
'Factor of revenue', 101–4
Factors of production, 44, 46,
  121, 173, 302, 400–403
  imperfections in the market for,
    175
Federal Trade Commission, 37,
  43, 55, 60, 82, 137, 144, 150,
  187, 190
Firm(s)
  barometric, 148
  and 'behaviourist' models, 16
  changes in number of, 108–15
  degree of concentration within
    industries, 74–7
  developments in the theory of,
    16
  dominant, 131, 135, 146–8
  'groups', 100, 107–8, 111, 116
  leverage or gearing of *see*
    Leverage
  market value of, 334
  measure of mobility of, 353, 357,
    358
  monopolistic, 48
  the objectives of, 16
  permanent growth model of,
    328, 329, 331–51
  size of *see* Size
  static theory of, 318, 318n

Profit(s), 49, 217, 285, 296, 371
  constraint, 325
  curves, 256, 261
  equalization of rates, of, 202
  excess, 206
  and growth and maximization
    of, 328–51
  maximization model, 339–41
  normal, 109, 111, 115, 202, 224,
    226
  optimal stream of, 325
  share of in income, 243
  static alternatives to
    maximization of, 249–86
  subnormal, 111
  supernormal, 115, 250, 288
  theory of, 218
  versus growth maximization,
    324–7
Proportionate effect,
  law of, see Gibrat's law,
  Size of firms

Qualitative
  calculus, 97, 106, 106n, 120
  comparative statics see
    Comparative
  economics, 105–6
  predictions, 97, 98, 118
  restrictions, 98, 106, 106n
Quality variation, 98–124

Raw materials
  basic, 228–32
  change in price of, 228–32
Reaction curve, 93, 94
Receipts
  gross and net, 88, 89
  maximum net, 88
Relative shares
  distribution of income, and,
    217–86
  of labour and capital, 11, 12

of manual labour in National
    income, 219–32
  alleged constancy of, 233–48
  and variance of aggregate
    wage-share, 238–48
  see also 'Widow's cruse' theory
Rent, 47, 48, 49, 250
  and existence of barriers to
    entry, 153
Resources
  allocation of, 9, 10, 201–15,
    258, 267, 268, 282, 384, 387, 401
  elimination of misallocation of,
    211
  optimal allocation of, 202, 268n
  see also Welfare
Resources, endowment of see
  Endowment
Retention, ratio, 330–47
Revenue
  adjusted marginal, 95
  annual, 87
  average, 111, 274, 279
  curves, 256, 274
  diminishing marginal, 257,
    320–23
  'factor of' see Factor
  iso-, curves, 258
  marginal, 92, 93, 130–35
  maximization of, 254, 269, 282
  net, 90, 320, 391
  present value of the expected
    stream of, 320–23

Sales
  discounted sum of future, 328,
    329, 339
  and growth and profit
    maximization, 328–51
  maximization of, 249, 251, 267,
    344–6
  subject to profit constraint,
    253–69